GREAT BRITAIN

MOSCOW

LONDON POTSDAM °BERLIN

°PARIS

E U R O

YALTA

A F R I C A

IN SEARCH OF PEACE

MR. BYRNES' TRAVELS ~ from Yalta to the Paris Peace Conference

1 Big Three Meeting, Yalta
Jan. 22, '45 — Feb. 12, '45

2 Big Three Meeting, Potsdam
July 6, '45 — Aug. 7, '45

3 Foreign Ministers Council, London
Sept. 4, '45 — Oct. 8, '45

4 Big Three Foreign Ministers, Moscow
Dec. 12, '45 — Dec. 29, '45

5 U.N. General Assembly, London
Jan. 7, '46 — Jan. 25, '46

6 Big Four Foreign Ministers, Paris
Apr. 23, '46 — May 18, '46

7 Big Four Foreign Ministers, Paris
June 13, '46 — July 14, '46

8 21-Nation Peace Conference, Paris
July 27, '46 — Oct. 17, '46

Total approximate mileage – 77,000
Dates cover from time of departure to return to Washington

K. VOUTE

Adapted from a map published in *The New York Times,* July 28, 1946.

SPEAKING FRANKLY

JAMES F. BYRNES

SPEAKING FRANKLY

By James F. Byrnes

Harper & Brothers Publishers

New York and London

To the Memory of

My Mother

Elizabeth E. Byrnes

Contents

Illustrations

Sample page of the shorthand notes taken by Mr. Byrnes at Yalta (February 9, 1945)

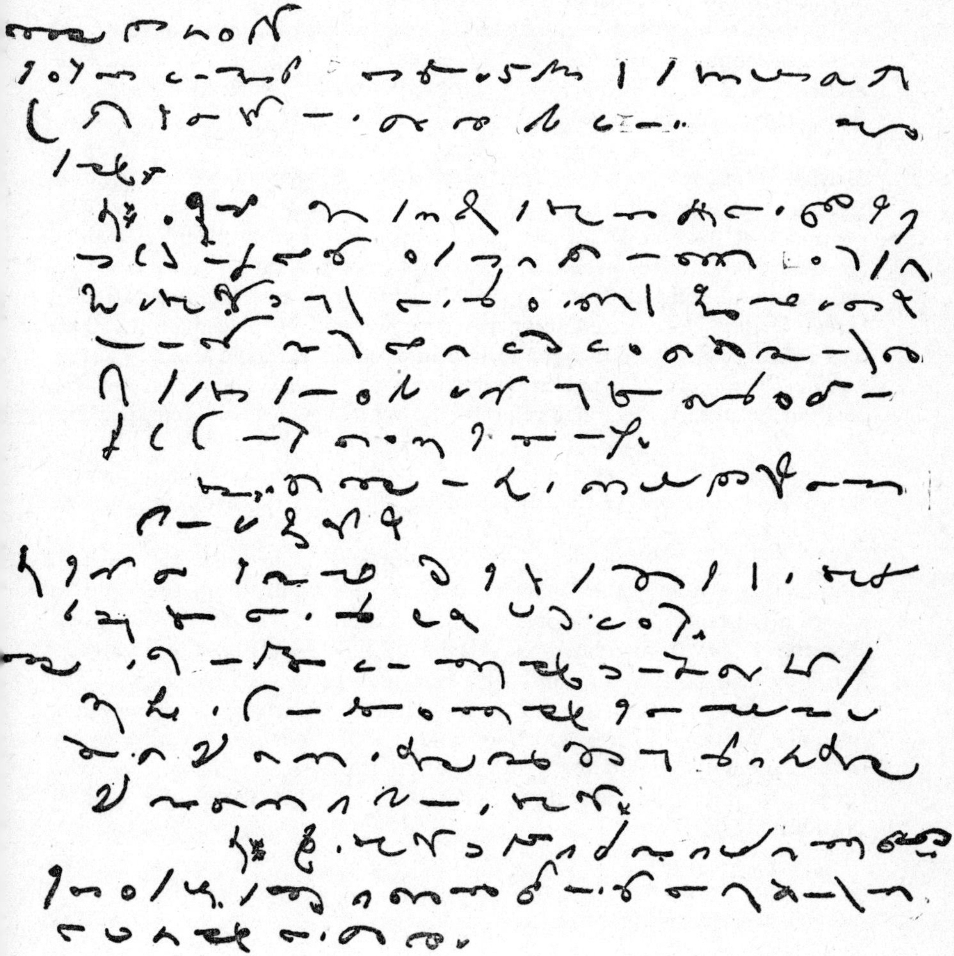

See other side for transcription of these notes.

Mr. Stettinius reads from a report:

"I have a brief statement as to Dumbarton Oaks. 'It is agreed that five governments which have permanent seats on the council should consult each other prior to the United Nations Conference as to the establishment of trusteeships.'"

Mr. Churchill: "I absolutely disagree. I will not have one scrap of British territory flung into that area. After we have done our best to fight in this war and have done no crime to anyone I will have no suggestion that the British Empire is to be put into the dock and examined by everybody to see whether it is up to their standard. No one will induce me as long as I am Prime Minister to let any representative of Great Britain go to a conference where we will be placed in the dock and asked to justify our right to live in a world we have tried to save."

The President: "I want Mr. Stettinius to finish the sentence he was reading because it does not refer to the matter you have been speaking about."

Mr. Churchill: "If we are out I have nothing to say. As long as every bit of land over which the British Flag flies is to be brought into the dock, I shall object so long as I live."

Mr. Stettinius: "The only thing contemplated as to territorial trusteeship is to provide in the Charter of the world organization the right to create a trusteeship if it desires to do so. Later on, we have had in mind that the Japanese mandated islands be taken away from the Japanese. We have had nothing in mind with reference to the British Empire."

Mr. Churchill: "So far as the British Empire is concerned, we ask nothing. We seek no territorial aggrandizement. If it is a question solely of dealing with enemy territory acquired during the war, it might be proper to put them into some form of trusteeship under the United Nations."

Foreword

> If we could first know *where* we are, and *whither* we
> are tending, we could better judge *what* to do and
> *how* to do it.
>
> Abraham Lincoln

THERE were a number of friends who beguiled me into writing this story. Their arguments were that while the events were fresh in my memory and I was still able to read my shorthand notes, I would, by speaking frankly, render a public service.

For some time I had been urging a people's peace and expressing the opinion that the people could not intelligently influence the peace unless they were told the facts about our negotiations. With this background, you can appreciate how easily I was flattered into believing that I might help the people who are interested in making peace to know where we are, so that they might better judge what to do and how to do it.

In the four months that have passed, as I have worked long hours on this manuscript, I have forgiven those friends but have not forgotten them. Also I have realized that writing is a profession and that it is not my profession. Instead of attempting to qualify as a professional and to acquire a literary style, I have tried to tell, in an informal and conversational way, of our efforts to make the peace settlements.

After completing the manuscript I was surprised and displeased to note the frequency of the capital "I." Now it is too late to do anything about it. In extenuation, I hope it will be recalled that this is a story of events and discussions in which the writer was a participant and it was difficult to avoid the frequent use of the "I."

This does not purport to be a story of our foreign relations since the cessation of hostilities. It is confined to our peace-making efforts and to events incident to those efforts. For example, there is no reference to our relations with our South American neighbors. This is because, in telling the story of the peace settlements, there is little reason to discuss our relations either with the South American Governments or the Canadian Government.

In writing this story I have had occasion to mention many persons who were associated with me in the various conferences. There were many others without whose assistance we could not have presented our cause, and whose names are not mentioned. Their services I warmly remember and deeply appreciate.

Many times during the preparation of this manuscript I also have had reason to thank those hard-working and nearly always anonymous members of the secretariat of the various conferences. Their carefully compiled records were invaluable in drawing together the many threads which form the pattern of our peace negotiations. I had many notes of my own, but only at Yalta, where I was serving as an adviser and not taking part in the debates, was I able to make a complete stenographic record.

Throughout the book there are many direct quotations. These are taken either from my notes, from the records of the secretariat or, in some cases, from memoranda made immediately after conversations. Nevertheless, they are subject to human error. This is particularly true in quotations of statements made by Soviet and French representatives. It should be remembered that, in those cases, the quotations are the words of the translator rather than those of the speaker. Wherever I had any reason for doubt, however, I have not used quotations but have tried instead to reflect the spirit as well as the letter of the statements, the events, and the atmosphere in which they occurred.

I have tried, in short, to give you a seat at the conference table. Some critics may say it is too early for these facts to be made known. My answer is that if it were possible to give the people of this world an actual, rather than a figurative, seat at the peace conference table, the fears and worries that now grip our hearts would fade away.

James F. Byrnes

Spartanburg, S. C.
July 1, 1947

BOOK I

INTRODUCTION TO WORLD LEADERSHIP

Chapter 1

Awakening to Danger—and Responsibility

A HUNDRED THOUSAND voices awakened me to danger. Acres of Germans in even furrows stretched before me and from them rose a chorus of praise for military might and its apostle, Adolf Hitler. It was no nightmare. It was Nuremberg, Germany, in September, 1937. Like most Americans, I had watched the rise of this man Hitler with a somewhat detached concern, but here was a scene that could not be regarded with detachment.

Domestic as well as international affairs had brought Mrs. Byrnes and me to Europe. I was a delegate to the Inter-Parliamentary Union meeting in Paris, and as chairman of the Senate Committee on Unemployment and Relief I wished to see how Europe was handling its unemployment problem. We had not planned to visit Nuremberg, but in Munich, an official of the German Foreign Office whom we had met on board ship, persuaded us we could not properly evaluate Germany's program for economic recovery without witnessing the Annual Congress of the Nazi Party.

What was spread before us, however, was a program not for economic recovery but for armed aggression. Twelve thousand troops marched past our stand, accompanied by the rumble of scores of tanks and motorized weapons, while 450 planes swept across the skies above the stadium. As the demonstration reached its climax, Hitler rode across the field in an open automobile standing erect and with right arm uplifted in the Nazi salute. An exultant cry arose from the multitude. But I was frightened—frightened by the specter of war.

While we were in Berlin the government announced the first civilian air raid drill. We heard women complaining because they had to buy blackout curtains. Two years before the war started, the German people already were doing what our people barely succeeded in doing two years after it started.

My concern mounted as we traveled through Germany. In Hamburg and Bremerhaven we witnessed the enthusiastic welcome given

the troops returning from Nuremberg. The people were proud of their
new and rapidly growing army. In rural districts and in the cities
there was talk of war. The older folks were fearful; the younger people
were enthusiastic. But nearly all supported the restoration of an armed
might they fervently believed to be a natural German right and a German necessity.

These impressions were in sharp contrast with what we had seen in
France. There, the contest between capital and labor was bringing
that country to an economic impasse. Stores and factories were closed
from Saturday noon until Tuesday morning. Demands were made in
some industries for even fewer working hours. But in Germany,
only an overnight train trip away, factories were working longer and
longer hours. The slogan JOY THROUGH WORK appeared everywhere.
The Germans were as busy increasing production as the French were
busy decreasing it.

We went to London. Because of what we had seen in Germany, I
asked the British officials we met what their government was doing in
the way of military preparedness. The alarm had sounded for them,
but only a few were responding. These few had succeeded in launching a preparedness program a few months earlier. Consequently, when
we visited the Birmingham area, I did find some plants producing
military equipment twenty-four hours a day.

Even Britain's limited program had aroused strong opposition from
the pacifists. The weekend we returned to London there was a huge
peace parade. I went to see it and to listen to the comments of the
other onlookers. The slogans were the same as those at home: WE
DIDN'T RAISE OUR BOYS TO BE CANNON FODDER, PEACE ON EARTH, and
the like. The marchers were good people—the same kind of people we
had in every state in our Union—who wanted to proclaim their desire
for peace and their hatred for war. As those earnest, uneven ranks
passed down the street, I saw again the thousands of tough disciplined
troops, goosestepping by Hitler at Nuremberg. And this parade for peace
seemed all in vain.

Surmise deepened into certainty when I combined the German display
of military power with what I had learned on a trip to the Pacific two
years earlier. A large Congressional party, headed by Vice President
Garner, had gone to Manila to witness the inauguration of Manuel
Quezon as the first President of the Philippine Commonwealth. There,
Americans in all walks of life had expressed to us their concern over
the increasing indications of Japan's aggressive intentions. Therefore,
when we stopped in Japan I made a special effort to inquire into
Japanese naval appropriations and naval construction. A study of the
Japanese budget for 1936 readily revealed that at least half of the total

was devoted to the army and navy. Members of our Embassy staff were convinced that the published budget disclosed only part of the naval appropriations. The published figures were alarming enough in themselves and when we returned to this country I urged the President to seek means for acquiring still more accurate estimates of Japan's naval strength.

Equally disturbing was the structure of Japan's political and economic life. I had begun by inquiring into the Japanese textile industry primarily because of its competitive relationship to the chief industry of South Carolina. I ended with a realization that industry, banking, shipping, in fact the whole economic and political life of Japan, were centrally controlled. The power of Japan rested with a small group of men who could set the entire nation on any course they desired.

It was clear that neither in Japan nor in Germany was there an opportunity to appeal to the judgment of the millions. It was the decisions of leaders and not the desires of people that prevailed.

On October 1, 1937, we returned from Europe and as soon as I could, I reported to President Roosevelt what we had seen and heard and my conclusion that we must immediately give serious thought to the nation's defense.

The President told me I only confirmed what he had concluded from the reports of our official representatives abroad. He was greatly disturbed about the developments in Europe. Even more, he was disturbed about the difficulties of awakening our people to a realization of the true situation.

I told him that the sentiment of the people, as reflected in the Congress, would make it difficult for us to secure increased appropriations for Army and Navy. He was determined, however, to do his best to make people see the necessity for increased appropriations, and I promised to help him.

It was on October 5, 1937, that the President made his famous Chicago Quarantine Speech. It was a strong speech. For many reasons it had to be. There was our traditional desire to be free of Europe's troubles and the belief, born of desire, that aggressive nationalism could be confined to the European continent. There also was the disillusionment from our venture into European politics after World War I which still lingered on. As a people we hated war and we prized our isolation.

There were other immediate factors.

Our support of our Army and Navy in peacetime was always a reluctant one. Reluctance in many cases turned to outright opposition in the years of the depression when there was great strength in the argument that the revenue we raised should be spent for relief and not for military preparedness. It was argued that the people of the world had enough of war in World War I. In addition, the Senate Munitions Committee had given encouragement to the pacifists; had helped foster the simple theory that war was a creature of the munitions makers' thirst for profits. Producers of military supplies were labeled "Merchants of Death." International bankers were charged with creating the markets for the products of those merchants.

Every time I brought a naval appropriations bill to the floor of the Senate, I had to face those pacifist slogans and arguments. They commanded large public support. To hear them, crowds with a high proportion of women and of students invariably would fill the Senate galleries. Senator Lynn J. Frazier usually spoke in criticism of the Navy, but the pacifists' outstanding spokesman was Senator Gerald P. Nye of North Dakota. His sincerity I never questioned; but I often wondered if he had ever considered why, out of all that large congressional group to visit Japan in 1935, he was the one member the Japanese Naval Command had wired prior to our landing seeking to honor him with a banquet. Nye declined the "honor." Later when we were leaving Japan on our return trip he showed me a book recording the story of the development of the Japanese Navy which had been sent to him at the ship by an admiral of the Japanese Navy. I am sure he was embarrassed. He should have been.

Since the early days of his administration, President Roosevelt had faced opposition as he sought to strengthen our defense establishment. He had allotted funds for public works to naval construction projects and he had obtained authority to increase the Army's enlisted strength from 115,000 to 165,000 men.

The President was disappointed by the failure of the people to respond to his Chicago speech. He waited until the turn of the year and then began in earnest the drive to arouse the Congress and the public.

"It is an ominous fact," he told the Congress in a special message on January 29, 1938, "that at least one-fourth of the world's population is involved in merciless, devastating conflict in spite of the fact that most people in most countries, including those where conflict rages, wish to live at peace."

He then called for a 20 per cent increase in the naval building program, construction of two battleships and two cruisers, experimental construction of small vessels and the pitifully small sum of twenty million dollars for Army materiel. Our regular Army then ranked eighteenth among the standing armies of the world.

But public sentiment was such that the campaign to increase our military and naval appropriations was an uphill fight. Attention was concentrated on the alphabet—WPA, PWA, AAA, CCC, NRA, and all the others. And the alphabet took all the revenues. It was hard to reduce them and impossible to abolish them. The nearest approach to immortality on earth is a government bureau.

The annexation of Austria in March 1938, the Munich agreement, and the consequent dismemberment of Czechoslovakia in September were shocks to the American people. But appropriations for the Army and Navy were still hard to get through Congress. To stimulate public interest, the President started the new year, 1939, with another special message to Congress on defense problems. This time he asked for an appropriation of half a billion dollars, primarily for the Army and Navy air arms.

On May 27, Secretary Hull submitted letters to the House and Senate asking for repeal of the act that placed an embargo on the shipment of arms to a nation at war. He explained that the law should be left flexible and that repeal would help us to stay out of war if it should, unfortunately, start in Europe. Shortly thereafter, during a conversation at the White House, President Roosevelt told me he greatly feared Hitler would start a war during the summer. When, on July 11, the Senate Foreign Relations Committee voted 12 to 11 to postpone consideration of the bill repealing the Arms Embargo, it was a keen disappointment both to the President and to Secretary Hull. Three days later, the President sent a message to Congress expressing his regret and appended a strong statement from Mr. Hull appealing for action without delay. It emphasized that without repeal our influence to preserve peace would be weakened. The appeal was in vain.

The Congress adjourned, but Hitler did not. He and his Foreign Minister, Joachim von Ribbentrop, were busily negotiating with the Soviet Union the nonaggression pact that was concluded on August 23. Seven days later the Nazi armies invaded Poland and the word "blitzkrieg" came into our vocabulary.

In accordance with existing law, President Roosevelt proclaimed our neutrality and invoked the Arms Embargo. At the same time he called a special session of Congress to convene September 21 to consider repeal of the embargo. And on November 4, Congress voted the repeal we had been seeking since May.

At the outset the President realized the necessity for bipartisan action in the emergency confronting him. In order to make such an appeal, he held a meeting in his office on the day preceding the opening of Congress, attended by representatives of the two political parties, including Vice President Garner, Secretary Hull, Alfred M. Landon, Colonel Frank Knox, Speaker Bankhead, Senate Leaders Barkley and McNary, and Senators Pittman, Byrnes, Minton and Austin, and Representatives Bloom, Rayburn, Martin and Mapes.

It was a serious meeting of serious men.

In response to his appeal for the co-operation of the two great parties, frank statements were made by those present. Landon thought the Congress should be kept in session. He thought the judgment of the Congress and the executive safer than the judgment of a single individual, meaning, of course, the President. Of the Republican representatives, no one made a more impressive statement than Frank Knox, the vice presidential candidate in the preceding election. A few days later the President remarked upon the splendid statement of Mr. Knox, who had said the war would spread, and that we neither were able to stay out of it nor prepared to get into it. He declared we should forget all about political parties, close ranks, and prepare to defend our country.

When the President made up his mind to appoint two Republicans to his Cabinet, I was not surprised that he selected Knox as Secretary of the Navy, and I was delighted at his choice of the talented and courageous Henry L. Stimson as Secretary of War.

The President asked me to ascertain from Senator Lucas of Illinois whether he would approve the confirmation of Knox. Lucas promptly advised me he approved the appointment and a few hours later said he also had talked with Mayor Kelly of Chicago. He quoted Kelly as saying that, although Knox's newspaper had consistently opposed him, political considerations must be entirely disregarded in the emergency we were facing. He then added he would be glad to see Knox appointed. This statement from Mayor Kelly, the head of a large Democratic political organization, was an encouraging demonstration that political considerations had become of secondary importance.

When the senatorial members of the group who had met with the President returned to the Capitol, Senator McNary, the Republican leader of the Senate, stated he wanted to advise me and I might advise the President that, while he had said little at the conference, the President could count on his wholehearted co-operation. McNary was one of the ablest Republicans in or out of Congress and in the days that followed, he lived up to his promise to co-operate. Time after time when some proposal connected with the preparedness program was pending, which by the enforcement of Senate rules could have been delayed, he would consent to immediate consideration and give his influential support to the legislation. He and Senator Austin, who was then the minority whip, quietly helped to speed the passage of many measures for our defense.

Notwithstanding the success of the Nazis in Poland, a large portion of the American public still was not aware of the danger confronting us. In the absence of action on the western front people began referring to the "phony war." The feeling was as widespread as the phrase, and was reflected in Congress. Early in the spring we had completed hearings on the Naval Appropriation Bill, providing for construction of additional battleships and cruisers. Conversation with my Senate colleagues forced me to conclude that passage of the bill without destructive amendments was very doubtful, so I deliberately delayed consideration of it in the Senate. Some of the appropriations were made immediately available. The Navy wanted them. But I wanted to be sure of getting the bill through without amendments reducing appropriations for new construction. From statements made by our Intelligence officers and from the opinions of our military leaders, I was convinced that with the coming of spring the Nazis would attack on the western front. They did. And when they did I brought up the Naval Bill in the Senate. It passed in three hours, as reported by the Appropriations Committee.

Our difficulties were not confined to materiel. The Army had in its higher ranks many officers who were good men, but who, in the opinion of General Marshall, were too old and not good enough for the terrific task ahead of us.

In August 1940, General Marshall appeared before the Senate Appropriations Committee to testify on a defense appropriation bill. During a recess, he told me that his greatest difficulty was his inability to promote younger officers of unusual ability. Possession of such authority, he said, was essential to the proper reorganization of the Army. He told me he had requested Chairman May, of the House Military Affairs Committee, to introduce the necessary legislation some months before but had been unable to get action on it.

His needs were so impressive that I requested him to have one of his technicians draft an amendment that would accomplish the purpose he desired and stated I would try to help him. Under the rules of the Senate, the amendment could not be added to an appropriation bill in committee but when the bill was reported to the floor, I offered an amendment, adopted without objection, providing that "In time of war or national emergency determined by the President, any officer of the Regular Army may be appointed to higher temporary grade without vacating his permanent appointment."

When we met in conference with the members of the House Appropriations Committee, I explained the urgency of the proposal and they accepted it. On September 9 it became law and under its provisions the War Department began the task of promoting over the heads of officers of high rank the younger officers who thereafter led our armies to victory. Before the end of the year, 4,088 of these promotions were made. Among the officers advanced were men like General Eisenhower, General George C. Kenney, General Carl A. Spaatz, General Mark Clark and the late General George S. Patton. Eisenhower was promoted over 366 senior officers.

It was the disaster at Dunkirk that at last aroused our people, but they reacted in a curiously divided way. Our hatred of war was at odds with our growing recognition that the conflagration was creeping ever closer to our shores. The compromise that emerged from this conflict of heart and mind was a willingness to build up our own defenses but a determination to avoid involvement.

The division of sentiment among the people was reflected in the political conventions.

The Republicans, meeting in Philadelphia on June 24, included in their platform a declaration: "The Republican Party is firmly opposed to involving the nation in foreign war."

The political leaders of the Democratic Party, appreciating what a strong appeal this declaration would make to the voting mothers, were exceedingly anxious that the Democratic convention should offset the Republican declaration.

The President had asked me to represent him on the floor of the convention. He was particularly anxious that I interest myself in the foreign relations declaration of the platform. When the Platform Committee met, it was apparent that we were in for a fight. Senator Burton K. Wheeler, an astute and able legislator, wanted a declaration against participation in the war. His views were shared by Senators David I. Walsh and Pat McCarran, as well as other members of the committee. Several proposals were offered. I asked Senator Wagner, the chairman of the committee, to postpone consideration of the foreign relations section until I could talk with the three Senators to see if we could agree upon a satisfactory declaration. Wagner appointed Mayor Kelly to confer with us also.

The three Senators were insisting upon a statement: "We will not participate in foreign wars and we will not send our armies, navies or air forces to fight on foreign lands outside the Americas." They advised me of threats from many delegates to bolt the convention if they didn't get a direct pledge of this kind. I finally told them that if they would agree to the words "except in case of attack" I would submit it to the President and the Secretary of State. They agreed. This, actually, was my third talk with the President on the subject and this time he had Secretary Hull with him. Hull was slow to agree. I pointed out that if we were attacked anywhere in the world we would fight and send forces abroad. After all, we would not send armies abroad to fight without declaring war, and it was the function of Congress to declare war. The President and Secretary Hull agreed.

The declaration was adopted unanimously by the committee and the convention. I did not like the "plank." I feared it would cause Hitler to conclude, as the Kaiser did in 1917, that we would not fight and that he would be encouraged to act on that assumption. But the views expressed by members of the Platform Committee made it clear it was the best we could hope for. The alternative would be a bitter fight in the convention that would disclose a serious split in the President's party and impair his prestige abroad. It was a good illustration of competition between the two political parties for the approval of a bloc of voters.

With France gone, and the grim bombardment of Britain in full swing, the President moved ahead on his own initiative. He sold to Britain rifles and other weapons from our World War I stockpile to help replace those left behind on the French beaches. The deal for exchanging fifty overage destroyers in return for bases was negotiated. There was a great protest that the President had no authority to dispose of these destroyers. When I talked to him about it, he called attention to a supporting legal opinion from Attorney General Jackson. However, from the President's attitude, I suspected he was more concerned whether public sentiment would support his action. He had determined to take that chance even with the election only a few months away.

It was about this time that Congress began its debate over the first peacetime military draft in our history. It was significant that this controversial legislation was being pushed by the administration a short time before a presidential election. The fact that Representative James W. Wadsworth, a loyal Republican, had joined with Senator Edmund R. Burke, a Democrat, in sponsoring the bill made the measure a bipartisan one. It passed just before the election, and it is doubtful if it affected many votes.

The acceptance of Selective Service by the people served to show that the public had responded to the developments in Europe.

From then on the people were often ahead of the President and the Congress. They saw the world-wide scope of the conflict. They realized the urgent necessity of aiding our friends and obtaining time in which to prepare.

Shortly before Christmas, 1940, President Roosevelt disclosed at a press conference his plan "to eliminate the dollar sign" from our aid to those fighting against Hitler. The idea was elaborated still further by the President when he appeared before the new Congress on January 8, 1941, to deliver his message on The State of the Union. Meanwhile, work had begun on drafting legislation to put the plan into action. A draft prepared by Oscar S. Cox, then an assistant to the general counsel of the Treasury, was used as a basis for soliciting advice and suggestions from many people.

On January 10, the bill was introduced simultaneously in the Senate and House by Senator Alben W. Barkley and Representative John W. McCormack, the majority leaders. In the House the symbolic number,

H. R. 1776, was attached to what finally became, on March 11, the Lend-Lease Act.

When the new Congress was organized there were two vacancies on the Senate Foreign Relations Committee, which was to handle the lend-lease legislation. Senator Carter Glass and I received the assignments. My principal activity from then on was to help secure passage of this legislation. Mr. Cox and Assistant Secretary of War John J. McCloy were assigned to furnish whatever information was desired by committees or by individual Senators and Congressmen. We had to admit to opponents that little of what we would lend and lease for use in the prosecution of the war would ever come back. Our justification had to be that it would enable other men to fight the enemy while we trained and equipped our own armed forces. The bill was brought to the floor of the Senate on February 17 after a favorable vote of 15 to 8 in committee. The ranking members of the Foreign Relations Committee conducted the debate on the floor and ably presented our cause which won by a vote of 60 to 31.

After passage of the legislation, the fight was transferred to the Appropriations Committee, of which, under the chairmanship of Senator Glass, I was also a member. An initial appropriation of seven billion dollars to implement the lend-lease program was approved.

In June 1941, Justice McReynolds, of Tennessee, announced his retirement from the Supreme Court, and I was appointed to fill the vacancy.

During the months that followed, I did not participate in any way in the preparations for national defense and had only such information as I got from the press and from visits with the President.

The invasion of Russia on June 22 left only one other major power free from war, but the sinking of the *Robin Moor* and the attacks on the *Greer* and the *Kearney* made it clear we would not escape much longer. Congress responded by further amending the Neutrality Act and voting more funds for defense. The President and Secretary Hull also were deeply concerned over the trend of events at the eastern end of the Axis. Japan's move into French Indo-China exposed aggressive intentions which could not be obscured by the "peace missions" of Ambassador Kurusu to the United States. The President finally was prompted to send an appeal for peace directly to the Emperor on Saturday, December 6. He received his response when the Japanese, without warning, attacked Pearl Harbor the following day.

The Tuesday after Pearl Harbor Sunday, the Supreme Court met to hear arguments in a case between the Bethlehem Shipbuilding Company and the United States of America. I must confess I found it very difficult to concentrate on the arguments that morning. The issue involved arose out of the company's construction of ships for the government during World War I. At any other time it would have seemed important, but right then it appeared of little consequence in the light of the news bulletins still pouring in from Pearl Harbor and our growing realization of their consequences.

Early Wednesday morning, I went to see the President. He was still in his bed, which was covered with dispatches and memos. Some of his papers were on the floor. He had been awake for hours studying the information and planning the future. I had hardly walked into the room before he began giving me the details of the disaster. Only then did I fully realize the extent of the damage to our ships. The President was alternately sad, determined, and hurt. He could not understand how such a thing could happen to the Navy of which he was so proud.

As we talked, he rang for his valet, arose, and began to shave. So our conversation was just moved to the bathroom. He had finished lathering when I changed the subject by saying:

"Mr. President, you know, before your fight on the Supreme Court was over I had concluded you were wrong, and my service on the Court has only confirmed that view."

His razor stopped in mid-stroke. It was a sore point with him. He turned to me with a look both of inquiry and annoyance, but I went right on.

"You urged that Justices be retired at seventy. From my experience, I've decided they shouldn't be appointed until they reach seventy."

His good humor was restored. He laughed as I told him about the case of the day before.

"I've been in the middle of crises ever since I entered public life," I told him, "but yesterday with the nation confronted with the greatest crisis in its history, the best I could do was to spend hours listening to arguments about the payment for ships that were built twenty-three years ago. I was thinking so much about those ships sunk at Pearl Harbor that it was difficult to concentrate on arguments about ships that were built at Bethlehem in 1918."

It was said half in jest. As we moved back into the bedroom the President made it clear he was taking me seriously. He pointed out that our entry into the war would require the passage of considerable legislation, the assumption of additional executive powers and the reorganization of much administrative machinery. Prompt action was required, he said, and because of my long experience in the Congress he wanted to call on me for help. The President thereupon ordered all war legislation cleared by Attorney General Francis Biddle, and asked him to consult with me.

This created a problem. The issues referred to me required consultation with leaders of the House and Senate as well as officials of the executive departments, and it was often difficult to explain how a Supreme Court Justice was connected with the heterogeneous questions that came my way. But we were at war—and we were frightened.

On December 15, I was studying the Overman Act of World War I, which had authorized President Wilson to reorganize government agencies for more effective prosecution of the war. It suddenly occurred to me that here was the solution to my problem. Reorganization was necessary now, and it would be easy for the President to announce that, since I had been chairman of the Senate Committee on Government Reorganization, he had asked me to make a survey and advise what changes were necessary. I recalled that back in 1913, during my second term in the House, President Taft had appointed Associate Justice Charles Evans Hughes to serve as chairman of a commission created by Congress to investigate second-class mail rates. So there was a precedent created by a Justice for whom I had the greatest admiration.

Acting on this impulse, I sent a brief memo to the President outlining both my problem and the suggested answer.

"I want to avoid the words 'liaison' and 'coordinator,' " I wrote him. "They would destroy even a good man."

But my message had hardly reached the White House when I began to fear that a public announcement might restrict my ability to help. The President agreed that I could work for him more effectively if I did so quietly and unobtrusively. So the announcement was never made.

Requests for emergency legislation came streaming in from virtually every agency of the government. The need for several of the requests was not readily discernible. Individual action on each of them would require consideration by at least a dozen congressional committees. Days and weeks of precious time would be lost.

In a conference with the Attorney General, and Oscar Cox, who had become his assistant, it was decided that these matters could best be handled in an all-inclusive bill. In that way, only one committee on each side of Capitol Hill would be concerned, and the popular proposals would carry along the more controversial issues. For example, Postmaster General Frank Walker had a proposal to extend free postage to all members of the armed forces. It was certain to win almost unanimous support—so it became Title X of the over-all bill.

Meanwhile, Speaker Sam Rayburn and Majority Leader Alben W. Barkley approved the idea of an omnibus bill. They selected the respective committees and conferred with the chairmen. As a result, the Second War Powers Act was sponsored by the chairmen of the Judiciary Committees of the House and Senate. It was approved by the Senate in eight days and was through the House by the end of February.

Organization of war production was another urgent problem. Labor had pledged its co-operation and William Knudsen was doing an excellent job in enlisting the support of the industrialists. But we simply were not organized for production on the scale necessary to supply our Allies and our own armed forces too. The divisions of power and the resultant conflicts were such that production actually was being delayed. There seemed to be more agencies than decisions. And there were as many suggestions on what should be done to remedy the situation as there were agencies. The press and public demanded a change.

Harry Hopkins was then chairman of the Munitions Assignment Board. He was living in the White House and was consulted by the President on many subjects. During a telephone conversation with Hopkins on January 2, Harry asked me to send him any ideas I might have on the production problem. That afternoon I sent him a two-page memorandum saying first that the proposal for a Ministry of Supplies, made popular by the current visit of Prime Minister Churchill and his Supply Minister, Lord Beaverbrook, would require transfer of the procurement organizations of the Army and Navy and thus would cause confusion, conflicts, and loss of time the nation could not afford.

Instead of still another board, my memo to Hopkins urged that the President appoint one man charged with the duty of supervising and expediting procurement. That man could have any type of board he wanted, but when a controversy arose, he should decide it. The memo to Hopkins continued:

"You say, 'All right—find the man.' If you demand perfection, you will never select a man. There are some things we do know. If you bring in an executive who has had experience only in a particular industry, he will have to be educated in the methods of government as well as to the needs of the various services. If you will recall how much you knew about the machinery of government when you first came to Washington, you will appreciate how little the average executive knows about the methods that must be pursued by the heads of the various agencies in the Production Organization. If you now have in the government service a man who has served his apprenticeship, who has some appreciation of the problems of the procurement divisions of the Army, Navy and other Services, and who has the ability to make other men work, appoint him, instead of bringing in another new man."

"We no longer need for political or prestige purposes a man with a big name," I wrote. "All you need now is a man who can do the job. If any one of the 'Stars' becomes temperamental and wants to resign— let him go. He will find it uncomfortable at home. . . . Pick the best man you now have on the team and let the heathen rage."

Monday, January 12, "Pa" Watson called to say the President wanted to see me. A few minutes later Hopkins telephoned to ask that I stop by his room before seeing the President. He was in bed, sick, but able to attend to business. He said he had discussed the problem briefly with the President but as the President had been reluctant to go into it he had not pressed him.

Hopkins said he had not shown the President my memorandum but had simply discussed the subject generally. I asked for the memorandum and presented it to the President.

"I've been considering the appointment of a commission," he said after he had read it, "but the more I think it over the closer I come to the conclusion you've expressed here."

I urged prompt action.

"If I had to make a selection this morning, I would pick Donald Nelson," he went on. "He was here last night for a dinner we had for Lord Beaverbrook. I hadn't known him too well, but last night I heard him discussing the sugar situation and a number of production problems, and I was impressed by the soundness of his views."

"I have not come to recommend any man but only to urge action," I told him. And warned, "The man will last only as long as it is recognized that he has your complete confidence."

With that, I had to leave as it was almost time for the Court to convene. The incident remains in my mind as this was the only time I ever arrived late either for a sitting or for a conference of the Court.

That afternoon General Watson asked me to come see the President the next morning. When I arrived Director of the Budget Harold Smith was there, and told me the President had asked him to draft an executive order embodying the ideas of the memorandum. Harry Hopkins joined us and we prepared a press release announcing the establishment of the War Production Board and Nelson's appointment as Chairman. Harry was anxious to have the President act at once.

"Every hour of delay gives more people an opportunity to know what the President is planning," Harry said. "The first thing we know somebody who has different ideas will be in here trying to change his mind. And," he added, "the news will leak to the press."

The President, however, insisted, quite correctly, that he must first advise Vice President Wallace, whose job as Chairman of the Economic Defense Board was being abolished by the order. He said he would see Wallace early that afternoon. I returned to the White House late in the day to see a final draft of the executive order. I learned there had been a delay. Wendell Willkie had called on Mr. Roosevelt. He enjoyed talking with Mr. Willkie, and became so engrossed in the conversation that he was behind his schedule of engagements. Consequently, it was not until almost six o'clock that he told the Vice President of his decision. The announcement was made shortly thereafter.

In the summer, while the Court was in recess, I was tired and wanted to go home for two weeks. But the President for some time had been worried about the wage and price situation and he requested me to confer, before I left, with Judge Samuel I. Rosenman, who afterwards became his personal counsel. Judge Rosenman had been designated to reconcile the various views on the best method of stabilizing our economy. The judge had worked out general outlines of a plan for an Office of Economic Stabilization, which reasonably satisfied the heads of agencies concerned. After making a few suggestions, I left at last for South Carolina.

Not many days had passed when a wonderful afternoon nap was interrupted by Mrs. Byrnes calling:

"Jim, the White House wants you on the telephone."

It was the President. It was essential, he said, to create without delay an agency with sufficient power to enforce ceilings upon prices and wages. He asked what I thought the Congress would think of his establishing by executive order the Office of Economic Stabilization and giving it such powers. He feared that, if the proposal were placed before Congress, it would take months to obtain its passage.

"Mr. President, I think you have got to submit this matter to Congress if you want it to succeed," I replied. "This regulation of wages and prices is so controversial, it touches so many people so directly, that enforcement will be difficult without congressional authorization. It's going to be tough enough with it."

A few minutes later Secretary Ickes telephoned. He had heard about the proposal the President was considering and the old "curmudgeon" wanted me to urge the President to submit it to the Congress. When I said the President indicated he would do so, Harold was genuinely pleased.

The legislation was introduced and the bill became law on October 2, 1942. That day, the President sent me a message requesting me to come see him the next morning.

It was another of our many bedside talks, but it is especially memorable to me because it marked the end of my service in the legislative and judicial branches of the government and my first entry into the executive department.

There was hardly time for a "good morning" before the President said he wanted me to get a leave of absence from the Court and accept the appointment as Director of Economic Stabilization.

I deeply appreciated his suggestion but told him no one had the power to give a leave of absence to a Justice of the Supreme Court, that the

Justice alone was responsible for the discharge of his duties. I stated that the job of regulating wages and prices would involve so many decisions with political implications that it would not be right for me to remain on the Court.

"But you will remember," I continued, "that the first time I saw you after Pearl Harbor, right in this room, I offered to assist in any way that I could. If you think this appointment is important to the prosecution of the war, I will, without hesitation, resign from the Court and accept it."

"Jimmy, most of my time is devoted to the consideration of problems intimately and directly connected with the conduct of the war. It just isn't possible for me to devote sufficient time to the domestic problems. All these new agencies we have had to create mean an increasing number of jurisdictional conflicts which come to me for decision. I want you to settle those conflicts for me; I'll issue an executive order giving you power to settle them, and I'll let it be known that your decision is my decision."

Then, with a quick flicker of a smile, he added:

"The Director of Economic Stabilization is an important job, but it will be less important than the other duties I want you to perform for me by direct delegation. Will you do it?"

I told the President I would, and within the hour sent him my resignation from the Supreme Court.

It wasn't easy to leave the Court. No man trained in the law could lightly do so. I liked the work and liked my associates. But as a young member of the House during World War I, I had been deeply impressed with the vital part the home front plays in the winning of a war. And I had seen what a tragic role the home front had assumed in losing the peace. This appointment, I felt, would give me an opportunity to help Franklin Roosevelt achieve for this country the dream of Woodrow Wilson.

How I felt is accurately reflected in my first speech as Director of Economic Stabilization. It was delivered to the New York *Herald Tribune* Forum on November 16, 1942, and dealt largely with the danger of inflation. It ended with these words:

"If anything like inflation happened, our people would not be ready to take the part which we are pledged to take to organize the world for peace. There could be no greater tragedy. After a while, by drastic national action and radical social planning we would recover, but there would have passed the time when our leadership must be asserted if peace and order are to be established in a prostrate world. This, the strongest and most powerful nation in the world, must keep its own house in order. We must be in a position, when the war is over, to turn our energies, our productive resources to the arts of peace. We must show the way to a world of expanding freedom. We must show the way to a lasting peace."

The fight to hold wages and prices was a bitter struggle. It was a struggle against the desires of producers to obtain increased prices and of workers to win increased wages. Senators, Representatives, labor leaders, businessmen, farmers, and spokesmen for groups of all kinds would present their special case. Whenever they could, they would go to the President to present their complaint.

The President was good at taking them on. After listening sympathetically, he would say, "You know, Justice Byrnes is temperamental on this subject. I do not want to talk with him about it but you should go over and see him." They would take his advice. I saw many people. In fact, it was a job in which I made many acquaintances and no friends!

The effort to hold the line on wages and prices should have started with the beginning of the war. Because we entered the fight late, it was always an uphill battle. I became tired of saying, "I'm sorry but it can't be done." The line was bent in many places but it held much better than I ever expected it would.

From October 15, 1942, when the office really began operating, until April 1943, the cost of living index increased 4.3 per cent. Then we drafted and the President issued what was known as the Hold-the-Line Order. It gave even greater power to hold prices and wages. It brought to my office in the White House all the leaders of organized labor and organized agriculture.

Shortly thereafter, I concluded that the job of mobilizing our resources for the prosecution of the war had become so big that I could not devote adequate time both to it and to the problems of economic stabilization. After talking with the President, he suggested I draft the order establishing the Office of War Mobilization.

At my suggestion he asked Judge Vinson to become Director of the Office of Economic Stabilization. Vinson didn't hesitate one minute. He resigned from the Circuit Court of Appeals and ably and courageously administered the Hold-the-Line Order. From April 1943, until his resignation in April 1945, the cost of living index rose only 3.2 per cent. In the twenty-two months following his resignation and the abandonment of the Hold-the-Line Order the increase was 20.2 per cent.

Day after day the problems faced by the Office of War Mobilization demonstrated the direct and often critical relationship between the economic power of this country and the fate of the world. The number of kilowatts we generated and consumed determined directly how many airplanes would be over European and Asiatic targets. The rate at which we produced and transported petroleum acted almost as a speedometer on the movement of our armed forces. The amount of steel that went into ships or war plants had to be weighed against the probable need for pontoons to bridge the Rhine or the Irrawaddy. Every statistic on our farm production was scanned anxiously because it determined not only the number of soldiers we could support abroad but also the balance between life and death for thousands of our Allies.

Dramatic evidence of this awful fact was placed on my desk on November 22, 1943. The President had radioed a message from Teheran. He urgently requested data on how much our output of landing craft could be expanded and how rapidly deliveries could be made. Every agency was immediately summoned because I knew the request involved a decision by the three heads of government at Teheran on the opening of a second front.

On November 24, I wired the President that by the end of May, 1944—six months hence—we could deliver to our own seaports the following: 570 LSTs, 665 LCILs, 950 LCTs, 8,469 LCMs, 12,496 LCVPs and 99 LCCs. But to do it, we would have to give them priority over all other munitions including supplies promised for the Russian front. And it would require, in addition, slowing down our output of army trucks, naval shipping and high octane gasoline. Actually we did better than was promised.

Information on this critical item helped the principals at Teheran plan for the invasion of the European mainland in the summer of 1944. It was America's ability to produce that made possible our landing in Europe on schedule. Stalin acknowledged it once in a toast by saying: "Without American production the United Nations could never have won the war."

Even so, our productive capacity ran a race with time. How close we risked disaster I saw on a visit to the European front in October 1944. Near Cherbourg was one of the launching sites for the Nazis' V-bombs. It was placed in what had been an old rock quarry and was well camouflaged. When the Germans were driven out they had not quite completed the construction of a concrete roof that would have been thoroughly bombproof. Had our invasion been delayed many months beyond June 6, it is entirely possible that from such sites as these, bombs would have rained on England so effectively that we might never have succeeded in gathering and launching our invasion force.

It was the daily collision with these facts that prompted me to say to the National Press Club at a lunch on September 27, 1944:

"This generation of Americans can nobly gain or meanly lose the hope of the world. If America can use her productive powers for peace as she uses them for war, we shall nobly gain that hope. If America cannot use her productive powers for peace, America and the whole world will lose. . . . It is not a theory to be held but a condition to be met."

Chapter 2

Yalta—High Tide of Big Three Unity

DURING Christmas week of 1944, I was in the President's study talking to him about the shipping problem. As he looked up from the memorandum I had given him, he said:

"Jimmy, I want you to go with me on this trip to the Crimea."

It was a complete surprise. He had talked with me about the forthcoming meeting with Stalin and Churchill a number of times, but there had been no hint that I should be a member of the party.

"You know what went on at the other meetings," he added, "and as Director of Mobilization you have acquired a knowledge of our domestic situation that will be of great service in settling the economic questions that are certain to come up."

"When you are out of town," I told him, "the machinery doesn't stop. Problems like the one we are now discussing constantly arise. I think I should remain here and work on those problems."

He insisted, however, that I should go. I agreed, but was not happy about it.

We did not discuss it again until the day scheduled for our departure. That afternoon the OWMR staff met to discuss the problems that were expected to arise during my absence. The discussion convinced me more than ever that I should not go. I left the meeting and went over to see the President. He was having his hair cut by John Mays, the colored man who has greeted guests at the front door of the White House on all formal occasions for thirty-six years. Mays came to the White House from South Carolina during the administration of President Taft, and ever since has acted as barber and enjoyed the confidence of the residents of the White House. He is not only courteous and dignified, he is wise and discreet.

As Mays continued clipping, I again urged that I should remain in Washington. I outlined the problems we anticipated during the month he would be away. He had been so absorbed in foreign affairs he did not appreciate the number of questions and decisions then devolving on

21

the Director of War Mobilization and Reconversion. In fact, I had tried, in so far as possible, to keep domestic issues from intruding upon his consideration of foreign problems. The President persisted in his view that I should go, and I finally agreed. That night we left for Norfolk, where, in the early morning darkness of January 23, we boarded the heavy cruiser USS *Quincy*, which was to take us as far as Malta.

When we left Washington the President was suffering from a severe cold. On board ship it grew worse and he stayed in his cabin most of the time. He would come to lunch and dinner and after dinner attend a moving picture. But only once or twice was he able to sit on deck, until we reached the Mediterranean.

We were at sea on the President's birthday, January 30, and his daughter, Mrs. John Boettiger, made the birthday dinner a gala occasion. Gifts purchased from the ship's commissary were presented to the President. His devoted Filipino chef insisted on providing a birthday cake. But others had the same idea. The commissioned officers presented one; so did the enlisted men and the warrant officers. When four cakes arrived, one of our group, who remembered that the President had just been inaugurated to serve a fourth term, went out and procured a fifth cake. A large candle was stuck into it which the President was challenged to blow out.

Although he responded to the gaiety of the occasion, I was disturbed by his appearance. I feared his illness was not due entirely to a cold and expressed this concern to Mrs. Boettiger. She thought my opinion arose from observing him during the moving pictures, when she usually sat on one side of the President and I on the other. She explained that, while looking at the pictures, the President would have his mouth open because of his sinus trouble and that this made him look badly, but he was not really ill. Dr. McIntyre also expressed the belief that the President's appearance was due to the combination of sinus infection and cold. Since he had so often "bounced back" after an illness, I dismissed my fears.

By the time we reached Malta he had improved greatly. As the *Quincy* approached its anchorage we saw Prime Minister Churchill, in navy uniform, waving a greeting to the President from the deck of the H. M. S. *Sirius* across the channel. Shortly thereafter he and his daughter, Section Officer Sarah Oliver, came aboard for lunch. There were ten of us at lunch and discussion of the approaching conference was only general. The President did, however, confide to Churchill his plans to visit King Ibn Saud on his return trip to discuss the Palestine question. He wanted to bring about peace between the Arabs and the Jews. Churchill wished him good luck but didn't seem very hopeful that the President would meet with success. He didn't,

That night the President traveled for the first time in the Sacred Cow. Months earlier I had tried to induce him to use this airplane, built for his use and provided with an elevator which could be lowered from the plane to the ground, for his trips to Hyde Park and Warm Springs. He told me he disliked to fly; he disliked the monotony of looking at the clouds. His other objection was more surprising. He thought an unnecessary expense had been incurred in fitting a plane solely for his personal use. He said he had not been consulted about it and he did not approve it. This from a man who often had been accused of being the greatest spender ever to hold the office of President!

So far as I could see, the President had made little preparation for the Yalta Conference. His inauguration had taken place the Saturday before we left and for ten days preceding that he had been overwhelmed with engagements. On the cruiser, the President, Admiral Leahy and I, on four or five occasions, usually after dinner, discussed some of the questions to be considered, particularly the proposal for the United Nations. But not until the day before we landed at Malta did I learn that we had on board a very complete file of studies and recommendations prepared by the State Department. I asked the President if the Department had given him any material and he advised me it was all in the custody of Lieutenant William M. Rigdon. Later, when I saw some of these splendid studies I greatly regretted they had not been considered on board ship. I am sure the failure to study them while en route was due to the President's illness. And I am sure that only President Roosevelt, with his intimate knowledge of the problems, could have handled the situation so well with so little preparation.

Secretary of State Edward R. Stettinius, who had gone ahead by air, joined us at Malta. We were met also by Mr. Hopkins who had been visiting in London, Paris and Rome. Harry was sick. He took off for Yalta in the first available airplane and during the conference was confined to his bed most of the time. His great courage caused him to attend every session of .the conference, but immediately after adjournment he would retire to his room. Members of our delegation frequently held meetings there because Dr. McIntyre insisted he remain in bed.

There were some uneasy minds in our party as we took off from Malta. Our pilots were unfamiliar with the airfield at Saki where, we understood, there had been a considerable snowfall. We had conflicting reports on the hazards of the drive from Saki across the mountains to Yalta. There also was some fear of typhus, as we were told the Germans had left the place infested with vermin.

These worries were based on an underestimation of the prodigious effort the Russians exerted to demonstrate their hospitality. The landing strip at Saki was swept clear of every snowflake. The road from the field to Yalta, eighty miles away, was guarded by an unbroken line of Soviet troops, many of them girls—girls with guns. Livadia Palace, which was our headquarters and the scene of the meetings, was immaculate. We were told the Germans had completely ransacked it, leaving behind only two paintings out of all the furnishings in the huge building which had been a summer home for the Czars. Although some of the conveniences we fortunate Americans are accustomed to were missing, the Russians, with only three weeks' advance notice, had done an amazing job in completely renovating the place.

As we were shown to our rooms we were told what they had been used for when the Czars were in residence. We soon learned Fleet Admiral Ernest J. King had been assigned to the Czarina's boudoir. He was reminded of it throughout the conference.

The Yalta Conference opened on Sunday, February 4, 1945, on a rising tide of Allied victories. The German counteroffensive in the west had been stopped in the bloody snow of the Ardennes Forest, and we were preparing to launch our drive across the Rhine. The Russians had begun the drive on Germany's eastern frontier that was to end in Berlin three months later. The situation was such that at one time President Roosevelt and Marshal Stalin engaged in light banter as to whether they should wager that the Red Army would get to Berlin before the American Army recaptured Manila.

Our chief objective for the conference was to secure agreement on the Dumbarton Oaks proposals for the creation of an international peace organization. But the rapid advance of our armies required also that urgent consideration be given to European political and military problems. It was natural, then, that the President, with the agreement of the other members, opened the conference with the suggestion to discuss "what we shall do with Germany."

Stalin immediately made it clear that he wanted to discuss the terms of the German surrender, the future form of the German state or states, reparations, and the allocation of a zone of occupation to France.

In the fall of 1944 the Soviet Union and the Provisional Government of France had entered into a treaty of friendship. It was immediately obvious at Yalta, however, that the treaty and the friendly words exchanged over it by the diplomats had not changed in any degree Marshal Stalin's opinion on the contribution of France to the war. He thought France should play little part in the control of Germany, and stated that Yugoslavia and Poland were more entitled to consideration than France.

When Roosevelt and Churchill proposed that France be allotted a zone of occupation, Stalin agreed. But it was clear he agreed only because the French zone was to be taken out of the territory allotted to the

United States and the United Kingdom. And he especially opposed giving France a representative on the Allied Control Council for Germany. He undoubtedly concurred in the opinion expressed to the President by Mr. Molotov that this should be done "only as a kindness to France and not because she is entitled to it."

"I am in favor of France being given a zone," Stalin declared, "but I cannot forget that in this war France opened the gates to the enemy." He maintained it would create difficulties to give France a zone of occupation and a representative on the Allied Control Council and refuse the same treatment to others who had fought more than France. He said France would soon demand that de Gaulle attend the Big Three's Conferences.

Churchill argued strongly in favor of France's being represented on the Council. He said the British public would not understand if questions affecting France and the French zone were settled without her participation in the discussion. It did not follow, as Stalin had suggested, that France would demand de Gaulle's participation in the conferences of the Big Three, he added. And, in his best humor, Mr. Churchill said the conference was "a very exclusive club, the entrance fee being at least five million soldiers or the equivalent."

Stalin, however, feared there would be such a demand. He said General de Gaulle was "very unrealistic," and reiterated that even though "France had not done much fighting in the war, yet de Gaulle has demanded equal rights with the Soviets, the British and the Americans, who have done the fighting."

President Roosevelt did not take issue with Stalin on de Gaulle. The President had great admiration for France and its people but he did not admire de Gaulle. On several occasions he referred to a conversation at Casablanca in which de Gaulle compared himself with Joan of Arc as the spiritual leader of France, and with Clemenceau as the political leader.

President Roosevelt's first opinion was not to insist upon giving France representation on the Allied Council if she were allotted a zone. As the argument proceeded, however, the President said he wished to consider further that phase of the question and asked that action be delayed. The following day Mr. Hopkins, Averell Harriman, our Ambassador to the Soviet Union, and I urged upon the President the view that France should be represented on the Council, that they could not accept a zone without such representation, and that any other action would greatly humiliate them. The President finally reached the same conclusion, and he later succeeded in inducing Stalin to agree with him.

The major problem in connection with the surrender of Germany arose from an informal suggestion, broached at Teheran, that the future security of Europe required Germany to be cut up into a number of individual states.

The discussion was brief but there seemed to be general agreement among all three that Germany should be divided into an unspecified number of states. Marshal Stalin was of the opinion that the Germans in surrendering should be told about this plan. Mr. Churchill suggested that the questions involved were so complex that further study should be made. The President then suggested that the Foreign Ministers study the matter and submit recommendations within the next thirty days.

At the later meeting in London, in which Ambassador John G. Winant represented the United States, no agreement was reached. When Mr. Hopkins saw Marshal Stalin late in May it was apparent that the Soviet leader had changed his views and had reached the conclusion that we and the British were opposed to dismemberment. He said it was evident there was no agreement at Yalta; and that at the London meeting the British had interpreted the Crimean discussions to represent not a positive plan but something to hold over Germany's head in case of bad behavior. He suggested that the matter be discussed at the forthcoming meeting of the Big Three at Potsdam. By the time that meeting occurred, however, the thinking of all three governments had veered away from dismemberment and the issue did not arise.

During all the consideration of the German question at Yalta, reparations were the chief interest of the Soviet delegation.

At the conference table Marshal Stalin sat between Mr. Molotov and I. M. Maisky, Deputy Commissar for Foreign Affairs. Maisky had served as the Russian Ambassador in London for eleven years, and at Yalta often acted as interpreter as well as adviser to Stalin. It was he who presented the Soviet proposal on German reparations.

"Our plan foresees that reparations in kind should be demanded from Germany in two ways," Mr. Maisky explained. "First, withdrawals from the national wealth of Germany. That means factories, land, machinery, machine tools, rolling stock of railways, investments in foreign enterprises, and so on. Second, yearly payments in kind after the war in the course of ten years."

He proposed that 80 per cent of all German industry should be withdrawn, specifying the iron and steel, engineering, metal and chemical industries. He added that aviation plants, facilities for the production of synthetic oil and all other military enterprises and factories should be withdrawn entirely.

"By withdrawal I mean to confiscate and carry away physically and use as reparations payments," he emphasized.

Retention of 20 per cent of Germany's heavy industry would be adequate to sustain the country's economic life, he said. All reparations should be terminated within ten years and the removal of factories and other wealth should be completed in two years. German enterprises important as war potentials should be internationalized with representatives of the three powers sitting on the boards of these enterprises for as many years as the three countries should desire.

Reparations funds should be paid only to those countries that had sustained direct material losses such as damage to factories, land and homes and the losses of personal property by citizens, Mr. Maisky maintained. Because such losses were so huge he proposed that a system of priorities be established among the countries to receive reparations based on their contribution to the winning of the war and the value of their direct material losses.

He then stated that reparations should be fixed at twenty billions of dollars and that the share of the Soviet Union in the reparations fund should not be less than ten billion dollars.

Mr. Churchill responded first to Mr. Maisky's statement. He recalled the experience of the United Kingdom after World War I.

"The process was a very disappointing one," he said. "With great difficulty about 1,000 million pounds was extracted from Germany, and that would never have been extracted if the United States, at the same time, had not loaned Germany a larger sum."

"Removal of plants and factories to a certain extent is a proper step," he declared, "but I am quite sure you will never be able to get out of ruined Germany for Russia alone anything like 215 million pounds a year." He pictured Britain's losses and heavy debts and referred to the severe losses of other countries which must be considered in allotting reparations.

"Secondly," Mr. Churchill continued, "there arises in my mind the specter of an absolutely starving Germany.

"If our treatment of Germany's internal economy is such as to leave eighty million people virtually starving, are we to sit still and say, 'It serves you right,' or will we be required to keep them alive? If so, who is going to pay for that? . . . If you have a horse and you want him to pull the wagon you have to provide him with a certain amount of corn—or at least hay."

"But the horse must not kick you," Mr. Maisky objected.

Mr. Churchill switched to a nonkicking illustration by saying:

"If you have a motorcar you must give it a certain amount of petrol to make it go. I am in favor of having a reparations inquiry committee set up to explore this subject with the object of getting the most we can in a sensible way."

In presenting the position of the United States, President Roosevelt pointed out that after the last war we loaned to Germany billions of dollars, and emphasized "We cannot let that happen again."

"We are in the position of not wanting any of Germany's manpower," the President said. "We do not want any of her machinery, tools, or her factories. There will be some German assets in the United States that might be credited against what Germany owes the United States, but it will amount to very little." After the meeting I advised the President that the best estimate placed the value of German assets in this country at 150 million dollars and that the value certainly would not exceed 200 million. He later used these figures to point out what an exceedingly small amount we would receive in contrast to other nations.

The American people want the Germans to live, the President told the conference, but do not want them to have a higher standard of living than other states, such as the Soviet Republic. He stressed that the United States would emerge from the war in poor financial condition and that we would have no money to send into Germany for food, clothing or housing.

"All I can say is that we will do the best we can in an extremely bad situation," the President said, and concluded by adding we would support the creation of a reparations commission as proposed by the Soviet Union.

Marshal Stalin then entered the discussion. "The root of the trouble the last time," he asserted, "was that reparations were demanded in money. Then, the question arose of transferring the German mark into foreign currencies. That was the rock upon which reparations broke down."

Marshal Stalin urged that the three powers that carried the burden of the war should have priority in reparations. He said it must be admitted that "France did not have any sacrifice to compare to the three powers I have in mind." And then to clinch the argument, he said, "France at this time has in the war eight divisions while the Lublin government has ten divisions." There is no doubt that his opinion as to the claims of a government was influenced by the number of its divisions. He is credited with having said at Yalta, when reference was made to the views of the Pope, "How many divisions does he have?" The Marshal did not make that statement at Yalta. But it was the yardstick he frequently used.

Stalin concluded his statement with a proposal that a decision be made as to whether reparations should be based upon the contributions made in the prosecution of the war or upon the losses sustained, or whether both should be considered. During the discussion, the President made a statement which still remains a source of misunderstanding between ourselves and the Russians. He said the Reparations Commission "should take, in its initial studies as a basis for discussion, the suggestion of the Soviet government, that the total sum of reparations should be twenty billions and that fifty per cent of it should go to the Soviet Union."

This language was later incorporated in the Conference Protocol, the document prepared by a committee appointed to set forth in writing the agreements reached during a conference. The protocol, which on the last day of the conference was submitted to the heads of government for final approval, also contained the statement that the Reparations Commission could consider "the use of labor" as a possible source of reparations. There was no discussion of this proposal at the conference table except a passing reference by the President in which he said the United States "cannot take manpower as the Soviet Republics can." Later I learned the language was added by Mr. Maisky, the Soviet representative, and subsequently agreed to by the other delegations. At any rate, I did not know of it at the time I left Yalta. Had I known it, I would have urged the President to oppose the inclusion in the protocol of any provision for the use of large groups of human beings as enforced or slave laborers. The program later drafted by the Reparations Commission contained no provision for "the use of labor." But I regret to say that Germans and Japanese still are being held in Allied hands for use as laborers.

In the days that followed Yalta, as our armies fought their way into Germany from the east and the west, and as our combined air power and artillery pounded the cities of Germany into rubble, it became fully apparent there was no adequate answer to Prime Minister Churchill's contention that Germany would be unable to reimburse the Allies for all the losses inflicted on the people in the various Allied countries.

Closely related to the reparations issue was the problem of fixing Poland's boundaries. President Roosevelt said, at the outset of the discussion, that the United States felt that Poland's eastern boundary should generally follow the so-called Curzon Line. He still held, he said, the view he had expressed at Teheran that it would be desirable to adjust the southern end of the line so that the city of Lwow and at least a portion of the oil fields should be inside Polish territory.

Prime Minister Churchill pointed out he had supported the Curzon Line in Parliament including the Soviet Union's retention of Lwow. The claim of the Soviet Union to this area, he said, "is one not founded on force but upon right." But if the Soviet Union made a "magnanimous gesture to a much weaker power" such as that suggested by the President, Mr. Churchill said, Britain "would admire and acclaim the Soviet position."

Marshal Stalin replied with an impassioned statement.

"The Curzon Line is the line of Curzon and Clemenceau and of those Americans who took part in 1918 and 1919 in the conference which then took place," Stalin declared. "The Russians were not invited and did not take part. . . . Lenin was not in agreement with the Curzon Line. . . . Now some people want that we should be less Russian than Curzon was and Clemenceau was. You would drive us into shame. What will be said by the White Russians and the Ukrainians? They will say that Stalin and Molotov are far less reliable defenders of Russia than are Curzon and Clemenceau. I could not take such a position and return to Moscow with an open face."

At this point, Stalin stood at the conference table as he spoke. It was the only time during the entire conference that he exhibited his strong feelings in such a manner.

"I prefer the war should continue a little longer although it costs us blood and to give Poland compensation in the west at the expense of the Germans," he continued. "I will maintain and I will ask all friends to support me in this. . . . I am in favor of extending the Polish western frontier to the Neisse River."

Mr. Churchill doubted the wisdom of extending the western boundary of Poland to the Neisse River. He agreed that Poland's western boundary should be moved into what had been German territory but asserted "it would be a pity to stuff the Polish goose so full of German food that he will die of indigestion." He estimated that the taking of territory in East Prussia as far west as the Oder would necessitate the moving of six million Germans.

Stalin protested that the number would be much smaller because "where our troops come in, the Germans run away."

Churchill reminded him that consideration must be given "to where those Germans are that run away," and asked, "will there be room for them in what is left of Germany?"

Privately, Churchill expressed to me the opinion that placing the line at the Neisse River would mean the transferring of nearly nine million Germans. Such a number, he asserted, could never be absorbed in what would remain of Germany.

The discussion was long and earnest but Stalin finally accepted the Curzon Line in principle and the following somewhat equivocal statement on Poland's frontiers was approved for inclusion in the protocol:

"The three heads of government consider that the eastern frontier of Poland should follow the Curzon Line with digressions from it in some regions of five to eight kilometres in favour of Poland. They recognize that Poland must receive substantial accessions of territory in the North and West. They feel that the opinion of the new Polish Provisional Government of National Unity should be sought in due course on the extent of these accessions and that the final delimitation of the western frontier of Poland should thereafter await the peace conference."

Not only Poland's boundaries but Poland itself was one of the most serious issues of the entire conference. More time was spent on this subject than on any other. Because of the intensity of the argument, Mr. Roosevelt would assume a role more of arbiter than of advocate although he, as well as Prime Minister Churchill, urged the establishment of a new Polish government in Warsaw.

The Soviet Union, on the other hand, wanted to continue the Lublin government. Stalin was willing to add a few persons but he wanted to make certain that those who were added did not affect the Soviet Union's control of the government.

The President said he favored a Polish government which would resolve all the political differences by "creating a government of national unity, a government which would represent all the political parties." Such a government, he maintained, should be provisional, and should regard as its primary duty the establishment of a permanent regime. He said the United States wished to have Poland on friendly terms with the Soviet Union and he felt if the conferees should solve the Polish question, they could make it easier to establish peace in the world.

"Britain," the Prime Minister said, "declared war on Germany in order that Poland should be free and sovereign. Everyone knows what a terrible risk we took and how nearly it cost us our life in the world, not only as an Empire but as a Nation. Our interest in Poland is one of honor. Having drawn the sword in behalf of Poland against Hitler's brutal attack, we could never be content with any solution that did not leave Poland a free and independent sovereign state."

He repeated the sentiment expressed by the President saying that Poland should not be "free to entertain hostile designs against the peace and safety of the Soviets."

Mr. Churchill eloquently painted the danger which arose from the continuing existence of two Polish governments. He urged that provision be made for a free election and that, in the meantime, effective guarantees could be made to secure the lines of communication of the Soviet army.

Stalin displayed great earnestness in replying.

"For the Russian people, the question of Poland is not only a question of honor but also a question of security. Throughout history, Poland has been the corridor through which the enemy has passed into Russia. Twice in the last thirty years our enemies, the Germans, have passed through this corridor. It is in Russia's interest that Poland should be strong and powerful, in a position to shut the door of this corridor by her own force. . . . It is necessary that Poland should be free, independent in power. Therefore, it is not only a question of honor but of life and death for the Soviet state."

In every subsequent discussion the Soviet Government has used this argument to justify what it has done in Poland. Their idea of a friendly government is a government completely dominated by them. The Lublin government fitted this description and Stalin did not want to take any chances with representatives of other political parties. Later I discussed the subject with Mr. Molotov. I could not impress him with my views that Soviet security would be better assured by having in Poland a people who were friendly, rather than a government that was friendly only because it was dictated to by the Soviet Union. Unsuccessfully, I argued that governments would come and go, but that if the Soviet Government's conduct in Poland won the friendship of the people, the friendship of the government would be assured.

After the first discussion of Poland, President Roosevelt wrote a letter to Stalin suggesting that delegates from the Warsaw and London governments, and representatives of the several political factions in Poland not represented in those governments, meet to consider the formation of a new Polish Government. The letter became the basis of further discussions.

The conferees debated the President's proposal for several days. Finally they agreed on a declaration providing, among other things: "The provisional government which is now functioning in Poland should therefore be reorganized on a broader democratic basis with the inclusion of democratic leaders from Poland itself and from Poles abroad. This new government should then be called the Polish Provisional Government of National Unity."

A commission, composed of Mr. Molotov, Mr. Harriman and Sir Archibald Clark Kerr, was appointed to consult, first, in Moscow with members of the Lublin government, with democratic leaders from within Poland, and others from abroad, with a view to reorganizing the government along the lines indicated.

The declaration pledged the Provisional Government to the holding of free and unfettered elections as soon as possible on the basis of universal suffrage and secret ballot.

As the conferees neared what we thought was agreement on this troublesome issue, President Roosevelt asked:

"How long will it take you to hold free elections?"

"Within a month's time," Mr. Molotov replied.

The election which, by our standard, was not "free," actually was held twenty-three months later on Jaunary 19, 1947.

The day we arrived at Yalta I learned for the first time of a draft declaration of policy on the liberated areas that had been prepared by the State Department. The President did not like the declaration as drafted, but it greatly impressed me and I undertook to see if it could be revised to meet his objections. After conferences with Secretary Stettinius and other State Department officials a draft was prepared which received the President's approval.

When Secretary Stettinius presented the paper, several amendments were suggested by Foreign Secretary Eden and Foreign Minister Molotov. These were accepted and the paper was placed before the Big Three.

The declaration referred to "a principle of the Atlantic Charter—the right of all peoples to choose the form of government under which they will live—the restoration of sovereign rights and self-government to those peoples who have been forcibly deprived of them by the aggressor nations."

It then asserted:

"To foster the conditions in which the liberated peoples may exercise these rights, the three governments will jointly assist the people in any European liberated state or former Axis satellite state in Europe where in their judgment conditions require (a) to establish conditions of internal peace; (b) to carry out emergency measures for the relief of distressed peoples; (c) to form interim governmental authorities broadly representative of all democratic elements in the population and pledged to the earliest possible establishment through free elections of governments responsive to the will of the people; and (d) to facilitate where necessary the holding of elections."

Agreement was quickly reached among the Big Three. At least, we thought there had been a meeting of minds, but, ever since, there has been continual disagreement between the Soviets and ourselves as to its proper interpretation.

The discussion of the proposal was brief. Stalin opened it by saying, "On the whole, I approve of the declaration."

The President called attention to the paragraph containing the agreement to "facilitate if necessary the holding of elections," and Stalin quickly replied: "I accept that."

"Poland will be the first example of operating under this declaration," the President said. . . . "I want the election in Poland to be beyond question, like Caesar's wife. I did not know Caesar's wife, but she was believed to have been pure."

Stalin smilingly replied:

"It was said so about Caesar's wife, but, in fact, she had certain sins."

I only hope the lady had fewer sins than, in our view, this declaration has had violations. It seems to me there is no question as to the intention of the parties to the agreement. We thought it was a step forward. But it proved to be a very faltering step.

When the draftsmen assisting the Foreign Ministers agreed to include in the declaration a statement that certain things would be done by the three governments "where in their judgment conditions require," the Soviets were able to say—as they so often did—whenever they disliked to act, that in their judgment conditions did not require action.

The American public greeted the publication of this declaration with enthusiasm. Editorial writers commented on it favorably. From the close of the Yalta Conference to the present day it has been a source of conflict between the Soviet Union and ourselves. But it is the basis on which we have shown the world that Russian actions in eastern Europe have been in violation of Russia's pledged word. In that respect it has been useful.

In October 1943, Secretary of State Cordell Hull had taken with him to Moscow the first proposal that finally developed into the Dumbarton Oaks plan for a United Nations organization. He and the President believed it would be far easier to obtain agreement on a plan for a peace organization while the war was still in progress. How right they were!

At the conclusion of the Dumbarton Oaks Conference, in the autumn of 1944, the only major point remaining at issue was the formula for voting in the Security Council. The Soviet delegation had insisted that all decisions in the Security Council must be by a unanimous vote on the part of the major powers. We agreed that no decision committing our military forces to action should be taken without our consent but did not believe the right of veto should extend to all matters.

We finally had devised a compromise formula which we hoped the Soviets could be persuaded to accept, and the President sent it direct to Marshal Stalin on December 5. At the same time, the State Department prepared and delivered to the Soviet and British embassies in Washington lengthy statements in explanation and support of the President's proposal.

We sought to meet the Soviet insistence that the votes of the five permanent members of the Security Council must be unanimous on all questions by suggesting that Paragraph 3 in the section of the plan dealing with voting procedure in the Security Council should state that unanimity would be required for all categories of decisions except one: in those decisions involving promotion of peaceful settlement of disputes, a permanent member of the council would not cast a vote if it were party to the dispute in question. Such cases, we believed, would be quasi-judicial in character and no nation should be placed above the law in an organization based on the principle of equality under the law. Where the decisions might require the use of force, we felt justified in placing the permanent members in a special position, since they would have to bear the principal responsibility for such action.

It was on the second day of the conference that Secretary Stettinius formally presented our proposal, and the President then asked for its immediate consideration. In supporting the plan, the President referred to the agreement reached at Teheran in which the three heads of government declared: "We recognize fully that supreme responsibility resting upon us and all the United Nations to make a peace that will command the good will of the overwhelming mass of the peoples of the world and banish the scourge and terror of war for many generations."

Conflicting reports of the exchange that followed were presented in the Security Council of the United Nations in the spring of 1947 by the Soviet and the British representatives during a discussion of the veto power and its relationship to the control of atomic energy. Because of this, and because the veto power has remained one of the most controversial issues of the United Nations structure, it may be of interest to present here the major portion of my shorthand record of the views expressed on the veto issue at Yalta.

Since the United States, as the author of the proposal, had clearly stated its position, the exchange was almost entirely between Prime Minister Churchill and Marshal Stalin. It follows:

Prime Minister: "The peace of the world depends upon the lasting friendship of the three great powers, but His Majesty's Government feel we should be putting ourselves in a false position if we put ourselves in the position of trying to rule the world when our desire is to serve the world and preserve it from a renewal of the frightful horrors which have fallen upon the mass of its inhabitants. We should make a broad submission to the opinion of the world within the limits stated. We should have the right to state our case against any case stated by the Chinese, for instance, in the case of Hongkong. There is no question that we could not be required to give back Hongkong to the Chinese if we did not feel that was the right thing to do. On the other hand, I feel it would be wrong if China did not have an opportunity to state its case fully. In the same way, if Egypt raises a question against the British affecting the Suez Canal, as has been suggested, I would submit to all the procedure outlined in this statement. I would do this without fear because British rights would be preserved under paragraph 3 when our veto would kill action if we chose to use it.

"I presume, Mr. President, if Argentina raises a question against the United States, that the United States will submit to all the procedure of the last five paragraphs and would not vote on the issue. However, the United States could raise its fundamental objections in respect to all the measures to be taken under paragraph 3. . . .

"His Majesty's Government see no danger from their point of

view in associating themselves with the proposals of the United States. We see great advantage in the three great powers not assuming the position of rulers of all of the rest of the world without even allowing them to state their case. It would not be right for us with the great power we possess to take that position, denying them the right to state their case, and to have measures taken to adjust difficulties short of the powers set out in paragraph 3, on which powers we rely if we are not convinced by our friends and colleagues on the Security Council."

The Marshal: "I would like to have this document to study because it is difficult on hearing it read to come to any conclusion. I think that the Dumbarton Oaks decisions have, as an objective, not only to secure to every nation the right to express its opinion, but if any nation should raise a question about some important matter, it raises the question in order to get a decision in the matter. I am sure none of those present would dispute the right of every member of the Assembly to express his opinion.

"Mr. Churchill thinks that China, if it raised the question of Hongkong, would be content only with expressing opinion here. He may be mistaken. China will demand a decision in the matter and so would Egypt. Egypt will not have much pleasure in expressing an opinion that the Suez Canal should be returned to Egypt, but would demand a decision on the matter. Therefore, the matter is much more serious than merely expressing an opinion. Also, I would like to ask Mr. Churchill to name the power which may intend to dominate the world. I am sure Great Britain does not want to dominate the world. So one is removed from suspicion. I am sure the United States does not wish to do so, so another is excluded from the powers having intentions to dominate the world."

Mr. Churchill: "May I answer?"

The Marshal: "In a minute. When will the great powers accept the provisions that would absolve them from the charge that they intend to dominate the world? I will study the document. At this time it is not very clear to me. I think it is a more serious question than the right of a power to express its intentions or the desire of some power to dominate the world."

Prime Minister: "I know that under the leaders of the three powers as represented here we may feel safe. But these leaders may not live forever. In ten years' time we may disappear. A new generation will come which did not experience the horrors of war and may probably forget what we have gone through. We would like to secure the peace for at least fifty years. We have now to build up such a status, such a plan, that we can put as many obstacles as possible to the coming generation quarreling among themselves."

The Marshal: "I think that the task is to secure our unity in the future, and, for this purpose, we must agree upon such a covenant as would best serve that purpose. The danger in the future is the

possibility of conflicts among ourselves. If there be unity, then the
danger from Germany will not be great. Now we have to think how
we can create a situation where the three powers here represented,
and China—"

Prime Minister: "—and France."

The Marshal: "Yes, and we will keep a united front. I must
apologize to the conference. I have been very busy with other matters
and had no chance to study this question in detail. As far as I understand what was said in the American proposal, all conflicts are being
divided into two categories—conflicts which demand sanctions of
a military nature; the other category includes conflicts which could
be regulated by peaceful means without military sanctions. Then I
understand that, in the consideration of conflicts of both kinds, it
is contemplated there should be first a free discussion of the conflict.
I understand, also, that in considering the disputes of the first
category, which demand military sanctions, that a permanent member
being a party to the dispute has a right to vote. But in conflicts of
the second category, which could be regulated by peaceful means,
and do not require sanctions, the party in dispute is not allowed
to vote.

"We are accused of attaching too great importance to the procedure
'how to vote.' We are guilty. We attach great importance to the
question of voting. All questions are decided by votes and we are
interested in the decisions and not in the discussions. Suppose China
is a permanent member and demands Hongkong be returned to her.
I can assure Mr. Churchill that China will not be alone. They will
have some friends in the Assembly. That would be true of Egypt in
the case mentioned."

Prime Minister: "I could say 'no.' I would have a right to say that
the powers of the World Security Organization could not be used
against us if we remained unconvinced."

The Marshal: "There is another danger. My colleagues in Moscow
cannot forget the case which occurred in 1939 during the Russian-
Finnish War, when Britain and France used the League of Nations
against us and eventually expelled us and isolated us."

The President: "It is entirely satisfactory for the Marshal to
have sufficient time to study the proposal."

I was deeply disturbed by the clear evidence that Stalin had not considered or even read our proposal on voting in the Security Council
even though it had been sent to him by diplomatic air pouch on December 5. This was February 6, and it occurred to me that if in those
sixty-three days he had not familiarized himself with the subject, he
could not be greatly interested in the United Nations organization. It
was all the more impressive since this certainly was the only proposal
on the agenda with which he was not entirely familiar. My concern
remained even though at the next day's meeting Mr. Molotov announced

the Soviet Union's acceptance of our proposal, which was later adopted in substantially the same form at San Francisco.

The discussion on the United Nations then turned to what governments should become members. There followed this colloquy:

The Marshal: "I have a list of the states that declared war on Germany. It means that they become future members of the Assembly. Among those states are ten which have no diplomatic relations with the Soviet union. [Most of these ten were South American republics.] We are to meet with them to build up international security. How is it possible to build up international security with states that have no diplomatic relations with us at all? Perhaps the conference would discuss this matter."

The President: "I think most of them would like to establish diplomatic relations with the Soviet Union. They just have not got around to it yet. At the same time it should be recognized that most of the states that have not recognized the Soviet Union have been sitting with the Soviet representatives at Bretton Woods and other places in conferences that have been held."

The Marshal: "That is right. But it is difficult to build up international security with states that do not want to have anything to do with the Soviet Union."

The President: "I think the easiest way to establish complete diplomatic relations with them is to invite them. This whole question involves a matter of history which should be explained.

"Four years ago the Acting Secretary of State, Mr. Welles, told the South American republics it was not necessary to declare war on Germany but that it was necessary to cut off diplomatic relations. So there are five or six republics which think they should be invited because they took the advice of the United States at that time. This matter was brought to my attention one month ago. As a result, I sent a letter to the Presidents of these six republics, explaining that if they want to attend the Conference of United Nations they should declare war. I think one, Ecuador, has done so, but has not yet had a chance to sign the Declaration of the United Nations. Paraguay will do so in a week or ten days. Peru and Uruguay will soon declare war. The result is that it would be a little embarrassing if, after they declared war, they should then be excluded from coming to the meeting. Quite frankly, it was a mistake of Mr. Welles in not advising them to declare war instead of merely breaking off diplomatic relations.

"In the meantime all these nations have helped us in the conduct of the war. A large part of the raw materials for the manufacture of munitions has come from them. The result is, I am in a difficult position.

"In addition to those nations that have signed, there are a small number called associated nations which have worked with us. They broke diplomatic relations but did not declare war."

The Marshal: "What about Argentina?"

The President: "The Argentines are not in it at all."

The Marshal: "But the Argentines broke relations with Germany."

The President: "But have not been accepted as an associated nation."

The Marshal: "I am not for the Argentines. I do not like them; but I do desire there should be no logical contradiction. If we invite the nations that declared war and also the associated nations that have broken relations, there is then a category of nations like Argentina. This means Turkey and some other countries would come. I think the nations which declared war would feel not quite at ease with those nations that have not declared war, but were saving all the time, trying to speculate on who would win and who generally were not straight in their behavior."

The President: "My idea would be to invite only those associated nations that have helped us on the condition that they declare war."

The Marshal: "When should they act?"

The President: "Right away. Put a time limit on them."

The Marshal: "Say, the first of March."

The President: "All right, the first of March."

Mr. Churchill also approved this solution, citing Turkey as an example of a state that had remained neutral heretofore and had been encouraged to do so. Although somewhat reluctant, Marshal Stalin likewise agreed.

Immediately after announcing the Soviet Union's acceptance of the President's proposal on voting procedure in the Security Council, Mr. Molotov expressed the hope that Byelorussia, the Ukraine and Lithuania would be admitted to the United Nations. In any event, he said, he hoped the first two would be admitted. Marshal Stalin made a forceful plea in support of the suggestion.

Prime Minister Churchill supported the Soviet request, stating: "My heart goes out to White Russia, bleeding from her wounds while beating down the tyrants."

Not wishing to agree, and yet not wanting to oppose Churchill and Stalin directly while the issue of the international organization was in the balance, the President made this statement: "The British Empire has great populations in its dominions, like Australia, Canada and South Africa. The Soviet Government has great masses of population like the three dominions mentioned. The United States has no colonies but has a large population. Brazil is smaller than the Soviet Union but larger in area than the United States. There are many countries with small population, like Honduras and Liberia. We must study the question of whether any country should be given more than one vote. I do not want to break down the principle of one vote to each nation. Therefore, we can decide on the general plan of a meeting to organize the association and then before the meeting, through the Foreign Secretaries, or at that meeting, we can decide these questions and I will be glad to take them up."

There was no dissent. Because I was strongly opposed to granting the Soviet request, I thought the President had done a good job and that we might hear no more of the proposal. But at the conference table the next afternoon the President began reading a report of the meeting of the Foreign Ministers which had just been handed him and said:

"Paragraph 2 is that it will be for the conference to determine the list of the original members of the organization. At that stage the delegates of the United Kingdom and the United States will support the proposal to admit to original membership two Soviet Socialist republics."

The report was agreed to.

I learned later that at the Foreign Ministers meeting, Mr. Eden, who wanted to be certain of the admission of all members of the British Commonwealth including India, which was not an independent state, agreed with Mr. Molotov on the votes for Byelorussia and the Ukraine. Mr. Stettinius then also agreed to the arrangement. As the meeting opened, the Secretary advised the President of the action which the President later announced, and the heads of government approved.

I was surprised at the agreement which, in my opinion, was very unwise. After the meeting I urged my view upon the President. I reminded him that before we left Washington he had told a group of Senators that if Stalin proposed granting membership to Byelorussia and the Ukraine, he would insist upon membership for each of our forty-eight states. The truth is, the Soviet republics are no more independent than the states of our Union.

I recalled to him how effectively the opponents of the League of Nations had argued that the British, because of their dominions, would have five votes in the Assembly while we would have but one. Our people had come to realize that the dominions were independent states and frequently held views different from the United Kingdom, but that was not true of the Soviet republics. I feared the opponents of the United Nations might use the allotment of three votes to the Soviet Union as effectively as the foes of the League had used the argument against the British votes twenty-six years earlier. I urged the President at least to ask that the United States be granted a number of votes equal to those of the Soviet Union. The President feared it was too late but said he would consider it.

I convinced Hopkins that, at the very least, we should secure such an agreement from Stalin and Churchill whether or not we afterward exercised the right. He then joined me in urging the President to withdraw his agreement regarding the two Soviet republics unless Russia agreed the United States also should have three votes. The President finally told us he would present it to Marshal Stalin. On the last day I spent at Yalta, February 10, the President wrote him a letter which stated:

> I am somewhat concerned lest it be pointed out that the United States will have only one vote in the Assembly. It may be necessary for me, therefore, if I am to insure wholehearted acceptance by the Congress and people of the United States of our participation in the World Organization, to ask for additional votes in the Assembly in order to give parity to the United States.
>
> I would like to know, before I face this problem, that you perceive no objection and would support a proposal along this line if it is necessary for me to make it at the forthcoming conference.

The following day Marshal Stalin advised the President that he entirely agreed with him that "since the number of votes for the Soviet Union is increased to three in connection with the inclusion of the Soviet Ukraine and Soviet White Russia among the members of the Assembly, the number of votes for the USA should also be increased.

"The number of votes for the USA might be increased to three as in the case of the Soviet Union and its two basic republics," he said. "If it is necessary I am prepared officially to support this proposal."

President Roosevelt also asked Churchill for his views, and Churchill stated he would support the President in any proposal he made to achieve American equality with other nations.

When I arrived in Washington there was waiting for me in the White House Map Room the following cable:

For Justice Byrnes from Mr. Hopkins
THE PRESIDENT HAS RECEIVED COMPLETELY SATISFACTORY REPLIES FROM THE PRIME MINISTER AND MARSHAL STALIN ON ADDITIONAL VOTES TO ACHIEVE PARITY FOR THE UNITED STATES, IF NECESSARY. IN VIEW OF THE FACT THAT NOTHING ON THIS WHOLE SUBJECT APPEARS IN THE COMMUNIQUÉ, THE PRESIDENT IS EXTREMELY ANXIOUS NO ASPECT OF THIS QUESTION BE DISCUSSED EVEN PRIVATELY.

I assumed he had some very good reason for not wishing this matter to be discussed, and I complied with the request.

The President and his advisers concluded not to ask at San Francisco for compliance with the agreement that we have as many votes as were given to Russia. He did not again discuss the subject with me, and I did not know he had changed his mind. I admit that the public opposition to Russia's three votes as against our one was not so great as I had expected. But nevertheless I think we should have insisted at San Francisco on the agreement made at Yalta. I felt then and feel now that the smaller states would have opposed the request of the Soviets and the United States. This course would have been just and it would have resulted in both governments having only one vote. That would have been the best solution.

In granting three votes to the Soviet Union, we established a precedent. The Soviets do not overlook precedents favorable to themselves. At the Peace Conference in Paris, for example, Byelorussia and the Ukraine were members. They will demand membership in every other conference. This means the Soviet Union has three arguments as well as three votes. They never fail to make the three arguments or cast the three votes.

The Paris Peace Conference agreed upon two kinds of recommendations, one requiring only a majority vote, the other requiring a two-thirds vote. The Soviet representatives announced that in the Council of Foreign Ministers they would not consider any recommendation adopted by less than a two-thirds vote.

There were twenty-one members of the peace conference. Therefore, eight votes in opposition to a recommendation would prevent its receiving the two-thirds endorsement. When the Soviets opposed a proposal, it was much easier for them to secure these eight votes because they had three votes to start with. Had the Soviets possessed only one vote, or had the United States been given three votes, as was agreed at Yalta, many of the recommendations which received thirteen votes, one short of two-thirds, would have been adopted.

Another agreement was made at Yalta which was to confront me later. This was the "Top Secret" Protocol in which it was agreed that in return for Soviet participation in the war against Japan, the Kurile Islands would be "handed over" to the Soviet Union. It also provided that "the former rights of Russia violated by the treacherous attack of Japan in 1904 shall be restored," and listed these as the return of the southern half of Sakhalin Island, internationalization of the Port of Dairen, the lease of Port Arthur as a Russian naval base, and joint Russo-Chinese operation of the Chinese Eastern and South Manchurian railroads. The United States was to use its influence to have China agree to that part affecting China's territory.

I did not know of this agreement, but the reason is understandable. At that time I was not Secretary of State. Mr. Stettinius was Secretary.

Because of problems that had arisen in Washington, the President wanted me to return with Admiral King, who was leaving at noon on February 10. We expected the conference would end that evening and that the President would leave the following day. But that afternoon Stalin requested the President to remain one more day. He said they could not conclude their work and he wished to discuss some matter he deemed important. The President complied. The agreement as to the Kurile Islands was reached in private conversations among the Big Three instead of at the conference table, and the protocols, including this one, were signed on February 11. Had I been in Yalta that day it is probable I would have learned of it.

When the President returned, he did not mention it to me and the protocol was kept locked in his safe at the White House. In the early summer I learned that President Roosevelt had undertaken to induce China to make the concessions affecting Port Arthur, Dairen, and the railroad, but it was not until some time after I became Secretary of State that a news story from Moscow caused me to inquire and learn of the full agreement. I presented the matter to President Truman and he requested Admiral Leahy to transfer to the State Department those documents at the White House containing agreements with foreign governments. I wanted to know how many IOUs were outstanding.

In considering the wisdom of these Pacific agreements entered into by President Roosevelt, one should be fair enough to consider the circumstances under which the promises were made. It was six weeks after the serious German counterattack on the western front. Although progress was being made in both the east and the west, neither the President nor anyone else at that time knew how long the Germans could hold out and how many casualties we would suffer before they surrendered. The President had with him at Yalta the Joint Chiefs of Staff. They knew the situation.

The evidence is clear that the agreement was, in great part, a military decision. The military leaders already had their plans for the invasion of Japan under way. They undoubtedly gave the President their estimate of what such an invasion would cost us in human lives with Russia in the war and what the cost would be if Russia were out of the war. They naturally wanted Russia in the war to engage the Japanese armies in the north. But once Stalin knew our plans for invasion were under way, he knew also that we would want his armies and he could demand more for them. Mr. Stalin is not bashful about making demands.

Nor should President Roosevelt be criticized for keeping the agreement secret. The Soviet Union was party to a treaty with Japan and we could not announce Russia's intention to go to war with her. Furthermore, Russia's military strength was then concentrated on the German campaign. Any hint of the agreement would have been an invitation to the Japanese troops on Russia's borders to launch an invasion. It was in the interest of all of us to allow the Soviets ninety days after Germany's surrender to transfer troops from the European front. It is, therefore, quite understandable that both Marshal Stalin and President Roosevelt wished to maintain strict secrecy.

Toward the end of the conference, Marshal Stalin entertained at dinner. At the time, the press quoted one of the Americans present as saying forty-five toasts were proposed. I am willing to believe it, but the simple statement certainly is misleading. Unexplained, it would indicate the diners were thoroughly intoxicated. The fact is that with each toast, the diners took only a sip of wine and many made the gesture without the sip. The dinner lasted four hours. Forty-five sips of wine in four hours, during which time enough food was consumed to last twenty-four hours, did not intoxicate any one of that group. As for me, I do not drink wine.

About the time we reached the soup course, I noticed Mr. Vyshinski, who was sitting near me, pouring water into his vodka glass. Since vodka is the color of water, I decided if he could do it, I could. In the confusion incident to everyone's standing up when a toast was proposed, I would pour water into my vodka glass. It was not very stimulating, but I do know what took place at the dinner. Because of some of the reports in the United States about Soviet officials getting intoxicated, it is only fair to say that all those with whom I have come in contact have been most temperate. Never have I seen a Soviet representative at a social affair who showed the slightest evidence of intoxication.

The Marshal was generous in the toast he proposed to Churchill and particularly generous in his remarks proposing the health of the President, whom he described as the "chief forger of the instruments which had led to the mobilization of the world against Hitler."

The Prime Minister toasted Marshal Stalin as the "mighty leader of a mighty nation whose people had driven the tyrants from her soil." The President spoke with pride of the unity that characterized the relations among the three countries, and expressed the hope it would continue.

One statement of Stalin's that interested me was: "It is not so difficult to keep unity in time of war since there is a joint aim to defeat the common enemy, which is clear to everyone. The difficult task will come after the war when diverse interests tend to divide the Allies. It is our duty to see that our relations in peacetime are as strong as they have been in war."

I can testify to the accuracy of his prophecy, and I share his views as to our duty.

When toasts had been proposed to all the military chieftains and the heroes of the war on land, sea, and in the air, I proposed a toast "to the people of our respective countries—the workers on farms and in factories—who did not wear the uniform but whose contribution made possible our victories." The Marshal left his place and came to clink his glass with mine in approval of the sentiment. The truth is, he is a very likeable person.

The report of the Yalta Conference was released simultaneously from London, Moscow and Washington on Monday afternoon, February 12. All the Allied nations responded favorably and American public opinion was especially enthusiastic. The Philadelphia *Record* called the conference the "greatest United Nations victory of the war." The New York *Herald Tribune* declared that "the overriding fact" is that the conference "has produced another great proof of Allied unity, strength and power of decision." And *Time Magazine* asserted: "all doubts about the Big Three's ability to co-operate in peace as well as in war seem now to have been swept away."

That was how I felt about it. There is no doubt that the tide of Anglo-Soviet-American friendship had reached a new high. But President Roosevelt had barely returned to American soil when the tide began to ebb.

Chapter 3

The Tide Begins to Turn

BACK home, in February 1945, there was a huge amount of work to plunge into. The shortage of manpower was critical and the proposed National Service Act, generally called the "work-or-fight" bill, was the center of controversy both on Capitol Hill and among the agencies concerned. Our entire production program was under review in anticipation of the end of the war in Europe. Plans for post V-E Day lend-lease, surplus property disposal and emergency relief were being made; and the policies for reconverting our industrial establishment from war to peacetime operations were being shaped.

During my absence these plans had been greatly advanced through the tireless efforts of the people in my office, including General Lucius D. Clay, whom I had induced the War Department to assign to my office a few months earlier. Assisting him was Fred Searls, a New York industrialist—a quiet, unassuming man, with extraordinary knowledge of industrial processes. Throughout the war, he ably filled a number of responsible positions, refusing salary and reimbursement for expenses and avoiding publicity. He served his country well.

The previous June, when the bill to expand the Office of War Mobilization into the Office of War Mobilization and Reconversion was under consideration in Congress, I had stated to the committee I was not asking for power for myself in the postwar era, because I would not remain in the government to administer the reconversion program. We then thought little would be done in the way of reconversion until the European war ended. However, immediately following our return from Yalta, we decided that the emphasis should immediately shift from mobilization to reconversion.

It was, therefore, necessary for me to give some thought to the manner and timing of my departure from government service. It seemed only fair that the man who would have to assume responsibility for administering the reconversion program should take charge as soon as possible, and should not be placed in the position of having to administer policies he had no part in drafting.

Nevertheless, the question of timing troubled me. We knew V-E Day could not be far distant, but there was a danger that what was evident in Washington might not be so clear to the GI, who still had to fight his way across the Rhine. I did not want to take any action, however desirable for domestic reasons, that would carry to the fighting fronts the remotest suggestion that there was a slackening of effort, enthusiasm or support by those in responsible positions at home.

By mid-March we had established a foothold on the east bank of the Rhine and had received word from Field Marshal Alexander that high German officers had proposed a meeting in Switzerland to arrange for the surrender of the German Army in Italy. Consequently, when we started moving across the Rhine in force on March 23, I concluded it was wrong to postpone action any further, and the following day I presented to the President a letter of resignation, asking that it become effective April 2. I fixed that date because the law required the filing of a quarterly report with the President and Congress on April 1, and necessarily I had to submit that report.

When the President tried to persuade me to remain, I reminded him of his promise the previous fall that with the end of the war in Europe I could leave. I told him that I had left the Court only to undertake a wartime task; that I did not want to become the head of an agency or bureau in time of peace. I convinced him that the man who was going to direct the reconversion program should be given an opportunity to share in drafting that program, and it was essential therefore that the change be made.

We discussed many things, including the plans for the occupation of Germany. He understood the War Department was planning to send Assistant Secretary of War, John J. McCloy, to Germany to head our organization. I informed him McCloy had decided to remain with Secretary Stimson and that my deputy, General Clay, had been selected by the War Department for the assignment. To my surprise, he did not know General Clay. I told him I had obtained his assignment to my office, because, after dealing with officials of all the departments, I had found no man more capable than Clay and no army officer who had as clear an understanding of the point of view of the civilian. The President remarked that I was unusually enthusiastic about Clay and asked that I bring him in for a talk. The President was leaving that day for Hyde Park but would be spending a day in Washington the following week en route to Warm Springs. We agreed the three of us would get together that day. Shortly after the President arrived in Hyde Park he telephoned me to ask that I reconsider my resignation, and then, when I did not change my mind, he asked that I suggest a successor. I recommended Judge Fred M. Vinson, who had succeeded me as head of the Office of

Economic Stabilization. The President indicated agreement and said we could discuss it when he returned.

The President was unusually nervous the day of his return. During our talk he told General Clay he was glad he was going to Germany and he wanted the general, who was an engineer, to know of his idea of establishing a TVA in Central Europe to develop greater electrical power and relieve Europe's chronic coal shortage. Clay stood at attention. The President did not give him a chance to say a word, and as soon as the President had finished Steve Early came into the room. I knew the President was behind his schedule and asked Clay to wait outside for me. I remained for a few minutes to ask about Vinson and the President told me he would appoint Vinson, and asked me to talk to him because he had a number of engagements to fill before leaving that afternoon for Warm Springs. He would telephone Fred later in the day.

When I left the President's office and rejoined Clay, I said jokingly: "General, you talk too much."

"Mr. Justice," Clay replied, "even if the President had given me a chance, I doubt that I could have talked to him because I was shocked at his appearance."

Clay had not seen the President for some time. For forty-one crowded, exciting months, I had been at work in the White House and, because I saw him frequently, I did not realize, as Clay did, the change in his appearance. Although, when we parted, I had felt that an eventful chapter in our relationship was ended, I certainly did not appreciate that for him the end of life's journey was only a few days away. While waiting for Judge Vinson's appointment to be confirmed, I talked to the President on our direct line to Warm Springs several times and he professed to be feeling much better. I concluded that he was staging a "comeback" as he had done on many previous occasions.

On April 8, I returned to Spartanburg, where the friendly people who are my neighbors gave me a warm welcome. Four days later, with millions of people all over the world, I was stunned by the radio announcement that President Roosevelt was dead.

The Secretary of the Navy, James V. Forrestal, telephoned that he was sending his plane to Spartanburg to bring me to Washington because he thought I might be of some service during the next few days and he knew I would want to attend the President's funeral.

Early the next morning I called to see President Truman. He was overwhelmed by the responsibilities suddenly thrust upon him but was rapidly familiarizing himself with the status of pending problems. That afternoon I returned to the White House and he requested me to ride with him the next morning to meet the train bringing the body of President Roosevelt, and to accompany him on the sad journey to Hyde Park.

On the train returning to Washington the President and I discussed many matters. As I had been out of the White House only a few days, I was able to acquaint him with the status of many serious problems in our foreign and domestic relations. In the course of this conversation the President said he would like me to attend the forthcoming United Nations Conference in San Francisco as his representative.

"Mr. President, I appreciate your suggestion very much, but I don't think you ought to send me," I replied. "The delegation already is appointed. It is a representative group and includes some very able people. Experience has shown that a personal representative of the President under such circumstances usually causes great dissatisfaction in a delegation. Almost invariably relationships become more personal than representative." President Truman agreed.

The following day he told me he wished to appoint me Secretary of State. I did not want in time of peace to be head of an agency considering reconversion problems but I did want to take part in the making of the peace. I said I would accept the appointment, and we agreed that neither the change nor the announcement should be made until the end of the San Francisco Conference which was just about to meet.

Probably no new President ever faced a swifter pageant of great events than did Mr. Truman in his first weeks in office. The collapse and surrender of Germany and the San Francisco Conference held the center of the stage before a world audience that was stirred by victory and filled with high hopes for the future.

But those of us who were familiar with Soviet activities following the Yalta Conference found our high hopes mingled with great concern.

Before President Roosevelt's death, in fact, even before his return from Yalta, difficulties had arisen with the Soviet Union regarding the action to be taken on the agreements reached. The two major points of difficulty were Poland and Rumania.

In the Declaration on Liberated Europe the three governments had exchanged pledges to "concert during the temporary period of instability in liberated Europe the policies of their three governments in assisting the peoples liberated from the domination of Nazi Germany and the peoples of the former Axis satellite states of Europe to solve by democratic means their pressing political and economic problems." It stated further that the three governments "will jointly assist" the peoples of this area "to form interim governmental authorities broadly representative of all democratic elements in the population and pledged to the earliest possible establishment, through free elections of governments responsive to the will of the people." And finally, it added that "when, in the opinion of the three governments, conditions in any European liberated state or any former Axis satellite state in Europe make such action necessary, to discharge the joint responsibilities set forth in this declaration."

Nevertheless, on February 24, only two weeks after the conference, when the American and British members of the Allied Control Council for Rumania requested a meeting of the council, their request was refused by the Soviet chairman. On that same day, Ambassador Harriman was instructed to indicate to the Soviet Government our desire to see an orderly development of the Rumanian situation under the Allied Control Council or else consultation among the three countries on a higher level.

Three days later we got our answer. Mr. Molotov's deputy, Andrei Vyshinski, went to Bucharest and presented a demand for the dismissal of the Radescu government and the formation of a new Rumanian government. At the same time, Mr. Molotov informed our Ambassador that the Radescu government was unable to maintain order and fulfill the armistice terms and that the Allied Control Council would take the necessary measures and keep the Allies informed.

Mr. Harriman was instructed immediately to inform the Soviet Government that we could not accept a provisional government in Rumania made up of representatives from one political party. His instructions also stated that measures should be taken to support the present government in maintaining order; that freedom of press should be granted in accordance with the armistice agreement; that all political groups should be disarmed; and that full three-member consultations should take place in the Allied Control Council on major political matters.

Mr. Molotov told Mr. Harriman that three power consultations were going on with Vyshinski in Bucharest.

On March 5, our Ambassador presented a letter to Mr. Molotov stating that the question of the Radescu government was a matter for direct consultation and agreement by all three governments. He advised Molotov that the Soviet member of the Allied Control Council had not kept the United States representative informed and that the Soviet military authorities had weakened the ability of the Radescu government to maintain order. He followed this with another note the next day rejecting the idea that the intermittent contacts with Vyshinski constituted the tripartite consultations agreed upon at Yalta.

While these exchanges were taking place between our Ambassador and Foreign Minister Molotov in Moscow, here is what was happening in Rumania:

On February 27, Mr. Vyshinski had arrived in Bucharest and requested an audience with the King that evening. He was received by the King and Foreign Minister Constantine Visoianu. Mr. Vyshinski stated that General Radescu was incapable of maintaining order; that the Soviet government was unwilling to interfere in Rumania's internal affairs but had the responsibility of seeing that order was maintained behind the front and, therefore, asked that the Radescu government be dismissed immediately and replaced by a government based on "the truly democratic forces of the country." He was told that consideration would be given his request.

Burton Y. Berry, our political representative in Bucharest, was unable to obtain an interview with Vyshinski. He then informed Vyshinski in writing of the American point of view—that no decisive action should be taken prior to consultation.

According to the information sent us by Mr. Berry, Mr. Vyshinski the next day demanded an audience with the King and asked for his decision on the suggestion of the previous evening. The King replied he had communicated this information to General Radescu and had started consulting party leaders for the purpose of choosing another Prime Minister. Vyshinski declared this answer was unsatisfactory. Then, the report stated, Vyshinski looked at his watch and told the King he had just two hours and five minutes to make it known to the public that General Radescu had been dismissed. By eight o'clock, he added in emphasis, the King must tell the public the name of his successor.

The Rumanian Foreign Minister reminded Mr. Vyshinski that the King was a constitutional monarch and had to proceed in a constitutional manner; that he could only consult party leaders and follow their advice in selecting some individual to form a government. Vyshinski retorted that Radescu was protecting Fascists and by retiring ten officers the previous day under a royal decree had performed an unfriendly act toward the Soviet Union. That decree, he said, must be annulled immediately. The King acceded to this request and Mr. Vyshinski left. In leaving he slammed the door so hard that the plaster around the door frame was cracked badly. It has never been fixed; it remains to testify to the strength of his feeling and of his arm.

The King announced that he had asked Prince Stirbey to form a government. Prince Stirbey tried to comply but could not induce the Communists to join in forming a government. Shortly afterward Mr. Vyshinski sent word to the King that the Communist leader, Petru Groza, was the choice of the Soviet government. Nevertheless, the King continued to consult party leaders and on the evening of March 1, Vyshinski again saw the King to inform him personally that the Soviet Union wanted Groza appointed. The King then decided to charge Groza with the formation of a government.

Because the first Cabinet suggested by Groza was not representative of the people, the King refused to accept it. Vyshinski then sent word that cancellation of the Groza appointments would be considered by the Soviet Government as a hostile act. Mr. Vyshinski was quoted as saying that unless the King accepted the Groza government by the afternoon of the following day, he would not be responsible for the continuance of Rumania as an independent state.

At the same time Groza announced that the Soviets had promised great improvement in relations between the Soviet Government and Rumania, mentioning the return to Rumania of control over its transportation system, the cession of Transylvania from Hungary and a relaxing in the terms of the armistice. The result was that the King summoned the leaders of the historic parties Monday night and appealed to them to disregard political considerations and support his action in accepting the Groza government.

The leaders of the historic parties could not agree and the King was urged by some to abdicate. However, he concluded he could best serve the people by not deserting the country. On Tuesday night, March 6, the Groza government was sworn in and immediately afterward Marshal Malinovsky arrived in Bucharest where he and Vyshinski had an audience with the King. They told the King that they could not concentrate upon front line activities if they had unrest behind the lines. The Rumanian government had failed in the past to maintain order, they said, and it would not be permitted again.

On March 7, the day after the Groza government was installed, Mr. Molotov informed our Ambassador in Moscow that the questions raised in his letter of March 5 had lost point since the crisis in Rumania had been overcome by the formation of a new government.

The following September, while in London, Mr. Molotov urged that we recognize the Rumanian government. I told him we had not recognized the Groza government because of the character of the government which had been installed by virtue of a two-and-a-half hour ultimatum given to the King by Vyshinski. Mr. Molotov then admitted that Mr. Vyshinski had "helped in the formation of the government," but said the Soviet Government had acted because "there was very serious danger of disorder and civil war."

These developments, of course, had been reported in full to President Roosevelt. As a result, instructions had been sent to Mr. Harriman to propose to Mr. Molotov the establishment of a joint committee in Bucharest to safeguard the application of the principles announced in the Declaration on Liberated Europe. Mr. Molotov's rejection of this proposal was blunt. In a note dated March 17 he stated that no action was required; that our proposal would emasculate the Allied Control

Council, and asserted it was untrue that our representative on the council had never been consulted.

All of this occurred while the Allied armies were closing in on Berlin and President Roosevelt was anxious to avoid giving aid and comfort to the enemy by a public display of disunity. The President told me he had grave misgivings about the future. However, he decided that, for the time being, our protest should be filed through our Ambassador and that he would resort to direct communication to Stalin only after other efforts were exhausted.

In the fall of 1944, Churchill and his Foreign Minister, Anthony Eden, had visited Moscow and, while there was no formal agreement, we knew they had reached the informal understanding that, if the British found it necessary to take military action to quell internal disorders in Greece, the Soviets would not interfere. In return, the British would recognize the right of the Soviets to take the lead in maintaining order in Rumania.

The British heartily disapproved of Soviet actions in Rumania but they did not want to take the initiative in protesting to Stalin. The President felt that the Rumanian situation did not offer the best test case of our relations with the Soviets. Great Britain and the United States had no armed forces in Rumania. It was under the exclusive control of the Red Army. The President knew that the Soviets had to maintain a line of communication from the homeland through Rumania to their armies in Germany. He knew the Soviets would claim the action taken was necessary to protect their armies and he knew we could not obtain from Rumanians, who were under the domination of the Red Army, information to contradict the Soviet claim of interference with the army. He felt that Soviet action in Poland was more clearly in violation of the Yalta agreement.

The Yalta decision on Poland contained the following sentence:

"Mr. Molotov, Mr. Harriman and Sir A. Clark Kerr are authorized as a commission to consult in the first instance in Moscow with members of the present Provisional Government and with other Polish Democratic leaders from within Poland and from abroad, with a view to the reorganization of the present government along the above lines."

On March 2, the day after President Roosevelt delivered his optimistic and widely acclaimed report on the conference to a joint session of Congress, a disturbing message was received from Ambassador Harriman. He reported that Molotov was insisting that only Poles who had been recommended by the Provisional, or Lublin, Government should be invited to consult with the commission. Molotov's list of those who should be invited to come to Moscow from London included only one name that appeared also on the list we had submitted. He stoutly refused to invite Mikolajczyk, the liberal leader of the Polish Peasant Party, who was with the exiled Polish Government in London and who had been warmly recommended to Marshal Stalin by Mr. Roosevelt.

The Soviet Foreign Minister was firm in his view that the Lublin government should be the "kernel" of the Provisional Government of National Unity. Our representative, together with the British member of the commission, refused to accept this interpretation of the Yalta agreement. They pointed out that the language of the Yalta Protocol and the discussion preceding it showed it was to be a "new" government, not an expanded Lublin government. The impasse which thus developed finally caused the President and Prime Minister Churchill to communicate directly with Marshal Stalin.

Toward the end of March, the Prime Minister had expressed to President Roosevelt the belief that the agreements at Yalta were breaking down and there would be serious consequences unless something were done to change the situation. On March 27, President Roosevelt replied that he too had been "watching with anxiety and concern the development of the Soviet attitude" since Yalta. He added he was "acutely aware of the dangers inherent in the present course of events, not only for the immediate issue involved but also for the San Francisco Conference and future world co-operation." He included in his message a draft of a telegram he proposed to send to Marshal Stalin.

President Roosevelt dispatched his message to Stalin on April 1, and the Prime Minister also sent a communication supporting the President's position.

The President opened his message by stating he could not conceal "the concern with which I view the development of events" since Yalta. He expressed his regret at "the lack of progress made in the carrying out, which the world expects, of the political decisions which we reached at Yalta, particularly those relating to the Polish question," and added that he could not understand the "apparent indifferent attitude" of the Soviet Union. The President said he felt the situation arose from the Soviet interpretation of the Yalta agreement as meaning that the new Provisional Government should be little more than a continuation of the present Warsaw government. The President emphasized that he could not reconcile that position either with the agreement or with the discussions preceding the agreement. He said he must make it plain to the Marshal that "any such solution which would result in a thinly disguised continuation of the present government would be entirely unacceptable, and would cause our people to regard the Yalta agreement as a failure." If the right of the commission to select the Poles to be invited to Moscow for consultation were either limited or shared with the Warsaw government, he went on, the foundation of the Yalta agreement would be destroyed. President Roosevelt said that he would not bar or veto any candidate proposed by Molotov for the consultation, and that our Ambassador should be accorded the same confidence. He told Stalin that there should be a maximum of political tranquility in Poland and that we should use our influence to see that dissident groups ceased measures and countermeasures against each other. He also urged that, in view of our responsibilities, representatives of the American and British members of the commission be permitted to visit Poland, reminding Stalin that Molotov himself had suggested this at an early meeting and subsequently withdrew the suggestion.

The President pointed out "how important it is, for the successful development of our program of international collaboration," to settle the Polish question. Otherwise, he warned, "all the difficulties and dangers to Allied unity" they had considered at Yalta "will face us in an even more acute form."

As for Rumania, the President said he could not understand why the developments there did not fall within the terms of the Yalta Declaration of Liberated Areas, and he asked Stalin "personally to examine the exchange of notes between our governments on this subject."

In concluding this message, the President took note of an exchange of messages about the desirability of having Mr. Molotov attend the San Francisco Conference. The President, on March 24, had sent a message urging that Molotov attend in which he had said "I am afraid Mr. Molotov's absence will be construed all over the world as a lack of comparable interest on the part of the Soviet Government in the great objectives of this conference."

After expressing regret that Molotov could not attend, Stalin added in the last paragraph of his reply:

"As regards various interpretations, you understand, this cannot determine the decisions which are to be made."

The President, after warning that the attitude of the Soviet Government on the Polish and Rumanian questions was having an adverse effect on public opinion, took note of Stalin's dismissal of possible public reaction to Molotov's absence, and concluded his message with this wise and true statement:

"I am sure you are aware that genuine popular support in the United States is required to carry out any government policy, foreign or domestic. The American people make up their own mind and no governmental action can change it. I mention this fact because the last sentence of your message about Mr. Molotov's attendance at San Francisco made me wonder whether you give full weight to this factor."

On April 7, Stalin replied, admitting that the Polish question had reached a dead end and charging this was because the Ambassadors of the United States and Great Britain had departed from the Yalta agreement. They had taken the position, he said, that the existing Provisional Government should be completely liquidated and an entirely new government formed. Mr. Harriman, he contended, had stated in the commission that it was possible no member of the Provisional Government would be included in the Polish Government of National Unity—a statement Harriman denied having made.

Stalin maintained the Big Three had agreed at Yalta to invite five persons from Poland and three from London, but that the British and American Ambassadors now urged that each member be given the right to invite an unlimited number of people from Poland and London. The Marshal said that only Polish leaders should be invited who would recognize the decisions of Yalta, including the decision about the Curzon Line, and who were "really striving to establish friendly relations between Poland and the Soviet Union." Knowing, as we did, Stalin's usual interpretation of the phrase "friendly relations" we were sure this could only mean a leader who would strive to establish a government willing to accept orders from the Soviet Union.

In his reply to Mr. Churchill, Stalin also indicated that he might withdraw his opposition to inviting Mikolajczyk provided Mikolajczyk would make a public statement recognizing the decisions of the Yalta meeting and declaring that he favored the establishment of friendly relations between Poland and the Soviet Union. Stalin refused to agree that American and British observers be allowed in Poland, taking the position that the Poles would consider this an insult to their national dignity.

The President and Churchill decided they would send a joint message in reply to Stalin. While the State Department and the Foreign Office were preparing the joint reply, President Roosevelt died.

In those closing days of his life he also was annoyed and particularly disturbed by still another incident; one which was on his mind when he wrote his last message to Mr. Churchill, just before his death.

On March 11, the Allied Commander-in-Chief in Italy, Field Marshal Alexander, learned through the Office of Strategic Services that General Kesselring and several German Staff officers were willing to meet in Switzerland to discuss the surrender of the German Army in Italy. The Combined Chiefs of Staff approved Alexander's plan to send his Deputy Chief of Staff to Bern but instructed him to wait until the Soviet Government was informed. When Ambassador Harriman gave this information to Mr. Molotov, the latter declared that the Soviet Government wished to take part in any such discussions and would send three Red Army officers. Thereupon, the Combined Chiefs of Staff informed the Soviet Government that nothing would be done at Bern except to arrange for a meeting at Allied headquarters in Caserta, Italy, where the Soviet representatives would be welcome. The directive also in-structed that it be made clear to the Soviet Government that, should the Germans offer to surrender, Alexander as supreme commander on that front, would conduct the negotiations and make the necessary decisions.

The Soviet Government replied that inasmuch as their officers could not participate in the discussions they would not be sent to Caserta. The message "insisted" that the negotiations be stopped.

A few days later Stalin sent a message to President Roosevelt stating that if the same situation had been presented on the Russian front he would not have objected to the participation of British and American representatives in the discussions. He recognized, he said, the great importance of the negotiation that had taken place because it affected the military situation on the eastern front.

President Roosevelt replied that no negotiations had taken place and assured Stalin that he would be kept fully informed. The next message from the Soviet leader was the one that deeply offended Mr. Roosevelt.

Stalin referred to the statement that no negotiations had taken place and asserted that it was evident the President had not been advised by his own military leaders. Stalin said the information given him by his Red Army advisers showed that negotiations had been completed and that, as a result of them, Kesselring was going to open up the German front to permit the American Army to advance. In return for this mili-tary assistance, Stalin said, the United States and Britain had agreed to secure easier peace terms for Germany. In accordance with this agreement, Stalin charged, the Germans already had moved three divisions from the Italian front to the Russian front, and the American Army had been permitted to advance in Germany.

Despite his personal reaction to this message, President Roosevelt managed to write a dignified reply. The movement of the three German divisions from the Italian to the Russian fronts, the President pointed out, had begun several weeks before the information regarding the desire of the Germans to negotiate had even reached Field Marshal Alexander and therefore the negotiations could not have been respon-sible in any way for the troop transfer. Stalin would have to believe him to be honest and truthful, the President declared. General Eisen-hower would not have entered into any negotiations without informing him. No negotiations such as Stalin described had taken place, and from the receipt of the first message from the Germans, instructions had been issued to keep the Soviet authorities fully informed.

In the last paragraph of his message, the President gave vent to some of his feelings.

He deeply resented, he said, the "vile misrepresentations" of Stalin's informers which reflected upon the President of the United States and his trusted subordinates, and indicated a belief that Stalin's informants wished to destroy the friendly relations between the two countries. He thought it would be a tragedy if, just as victory for the Allies seemed assured, such misrepresentations should disturb the unity that had existed and that was necessary for complete victory.

To this message Stalin replied that he did not question the President's honesty or truthfulness but repeated his belief that he had received accurate information from his Red Army advisers. He had reason to regard them as accurate, he said, because only a short time earlier General Marshall and the general of the British Army had been kind enough to send word to the Russian commanding general that the Germans were concentrating at a certain point in preparation for attack upon the Russian lines. The Russian officers, however, knew that the information was wrong and that the German drive was to take place at another point. The Red Army had concentrated its forces at the place it thought best and had stopped the German drive. He recognized, he said, that the Germans may have misled the American and British officers deliberately, but the incident served to show the accuracy of his Red Army officers. He wished, nevertheless, to thank the Americans for this effort to be helpful. On the whole, Stalin's message was more conciliatory than the previous ones and President Roosevelt, on April 11, sent Stalin a message saying he was glad the unfortunate incident was now over.

Meanwhile, the negotiations with the Germans had been postponed for other reasons and in the interim the Combined Chiefs of Staff made a proposal that was accepted by the Soviet military leaders. It provided that each of the three powers should observe all surrender negotiations, but that a surrender on any one front would not be delayed because of the absence of any one of the powers.

Nevertheless, Stalin's charges and his apparent willingness to believe we had secretly concluded a separate peace, coupled with the exceedingly objectionable language of at least one of his messages had greatly offended Mr. Roosevelt. And when President Truman assumed office and read these messages he fully sympathized with the view and attitude of President Roosevelt.

On the same day that President Roosevelt received his last message from Stalin, he received one from Prime Minister Churchill. It stated that he had to make a statement in the House of Commons within a few days, dealing primarily with Poland but necessarily requiring a discussion of Russian relations. He was exceedingly anxious not to say anything that would affect adversely the military situation at that critical hour and he asked President Roosevelt for advice.

Although the President by that time was greatly disappointed by the Soviet attitude, he was philosophical about it. He had reached the conclusion—which I was to reach months later—that there is no easy formula to guide one in getting along with the Soviets. Thus, on April 12, an hour before he died, President Roosevelt, replying to the Prime Minister's request for advice about his speech to Commons, sent this message:

I would minimize the general Soviet problem as much as possible because these problems, in one form or another, seem to arise every day and most of them straighten out as in the case of the Bern meeting.

We must be firm, however, and our course thus far is correct.

The message was sent from Warm Springs and bears all the earmarks of having been written by the President himself. The advice is as good today as it was on the day it was written.

It is idle to speculate on what the course of history would have been had President Roosevelt lived, but these messages dispose of the legend that our relations with the Soviet Union began to deteriorate only after his death.

The President's deliberate efforts to cultivate the good will of Marshal Stalin have led some observers to underestimate the strength of his affection and admiration for Mr. Churchill. It was a feeling that was genuine and that was cordially reciprocated. It was the kind of friendship that permitted frankness in their conversations with each other and about each other.

Whenever Mr. Churchill was a guest at the White House, the President would complain to those of us who had to carry on business with him that Mr. Churchill had kept him up late. But even as he complained about his guest, it was clear that the President had greatly enjoyed the conversation of the previous evening. Once at Yalta, when we were preparing for dinner at the end of a long session, the President grumbled that the lengthy session was "Winston's fault because he had made too many speeches."

"Yes, he did," I replied, "but they were good speeches."

The President chuckled and replied:

"Winston doesn't make any other kind."

It is true, if my observations at Yalta provide a typical example, that the President used all his charm and his genius for promoting human relationships to make the Big Three meetings harmonious. The value of these qualities in those early days cannot be overestimated. But the Soviet leaders did overestimate the ultimate extent of the President's generosity and his willingness to compromise on principles.

Two other elements figured in the deteriorating situation. During the war the issues that faced the Big Three and the decisions they made together were primarily military. As we approached the end of hostilities, political questions began coming to the fore and these, of course, became issues between victors. President Roosevelt had sensed this. In fact, in his speech on The State of the Union made on January 6, 1945, he warned that "the nearer we come to vanquishing our enemies the more we inevitably become conscious of differences among the victors." That was why he was so insistent that the United Nations should be established while the war was still in progress.

The second element is a corollary of the first. This is the fact that the end of the war and the lifting of censorship brought to public attention differences that had been known to few except a restricted group of officials.

Just after the President's death, there was, in fact, a momentary rise in our hopes that the barometer of our relations would cease falling. This was caused by an interview with Marshal Stalin in which Ambassador Harriman requested that Mr. Molotov be sent to the San Francisco Conference.

"President Roosevelt has died but his cause must live on," Marshal Stalin told our Ambassador. "We shall support President Truman with all our forces and with all our will."

He then asked the Ambassador to inform President Truman of his statement and say that he would send Molotov to San Francisco to let the world know his attitude.

Meanwhile, the State Department had prepared the joint message on Poland in answer to Stalin's communication of April 7. This message, which President Roosevelt had directed the State Department to prepare, was sent by President Truman and Mr. Churchill on April 18. It began by seeking to correct the "completely erroneous impression you have apparently received in regard to the position of the British and United States governments" and by denying that our Ambassadors had asked for the right to invite to Moscow for consultation an unlimited number of Poles. They called attention to the statement in President Roosevelt's message of April 1 that "in order to facilitate the agreement, the commission first of all might select a small but representative group of Polish leaders who could suggest other names for consideration by the commission." "The real issue between us," said Truman and Churchill, "is whether or not the Warsaw government has the right to veto individual candidates for consultation." No such interpretation could be found in the Yalta agreement, they said, and they expressed the belief that the Soviet Union was reverting to the position it had assumed originally at Yalta but which had been modified in order that agreement could be reached.

By the time Mr. Molotov reached Washington, President Truman had

studied the agreements at Yalta and had read much of the correspondence between President Roosevelt and Marshal Stalin, particularly those
messages dealing with Rumania, Poland and the Bern incident. He was
so disturbed by the swift collapse of what we thought had been agreements and the consequent dissipation of the cordial spirit of Yalta that
he called a meeting of the Secretaries of State, War and Navy, the
Chief of Staff and Admiral Leahy to discuss our relations with the
Soviets. Later when Mr. Molotov called at the White House, President
Truman spoke very frankly about some of our problems, and the Polish
situation in particular. From what I learned upon my return to Washington, it was not a very harmonious meeting and ended rather abruptly.

At San Francisco, efforts at collaboration were marred by disagreement on almost every issue. It started the first day with the question of
the chairmanship. With the announcement that sixteen Polish resistance
leaders, who were discussing problems of reorganizing the government
with the Russians, had been arrested, President Truman decided some
action had to be taken to halt the increasing deterioration in our relations. He therefore suggested to Marshal Stalin that Harry Hopkins
go to Moscow, on what was to be his last mission.

Hopkins had served his government well on many occasions, but the
record of this mission does him special credit. Ambassador Averell
Harriman, who had come home to confer with the President on the
Polish problem, returned with Hopkins to take part in the talks. And,
of course, Chip Bohlen went along to interpret for them and to advise
them. The report of their conversations with Marshal Stalin, which they
sent to the President, is an illuminating chapter in the story of our relationships with the Soviet Union. It was of great interest to me as I was
educating myself for the work ahead.

The conversations were marked by the frank exchange of views and
the interesting revelation of Soviet thinking.

Stalin expressed concern over what seemed to be a cooling of American friendship once it became clear Germany was defeated and Russia's
help was no longer needed. He gave examples he felt supported this
impression.

He cited the action of the United States in agreeing to the admission
of Argentina to the United Nations in violation of President Roosevelt's
statement at Yalta and declared he was forced to question the value of
agreements between the major powers if their decisions could be upset
by votes of such countries as Honduras.

He said our stand that France should be made a member of the
Reparations Commission was an insult and an attempt to humiliate
the Soviet Union, since France had concluded a separate peace with
the Germans and opened her frontier to them.

The Yalta agreement, he insisted, contemplated that the Lublin government would form the basis of the new Polish government and that no other procedure was reasonable. "Even though the Russians are a simple people," Stalin added, "the West often made the mistake of regarding them as fools."

He was particularly irritated by the manner in which lend-lease shipments had been suspended at the end of the European war. The fact that ships with supplies bound for Russia even had been unloaded indicated to him that the cancellation order was an effort to put pressure on the Soviet Union. This, he declared, was a fundamental mistake and the United States should understand much could be gained from the Russians only if they were approached on a friendly basis.

In the case of the German Navy and merchant fleet, he had sent a message to the President and the Prime Minister suggesting that one-third be turned over to the Soviets. Not only had he received no reply, he said, but he had acquired instead an impression that the request was to be rejected.

These complaints were surprising to us at home. They revealed an extreme sensitivity and an amazing degree of almost instinctive suspicion.

Mr. Hopkins forcefully and tactfully presented the position of the United States. As for the German ships, it was our intention that they should be divided equally among the three and we thought that the matter could be settled at the forthcoming meeting of the Big Three. He explained that the cancellation of lend-lease was necessary under the law because lend-lease was authorized only for the purpose of prosecuting the war. With the German war ended and with the Soviet Union not yet a participant in the Japanese war, further shipment could not be justified. The order to unload the ships was the mistake of an official who had nothing to do with policy, and the order had been withdrawn quickly. He reminded the Marshal of how liberally the United States had construed the law in sending foodstuffs and other nonmilitary items to their aid.

Stalin readily acknowledged the accuracy of Hopkins' statement. If proper warning had been given there would have been no feeling about the matter, he said, pointing out that advance notice was important to them because their economy is based on plans. The way in which the shipments had been halted made it impossible for him to express, as he had intended, the great appreciation of the Soviets for the lend-lease aid given to them.

Hopkins told the Marshal that what disturbed him most was the revelation that Stalin believed the United States would use lend-lease as a pressure weapon. The United States, he asserted, is a strong nation and does not need to indulge in such methods. With this, Stalin said he was fully satisfied with our explanation.

Ambassador Harriman explained the Argentine question. The difficulty was due to the fact that, after Secretary Stettinius had obtained the agreement of the South American republics for the admission to membership of the Ukraine and Byelorussia, Mr. Molotov had also raised the question of inviting the existing Polish Government to the conference. There certainly had been no agreement at Yalta to invite the Polish Government, and this action by Mr. Molotov caused the South American republics to insist that the Argentine be admitted. We not only had fulfilled our commitment to support the admission of the two Soviet republics, but we had gone further and had obtained support for the motion from the South American republics. Mr. Stettinius had therefore felt that, since our neighbors had supported him in his efforts in behalf of the Ukraine and Byelorussia, he should accede to their wishes and support the admission of Argentina.

Stalin said simply that what had been done could not be changed and it all belonged to the past.

With these questions out of the way the discussion proceeded to the principal cause of Hopkins' trip—the situation in Poland.

Throughout the conversations Hopkins kept emphasizing that, in the eyes of the American people, the Polish question had become a symbol of our ability to work out mutual problems with the Soviet Union and that an impasse on this issue would threaten our whole relationship with our Soviet Allies. Our people were deeply disturbed, Hopkins said, because the Soviet Union was acting independently on a problem that should be worked out jointly. He stressed that we had no interest in Poland other than a desire to see a truly independent government established which would protect what we regarded as basic freedoms and which would be friendly to the Soviet Union.

Marshal Stalin repeated the statements he had made at Yalta on the vital interest of the Soviet Government in Poland. He felt that before the war the policy of European governments had been to keep Poland hostile toward Russia, and that this could not be permitted again; Poland must be friendly and must be strong. He admitted unilateral action had been taken but asked Mr. Hopkins to consider that the Soviet Army was in Poland, that an army's lines of communication must be protected and its authority maintained.

During this discussion, Stalin made a very interesting reference to his conception of the United States in world affairs. Whether the United States wished it or not, he said, we were a world power and would have to accept world-wide responsibilities. Without our intervention in the last two wars, Germany could not have been defeated.

In fact, he added, the history of the last thirty years shows that the United States has more reason to be a world power than any other state, and he therefore recognized our right to participate in the Polish question.

There was considerable discussion as to which Poles should be invited from outside and inside Poland to meet in Moscow and consider establishing a provisional government which would carry out the Yalta pledges on the holding of elections.

During these talks Stalin revealed a willingness to believe that we would secretly sponsor the names of men hostile to the Soviet Union or associated with hostile groups. In the strongest terms Hopkins assured him we had no such intent and would drop from consideration any person who appeared to fall in either category.

Stalin agreed to invite Mikolajczyk and an agreement was reached on the personnel of the Polish Committee. As a result, a new government was subsequently formed which pledged itself to hold free elections. On the basis of the new government's pledges, Poland was admitted to the United Nations and the first official telegram I signed as Secretary of State dealt with diplomatic recognition of the Provisional Polish Government.

While Hopkins and Harriman were conferring with Stalin, in the San Francisco Conference a controversy over voting procedure in the United Nations organization had arisen. The Soviet delegation insisted that a dispute could not even be discussed by the Security Council without the unanimous vote of the five permanent members, unless the situation clearly was one that could be settled by peaceful means. In effect, the Soviet position meant that even the council's agenda could be subject to a veto. To many at the conference it seemed that the deadlock was complete.

On one occasion during this period, our former Ambassador to Russia, Joseph E. Davies, and I were talking to President Truman. Davies was telling the President of some matters connected with his mission to London. The President mentioned his concern over the impasse at the San Francisco Conference. I suggested he take advantage of Hopkins' presence in Moscow to present directly to Marshal Stalin our view that the veto should not apply to procedural questions. The President sent a message to Hopkins who presented it to Stalin.

As soon as our point of view had been presented, Mr. Molotov intervened to defend the Soviet position. The conversation between Marshal Stalin and his Foreign Minister, as interpreted by Bohlen, made it clear that the Marshal had not understood the issue involved. He told Molotov he thought it was an insignificant matter and that the American position should be accepted. In expressing his agreement, he cautioned against what he termed a tendency on the part of small nations to create and exploit differences among the great powers in order to gain the backing of one or more of them for their own ends. "A nation need not be innocent just because it is small," he said.

This incident was especially interesting for two things: First, it revealed that the Russian leader was not informed on what was the crucial issue of the San Francisco Conference on International Organization; and, second, it demonstrated that when matters are brought to Stalin's attention it frequently is possible to get a quick decision even when it requires reversing openly the decision of his Foreign Minister.

The agreements reached in the Hopkins conversations constituted an advance over the deadlock of the preceding ninety days, but it was clear they constituted no advance over Yalta. It meant that in June we would establish in Poland the Provisional Government that we had agreed in February should be established promptly. It did not mean we had solved the Polish problem.

Not only Poland and Rumania but other developments worried us. On April 18, the Soviets invited the other Allies to send representatives to Vienna, but then took the position that they could not proceed until an agreement was reached by the European Advisory Commission regarding zones in the city of Vienna and the provisional control machinery. The British, supported by the United States, maintained that it was impossible to agree about zones until our representatives reached Vienna and learned what conditions were there. Finally, on May 19, Stalin agreed that our representatives could visit Vienna for that purpose and with the understanding that the zones would be determined by the European Advisory Commission. When our representatives reached Vienna they were not allowed to see anything outside the city limits and after a short stay were ordered to leave by June 10 or 11.

We continued to worry about the differences revealed by the San Francisco Conference, the difficulties being encountered in the Reparations Commission meeting in Moscow, the conflicting points of view already arising in the Allied Control Council in Berlin, Marshal Tito's bellicose behavior in the Trieste area, and growing tension in Iran, Greece and Turkey.

The successful conclusion of the San Francisco Conference was a big factor on the credit side of the ledger as we analyzed the situation in preparation for the forthcoming meeting of the Big Three. It had been agreed, during Hopkins' visit in Moscow, that this would be held in Berlin on July 15.

On Tuesday, July 3, my lifelong friend, Chief Justice Richard S. Whaley of the United States Court of Claims, administered the oath making me Secretary of State. To the friends who had gathered for the ceremony on the rose-covered east portico of the White House, I made this statement:

"The making of enduring peace will depend on something more than skilled diplomacy, something more than paper treaties, something more even than the best charter the wisest statesman can draft. Important as is diplomacy, important as are the peace settlements and the basic charter of world peace, these cannot succeed unless backed by the will of the peoples of different lands not only to have peace but to live together as good neighbors. . . .

"Today there can be no doubt that the peoples of this war-ravaged earth want to live in a free and peaceful world. The supreme task of statesmanship the world over is to help them to understand that they can have peace and freedom only if they tolerate and respect the rights of others to opinions, feelings and way of life which they do not and cannot share."

Three nights later I boarded the President's special train for the journey to Newport News, where the USS *Augusta* was waiting to take us to Europe, to Potsdam—the first step down the long road toward peace.

Chapter 4

Potsdam—The Success That Failed

WE WORKED hard on board the *Augusta*. Memoranda had been prepared in the State Department to cover every subject which conceivably could arise at the conference. Every morning throughout the trip, Ben Cohen, H. Freeman (Doc) Matthews, and Charles E. (Chip) Bohlen would meet with me in my cabin to consider these papers. A new Secretary of State could not have asked for a finer trio of advisers.

Ben, in his quiet, shy way, has had a hand in important issues ever since the early days of the Roosevelt administration. He was with me through all my work at the White House. In addition to having a genuine affection for him, I regard his mind as one of the best I have ever encountered. There is no more selfless and devoted public servant than Ben Cohen. Doc, the chief of the State Department's European Division, is a veteran foreign service officer, who combines with his vast and intricate knowledge of foreign affairs keen political sense and sound judgment. He is representative of the finest men in our career service and I relied upon him heavily. Chip is another in this category. After spending some years in the Soviet Union, he has served through a crucial period as the State Department's expert on Russian affairs. Chip, I believe, is the only man who has attended all the Big Three meetings with President Roosevelt and President Truman. He has seen these meetings from the unique position of both interpreter and adviser. He was invaluable to me.

The four of us spent many hours in long and earnest discussion of the State Department memoranda. On many issues, President Truman's Chief of Staff, Fleet Admiral William D. Leahy, would join us. In these meetings we would agree on recommendations to present to President Truman. At least once a day during the entire trip the President and I would go over them. When the President approved a proposal, it was then prepared for presentation to the conference. Consequently, by the time we landed at Antwerp on July 15, 1945, we had our objectives thoroughly in mind and had the background papers in support of them fully prepared.

We wanted to reach agreement on four major issues: *first,* the ma-

chinery and the procedures for the earliest possible drafting and completion of peace treaties; *second,* the political and economic principles which
would govern the occupation of Germany; *third,* plans for carrying out
the Yalta Declaration on Liberated Europe, with the hope of ending the
constant friction which had prevailed over Russian policy in eastern
Europe since the Crimea Conference; and, *fourth,* a new approach to the
reparations issue in view of the inability of the Reparations Commission
to reach agreement.

There were other goals, also. Among them was our desire to speed
Italy's entry into the United Nations in recognition of the part her
people played in the last year of the war in Europe and her declaration
of war against Japan. Then, we had a plan for insuring free navigation of all of Europe's inland waterways.

When we arrived at the "Little White House" in Babelsberg, the
Berlin suburb that had been the center of the German film colony, we
learned that Marshal Stalin would be delayed a day. This gave us a
chance to do a little sightseeing; the President, Admiral Leahy and I
drove into Berlin. We were greatly impressed by the streams of people
walking along the road. They were mostly grandparents and children.
As a rule they carried their possessions on their backs. We did not know
where they were going and it is doubtful that they did, but when we
reached Berlin we were convinced they were headed in the wrong
direction. Despite all we had read of the destruction there, the extent
of the devastation shocked us. It brought home the suffering that total
war now visits upon old folks, women, and children, besides the men in
uniform.

Shortly after his arrival, on July 17, Stalin came to call on the President. We had to remember to call him Generalissimo rather than
Marshal Stalin, for he had been accorded the new title in recognition
of the Red Army's great successes. It was the first time the President
and Stalin had met. After a very pleasant conversation, the President
quite informally asked Stalin, Molotov, and Pavlov, the capable Soviet
interpreter, to stay and have lunch with him. They accepted. The conversation was general in nature and cordial in spirit. The President was
favorably impressed by Stalin, as I had been at Yalta. In speaking of our
visit to Berlin, I asked the Generalissimo his views of how Hitler had
died. To my surprise, he said he believed that Hitler was alive and that it
was possible he was then either in Spain or Argentina. Some ten days
later I asked him if he had changed his views and he said he had not.

At lunch the Generalissimo was as entertaining as he usually is on
such occasions. He complimented the President on the wine that was
served. While the President was thanking him, Stalin asked the Filipino

waiter to unwrap the towel from the bottle, because he wanted to see the label. I was glad he did; it was a California wine.

Shortly after lunch, we left for the first of our many three-mile drives to Potsdam and to Cecilienhof Palace where the meetings were held. As always, when they are hosts, the Russians had made painstaking preparations. Cecilienhof Palace had been the country estate of the former Crown Prince Wilhelm, and provided ample accommodations for the conference. It is a two-story brown-stone mansion beautifully situated on Gribnitz Lake. Its four wings form a square with a courtyard in the center, which the Red Army had brilliantly carpeted with a twenty-four-foot wide Red star of geraniums. Each head of government was provided with a suite of rooms for his personal use and each delegation had a conference room and offices for its staff.

The conference room itself was impressively large and pleasantly bright. At one end a huge window reached up the full two-story height of the room, letting in light and giving the conferees a sweeping view of beautifully landscaped gardens.

The group that sat down at the large oaken table at 5:10 P.M. on July 17 included, besides the President and me, former ambassador Joseph E. Davies, Admiral Leahy and Chip Bohlen from the United States delegation; Prime Minister Churchill, Foreign Minister Anthony Eden, Mr. Attlee, Sir Alexander Cadogan, and an interpreter from the United Kingdom delegation; and from the Soviet Union, Generalissimo Stalin, Foreign Minister Molotov, Mr. Vyshinski, Mr. Andrei A. Gromyko, who was then the Soviet Ambassador in the United States, the Soviet Ambassador to Great Britain, F. T. Gousev, and Mr. Pavlov.

It was fortunate that the room was large because each of these delegations had grouped behind them other members of their delegations. This group would change as various issues before the conference called for the aid of different technical advisers. As I recall it, our delegation that opening day included Ambassador Averell Harriman, Under Secretary William L. Clayton, Reparations Commissioner Edwin W. Pauley, Counselor Ben Cohen, Assistant Secretary of State James C. Dunn and Doc Matthews.

At Stalin's suggestion, President Truman was made chairman and he immediately presented for consideration some of the proposals we had prepared aboard the *Augusta*. It was evident that the other heads of government appreciated the President's efforts in having proposals ready for discussion.

The first of these papers was the proposal to establish the Council of Foreign Ministers. It had been agreed at Yalta that there should be regular consultation of the Foreign Ministers to deal with the difficulties we knew would arise after the war. But it had not been intended that those meetings should be concerned with peace treaties. At Yalta, peace had still seemed so remote that the question of how it should be brought about was not, to my knowledge, ever discussed. The machinery for making the peace was, therefore, one of the first things we began to work on in planning for the Berlin Conference.

As a Member of Congress I had followed closely the peace conference proceedings at the end of World War I and I was convinced that this time we had to follow a different procedure. If we waited until the end of the war with Japan and then held one peace conference, attended by all the states at war, with no preliminary draft to use as a basis for the treaties, there would be endless bickering. The logrolling, the interplay of conflicting interests, plus the sheer number of issues and people, would result, I was sure, in such confusion that the conference would last a year if, indeed, it could ever end successfully. Even the Versailles Conference had finally found it necessary to assign to a few of the great powers the duty of treaty-drafting. Those states not represented on the drafting committee had little opportunity to know what was in a treaty and why. Consequently, when agreement was reached among the great powers, the smaller Allied nations had little more opportunity to examine or amend the treaties than did the defeated Germans.

We had to devise a system that would facilitate agreement among the major powers and at the same time provide the smaller states with ample opportunity to express their views.

Fortunately, the procedure initiated by Secretary Hull and carried out by Secretary Stettinius in the establishment of the United Nations organization provided good precedent. The accomplishments at San Francisco demonstrated the wisdom of the earlier conversations at Dumbarton Oaks and at Yalta where the big powers had reached agreement on the more important points at issue.

Ben Cohen and I prepared the plan for the creation of the Council of Foreign Ministers. When I presented it to President Truman for his consideration, we suspected what later we found to be true: the Soviet Union did not wish to act promptly on a German treaty. We knew that because of the many serious problems presented, and because there was no German government, some delay was inevitable. But we thought a start should be made promptly and that our experience with the Italian and Balkan treaties would make it easier for us to agree on Germany's problems.

I visualized for him the council's operation, in these terms: The council would consider first the treaties with Italy and the Balkan enemy states because these were the least controversial. The Foreign Ministers would agree on certain general principles and appoint deputies to draft treaties based on these principles. The Foreign Ministers, shortly thereafter, would take up the German treaty, agree on fundamental problems such as frontiers, and local governments, and then appoint different deputies to begin drafting a German settlement. The peace treaties based on these general agreements would then be presented to all the United Nations for their consideration and amendment in the same way the Dumbarton Oaks proposals were reviewed at the San Francisco Conference. A similar course ultimately would be followed for Japan.

After consideration the President approved the plan. This was shortly before I became Secretary of State. The President submitted our memorandum to the State Department for comment. The Department officials had been thinking along similar lines and recommended the procedure.

It was a good theory. But it was faulty in one assumption. I had assumed that at the end of hostilities an era of peace would be so deeply desired by those nations that had fought the war in unity that the inevitable differences of opinion could be resolved without serious difficulty.

It is true that following Yalta we had been somewhat disillusioned. Such things as the Bern incident and the Soviet violation of the agreements on Poland and Rumania warned us that in the days to come we would encounter serious differences and would have to overcome deepseated suspicion. However, fresh in our minds were the words of President Roosevelt's last message to Prime Minister Churchill, based upon his experience with the Russians, that such difficulties would straighten out.

Today it is easy for one to say that President Roosevelt's advice and our assumption were not warranted. It is a trite but true statement that "hindsight is better than foresight." But, if one can recall the attitude of the people of the United States toward the Soviets in the days immediately following the German surrender, he will agree that, as a result of our sufferings and sacrifices in a common cause, the Soviet Union then had in the United States a deposit of good will, as great, if not greater than that of any other country. It is little short of a tragedy that Russia should have withdrawn that deposit with the recklessness and the lack of appreciation shown during the last two and a half years. Our assumption that we could co-operate, and our patience in trying to co-operate, justify the firmness we now must show.

Our optimism certainly was not lessened by the speed with which the proposal to establish the Council of Foreign Ministers was approved at the conference table. Both Churchill and Stalin asked questions on our inclusion of China on the council; the Russian delegation continued to oppose the admission of France to the ranks of the great powers. When Churchill suggested that the Foreign Ministers consider whether the council should be composed of four or five members, Stalin quickly added, "or three members."

The Foreign Ministers met the following morning, and we agreed that China's part should be limited to Far East problems and those of world-wide importance. Mr. Molotov reiterated the view that France should participate in the drafting of only the Italian and the German treaties. We finally agreed that each treaty should be drafted by the states which signed the armistice with that particular enemy, and, that in the case of Italy, France would be regarded as a signatory of the armistice.

We submitted our recommendations to the chiefs of state that afternoon. Churchill inquired about a phrase stating that the council should draft treaties "with a view to their submission to the United Nations." I explained that this was required by the Declaration of the United Nations, which all of us had signed. Stalin then made a statement which carried a significance that we did not appreciate until later months. The inclusion of such a phrase in the document, he said, made no difference as "the three powers would represent the interests of all."

With this brief exchange, the proposal of the American delegation for the creation of a Council of Foreign Ministers charged with the responsibility of preparing peace treaties became the first approved act of the Berlin Conference.

The high state of our hopes is indicated by my notes of a luncheon conversation with Mr. Molotov on July 24. We discussed plans for the first meeting of the council to be held in London in September. I expressed the belief that we should organize the council and agree upon directives to guide our deputies and their staffs in the preparation of treaty drafts. I then added that the Ministers should be able to finish their work in about ten days, and that the effective performance by the deputies of their work would keep our subsequent meetings as short. Mr. Molotov appeared to be very pleased with this view. We discussed the appointment of deputies, the relationship of the council to the United Nations and the desirability of beginning work on the Italian treaty upon our return home. On all these points we appeared to be in complete accord.

We went to the meeting of the heads of government encouraged by our apparent agreement. The debate that followed perhaps should have stifled my optimism, but it didn't. It dealt with another of the proposals that President Truman had presented at the opening meeting of the conference—the implementation of the Yalta Declaration on Liberated Europe.

Our paper stated flatly that the obligations assumed in the Yalta Declaration had not been carried out. A continuation of this situation, it went on, would be regarded throughout the world as evidence of lack of unity and would undermine confidence in the sincerity of the jointly proclaimed aims. We proposed joint action in reorganizing the governments of Bulgaria and Rumania to permit participation of all democratic groups as a prelude to establishing diplomatic relations and concluding peace treaties. We also suggested that our three states should help the interim governments in holding "free and unfettered elections."

The discussions that churned around this paper and the issues it raised are worthy of note. They form the background for many weary hours of negotiating.

Stalin's initial response to our paper was simply that the Soviet Union had a proposal of its own to present on the subject. Molotov presented it at the meeting of the Foreign Ministers the next morning. It was devoted largely to a severe attack on Greece. Eden angrily termed the attack a "travesty of fact," pointing out that international observers, including representatives of the Soviet Union, had been invited to observe the Greek elections. Unfortunately, the same could not be said of Rumania or Bulgaria, he added. And he concluded by saying that the British Government "took the gravest exception" to the charges in the Soviet paper, and the matter could only be reported to the Prime Minister.

Mr. Molotov replied that the charges were directed only against the Greek Government. He asserted that the British had more representatives in Rumania and Bulgaria than the Soviet Union, and, citing British and and American press reports as evidence, he charged that there were greater excesses in Greece than in either Rumania or Bulgaria.

My contribution to this exchange was to repeat a statement which I was to make many times. It is one which, I fear, Mr. Molotov never fully understood or believed. "The United States," I told him, "sincerely desires Russia to have friendly countries on her borders, but we believe they should seek the friendship of the people rather than of any particular government. We, therefore, want the governments to be representative of the people. If elections are held while there are restrictions not only on newspaper and radio correspondents but upon our own governmental representatives as well, the American people will distrust any government established as a result of such an election. We do not wish to become involved in the elections of any country, but, because of the postwar situation, we would join with others in observing elections in Italy, Greece, Hungary, Rumania and Bulgaria."

This discussion contains arguments heard scores of times during ensuing months. Whenever the Soviets were faced with an issue that annoyed them or placed them on the defensive it was standard operating procedure for them to gather up a sheaf of British and American press reports from Greece and launch a counterattack. Mr. Molotov always seemed ready to enjoy the blessings of other nations' free press.

A few days later our paper came up for discussion again, providing an interesting demonstration of the Soviet bargaining technique.

"The Soviet Union," Molotov said, "can not agree to the supervision of elections. I can understand, though, that other Allies want better facilities for their representatives in these countries. Now that the war is at an end, there is every reason to give greater freedom both to these representatives and to the press. They will have every opportunity to be informed fully regarding the elections."

Having stated an opposition and a promise, he then lodged a complaint that the Soviet representative on the Allied Control Council in Italy was not receiving proper attention. He followed these parries and thrusts with an offer to discuss our proposal regarding elections *if* we would agree to accord diplomatic recognition to Rumania and Bulgaria.

Eden explained that formal recognition was constitutionally impossible for Britain until peace was concluded. I told him that our recognition of a country had to be based on our own estimate of it rather than on its value as a bargaining point. But Mr. Molotov is a difficult man to discourage and the effort to effect a trade of diplomatic recognition in return for the ends we desired went on and on.

Most of the Soviet bargaining effort was centered on Italy. We had asked for modification of Italy's armistice terms in recognition of her help in the war against Germany and of her declaration of war against Japan. We had proposed that the drafting of an Italian peace treaty be the first order of business for the Council of Foreign Ministers.

Both Generalissimo Stalin and Mr. Molotov were determined that no favor should be granted to Italy that was not also granted to Hungary, Rumania and Bulgaria. One essential difference was pointed out to them constantly: all foreign representatives were free to travel about in Italy and report their observations. During one of these exchanges, Mr. Churchill was stating that the British mission in Bucharest had been "penned up with a closeness approaching internment," when Stalin broke in to ask him how he could make such unverified statements.

Mr. Churchill reddened slightly; he said that the Generalissimo would be astonished at the catalogue of difficulties encountered by the British mission. "An iron fence has come down around them."

"All fairy tales," Stalin exclaimed, and maintained that British representatives in Rumania were accorded the same courtesies received by Soviet officials in Italy.

Not until the end of the conference, when we linked this question to that of reparations, did we secure Soviet acceptance of Section 10 of the protocol. This stated, first, the desirability of concluding peace treaties and resuming normal relations with all five countries. It then stated that the three powers "have included the preparation of a peace treaty with Italy as the first among the immediate important tasks to be undertaken by the new Council of Foreign Ministers." It then referred to the other four countries, in a way that permitted concurrent preparation of peace treaties with them if this were found feasible. We met the problem of recognition with the statement that "the three governments agree to examine each separately in the near future, in the light of conditions then prevailing, the establishment of diplomatic relations with Finland, Rumania, Bulgaria and Hungary to the extent possible prior to the conclusion of peace treaties with those countries."

The problem of the press was met by this statement: "The three governments have no doubt that in view of the changed conditions resulting from the termination of the war in Europe, representatives of the Allied press will enjoy full freedom to report to the world upon developments in Rumania, Bulgaria, Hungary and Finland."

I must admit we did have some doubt, but this was the strongest commitment for freedom of the press that we were able to achieve after many hours of discussion devoted to the issue.

In the meantime, the Soviet Union had placed on the table a second series of charges against Greece in obvious retaliation for a British paper directed against Yugoslavia. When agreement was finally reached on the foregoing section of the protocol, Mr. Bevin pointed out that the agenda carried two papers against Greece and one against Yugoslavia. He proposed that all three be dropped. Stalin quickly replied "Yes, welcome." It was a good demonstration of the seriousness with which some of the charges and countercharges were made.

Another irritant running throughout the conference was the question of American- and British-owned industrial equipment in Rumania that had been seized by the Russians. As an example of the Soviet conception of property rights, it was a forewarning of the difficulties we were to encounter on reparations. Before the war American and British firms had substantial holdings in Rumanian oil enterprises involving the ownership of highly valuable equipment. The Germans, of course, confiscated this equipment when they overran Rumania; our people assumed that when Rumania was liberated this equipment naturally would be returned to them. We were amazed to find, however, that the Red Army had carried off much of the equipment as war booty and insisted on the right to a large quantity of what remained. We could not admit that the Russians had a right to take, as war booty, property owned by their Allies. Stalin, Molotov and Vyshinski all stoutly maintained that this equipment did not belong to our nationals but was German property which they had a right to confiscate. Some of it had been bought in Germany before the war by American and British interests. But the Soviets insisted that since the property was German in origin it did not belong to us.

Mr. Vyshinski presented much of the Russian case. He is an able and aggressive lawyer. When he sits across the table looking at you with his cold, gray, piercing eyes and arguing his case with relentless precision, it is easy to understand his selection as Chief Prosecutor in the Soviet Union's great "purge" trials.

The question of ownership became fairly technical in such problems as equipment replacement and identification. Only after long argument were we able to appoint Soviet-American and Anglo-Soviet committees of experts to investigate the legitimacy of our claims.

On the opening day of the conference, Stalin announced his desire to discuss the question of trusteeship, stating that the Soviet Union "would like some territory of the defeated states." His delegation accordingly submitted a paper proposing that the Soviet Union be named trustee of one of the Italian colonies. The Atlantic Charter was a forgotten pledge. He wanted territory—indicating his conception of a trusteeship.

When the item was reached on the agenda, Mr. Churchill was reluctant even to discuss it. The President immediately made clear our belief that it was a matter for the peace conference and the United Nations but that no bars should be raised against discussion. Thereupon, Mr. Churchill delivered an impassioned statement.

"Britain," he said, "expects no gain out of this war. We have suffered terrible losses. Our losses have not been so heavy in human life as those of our gallant Soviet Ally. We have come out of the war, however, a great debtor in the world. There is no possibility of our regaining naval equality with the United States. We built only one capital ship during the war and lost ten or twelve. But in spite of the heavy losses we have suffered, we have made no territorial claims—no Königsberg, no Baltic states, nothing. We therefore approach the question of the colonies with complete rectitude.

"The British, of course, have great interests in the Mediterranean," Mr. Churchill added, "and any marked change in the status quo will need long and careful consideration," and he asked the Generalissimo to state what it was the Soviet Union desired.

"We would like to learn if this meeting will consider whether Italy is to lose her colonies," Stalin replied. "In that event, we can decide to what states they should be transferred for trusteeship."

"I had not considered the possibility of the Soviet Union desiring to acquire a large tract of the African shore," Mr. Churchill declared. "If this is the case, it will have to be considered in relation to many other

problems." The question, he said, properly belonged to the peace conference and the ultimate administration of the colonies was a matter for
the United Nations.

The President finally intervened. He suggested that the question be
referred to the Foreign Ministers for further discussion, and there was
a noticeable relaxation of tension around the big table as this suggestion
was accepted.

When the Foreign Ministers met to consider it, Mr. Molotov immediately proposed that a definite determination be made of the future
status of these colonies. I reminded him of President Truman's declaration that such a decision could be made only in connection with the
peace treaties. When I pointed out that work would begin on them
within one month, he agreed to wait.

The Soviet desire to reach into the Mediterranean was more modestly
but nonetheless importantly expressed in connection with the control
of the Dardanelles. Mr. Churchill first raised the issue. He had discussed it previously with the Generalissimo and now he expressed once
again his willingness to join in a revised agreement that would insure
free passage through the Straits for both the naval and the merchant
ships of the Soviet Union in peace or in war. He felt it important, however, that Turkey should not be alarmed unduly, and pointed to the concern aroused by Russia's requests for the provinces of Kars and Ardahan,
and for a naval base in the Straits.

"This," Mr. Churchill said, "has led Turkey to fear for the integrity
of her empire and her power to defend Constantinople."

Both Stalin and Molotov explained that the request for the provinces
had resulted from Turkey's proposal to the Soviet Union of a treaty
of alliance. They contended that, aside from the fact that these provinces
had been part of Russia under the Czar, the Soviet Union was justified,
when entering into a treaty of alliance, to fix the boundaries it would
thereafter be obliged to defend. The Montreux Convention, Stalin
described as "inimical" to the Soviet Union since it gave Russia the
same rights granted the Japanese Emperor. Turkey, he maintained,
was too weak to give any effective guarantees of free passage and it
was, therefore, only right that the Soviet Union should be enabled to
defend the Straits.

"The American government will agree to a revision of the Montreux
Convention," the President said. "We believe, however, that the Straits
should be a free waterway open to the whole world and guaranteed by
all of us."

That presented the issue. The Soviets wanted the free navigation of
the Straits guaranteed by the Soviets, or by the Soviets and Turkey.

This meant their armed forces would be on Turkey's soil. We wanted the free navigation of the Straits guaranteed by the United Nations.

The thinking of the Soviet leaders in connection with the Dardanelles is unrealistic. For a hundred years Russia has coveted this section of its neighbor's territory. A hundred years ago the fortifications they now seek would have been of great military value. Today, without complete air superiority, their fortifications in the Straits would be of little value.

At this point, President Truman declared he was convinced that a great step toward ending Europe's recurring wars could be taken if the barriers to free passage of goods and vessels could be eliminated. He then presented the proposal we had prepared providing for free and unrestricted navigation of inland waterways.

This proposal, Stalin said, he was not prepared to discuss, since it had not been on the agenda. Despite several subsequent efforts by the President and by me, the best we could obtain was an agreement to refer the proposal to the Council of Foreign Ministers for later consideration. When it came to drafting the communique of the conference, Stalin objected to any mention even of this action, giving no reason other than that it was unnecessary and that the communique was already too long.

On July 25, the conference recessed, because the votes cast in the British election several weeks earlier were to be counted the following day. Mr. Churchill had brought the leader of the Opposition, Mr. Clement R. Attlee, to the conference, so that there would be continuity of representation regardless of the outcome of the election.

The day before the two Britons left for home to hear the results, I asked Mr. Churchill what he thought of his chances of remaining in office. He said he had no idea of the result but that the people who professed to know about elections had been betting that the Conservative Party would maintain a sizeable majority of the seats in the House of Commons. He felt very confident of victory. Mr. Attlee, on the other hand, impressed me as believing that his party would make a fine showing but would be defeated.

It made an interesting point that in the midst of our wrangling over how elections should be conducted in the liberated areas, these two leaders, weeks after the votes had been cast in England and by the armed forces overseas, were entirely unaware of the landslide that had taken place to sweep the Labor Party into power. The result was a surprise to all of us who had discussed the matter with them.

When the new Prime Minister returned to Potsdam, he brought Ernest Bevin to succeed Anthony Eden as Foreign Minister. As personalities, Attlee and Bevin differ from Churchill and Eden about as much as it is possible for people to differ. Mr. Attlee, in appearance and certainly in manner, gives one the impression of being a university professor. In speaking, he makes no pretense of oratory but presents his ideas clearly and carefully. He is exceedingly modest; there is nothing of the actor in him, and it is difficult to picture this earnest, serious man having great appeal for masses of people.

Soon after their arrival, Mr. Attlee and Mr. Bevin called on the President and the four of us discussed the work of the conference. The President mentioned the Soviet demand for East Prussia and indicated on a map the changes in the boundary lines of Germany, Poland and the Soviet Union that thus would be effected. Mr. Bevin immediately and forcefully presented his strong opposition to those boundaries. His manner was so aggressive that both the President and I wondered how we would get along with this new Foreign Minister. Some time later I told Mr. Bevin of the impression he had made on us at our first meeting, adding that we soon came to admire his bluntness and directness. He rather enjoyed my statement. And indeed it did not take me long to learn to respect highly his fine mind, his forthrightness, his candor, and his scrupulous regard for a promise. I have not only a high regard for his ability but a genuine affection for him as a man.

Britain's stand on the issues before the conference was not altered in the slightest, so far as we could discern, by the replacement of Mr. Churchill and Mr. Eden by Mr. Attlee and Mr. Bevin. This continuity of Britain's foreign policy impressed me. Later, in London, an incident occurred which demonstrated that I was not the only one so impressed. During the session of the United Nations General Assembly, Mr. Bevin made an important speech on British foreign policy. An Englishwoman, who had followed foreign affairs closely and who, naturally, had contrasted Ernest Bevin's bulk of at least 250 pounds with Anthony Eden's tall slender frame, sat in the gallery with an American friend listening to Mr. Bevin's speech. During the course of it, she turned to her companion and remarked, "Anthony Eden is making a good speech, but he seems to have gotten a little stout."

With the arrival of the new British leaders, the conference resumed and we started work in earnest on the most difficult issue before us— Germany.

We had arrived in Potsdam to face what amounted to a *fait accompli,* so far as the Polish-German frontier was concerned. Prior to Yalta, the three powers had agreed to divide Germany into four zones of occupation, and they had made a positive declaration in Section VI of the Yalta Protocol that the final delimitation of the western frontier of Poland should await the peace conference. Although the protocol would seem to permit no misunderstanding, we learned before leaving the United States for Germany that, without any consultation either with the United Kingdom or with the United States, the Soviets had transferred all the German territory east of the Neisse River to Poland for administration.

Both President Truman and Prime Minister Churchill promptly asked for an explanation of this unilateral action in establishing, for all practical purposes, another zone. Such a course, the President maintained, not only was contrary to agreement but would make the settlement of problems such as reparations far more difficult.

The Soviet defense was that the Germans had fled before the Russian armies, and, since it was necessary to have some government in the area, they had permitted Poland to take over its administration. Generalissimo Stalin agreed that no one of the powers had the right to create a new zone, but said that the Soviet government had to be assured of stable conditions in the rear of the Red Army. He then admitted that Poland was actually removing from this area substantial amounts of coal, which we contended certainly should be considered part of reparations payments.

The President asked how the reparations issue could ever be settled "if part of the German territory is gone before we reach agreement on what reparations should be."

Stalin remarked that everything the President said was irrelevant since "no frontiers had been ceded at the Crimea Conference except for the provisions that Poland would receive territory."

"The western frontier question is open," Stalin said, "and the Soviet Union is not bound."

The President repeated: "You are not?"

"No," Stalin replied.

We were concerned also by the huge displacement of population resulting from this action of the Soviets. Although Stalin claimed "no single German remained in the area to be given to Poland," an area that had a prewar German population of nearly nine million, our information indicated that there were at least two million Germans left there. Later, representatives of the Polish government admitted the presence of approximately a million and a half Germans, but contended that many of them would leave voluntarily if the area were assigned to Poland.

President Beirut of Poland argued his country's claim to eastern Germany at a meeting of the Foreign Ministers on July 24. He pointed out that, if all the area they asked were given them, Poland would still be smaller in total area than before the war because, in accordance with the Crimea decision, 180,000 square kilometers of territory in the east would be transferred to Russia. He asserted, however, that the eastern German area would give Poland a sounder economy and a more homogeneous population.

Mr. Churchill had pointed out that this Soviet-supported plan would take nearly one-fourth of the arable land within Germany's 1937 frontiers. Not only would the German food supply be cut, he stressed, but more than a million Germans would be forced into the western zones, "bringing their mouths with them."

Time after time, in discussing the claims of Poland and the question of recognizing the existence of Polish administration of the area during the occupation, the President repeated that there could be no transfer of territory until there was a peace conference. In addition, we specifically refrained from promising to support at the German Peace Conference any particular line as the western frontier of Poland.

Our deliberate avoidance of a promise on the Polish border is emphasized by the promise we did make in the protocol about the transfer of the city of Königsberg to the Soviet Union, when we said: "the President of the United States and the British Prime Minister have declared that they will support the proposal of this conference at the forthcoming peace settlement."

To remove even an excuse for Poland or the Soviet Union to claim that the line had been established or that there was any promise to support a particular line, the Berlin Protocol declared: "The three heads of government reaffirm their opinion that the final delimitation of the western frontier of Poland should await the peace settlement."

In the light of this history, it is difficult to credit with good faith any person who asserts that Poland's western boundary was fixed by the conferees, or that there was a promise that it would be established at some particular place.

We had recognized from the outset, however, that we would have to accept for the time being the Polish administration of this part of the Soviet zone. It was an accomplished fact and we could not force the Russians to resume the responsibilities they had voluntarily resigned. However, no agreement even on the temporary administration was reached until we came to grips with the issue of reparations.

Ever since Yalta the great variance between the Soviet Union and ourselves on the subject of reparations had been apparent. We agreed that reparations should be obtained through payments "in kind" rather than in currency. But the meetings of the Commission on Reparations between the Yalta and Potsdam meetings had demonstrated that our agreement extended no further.

There was, first of all, the figure of twenty billion dollars, with one-half, or ten billion dollars, to go to the Soviet Union. Mr. Maisky had advanced this figure at Yalta and President Roosevelt had accepted it as a "basis for discussion" in the Reparations Commission. When the commission met at Moscow repeated efforts by our representative, Mr.

Edwin Pauley, failed to elicit from Mr. Maisky any data to support this figure. At Potsdam, both Generalissimo Stalin and Mr. Molotov kept pressing for the establishment of a definite figure. We finally succeeded in eliminating from the agreed declaration any mention of a total amount either in terms of dollars or tonnages of equipment.

The major impasse at the Moscow Reparations Commission meetings arose from our insistence that there could be no reparations from current output until Germany exported enough goods to pay for essential imports. Here, too, we were guided by our experience in World War I when American loans paid for German purchases of raw materials, which were then converted into goods for delivery to other countries as reparations payments. We were determined that we would not again pay for Germany's reparations and, therefore, maintained that necessary imports and advances must constitute a first charge against any German production available for export.

Our desire to treat the reparations issue as one part of the over-all economic planning struck a snag of reality. We had expected that no property other than war booty would be removed from Germany by any of the armies of occupation without a strict accounting so that its value could be charged against whatever reparations program was later agreed upon. But, even before the conference opened, we had received reports that the Soviet army was removing property and equipment that could in no sense be classified as war booty. Some of these reports were such that we were reluctant to believe them. But there was little room for doubt after our arrival in Germany where we not only received eye-witness accounts but ourselves encountered corroborating evidence.

The house assigned to the President and his party had been the home of a motion picture executive who, we were told, had been taken to Russia. His wife was acting as charwoman in one of the homes assigned to other members of the American delegation. "The Little White House" had been completely stripped of its furnishings, but had been refurnished for the conference with furniture taken from still other homes.

Assistant Secretary Clayton and Mr. Pauley were shown a point on the line between the American and Russian zones where the Soviets, before the dividing line was finally fixed, had taken machinery from a plant which eventually was left in our zone and moved it into their area not more than two-hundred yards from the line. There it was left in an open field. The International Telephone and Telegraph Company's plant in Berlin, they found, had been stripped of nearly all its machinery. They visited other plants where rayon, ice and optical instruments had been made, and observed similar conditions.

Mr. Pauley had discussed the matter at length with Mr. Maisky, who admitted that the occupying power could not rightfully remove property without accounting to the other powers unless that property could be classified as war booty. Mr. Maisky tried to devise a definition of war booty that would include furniture, bath fixtures, silverware, coal, and other nonmilitary supplies. He found it an impossible task.

Finally, at a meeting of the Foreign Ministers on July 23, I asked Mr. Molotov whether it was true that the Soviet authorities had taken large quantities of equipment and materials, including even household goods, out of their zone.

"Yes, this is the case," Mr. Molotov replied. If it was worrying me, he went on, he would agree to deduct from their reparations plan a suitable figure to cover removals already made and he suggested 300 million dollars as a proper amount. When I objected, he quickly responded with an offer to reduce their reparations claims from ten to nine billion to cover removals already made "and thus dispose of the question."

But at Paris, at New York and at Moscow in the spring of 1947, Molotov was again demanding ten billion dollars.

Further complicating the problem of property removals was Poland's action in eastern Germany, where, Stalin admitted, the Poles were taking coal from the Silesian mines. This area, Mr. Molotov maintained, "must of necessity be considered differently."

We considered these practical problems in our delegation at considerable length. We knew that, if reparations were to be drawn from all Germany we would have to demand an accounting from the Soviets. We were sure they could not even approximate an accurate valuation of what had been taken, and we realized that the effort to establish and maintain such an accounting would be a source of constant friction, accusations and ill-will.

Mr. Clayton, Mr. Pauley and I concluded that the only way out of the situation was to persuade each country to satisfy its reparations claims out of its own zone. I discussed this idea with former Ambassador Joseph E. Davies and he, too, thought it was the solution. Then, with the approval of the President, I arranged for a private interview with Mr. Molotov on July 23.

The United States, I said, was "deeply concerned" at the development of the reparations issue. We had always favored the adoption of a policy by which the three powers would treat the entire German economic question as a whole, but we did not see how the Soviet Union's position on war booty, removals, and so on, could be reconciled with an over-all reparations plan. We were very much afraid, I stressed, that "the attempt to resolve these conditions in practice would lead to endless quarrels and disagreements between the three countries at a time when unity between them is essential." Therefore, under the circumstances, we believed it wise to consider the possibility of each country's taking reparations from its own zone.

Approximately 40 per cent of the value of "industrial equipment

deemed unnecessary for a peace economy" was located in the Soviet
zone. We proposed that 10 per cent of such industrial equipment in the
western zones be given to the Soviets. If the Soviets desired certain
additional equipment or materials from the British or American zones,
these could be exchanged for food or coal needed for the German population in the west.

Mr. Molotov promised to give this proposal to Generalissimo Stalin
for his consideration.

The day before Mr. Attlee and Mr. Bevin were to arrive, Mr. Molotov
returned to the subject with the complaint that we were seeking to
reverse a decision made at Yalta by not accepting the twenty-billion
dollar total reparations proposal. I tried many ways to help him understand that acceptance by Roosevelt "as a basis for discussion" was not
a commitment.

"If you ask me for a million dollars and I tell you I will discuss it,"
I told him, "it does not mean I will write a check for it." That didn't
get the point over. So I pointed out that we not only had accepted the
proposal as a basis for discussion but that Mr. Pauley had been in
Moscow for thirty-five days and discussed it; then he had come to
Berlin and we had continued to discuss it, and for the many reasons I
had previously explained to him we had decided, after this discussion,
that the figure was not practical.

As soon as Mr. Attlee and Mr. Bevin returned I visited them and,
after several hours discussion, obtained their agreement in principle to
our proposal. The next day the President and I arranged to see Generalissimo Stalin and Mr. Molotov, but the Generalissimo was ill with a
cold. Molotov came.

We declared our agreement to an equal division of the German fleet
and merchant marine among the three powers, for which the Russians
had been pressing very vigorously since the beginning of the conference.
We urged him to accept our plan for reparations. Mr. Molotov thereupon announced that the Soviet Union was prepared to accept our proposal "in principle" but wished to settle certain "details." The major
"detail" was the amount of equipment that would be turned over to the
Soviet Union from the Ruhr and he suggested two billion dollars' worth
as an appropriate amount!

We explained that the placing of a dollar value on the equipment was
impossible and we could only agree to offer a certain percentage of the
equipment to be declared available for reparations. Mr. Molotov was
most insistent about having a total dollar value set because otherwise
"a percentage figure would be meaningless."

During this conversation he asserted that the Economic Committee
had not done so well. I knew this was a criticism of his representative,

Mr. Maisky, for his inability to justify in some way the removals from the Soviet zone. But I did not realize how serious a matter it is for a Soviet representative to fail to have the right answers. Since that criticism, Mr. Maisky, who had served as Ambassador at London for ten years and spoke English fluently, has not been seen at a conference.

On July 31, I told Mr. Molotov there were three outstanding issues: reparations, Poland's administration of a part of the Soviet zone, and our paper entitled "Admission to the United Nations" dealing with Italy and the Balkan states. I submitted a proposal containing the only concessions we were willing to make and requested that Mr. Molotov present the three proposals to Generalissimo Stalin so that they might be discussed at the afternoon session. I told him we would agree to all three or none and that the President and I would leave for the United States the next day.

When the conference opened that afternoon the President immediately suggested that the three proposals be discussed and called on me to present them. I did so, emphasizing that it was all one proposition.

Generalissimo Stalin expressed disapproval of "the tactics of Mr. Byrnes," in asking for consideration of the three proposals at one time. I replied that we had been considering them one at a time for three weeks; that we were now making concessions in one solely for the purpose of reaching a compromise on the three in order to bring the conference to an end. Therefore, we insisted on this procedure. The Generalissimo renewed his protest and then began to bargain. First, he suggested a fantastic increase in reparations. Then, he proposed that the amount of capital equipment to be removed from the western zone in return for products such as food, coal, timber, and so on, be increased from 12 per cent to 15 per cent. I said if he would withdraw his other demands and agree to the other two proposals in dispute, we would agree to the 15 per cent. He agreed and the conference ended shortly thereafter.

Molotov dropped, for the time being at least, his proposal for the joint administration of the Ruhr, a major objective of the Soviet Union in western Europe. Agreement quickly followed on such matters as the economic principles to govern the occupation of Germany, including the compact to treat the country as an economic unit; the orderly transfer of German population; and the revision of the Allied Control Council procedure in Rumania, Bulgaria and Hungary to meet, in part, some of the requests made in our paper on implementing the Yalta Declaration on Liberated Europe.

We agreed to urge our representatives to act promptly on the procedure for the trial of major war criminals. It would take some of the joy out of war if the men who started one, instead of a halo around the head, got a rope around the neck.

Note that nowhere in the Potsdam Protocol is there any provision for the payment of reparations from current production. All prior discussions were superseded by the formal reparations agreement at Potsdam. The Soviet Union's renewal one year later of its demand for ten billions of dollars of reparations from current production and its continued use of German labor is inexcusable.

There is even less justification for requiring Germany to pay reparations out of current production when it is considered that the prewar value of taxable property in the Silesian area alone, which is only a part of the region now administered by Poland, was 11,300,000,000 dollars. Poland invariably argues that it is entitled to this area because of the 180,000 square kilometers of its territory east of the Curzon Line transferred to Russia by the Yalta decision. In addition there is East Prussia, which we have pledged to the Soviet Union and which had taxable property valued at two and a half billion dollars. The resources of these areas certainly should be considered as part of the reparations settlement.

Even if the figures were less generous, I think we should realize that, modern war being what it is, it is shortsighted and futile for any country to seek approximate compensation for losses it has sustained.

Because Generalissimo Stalin made so clear in the discussion of reparations at Potsdam that he "disliked the tactics of Mr. Byrnes," I thought he was seriously offended. It was therefore a surprise and a good indication of Russian appreciation of firmness in negotiating that just before the final gavel was to fall on the Potsdam Conference he asked the President for permission to say a few words about "Mr. Byrnes who has worked harder perhaps than any of us."

"He has brought us together in reaching so many important decisions," Stalin added.

The President expressed the hope that the next time the Big Three met it would be in Washington.

"God willing," Stalin replied.

The conference ended in good spirits. But the American delegation that headed for home probably was less sanguine than the one that had departed from Yalta. Events had shown that agreements reached in conference must be hammered out on the hard anvil of experience. We thought, however, that we had established a basis for maintaining our war-born unity. Our efforts in relation to eastern Europe had been less successful than we had hoped. We had failed to exempt Italy from reparations. We thought we had succeeded in the case of Austria. We felt we had made genuine progress in the agreements about Germany, although there was ample ground for our fears that it would be a long time before we could get the Soviets to start work on a German settlement. Nevertheless, we believed our agreement on reparations enabled us to avoid denouncing their unilateral action in removing people and property from their zone.

Certainly, no one of us suspected that the first treaties of peace would be concluded only after sixteen more months of almost continuous negotiation. We considered the conference a success. We firmly believed that the agreements reached would provide a basis for the early restoration of stability to Europe.

The agreements did make the conference a success but the violation of those agreements has turned success into failure.

WORKING ON BOARD USS AUGUSTA ON THE WAY TO POTSDAM

Charles E. Bohlen, H. F. Matthews, James F. Byrnes and Benjamin V. Cohen

BOOK II
THE TREATIES—FIVE STEPS
TOWARD PEACE

Chapter 5

Setback at London

ON MAY 9, 1947, I appeared before the Senate Foreign Relations Committee which was considering the peace treaties with Italy, Bulgaria, Rumania and Hungary. The committee was under considerable pressure, primarily from Italian-American groups, to delay action. The arguments for delay were really intended to accomplish the defeat of the treaties. After describing how the United States had held the initiative throughout sixteen months of difficult negotiations, I urged the committee to consider the consequences if the treaty were to be delayed and we were to give up our leadership. I then asked the Senators to remember the words of President Roosevelt in his last State of the Union message on January 6, 1945.

Perfectionism, no less than isolationism or imperialism or power politics, may obstruct the paths to international peace. Let us not forget that the retreat to isolationism a quarter of a century ago was started not by a direct attack against international co-operation but against the alleged imperfections of the peace.

In our disillusionment after the last war we preferred international anarchy to international co-operation with nations which did not see and think exactly as we did. We gave up the hope of gradually achieving a better peace because we had not the courage to fulfill our responsibilities in an admittedly imperfect world.

We must not let that happen again, or we shall follow the same tragic road again—the road to a third world war.

We should remember these words as we seek to conclude treaties of peace with Austria, Germany and Japan, and as we watch the evolution of international relations within the framework of the United Nations.

Happily, the committee and the Senate acted in the spirit of these words and President Roosevelt's wisdom. The committee unanimously endorsed the treaties, and the Senate, on June 5, 1947, approved the Italian treaty by a vote of 79 to 10, and ratified the others by a voice vote.

Good government lies in seeking the highest common denominator.

This is as true in international councils as it is in the county court house. The story of our effort to obtain this common denominator in the four European treaties is told here not only for its intrinsic interest and importance but as one means of evaluating the solution to the many problems that lie ahead.

I had been Secretary of State two months when we boarded the *Queen Elizabeth* on September 5, 1945, for London and the first meeting of the Council of Foreign Ministers. Those twenty-eight days spent in the United States after the return from Germany were full of action. There had been the second atomic bomb; Russian entry into the Japanese war; Japan's surrender; arrangements for the occupation of Japan; the visits of the French President, General de Gaulle, and his Foreign Minister, Georges Bidault; postwar lend-lease settlement problems; intensified efforts to bring China's divided factions together; departmental appointments, including the nominations of Dean Acheson as Undersecretary, Ben Cohen as counselor, and Donald Russell, Spruille Braden and William Benton as Assistant Secretaries; and, finally, the very important preparation for the London Conference.

On the boat we started to work in earnest on the proposals and alternative proposals that had been prepared by the State Department experts. John Foster Dulles, a leading Republican spokesman on foreign affairs, had accepted my invitation to join the delegation, and together we met with the State Department advisory staff twice a day to plan the position of the United States on all the issues before the Council.

One of the things that gave us particular concern in these talks was the unmistakable evidence of Russian expansion. I had secured the Yalta agreement on the Kuriles, Sakhalin, Dairen and Port Arthur from the Map Room, in the White House. At Potsdam we had encountered the Soviet demands that Poland be given a large portion of eastern Germany to compensate for the Polish territory east of the Curzon Line taken over by the Soviets; her demands for Königsberg; for a share in the administration of the Ruhr; and for control of the Dardanelles. Her determination to dominate the Balkan states had become apparent, and at Potsdam she had made a bid for control of one of Italy's North African colonies, preferably Tripolitania.

This last request was especially disturbing because events had convinced me that the Soviets' interest in this territory was primarily military. Throughout the war they had shown a tendency to enter into multilateral arrangements when they were economic in character and demonstrably of direct benefit to them, but to prefer unilateral action where military and security considerations were involved.

We finally decided that our policy should be to promote the independence of these colonies, which covered over a million square miles of territory and had more than three million inhabitants. While preparing for independence they should be administered under a trusteeship set up within the United Nations Charter. The problem was: Who should be the trustee? Some of the State Department officials had recommended that Italy continue as trustee for the United Nations. At first that seemed the easiest solution but there were strong reasons against it.

Italy's record of administering the colonies was one of inefficiency and oppression. Consequently, in the African campaign the native inhabitants were sympathetic to the Allied cause and had given great assistance to the British. The British had promised the Senussi tribes, in recognition of their help, that Italy would never again be placed in control of their territory and their people. Investigation disclosed that every year Italy had been in control of the colonies she had incurred financial loss, notwithstanding the fact that her civilian employees were paid pitifully small salaries. As long as the United States was appropriating relief funds for Italy, it did not seem wise to allow Italy to assume such a financial burden.

It was difficult to foresee what kind of government would prevail in Italy. The colonies had proved of no value to her except as a place for military training and, under the treaty we were considering, she would have no need for great areas for training troops. But above and beyond these considerations was our belief that a trusteeship should be established solely to assist the inhabitants of the colonies to develop the capacity for self-government so that the people might be granted independence. With these thoughts in mind, I asked one of my aides to prepare a draft of a proposal for a collective trusteeship under the United Nations.

I was glad we had come to London to begin work on drafting treaties of peace. The devastation of war that surrounded us seemed to me to be a desirable reminder of the grave responsibility that was ours. From my observations on short walks or quick drives around the city I concluded that fifteen years at least would be required to repair the damage. But I am always more impressed with people than with buildings and I was deeply moved by the patience and the courage of the British people. About all the end of the war had brought them was a reduction in casualty lists, but they accepted all the rationing and regulations in a spirit that was in sharp contrast to the clamor at home over the few remaining shortages and controls.

The council convened on September 11, and we immediately encountered serious differences of opinion over its organization and its agenda. There was even, to my surprise, a request from Molotov to discuss the control of Japan. Two days passed before we were able to get started on the Italian treaty.

It was agreed that a British draft would be used as the basis for our work. Issues which were to become old friends immediately appeared. They were the Italo-Yugoslav border, the Dodecanese Islands, and the Italian colonies. Mr. Molotov would not discuss the border problem unless the Yugoslavs were present; he would not discuss the Dodecanese until we discussed the Italian colonies. So I suggested that we invite the Yugoslavs and the Italians to come and present their case, and proceeded to present the proposal on the Italian colonies, which we had completed immediately after our arrival.

Our proposal provided that an administrator be appointed by the United Nations Security Council of which the Soviet Union was a permanent member. This administrator would be an international civil servant appointed from any one of the member nations. He would have an Advisory Council composed of one representative each from Britain, France, the Soviet Union, and the United States, plus Italy, and a representative of the people of the territory. Should the administrator fail to discharge his responsibilities in a manner satisfactory to any one of the states on this Advisory Council, any one of them could bring the matter to the attention of the Trusteeship Council. Our plan also called for the termination of the trusteeship at the end of ten years.

"This plan would give assurance that the Italian colonies will not be developed for the military advantage of anyone," I stated. "It would be left to the Security Council to determine, if necessary, the points in these colonies at which strategic bases might be established. This plan would give heart to the peoples of the world, since it shows that the states on this council intend to carry out their promises and permit these peoples to select at the earliest possible moment the government under which they would live."

Mr. Bidault preferred to make Italy the trustee power, particularly since the Trusteeship Council had not yet been established and there was no indication of how a collective trusteeship would work. Dr. Wang Shih Chieh immediately expressed the Chinese delegation's full approval of our proposal. Mr. Bevin said this was a new proposal and he would have to study it. He referred to Britain's wartime promise to the Senussi tribes. He was not ready to commit himself. He wished to know if other proposals would be considered because he wanted the dominions to have the opportunity to give their views to the deputies. It was then Mr. Molotov's turn.

The Soviet delegation, he said, proposed that the principle of trusteeship be applied to some of the Italian colonies with individual countries being made trustee for each of the colonies. He doubted our ability to agree on an administrator. He would not conceal, he added, the desire of the Soviet Government to claim an individual trusteeship, and proceeded to base his claim on the damages inflicted by the ten divisions and three brigades of Italian Blackshirts that had invaded the Soviet Union. Pointing to the "wide experience" of the Soviet Government in "establishing friendly relations between different nationalities," he proposed this experience be applied to Tripolitania and assured the council that ten years would be adequate to prepare the territory for independent existence.

In a private conversation, Mr. Molotov proposed to me that each of the three powers: the United States, United Kingdom and Soviet Union, should administer one of the colonies. I told him we could not agree to that.

Our delegation, I told him, had concluded it would be far more difficult to agree on administration by individual governments than on an individual administrator who could not be charged with exploiting the colony for commercial or military advantage. These areas must constitute a trust and must not be regarded as spoils of war or compensation for damage done in the war. Dividing these three colonies among three states without restrictions on military developments would not serve peace but would sow the seeds of trouble.

The following afternoon Mr. Bevin presented the British position. With characteristic bluntness he said that Britain could not agree to the Soviet claim to an individual trusteeship over Tripolitania. Since the claim was based on the damage caused by Italian troops in Russia, he was forced to point out that Britain and the dominions were fighting Italy long before Italy and Russia were at war. Britain, he went on, recognized the interest of the Soviet Union in eastern Europe and had therefore supported Russia's claims, and he expressed his surprise that Russia did not recognize a similar interest on the part of his country in the Mediterranean. Bevin then declared his support for our proposal, subject to modifications. He did not want to be tied to the American draft as it applied to Somaliland and Eritrea. But as for Libya and Tripolitania, he agreed "because it was a great, new and untried experiment and because Britain wished to avoid conflict in this area between the great powers." With regard to Eritrea and Somaliland, he suggested that the deputies consider the right of Ethiopia to an outlet on the sea and seek territorial adjustments among those countries that would "give these peoples a better chance to live."

This latter suggestion, of course, was acceptable to us. Mr. Bidault's opinion was still reserved. France, he said, could not accept our proposal, "even in principle" until the details were more definite and he pointed out that Libya was bordered by an important part of the French Union. Obviously, he feared the effect that the promise of independence for Tripolitania would have in French territory.

Mr. Molotov was precise and specific. He wanted to discuss Tripolitania. The Soviet Union had a sea outlet in the north, he asserted, and in view of its vast territory should have one also in the south, "especially so since we now have the right to use Dairen and Port Arthur in the Far East."

"The Soviet Union should take the place that is due it," he said, "and therefore should have bases in the Mediterranean for its merchant fleet. We do not propose to introduce the Soviet system into this territory apart from the democratic order that is desired by the people." And then, he added, "This will not be done along the lines that have been used in Greece."

In a private conversation with Mr. Molotov it became apparent that another difficult misunderstanding in language had arisen between ourselves and the Russians. At the San Francisco Conference when the question of establishing a trusteeship system within the United Nations was being considered, the Soviet delegation had asked Mr. Stettinius what the American attitude would be toward the assumption by the Soviet Union of a trusteeship. Mr. Stettinius replied in general terms, expressing the opinion that the Soviet Union was "eligible" to receive a territory for administration under trusteeship. Mr. Molotov took this to mean we would support a Soviet request for a trusteeship. He told me he was surprised that we were opposing his request for Tripolitania. He admitted the letter contained no specific commitment as to the Italian colonies, but asserted that these colonies provided the only opportunity that the Soviet Union would have to acquire a trusteeship, and therefore a commitment was certainly implied.

He repeated this so often I finally said:

"In the United States any citizen is eligible to become President, but that does not mean every citizen is going to be President. If you keep repeating that there is a commitment to support any request you make, for a trusteeship, you will soon come to believe it yourself."

I saw I had not convinced him, so I tried again.

"If I tell a man I think he is eligible to own a house, I do not mean that if he asks for the Soviet Embassy, I must support his demand for the house."

That did not help. He still professes to believe that because of Secretary Stettinius' statement it is our duty to find a satisfactory territory that the Soviet Union can administer as trustee.

Those were the opening arguments. With variations and embellishments they were repeated throughout the next sixteen months until it became clear the issue could not be settled at present. Consequently, unless there is a prior agreement, the military government will continue for one year after the Italian treaty comes into force. If the four states do not reach agreement within that year, the disposition of the colonies will be decided by the General Assembly of the United Nations, where unanimous agreement is not required.

Nor could we reach any agreement on the Dodecanese Islands. Four members of the council believed they should go to Greece but Mr. Molotov insisted that a decision on these islands could be made only in connection with a decision on the Italian colonies.

As to the Italo-Yugoslav border, the initial statements of position disclosed that all members of the council were generally agreed that Trieste should be made a free port. The chief problem was Mr. Molotov's lone stand that the city be placed under Yugoslav sovereignty despite the fact that its population was overwhelmingly Italian. The position of the council members was not changed in any marked degree by the arguments presented on September 18 by the representatives of Yugoslavia, Italy, South Africa, Australia and New Zealand. But immediately after this hearing I proposed that experts be sent to the territory with directions to determine a line that would, primarily, follow ethnic divisions but which would also take economic factors into consideration. Molotov accepted this suggestion but afterward regretted the action because the line his expert recommended could not be justified under the directive.

Another issue on which Mr. Molotov faced four-to-one opposition was that of reparations. The Soviet proposal called for payment by Italy of reparations totaling 600 million dollars of which 100 million would go to Russia. The other members of the council held that after Italy repaid advances for relief there would be little left for reparations payments.

Although I had come to the conference thinking the Foreign Ministers might reach agreement on general principles to guide the deputies in detailed work on the treaties within ten days or two weeks, it was apparent by the end of the first week that this was a vain hope. We had spent hours talking about procedure. France wanted to discuss the control of Germany. Molotov wanted to discuss German reparations. He also raised the question of the Control Council in Japan. We had made little progress on the Italian peace treaty and the Soviet delegation was insisting that Britain and the United States extend diplomatic recognition to their puppet governments in eastern Europe.

It was the latter demand that appeared to me to be the main stumbling block of the conference. On Sunday morning I determined I must make Mr. Molotov understand why we refused to recognize governments installed and maintained by the Soviet Union. The Soviet official was spending the day in the country but arrangements were made for us to meet at the Russian Embassy at 5:30.

I opened the conversation by saying "It is essential for the future of the world that our nations continue to co-operate and that we should endeavor to adjust our differences in such a way as to preserve our unity of purpose." I then emphasized that "the United States is not interested in seeing anything but governments friendly to the Soviet Union in adjacent countries."

"I must tell you I have doubts as to this, and it would not be honest to hide it," Mr. Molotov replied. He went on to say that the doubts rose from the attitude of the United States in the case of Rumania. The former Radescu government, he said, "was hostile to the Soviet Union and yet received British and American support but when the Groza government, which was friendly, had been established, both the United States and Britain had withdrawn support."

"The Yalta Declaration on the Liberated Countries had been warmly received by the American people," I told him. "You will remember, I am sure, that the Groza government was installed during President Roosevelt's administration. We know it was installed as a result of a two-and-a-half hour ultimatum to the King by Mr. Vyshinski. Since that time, the exclusion of our press representatives, the treatment accorded our official representatives and other actions has confirmed our doubts as to the character of this government.

"Our objective," I said, "is a government both friendly to the Soviet Union and representative of all the democratic elements of the country." I pointed out that the misunderstandings that had arisen after Yalta over Poland had been worked out and I suggested we try to agree on the composition of a Rumanian government as we had in the case of Poland.

Mr. Molotov refused to accept the Polish case as a precedent. In Rumania, he said, such a course would lead to civil war. Only after an election was held, he maintained, would it be possible to consider reorganizing the government.

I pointed out that the government then would not be a provisional one but an elected one and that if we joined in establishing a representative provisional government, the results of an election held by such a government would be accepted by our people.

"Are all parties represented in the British and American governments?" Mr. Molotov inquired.

"No," I replied, "but in the case of Rumania we are speaking of a temporary government and not one based on elections. Because of the manner in which the Groza government has been established and because of its subsequent actions, any elections held under its auspices would be suspect in the eyes of the American people."

Mr. Molotov then attacked Greece and asked why we should maintain a different attitude toward one country than toward the other.

"It is a question of facts," I told him. "In Greece correspondents had been allowed to go in, move about freely, and report without censorship what they had seen. As a result, the American people were informed about Greece and felt the situation was not the same as that described by you. In Rumania, correspondents have not been allowed any such facilities and the actions of the Groza government have led us to believe it is not representative of the people."

"Apparently," Mr. Molotov remarked, "in Greece the correspondents are happy but the people are not; whereas in Rumania the people are happy but the correspondents are not. The Soviet Government attaches more importance to the feeling of the people."

Although our representatives believed an overwhelming majority of the people in Rumania opposed the Groza regime, I chose not to argue this with him but rather to seek some formula for resolving our differences. But he kept insisting that our refusal to recognize Groza could only mean we desired to see established a government hostile to the Soviet Union. After repeatedly insisting this was not true and failing in every effort to reach an understanding, I finally gave up and went home.

It was a gloomy Sunday evening for the American delegation. We talked over this interview and the problems it raised for a long time. It seemed that the Soviet Union was determined to dominate Europe. We could see no solution to our problems but we knew we must continue to search for one.

The events of the following day gave us no encouragement. In all the treaties, we had proposed a strict limitation on armed forces and the establishment of inspection commissions to insure that the limitation was observed. The Rumanian treaty was under consideration, and Mr. Molotov immediately announced his opposition to our proposal.

Mr. Bevin pointed out that the last two wars had started in small states, Serbia and Poland, and we must hereafter see that small states neither start war nor become the first victims of war.

"If we encourage these small states to maintain peace rather than armies, and to develop their economies," he said, "it will also keep the big states out of trouble."

Mr. Molotov said it had never occurred to him that "if one disarmed a state it could lead a quieter life." And, in the same note of sarcasm, he asked:

"Do you really have so many people in your countries that you can send them out as inspectors, and consuls and so on?"

Mr. Bevin, who felt very strongly about the activities of the Red Army in Rumania, inquired how that country had acquired all the people it had there now.

I interrupted to say that I regarded the issue as a serious one.

"The world is war weary," I stated. "In every country soldiers want to return home. In the countries where they are in occupation, they

should return home as soon as possible. The peoples of the world look
to this council for action that will establish permanent peace. It would
be the greatest favor we could do these countries, all of which are poor,
if we relieve them of the burden of armaments. We have given assurances through the United Nations to prevent aggression against any
country. Why, then, do any of these countries need large armies?"

But we made no progress and so proceeded to equally fruitless discussions of other treaty clauses.

Wednesday evening Mr. Molotov came to my office and we went over
the same ground in almost the same terms. He persisted in believing
that there was some hidden motive in our stand based on hostility
toward the Soviet Union. Nothing I could say would dissuade him and
I understand he later said he wished he could find out what it was I
wanted so we could negotiate.

I was impressed by the repeated statements made by Stalin, Molotov,
and others that the Soviet Union sought security. Ever since Yalta,
when Marshal Stalin recounted how Poland twice within twenty-five
years had been used as a corridor for invading Russia, this fear had
kept cropping up in Russian policy. It was present in Molotov's demand
that governments wholly subservient to Russia should be maintained
in Rumania, Bulgaria and Hungary. Therefore, I thought that if we
could give them assurance on this score perhaps the obstacle blocking the
conference could be removed. In any event, we would eliminate that
argument. So, the following morning, I arranged for another private
talk with the Soviet Foreign Minister.

I recounted my conversation with Generalissimo Stalin at Yalta and
said that I had been impressed by his observation that twice within
twenty-five years Russia had been invaded through the Polish Corridor
and by his fear of a revival of German military power.

"As you know," I went on, "the United States, historically, is reluctant to enter into political treaties, but I want to ask you if the
Soviet Government would consider desirable a twenty-five-year treaty
between the four principal powers for the demilitarization of Germany.
If the Soviet Government thinks this a good idea, I am prepared to
recommend it to the President and both of us could recommend it
to the Congress. The details we will have to work out, but I
would like your views as to whether such a treaty would be a real
contribution toward removing the fear of a recrudescence of German
aggression—a fear that plays a large part in the policies of various
European states.

"If you think well of the idea," I concluded, "we can then talk to the
French and the British."

He said he could not give the definite views of his government but personally he thought it was "a very interesting idea." He would report it to Moscow and we could discuss it again in a few days. With that, he returned to the question of Rumania and told me that unless we withdrew our paper he would have to reply to it because it was, in effect, a challenge directed against the Soviet Union.

I told him he had every right to make a statement but that he could rest assured I would reply to him.

There were two meetings the next day and both of them were tense as the arguments that Mr. Molotov and I had been having privately were at last brought out into the open.

"In Rumania," Mr. Molotov asserted, "there is the Groza government which enjoys the support of the overwhelming majority of the population, and no one can deny this. . . . I ask; is not the reason that the American Government opposes this government the fact that it is friendly to the Soviet Union?"

He declared that our feeling that the Rumanian Government is undemocratic "does not correspond with the facts," and then added:

"The Rumanian Government is liked by the Rumanian population but not by the American Government. What should be done? Should we overthrow it because it is not liked by the United States Government, and set up a government that would be unfriendly to the Soviet Union? In such an undertaking the Soviet delegation will not be able to assist the American delegation."

I pointed out to Mr. Molotov that at Yalta the heads of government had agreed to favor interim governments that would be broadly representative and committed to the holding of early elections.

"At Potsdam," I continued, "the President had stated not once but a dozen times that the United States could not recognize the present governments of Rumania and Bulgaria. There was difference of opinion between the President and Generalissimo Stalin, but Generalissimo Stalin never once questioned the motives of the United States." I pointed out the steps we had taken to extend recognition to Poland, Finland and Hungary, and asserted these actions proved conclusively that "the statements made by Mr. Molotov regarding the motives of the United States Government are both unfair and untrue."

This exchange was typical of the debate throughout the morning. That afternoon, Mr. Bevin declared his support of the United States' position. Mr. Molotov, of course, rose to the challenge, but I could see that further discussion would only contribute bitterness and therefore declined to make any additional statements about Rumania. Mr. Molotov then concluded the discussion by charging that the other members of the council were "conducting an offensive" against him on the issue of Rumania.

It was the next day, September 22, that broke the back of the London Conference.

Just before 10 A.M. Mr. Molotov's secretary called to say that the Russian delegation could not be present for the scheduled meeting at 11, but asked if I would meet Mr. Molotov at 11:30. I arrived promptly and discovered he wanted to discuss Japan. The instructions he had received from Moscow undoubtedly had been sent before the receipt of his message regarding my suggestion for a nonaggression treaty, he explained. His government had informed him that it was timely to conclude a treaty directed againt a revival of Japanese aggression, particularly in view of the manner in which terms of surrender were being carried out in Japan. He urged the establishment of a Control Council for Japan.

This was not the first time Molotov had raised the question of the control of Japan and it was not the last. I thought it was just an element in his campaign of counterattack. Nevertheless, we were placed in an embarrassing situation.

The British also had previously proposed the establishment of a Control Council for Japan. Australia was pressing hard for a greater share in the determination of occupation policies. Japan was not on the agenda for the London meeting. I wanted first to get the views of our occupation forces, and therefore was not prepared to discuss it. I said that the heads of government at Potsdam had instructed us to devote ourselves to the immediate task of drafting the five European treaties. I assured Mr. Molotov I would take up the Japanese question as soon as I returned home and would communicate with him.

While our conversation was in progress, Mr. Bevin walked in. It was obvious that Molotov had asked him to come in at noon and that he had arrived too early. Mr. Molotov made it clear that he wanted to continue the discussion with me, and Bevin withdrew. When, at noon, he rejoined us, Mr. Molotov immediately said that he wished to propose a reorganization of the Council of Foreign Ministers on the ground that the work was being retarded through an initial mistake which had in effect violated the decisions of the Berlin Conference. This mistake, he said, had been made on the opening day, September 11, when it had been decided that France and China could participate in the discussion of the peace treaties for Finland, Rumania, Bulgaria and Hungary. He took the position that France and China should absent themselves completely except when the council was discussing treaties for countries with which they had signed armistice terms as provided in the Berlin declaration. This would exclude China from all the European treaties and France from all except the German and the Italian treaties.

Mr. Bevin and I both asserted that our clear understanding of the

Berlin decision was that while France and China could not vote upon any proposal under the circumstances cited, they could certainly take part in the discussions, and that to ask them to withdraw now would be an unnecessary humiliation.

As soon as I could get away I put in a telephone call to the President. He was at the Jefferson Islands Club, so I outlined the situation to Admiral Leahy and asked him to communicate with the President as soon as possible and make sure the President's understanding of the Potsdam decision was the same as mine. Then I drafted a message to Generalissimo Stalin which I suggested the President send. It urged Stalin to agree that China and France could continue participating in discussions on all treaties but could vote only on treaties for those countries with which they had signed armistice terms. The message, which the President sent, asserted that Mr. Molotov's stand would create a bad impression throughout the world.

"It would be charged," it said, "that the three big powers are denying the other members of the council even an opportunity to present their views." It argued that this was "too small a matter to disrupt the council and delay progress toward peace and better understanding."

When Mr. Molotov presented his proposal at the late afternoon meeting of the council it was, of course, a shock to the other members. Our most earnest persuasion had no effect whatever on Mr. Molotov. Late that evening, I arranged to see Mr. Bidault who, I knew, was furious. I was afraid he would walk out of the council and deliver a public blast, which I was anxious to avoid while there was any chance of receiving a favorable reply from Generalissimo Stalin. Despite his justifiable anger, Mr. Bidault promised to co-operate, and he did.

Stalin's reply confirmed the position taken by Mr. Molotov against the participation of France and China. The conference had come to an impasse.

I made several efforts to compromise our differences. On September 28, at a meeting with Mr. Molotov and Mr. Bevin, I submitted a compromise which I hoped would work. In the first step, it gave in to Mr. Molotov's insistence that the first draft of the treaties should be prepared only by those countries which had signed surrender terms. This meant only Britain and the Soviet Union in the case of Finland; Britain, the Soviet Union and the United States for the Rumanian, Hungarian, and Bulgarian treaties, with France joining the group only for the Italian treaty. But, because of our interest in participation by the small states, we proposed a second step on which, I served notice, we would be most insistent.

It provided that, after the treaties had been drafted, all of them would be submitted to a peace conference that would include "the five members of the Security Council, together with all European members of the United Nations and all non-European members of the United Nations which supplied substantial military contingents against European members of the Axis."

This was so worded because Molotov took the position that the Soviet Union would not attend if Argentina were invited.

Mr. Molotov wanted three separate peace conferences. He said the Soviets could not be prepared to discuss the Italian treaty during 1945. When Mr. Bevin asked him why, he replied it would be easier for him to get ready if the United States agreed to an Allied Control Council for Japan! This was in addition to his earlier demand for recognition of the three Balkan governments as a prerequisite for an Italian peace treaty. It illustrated his technique. Because we wished to proceed with the peace treaty he would delay the treaty, hoping thereby to force us to agree to various proposals in which he was interested.

The following day, I made one more effort. I submitted an additional paragraph to our peace conference proposal. It provided that "after full and free discussion by the invited states the final approval of the terms of the treaties of peace will be made by those of the invited states which were at war with the enemy states in question."

This, I hoped, might satisfy Mr. Molotov's desire to restrict the number of states sharing in the final decisions. My hope was in vain.

We had come to the crossroads. We saw there would be no agreement unless we yielded to the Soviet demands. We were determined to yield no further. Yet we were reluctant to let the first test of the peace-making machinery result in complete breakdown.

The people were anxious for peace. The public at home did not have the clear view of Soviet ambitions that the President and I got at Potsdam, and which was revealed even more clearly here at London. We had refrained, after Potsdam, from publicly expressing our concern because of our desire to maintain friendly relations with our Russian Allies. The first meeting of the council would be a complete failure and I realized that the failure would be attributed to me.

Mr. Molotov had concluded that I was unfriendly to Russia, and he declared that our policy had changed since President Roosevelt's death. His attitude was understandable. At the first meeting in Teheran, his need was for a second front and for further lend-lease aid. Both of these requests were agreed to by President Roosevelt. At Yalta the President had agreed to the transfer to Russia of the territory east of the Curzon Line and to offset this had agreed that there should be some extension of the western boundary of Poland. He had agreed to the transfer of the Kuriles and the remainder of Sakhalin, and to the transfer by China of Port Arthur and of certain rights in Dairen. At Potsdam, we had agreed to support at the peace conference the claim of the Soviets for Königsberg and the valuable territory of East Prussia. We had recognized for the time being their *fait accompli* in eastern Germany, and had made a reparations settlement they then regarded as acceptable.

Now, at London, Mr. Molotov saw no chance of taking home any packages. He could not understand why we would not accept his interpretation that "friendship" between our governments required that we let the Soviets establish complete suzerainty over the Balkan states. As far as I was concerned, Christmas was over—it was now January 1, and we had many bills to pay. Instead of issuing more I.O.Us, I wanted to collect some we held. One of these I felt was the Yalta pledge on the treatment of the liberated states.

To make the sacrifice Mr. Molotov demanded, I was convinced, would constitute a defeat for the Allies and the principles we had espoused. Only by refusing to bow to Soviet domination could we establish sound relations for the future. Our attitude was a shock to them. At that time, immediately after the end of hostilities, the Soviet Union enjoyed the admiration and the good will of most of our people. The Soviet leaders knew of our people's strong desire for peace and they thought we would not dare let the conference fail.

Our stand at London required them to make a re-evaluation; it made them realize they could not force us to accept their position. It was, in a very real sense, a test of strength. Most of all, it was a test of whether we really believed in what we said about one world and our desire to build collective security, or whether we were willing to accept the Soviet preference for the simpler task of dividing the world into two spheres of influence.

Our fight to have France and China remain in the council was generally applauded, and our fight for the peace conference and for the right of the smaller states to participate in the peace won for us the good opinion of those states. And it forced the Soviets to begin to reorient their policy. Their shift toward collective action within the United Nations is slow and grudging; it is still in process, but it will continue only so long as and only to the extent that the Soviets are forced by world opinion to co-operate.

Before closing the conference we tried to reach agreement on the customary protocol enumerating the questions on which agreement had been reached. But Mr. Molotov refused to sign any agreement which was based on the decision of the council on September 11 making France and China participants in the discussion. In one of the several heated discussions on the protocol, Mr. Bevin referred to Mr. Molotov's denunciation of his own previous action as "the nearest thing to the Hitler theory I have ever heard."

The effect was electric. Mr. Molotov rose from the table and started angrily toward the door. He slowed down a little as he approached it and gave the blunt Briton a chance to call him back and withdraw the statement—which he did.

Five more meetings failed to bring any further progress. Actually, we had realized for several days that no agreement was possible, but Dr. Wang Shih Chieh had urged us to continue our efforts a little longer. The final day of the conference Dr. Wang was presiding. It soon became apparent to all of us that a Russian filibuster was under way. The only plausible reason for it was the fact that the next day I was scheduled to be chairman and Mr. Molotov seemed to feel it would be desirable to have the council break down while an American was presiding. During a recess I expressed this opinion to Dr. Wang. He said that since the sessions had been extended at his request, he was willing to assume the responsibility of presiding at the breakdown.

The session extended fruitlessly into the late evening hours and, finally, Dr. Wang picked up his gavel and declared:

"I happen to be the man who has prolonged the session until today. As I hear no request for another meeting, I declare the council adjourned. My earnest hope is that a future meeting of the council will be arranged by the governments concerned."

It was courageous action by Dr. Wang. It is typical of the statesmanship exhibited by Chinese diplomats wherever I have observed their work. China's difficulties certainly cannot be attributed to the caliber of its foreign representatives. From my experience, I know of no nation which has been more ably represented in international conferences than China.

As I look back on this London meeting now, about the only pleasant experience of the entire meeting that I can recall occurred during a state dinner given by Prime Minister Attlee. Despite the splendor of the setting and the friendly efforts of our host, the tense mood of our meetings pervaded the dinner. The speeches were short and restrained and were finished long before it was time for the dinner to end. During an especially long lull in the proceedings, Mr. Bevin began quietly to sing. "Ernest," I said, "you can't sing and neither can I, but I have a military aide here who can sing."

"If you have such a man, why don't you produce him?" he immediately responded.

"You won't like him," I joked, "because all he knows is Irish songs. It's too bad, though, that this is St. James Palace, because he is the best singer of Irish songs you ever heard."

"Go ahead," Bevin urged, so I told Colonel Hugh A. Kelly, an architect and old friend from Jersey City who was the security officer of the American delegation, that Mr. Bevin wished him to sing an Irish song.

He must have been taken aback, but he rose to the occasion splendidly. Soon, he was standing in the middle of the room and was directing the whole group of nearly a hundred, including the Prime Minister and Mr. Molotov, in a hearty "community sing." Mr. Molotov asked for a repeat performance of "Johnny Doughboy Found a Rose in Ireland."

Everyone had a wonderful time. The final and most conclusive evidence of this fact came as we were leaving. The dinner had been served by a butler who was as stiff, correct, and impassive as we always imagine British butlers to be. Colonel Kelly was getting into his coat when the butler suddenly bowed and said:

"Begging your pardon, sir, I wish to say that precedent was set here tonight. But all of us had a ripping good time."

With the break-up of the council I headed for the United States knowing I had to face criticism. The public's disappointment was quite understandable. Immediately upon my return, I delivered a report to the people by radio in which I presented as complete a picture as possible without stimulating a wave of disillusionment that would adversely affect our future relations with the Soviets. The public response was gratifying. I decided then that hereafter the people would have to be more fully informed if we were to maintain a firm position in international affairs with full public support.

I resolved, too, that the deadlock had to be broken; peace was too important to be lost by default.

The chief cause of our difficulties appeared to be our failure to agree on the recognition of Rumania and Bulgaria; so that problem was tackled. I wanted to make certain that our views on conditions in these countries were not based on erroneous or prejudiced information and therefore arranged for Mark Ethridge, editor of the Louisville *Courier-Journal*, an outstanding liberal, to visit the Balkans. I instructed State Department officials not to give him the information sent in by our representatives in these two countries, as I wanted him to approach his investigation with an open mind.

Simultaneously, we sought to demonstrate to the Soviets that, where efforts were made to comply with the spirit of the Yalta agreement, we would not withhold diplomatic recognition. Therefore, on October 20, we joined with the other three powers in recognizing the Provisional Government of Austria. And on November 2 we recognized the Provisional Government of Hungary.

In accordance with our Potsdam agreement, we initiated discussions on a revision of the Montreux Convention. On November 7, we sent a proposal on the control of the Dardanelles to the signatories, which stated our willingness to join in a multilateral guarantee of free access to the Straits and our opposition to a settlement confined to the Black Sea powers.

In addition, I accepted an invitation to speak before the New York *Herald Tribune* Forum on October 31, in which my message was directed largely toward the Kremlin. I emphasized our recognition of the importance to the Soviet Union of having friendly states as neighbors. I declared "America will never join any groups in those countries in hostile intrigues against the Soviet Union," but went on to say: "The policy of the good neighbor, unlike the institution of marriage, is not an exclusive arrangement. The best neighbors do not deny their neighbors the right to be friends with others."

The speech stressed the importance of the United Nations in promoting security, and then asserted: "We cannot have the kind of co-operation necessary for peace in a world divided into spheres of exclusive influence and special privilege." And I closed the speech with words I hoped the Kremlin would ponder: "There must be one world for all of us or there will be no world for any of us."

Meanwhile, I had asked Ambassador Harriman to request an interview with Generalissimo Stalin who was then on vacation in the Gagri. I wanted him to present to Stalin directly an amended proposal for a peace conference, setting forth the list of states to be invited, and to discuss the situation in Rumania and Bulgaria in the light of the steps we had taken to show our desire for co-operation.

The result was a revelation. When the Ambassador started to present our views on these European questions, Stalin interrupted to say that what he wanted to hear about was our view on the control of Japan. Mr. Harriman was as surprised as he was unprepared, and my surprise was even greater.

At London when Mr. Molotov had raised the question of Japan at the same time that he was killing days discussing procedural questions, we had concluded it was simply part of his war of nerves. Ambassador Harriman, who was present at London, agreed with me that the Balkan issue was the crucial one. Now, we suddenly realized we had been wrong. The remarkable performance that had led to the breakdown of the London Conference had been stimulated by the Russians' belief that they were not being consulted adequately by our officials in Japan. There was confirmation of the Russian attitude in the fact that the Soviet military representative in Tokyo, General Kuzma N. Derevyanko, had returned to Moscow.

Shortly after we had received this surprising information from Ambassador Harriman, Prime Minister Attlee and Prime Minister King came to Washington to confer with the President on procedure for controlling atomic energy. The agreement that emerged from this meeting injected still another important element into the already complex problem of international relations.

A few days later it was Thanksgiving Day and I was alone in my office, taking advantage of the holiday quiet to think over several problems. Suddenly I recalled that at Yalta it had been agreed that the three Foreign Ministers should meet every three months. So many things had taken place thereafter that there had been no need to schedule a specific meeting. A meeting of the three Foreign Ministers might get the peace-making machinery in motion again. I thought it was worth a try, so next morning a cable was sent to Mr. Molotov referring to the Yalta agreement that the three Secretaries should meet regularly and pointing out that they had met informally at San Francisco, Potsdam, and London, but not in Moscow. I suggested, therefore, that a meeting be held in the Russian capital. I felt sure that, Russian hospitality being what it is, the Soviet Government would extend the invitation and I believed that if we met in Moscow, where I would have a chance to talk to Stalin, we might remove the barriers to the peace treaties.

Of course, a proposal for a meeting under such circumstances was in violation of accepted diplomatic procedure. Many of the diplomats and columnists reminded me of that procedure and declared that no such conference should be held without first having diplomatic exchanges to assure agreement on the questions at issue. But in view of what had taken place, I knew there was no chance of reaching agreement by correspondence or through Ambassadors. The peace of the world was too important for us to be unwilling to take a chance on securing an agreement after full discussion. Furthermore, the first General Assembly of the United Nations would meet in January, and this would be our only chance personally to urge Stalin and Molotov to join with us in sponsoring our proposed resolution on atomic energy control.

So, against the advice of the diplomats and the columnists, I went to Moscow.

Chapter 6

Moscow Ends an Impasse

EVEN the journey to Moscow was tense. We were told that we could not fly over the Soviet Union without Russian navigators, and they met us on a snow-covered runway at Berlin on December 14. There was no usable airport between Berlin and Moscow, so our plane had to carry enough gas to make a return trip if an emergency developed. When we were supposed to be about sixty miles from Moscow, the navigators told Mr. Bohlen that they had lost their way. They were trying to identify farm homes projecting from the snow-covered earth. It would have been difficult under any circumstances, but it was virtually impossible in the heavy snow storm. They had us flying so low that I was afraid we would collide with the first sizable hill that came along.

"There are no mountains here," Bohlen told me.

"I could accept your assurance," I told him, "if only you could tell me where 'here' is."

The navigators and pilot asked for permission to "shop around" for ten additional minutes. The pilot said there was just enough gas to permit that and still have a margin for the return to Berlin. I agreed, but told them that Napoleon and Hitler had tried to reach Moscow and had failed and that I, too, would have no objection to an immediate retreat.

When the ten minutes were almost gone, the navigators sighted a familiar building. They knew then where we were, and in a few more minutes we were back on the route to Moscow. Even then we landed at the wrong airport, but no airport has ever looked so good to me.

Russian hospitality, however, was equal to the challenge of the weather. The officials of the Foreign Office had foreseen the possibility of our landing at a different airport and had divided the group of official greeters, so, although Mr. Molotov was not on hand, we were received with appropriate ceremonies.

On our drive to Spasso House, the home of the American Ambassador, the snow storm prevented me from seeing much of the city. I was disappointed, because, as one feels about all places that are difficult to get to, I was curious about Moscow. But I consoled myself with the thought that I would get to see it later. As usual, I was an optimist. I doubt if anyone else has spent even a fraction of the time I did in Moscow and has seen so little of the city. Besides Spasso House, where we worked and managed to get a few hours of sleep each night; Spridinovka House, where the council held its sessions; and the Kremlin, where we had our meetings with Stalin, the only other thing I saw in Moscow was the Opera House where the Foreign Ministers were entertained by the Soviet Government.

The meeting opened at 5:00 P.M., December 16, and at my suggestion Mr. Molotov was made chairman. In recognition of Generalissimo Stalin's concern over the situation in the Far East, I had suggested including on the agenda proposals for the creation of a Far Eastern Commission to function in Washington and of an Allied Council to be located in Tokyo; a paper on the creation of a unified administration for Korea as a prelude to the establishment of an independent Korean government; and a review of American policy in China, including the disarming of Japanese troops in North China. We agreed also that there would be informal discussions on the Soviet occupation of Manchuria, the withdrawal of British troops from Indonesia and from Greece, and the withdrawal of Soviet troops from Iran. The remainder of the agenda included in accordance with my original suggestions, proposals for a United Nations Commission to consider the control of atomic energy, the reconvening of the Council of Foreign Ministers and the resumption of the work of their deputies, and, conditions permitting, the recognition of the present governments of Rumania and Bulgaria. At Mr. Molotov's request, the first item on our list, atomic energy, was placed at the end of the agenda. It was just his way of informing me that he regarded the subject as one of little importance.

Our proposal on peace conference procedure was based on our last position at London in which we had acceded to the Russian stand on the preparation of first drafts but had insisted that these drafts be submitted to a peace conference. The only change was in the final paragraph. It now provided that, after the peace conference had considered the draft treaties and made recommendations, the final drafts would be prepared by the states that had signed the armistice terms; in other words, Britain, the Soviet Union, the United States and France for the Italian treaty, with France dropping out for the Rumanian, Bulgarian, and Hungarian treaties, and both France and the United States dropping out for the Finnish treaty.

This final paragraph was in accordance with a proposal Stalin had advanced in his vacation meeting with Ambassador Harriman. We had accepted it reluctantly but we knew it was the only way we could get the Soviets to agree to call a peace conference.

The following day Mr. Molotov presented his counterproposal which failed to advance the situation beyond the London stand of the Soviet delegation. It provided that at the peace conference each treaty could be considered only by those countries which actually had waged war against that particular enemy. As a practical matter, this meant that there really would be a separate conference for each treaty. For the Bulgarian and Hungarian treaties only five countries would be qualified, under Mr. Molotov's definition, even to take part in peace conference discussions. They would be the Big Three, Yugoslavia and Greece for the Bulgarian treaty, with Czechoslovakia replacing Greece for the Hungarian treaty. Discussions on the Rumanian treaty would be limited to the Big Three, and only the Soviet Union and Britain would consider the Finnish treaty. In the case of Italy, the participants would be the Big Three, France, Greece, Canada, Yugoslavia, Australia, New Zealand, South Africa, Brazil and Ethiopia—a maximum of twelve states.

This was clearly so unacceptable that I simply proposed that we pass to the next item on the agenda, and waited until the next day when a private conversation was arranged between Mr. Molotov, Mr. Vyshinski, Ambassador Harriman and myself. Then I frankly expressed my disappointment at the Soviet proposal, especially since our paper had been prepared with regard for the views expressed by Generalissimo Stalin in his conversation with Mr. Harriman. Mr. Molotov protested that his proposal corresponded exactly with the Generalissimo's statements. Mr. Harriman then outlined his understanding of the conversation, pointing out that on the first day of his talks with Stalin, the Generalissimo had presented views in accord with the current Soviet proposal. On the second day, however, Stalin had agreed that there should be one conference, at which states included on a list we had presented would have an opportunity to present their views—provided the appropriate members of the Council of Foreign Ministers retained the right to "determine the final peace terms."

Mr. Molotov was willing to concede the right of the United States to express its opinions in connection with the Finnish treaty, but no further progress was made.

When we met on December 18, I immediately presented a list of states eligible for invitation to a peace conference under the terms of our proposal. This list included "all members of the United Nations which actively waged war with substantial military forces against the European members of the Axis." There were twenty-one.

"The war was one war," I stressed. "As partners in a common venture each of the Allies served where it could serve best. China performed a great service by holding the Japanese and giving the United States an opportunity to furnish more aid to those engaged in Europe. Norwegian shipping helped to supply our air force in its bombing operations. These states should have the opportunity to come to a peace conference and present their views. This would do no harm and would give the world confidence in the fairness of the Big Three."

Mr. Bevin supported me, declaring it would be unjust if Norway, for example, which had lost one-third of its seamen in the war, should be excluded from taking part in the peace. A long meeting brought no results, so we decided to try one of our "informal" meetings at which attendance is restricted. Mr. Molotov referred to my list and said India would have to be dropped—"it is not an independent state; it has no Foreign Office of its own," and, if India were to come, the three Baltic Soviet republics—Latvia, Lithuania and Estonia—would have to be invited. Mr. Bevin, of course, could not agree to exclude India, which had sent large contingents of troops to the European theater.

That night, Ambassador Harriman, Mr. Bohlen and I went to the Kremlin for the first of our meetings with Generalissimo Stalin. I wanted to present my views to Stalin before Molotov took positions from which he would find it difficult to withdraw. I wanted to see the man who had the power to decide.

The Kremlin, of course, has a reputation as a place of mystery and, being an appreciative reader of good mysteries, I looked forward to my first journey into its inner chambers. Before we reached Stalin's office we were ushered through three successive chambers, each with several identical doors. I had just begun to ponder on how carefully Stalin was guarded when it suddenly occurred to me that any foreigner might get a similar impression on a visit to the White House. When one goes to see President Truman, there is a large outer hallway to pass through. Then one is escorted into the waiting room presided over by Bill Simmons, the tactful White House doorkeeper. After that, one goes through the office of the President's secretary, Matthew J. Connelly, and finally reaches the President's oval office. The principal apparent difference was that in the Kremlin everyone was in uniform.

Stalin's greeting was businesslike, but cordial. After presenting a personal letter from the President, I assured him of our belief that there were no conflicts between us we could not solve.

"Our only desire," I said, "is to live in peace, increase the comfort of the American people, and help our friends abroad restore the damages of war through economic assistance."

Stalin replied that he fully shared this desire, and we agreed that in view of our different customs and traditions it was understandable that we should sometimes interpret the same question differently. He volunteered the belief that so far we had succeeded quite well in settling our differences.

I then sketched the discussions with Mr. Molotov on our proposed list of states, which I noticed he had before him. I pointed out that if India and the three Baltic states were admitted to the peace conference "this would mean that Britain would be there with five dominions and the Soviet Union would be there with five republics.

"It would be difficult for me to explain such a decision in the United States," I told him. "I would have to add to the list five states, including my own state of South Carolina!"

Molotov interjected that even if India were dropped, Britain would still have four dominions represented.

"The Soviet Union and the United States are strong enough to stand alone, and I am sure Mr. Molotov can adequately protect the interests of the three Soviet republics at the conference," I replied. "We have made important concessions in this matter of the peace treaties, and it is not too much to ask that our list for the conference be approved."

Stalin said he could see no concession on our part since the list was identical with the one Mr. Harriman had shown him in October. I explained that the concessions related to the preparation and final approval of the treaties rather than to the list. He contended that the Armistice in each case had been signed by those who had shed blood in the war against that country, and that they should be the ones to sign the peace. Belgium and Holland, for example, had not fought against Rumania and Italy. He then recounted the contributions of the Baltic republics and offered to accept our list with the addition of these states. He was sure, he said, that we would soon have to recognize these republics, but he realized it would be embarrassing for the United States if the United Kingdom and the Soviet Union had six votes while the United States had but one. This situation, he said, must be met. One way was to give the United States six votes. He recalled that he had agreed with President Roosevelt at Yalta that the United States could have two additional votes in the General Assembly of the United Nations if we wished.

I concluded he would not want to reverse Molotov's decision that night but might do so later, so I urged him to give the matter further thought in the hope that we could find a solution. He agreed to do so.

The next afternoon, Mr. Molotov excused himself from the conference table. When he returned, he came to me and said that the Generalissimo had just telephoned to inform me that he would accept our list of states.

The conference then quickly agreed that a peace conference should be held in Paris not later than May 1. But this agreement was followed by a long wrangle over who should sign the peace treaties when they were concluded, and whether China and France should be invited to concur in this Moscow agreement or should merely be informed of it. We finally compromised by both informing *and* inviting concurrence!

The day before Christmas, we received China's favorable reply. There was no word from the French. I was anxious that, as a Christmas gift, the world should know that a peace conference would be held. Unsuccessfully I tried to reach Mr. Bidault by telephone. I learned he was very busy—getting married to his charming wife. Finally, I suggested we simply announce our own agreement and state that France and China had been invited to concur. I had suggested Paris as the site of the conference but we deleted mention of it pending a French reply.

And so, on Christmas morning, 1945, people throughout the world learned that five months of negotiation had at last brought agreement on the holding of a conference to help restore "peace on earth."

The solution we reached was not ideal, but it did assure the small states an opportunity to be heard. While the larger states were not to be bound by the recommendations of the peace conference we were in a position, by exercising the unanimity rule, to refuse a final treaty which arbitrarily rejected the recommendations of the peace conference. Experience proved the value of the peace conference, and the record shows that practically all of its recommendations adopted by a two-thirds vote were written into the treaties.

With this agreement reached, we turned again to the question of Rumania and Bulgaria. On the third day of the conference I had called on Mr. Molotov and presented to him a copy of the report Mark Ethridge had submitted on Rumania and Bulgaria. We had intended to publish it, I told him, but instead we had held it for discussion, in the hope that Mr. Ethridge's findings furnished a basis for an understanding.

Even before looking at it, Mr. Molotov deprecated the report, saying that Ethridge, of course, knew I was opposed to recognizing these governments and therefore must have been influenced in his judgment.

I pointed out to him the instructions I had given Mr. Ethridge, which were repeated at the opening of the report, and which made it clear he was a completely free observer. After an independent, unprejudiced investigation Mr. Ethridge found not only that these governments failed to meet the Yalta Declaration, I told him, but that they were authoritarian, dominated by one party, and forcibly excluded from representation large democratic segments of the population. I asked him particularly to note that in Rumania Mr. Ethridge had found former pro-Fascist collaborators and even pro-Nazi Iron Guardists occupying key government posts.

Mr. Molotov had made quite a point of the fact that elections had been held in Bulgaria, and I asked him to note Mr. Ethridge's comment that these elections signified nothing and that Ethridge had, in fact, been told a month in advance how they would come out. As for Rumania, Mr. Ethridge merely confirmed what both of us knew about Mr. Vyshinski's activities and the repressions which had followed the installation of the Groza government.

I asked him to give special consideration to Mr. Ethridge's recommendations that the Soviet Union join with us in an agreement similar to those reached on other former enemy countries in eastern Europe.

After giving Molotov two days to consider the Ethridge report, I submitted papers to the Foreign Ministers suggesting action to be taken toward each of these countries. These papers proposed, with variations necessitated by differing conditions, that the three powers join in suggesting a reorganization of the present governments to include all leading democratic elements. Mr. Molotov strongly objected. He contended that nothing could be done in Bulgaria as elections had taken place which the Soviet government considered free and unfettered. Any interference after these elections, he maintained, would be greatly resented by the Bulgarian people. He dismissed the opposition to the government with the observation that opposition parties always are dissatisfied. As for Rumania, he contended that King Michael's request for three-power assistance in establishing a government would never have been made except at the instigation of the American and British representatives there. This, I assured him, was untrue, but he chose not to believe me. The Ethridge report he also dismissed, saying it merely reiterated my views and could have been written without the trip ever having been made.

Once again it appeared that the only hope was to take up the matter directly with the Generalissimo, and I went to see him the following night. The engagement was set for 10 P.M. This is just about the time I usually go to bed, but is about the time the Generalissimo starts to work.

We first discussed the question of withdrawing all foreign troops from Iran, and then I expressed a desire to talk about the Balkans "as I have been having a difficult time with Mr. Molotov on this subject."

Stalin smiled broadly and said that this was unexpected news.

"It is terribly important to settle this matter and to proceed with the peace treaties so that we can be in a position to render them economic assistance," I asserted. Then I quickly outlined the situation. I concluded by saying that if we could reach no agreement I would be compelled to publish the Ethridge report.

Stalin replied that if I felt it necessary to publish the Ethridge report he would ask Mr. Ehrenberg, who also was an impartial man and had visited these countries, to publish his views.

This would be most unfortunate, I told him, as the two reports would tend to separate rather than unite our two countries on this question. I expressed my confidence that with his help and understanding we could find representatives of the democratic parties who were also friendly toward the Soviet Union.

Given a mutual desire to settle the problem, means could be found to do so, he said, and then referred to accusations in our press that the Red army had exerted pressure on the Bulgarian elections. This, he declared, was untrue and he pointed to Hungary, where, despite the presence of Soviet troops, the election had not resulted in a Communist victory. The alleged action, he stressed, was unworthy of the Soviet Union which asked only that near-by states should not be hostile. This did not mean that only Communist parties could be regarded as friendly, he said, but he asked me to remember that during the war Hungarian troops had reached the Don River and Rumanian troops had reached the Volga.

Since elections had been held in Bulgaria it was impossible to ask for a reorganization there, but he finally agreed it would be possible to advise them to include in the government two truly representative members of two important political parties not then represented. He stressed that there could be no pressure—merely advice. He assented to my suggestion that the advice should come from the Soviet Union. I made it clear that we would reserve the right to decide whether necessary conditions had been created to warrant recognition. In the case of Rumania, he conceded it would be less difficult to make changes. After considerable discussion it was agreed to send a commission, composed of the American and British Ambassadors in Moscow and Mr. Vyshinski, to Bucharest to work out with the government the addition of representatives of other parties, and to insure the restoration and maintenance of civil liberties. Stalin asked me to convey his acceptance of this proposal, which I originally had made in London, to Mr. Bevin. I agreed to inform the British Foreign Minister and added jokingly that even though we were supposed to have a bloc with Britain I had not informed Bevin about my proposal to Mr. Molotov for this meeting in Moscow as soon as I should have.

The Generalissimo smiled and, in the same spirit, replied that this obviously was only a cloak to hide the reality of the bloc.

The next day I presented to the meeting the proposals regarding Rumania and Bulgaria which we believed Stalin had agreed to. However, we immediately entered into an all-day argument with Messrs. Molotov and Vyshinski over the wording of them. The argument was still under way when we adjourned for the Christmas Eve dinner given us by the Generalissimo.

At dinner I was seated on Stalin's right and Bevin was on his left. I told him that our newspapers had represented him as being ill and that I was happy to see him looking so well. He said his recent vacation had been his first one in many years and that he realized, after the strain of the war, that he was not so young as he once was. He had attended to many important matters while away, he continued, but he had rested also and now felt better than he had in years. He was determined, he said, to take a vacation every year.

In all sincerity I proposed a toast to him, expressing the hope that he would continue to take vacations for many years to come and continue to enjoy good health. I added: "whom war hath joined together, let not peace put asunder." I thought it was good, but from the Russian's lack of appreciation, I concluded they were all bachelors or, in any event, were not familiar with our marriage ceremony. I felt sure they did not dissent from the sentiment.

My talks with the Generalissimo that night, like those during the two earlier interviews, were marked by their encouraging combination of frankness and cordiality. One of the issues on which I placed particular emphasis was the situation in Iran.

At our first meeting on December 19, I told him we were concerned about the events in Iran because of the pledge President Roosevelt had entered into with him and Prime Minister Churchill at Teheran in 1943. In that pledge, the three leaders recognized "the assistance which Iran has given in the prosecution of the war against the common enemy, particularly by facilitating transportation of supplies from overseas to the Soviet Union." The declaration promised that "any economic problem confronting Iran at the close of hostilities should receive full consideration" along with those of other members of the United Nations. It expressly declared that they were "at one with the Government of Iran in their desire for the maintenance of the independence, sovereignty and territorial integrity of Iran."

Developments within Iran prior to the Moscow meeting indicated that the pledge was in danger of being broken. The Iranian Government had protested that when it dispatched 1,500 troops toward the province of Azerbaijan to quell what the Iranians said was an insurrection encouraged by foreign sources, the force had been stopped en route and ordered by the Red army to turn back. The Iranian Government thereupon asked for the withdrawal of all foreign troops. We promptly issued an order to the remaining American troops to evacuate and I sent a message to the Soviet Union and the United Kingdom urging that they take similar action.

The Iranian protest was still pending and I told the Generalissimo that, unless we fulfilled the Teheran Declaration, Iran very likely would place its complaint before the forthcoming meeting of the United Nations in London. As a signatory of the declaration, the United States would feel obliged to support Iran's right to be heard. We felt it would be difficult to explain how the Soviet Army of 30,000 would have been endangered, as they had asserted, by the presence of 1,500 Iranian soldiers.

Stalin outlined what he termed "the pertinent facts" in the matter. The Baku oil fields in the south of Russia lay close to the border and this created a special problem. These fields had to be safeguarded against any possible hostile action by Iran against the Soviet Union, and no confidence could be placed in the Iranian Government. Saboteurs might be sent to the Baku oil fields to set them on fire, he continued. Since the Soviet Union had a right, by treaty, to maintain troops in Iran until March 15, it did not want to withdraw before that date. At that time, he said, it would be necessary to examine the situation and see whether or not it was possible to evacuate the soldiers. The decision would depend upon the conduct of the Iranian Government. He pointed out that a 1921 treaty with Iran gave the Soviet Union the right to send troops into northern Iran if there was a possible danger from an outside source.

I told him I was greatly surprised to learn that he considered the Iranian Government hostile in view of his declaration at Teheran, and in view of the report made to me by General Connolly, the commanding general of our forces in Iran, that the Government had co-operated well with both the Red Army and the American forces in moving supplies through to the Soviet Union. While he had a right to maintain his troops in Iran until March, I pointed out that he was not required to do so. The United States, incidentally, had always regarded March 2 as the deadline date rather than March 15, as cited by Stalin.

Stalin told me that the Soviet Union had no designs, territorial or otherwise, against Iran and would withdraw its troops as soon as they felt secure about the Baku oil fields.

The more I thought about Generalissimo Stalin's excuse for retaining troops in Iran, the less confidence I had in the Soviet position. It was absurd to claim, as he had, that the Red Army of 30,000 well-trained and fully equipped troops must stop the poorly trained and inadequately equipped Iranian force of 1,500 from marching toward Azerbaijan on the public highway because it feared a disturbance would be created. His statement that he feared saboteurs from little Iran would come over into the Soviet Union and set fire to the Baku oil fields seemed an equally poor excuse for maintaining a large army inside the borders of Iran. And his admission that the question of withdrawal would be examined on the evacuation date showed that our worries about his fulfilling the Teheran Declaration were justified. Consequently, I determined to make another effort to get him to understand our position regarding that obligation.

Iran was the first thing I took up with him at our second meeting. I told him I was "seriously disturbed" at the prospect that the issue would be raised at the first meeting of the United Nations. It was exceedingly important, I added, that the great nations keep their pledges to the smaller powers. If Iran raised the issue at London it would be unfortunate, I warned him, because, under the facts as we knew them and in view of our solemn pledge, we would be forced to support the position of Iran. The United States would greatly regret having to oppose the Soviet Union in the very first meeting of the United Nations and I hoped, therefore, that we could take action at Moscow that would forestall this possibility.

We discussed Mr. Bevin's proposal that a Three-Power Commission be appointed to go to Iran and seek a solution to the numerous aspects of the problem. He was noncommittal regarding the Bevin proposal, and I said once again that we hoped no action would be taken in Iran that would cause a difference between us. To this, the Generalissimo replied: "We will do nothing that will make you blush."

On Christmas Day, the council resumed the argument on the Balkan and Iranian problems. We finally reached substantial agreement on Rumania but were at a complete impasse on Bulgaria. Molotov and Vyshinski argued for a draft stating that the Cabinet could include only people loyal to the existing government. Mr. Bevin and I pointed out that this wording could exclude all prodemocratic elements except those that had sworn allegiance to the government we were seeking to broaden; in practice, it could be used to nullify our agreement. Mr. Bevin pointed out that he had been fighting Mr. Churchill for thirty years and that, under such a ruling, he could not now be in the British Government.

The afternoon of December 25, I had a private conversation with Mr. Molotov. Among other things, he said he thought that "the British proposal on Iran in general is acceptable." He asked for my views. I told him I would accept it because I was particularly anxious to avoid having the Iranian question raised in the General Assembly. When the conference met that night, Molotov offered several amendments to Mr. Bevin's proposal. Bevin accepted all except one which left in doubt the date for the withdrawal of troops. He claimed that that date had been fixed by treaty and that the proposed amendment, therefore, was unnecessary.

In view of our private conversation I thought Molotov would finally agree to Bevin's language. However, when we met the afternoon of December 26, it was clear that the Soviet High Command had changed its attitude. Molotov announced that the Iranian case was not properly on the agenda and "cannot be considered." Bevin complained that he had accepted practically every amendment the Soviets had proposed. He said he had understood, as a result of a conversation he had had with Stalin, that the Soviet Union would agree to his proposal.

"It is sufficient that views have been exchanged," Molotov replied. "No decisions have been reached. The question was not on the agenda and there is no need to mention it in the communiqué."

"What is my next step?" Bevin asked.

"You know that well," Molotov answered.

Bevin, with some feeling, said he thought he understood the situation and greatly regretted it.

The heated arguments on Bulgaria and Iran were jeopardizing our agreements on other issues, so I suggested that we resume, in London, consideration of the pending problems. Members of the staff were asked to prepare the protocol to be signed by the three Foreign Ministers. This was completed about 2:30 in the morning and in a formal meeting the protocols in two languages were presented for signature. That meant there were nine copies that each of us had to sign. Mr. Bevin signed first and the papers were passed to me. After signing, I arose to say good-by to a member of the British delegation seated near me.

Suddenly Mr. Molotov sent one of his aides to me and asked that I return to the table. He said that his staff had, "by mistake," included the Soviet document on Bulgaria in the Russian text of the protocol. He asked if, after all, it could not be accepted. We promptly said it could not. He then suggested that we might combine the first half of my proposal with the second half of his draft. I told him we could not do things by "halves"; that since he had come halfway, he should accept the American proposal. To my amazement, he did.

Mr. Bevin then facetiously asked him to look in his pocket to see if he could not find another "mistake" that would satisfactorily end our discussions on Iran. In good humor, Mr. Molotov said he regretted that he could not. The protocol was then amended for signature.

It was 3:30 A.M. December 27. I was dead tired; all of us were. Mr. Molotov and Mr. Vyshinski probably were less exhausted than the rest of us because they customarily begin their working day at noon and often extend it past midnight. They were more accustomed to a steady succession of late hours than an American who long ago had learned that his constituents expected him to be at his office at nine in the morning. Our airplane was scheduled to take off at 7:30. I packed, had a short nap, talked to the American newspaper and radio correspondents, and got to the airport on time. It seemed terribly early, but Messrs. Molotov and Vyshinski were there to see us off.

The man who, three nights later, sat before a radio microphone in Washington to report to the American people was far happier than the one who had sat before the same microphone upon his return from London only fifteen weeks earlier. The proposal for a peace conference, rejected at London, had been accepted at Moscow, with the participating states selected in accordance with the American list. After ten months' experience in trying to secure Soviet compliance with the Yalta agreement on the Balkans, we fully appreciated the difference between promise and performance. But Ambassador Harriman, Chip Bohlen and others, who had been living with this problem, felt we had made progress in securing a much more specific agreement than that made at Yalta.

On the question of Japanese policy, which had been an important factor in Soviet obstinacy at London, we had won full approval of the plans President Truman and I had prepared prior to my departure for Moscow. We had secured agreement on the presence of our troops in China and had stimulated a restatement by Stalin of his support of the National Government of China. Coming at a time when General Marshall was beginning his effort to bring about a unified and democratic China, this seemed an important gain.

And on the subject of atomic energy, which I had expected to make difficulties, the Soviet Union had agreed to join in sponsoring, with no material change, the resolution previously approved by the United Kingdom and Canada for the creation of a United Nations Atomic Energy Commission.

The only important question on the conference agenda not resolved was the proposed appointment of a commission to try to solve our common problems in Iran. I was therefore surprised and disappointed to find a portion of the press criticizing our agreements as "appeasement." Some of the criticism I recognized as personal in character. Some of it came from people who obviously had been misled in their thinking—largely as a result of Soviet censorship of the news from Moscow on the conference. But much of the criticism, unfortunately, came from people so unreasonably anti-Soviet in their views that they would regard any agreement with Russia on any subject as appeasement.

No one who had shared my experience at Potsdam, London and Moscow doubted that there were still many trying days ahead. But we did face the new year of 1946 with greater hope as a result of the Moscow Conference. Perhaps the rest of the world did too. I hoped so.

Chapter 7

London Again and Paris Twice

FIVE days after returning from Moscow I had to fly back to London for the first session of the General Assembly of the United Nations. My primary concern was the adoption of the resolution to establish a United Nations Commission on the control of atomic energy, and I announced before leaving Washington that I would return as soon as the Assembly acted on this issue.

But life in London was not to be so simple. The problems of Moscow followed us there. Ambassador Harriman came to London to report that the committee composed of Mr. Vyshinski, Sir Archibald Clark Kerr and himself had made no progress in Bucharest toward a reorganization of the Groza government. The efforts to broaden the Bulgarian Government were equally unproductive. And the problem of Iran was becoming more acute.

Iran's representative in London called on me and asked whether he should file his country's complaint against the continued presence of Soviet troops in Iran and interference in Iranian affairs with the Security Council. He said Mr. Bevin had declined to advise him and he therefore hoped that I would. I told him that I, too, hesitated to offer advice, that the Security Council was just being organized, that it had not even adopted rules of procedure, that only the most urgent matters should be placed before the Security Council while it was being organized. However, I told him I would gladly listen to the facts of his case, give the matter consideration, and advise him the following day. Without waiting, he filed his complaint. The Soviet delegation conceived the idea that Mr. Bevin had inspired the Iranian representative to do this. From the latter's statements to me, I am sure the Russians were mistaken. Nevertheless, because of their suspicion, the Soviet delegation two days later filed a complaint against the presence of British troops in Greece; the Ukrainian delegation filed a similar charge against the British troops in Indonesia. The debates that ensued were acrimonious and created a situation conducive to anything but agreement.

This was the atmosphere that prevailed when the deputies of the Foreign Ministers gathered at Lancaster House, a few blocks away from the United Nations meetings, on January 18, 1946, to begin the actual drafting of the peace treaties.

With the unanimous adoption by the General Assembly of the atomic energy resolution on January 24, I left for home. But already there were indications the deputies would encounter the same barriers that had blocked the Ministers' agreement at the September meeting. At our suggestion, the Italian treaty was taken up first, not only because the Potsdam agreement had named Italy as first, but also because the question of France's right to take part in discussions on the others remained unsettled.

March arrived and the deputies were still as far apart as ever on the three main issues: reparations, the colonies, and the Italian-Yugoslav border. On the latter issue, there had been at least some action. A commission of experts was appointed to visit the area with instructions to determine a frontier that would (a) leave a minimum number of Italians and Yugoslavs under alien rule and (b) take into account local geographic and economic factors. Our able deputy, James C. Dunn, appointed Philip E. Mosely to represent us on this commission; the commission arrived in Trieste on March 9.

The deputies then turned to a study of draft treaties for the three Balkan states, submitted by the Soviet delegation. At this point, the French deputy tactfully withdrew. The Soviet drafts were very brief documents; in fact, little more than an extension of the armistice terms. Nevertheless, some progress was made toward securing agreement to the amendments offered by the British and the United States.

At Moscow we had agreed there would be a peace conference "after the completion of the drafts" and "before May 1." As the weeks went by, the deputies reached agreement on so few clauses it was clear that drastic action would have to be taken if we were to keep our promises to the world. I sent a message to the other members proposing that the council meet in an effort to speed up the work of the deputies and suggested that this meeting be held in Paris. We had agreed that Paris should be the site of the peace conference and I was eager to have the council meet there also. I was reasonably sure that in Paris, where the Communists were very active in French politics, Mr. Molotov would be much less obdurate in opposing French participation in discussions on all treaties. The earliest date we could agree on was April 25.

At the first session, Mr. Bidault proposed rules of procedure that provided for the participation of all four delegations in the discussions of all five treaties. Although he had opposed such an arrangement for months as a matter of vital principle, Mr. Molotov quickly agreed. This, however, marked about the limit of his concessions.

The agenda was the subject of our first disagreement. Mr. Bidault was eager to discuss questions involving Germany and I had submitted the United States' draft treaty for the disarmament and demilitarization of Germany for a period of twenty-five years. In addition, we proposed that special deputies begin work on a peace treaty for Austria. Mr. Molotov was willing to discuss Germany, but he dismissed our treaty proposal as wholly inadequate and flatly refused even to put the question of Austria on the agenda.

I saw that if we were going to make any progress Mr. Molotov and I must try to get together. So I invited him, Mr. Vyshinski and Mr. Pavlov, the interpreter, to dine with Mr. Cohen, Mr. Bohlen and me.

Although our dinner was to be a quiet private affair, the constant effort made to protect Mr. Molotov, as well as Generalissimo Stalin, was not relaxed. The afternoon of the dinner, Soviet security officers came to the United States delegation office in the Hotel Meurice and asked to be shown the suite where we were to dine. My secretary, Miss Cassie Connor, gladly showed them through the apartment which Mrs. Byrnes and I occupied. As no criticisms were made, we assumed they were entirely satisfied with the arrangements.

That evening when the guests arrived, the security officer who accompanies Mr. Molotov wherever he goes was with them. Even though we had an American MP at each end of the hall, Mr. Molotov's guard took his station in the hall where he had a view of all doors to the five-room suite, which included my offices.

Mrs. Byrnes and Miss Connor left the apartment to go down to the hotel dining room for dinner. The guard evidently paid little attention to those leaving the apartment because, when they returned and Mrs. Byrnes tried to enter the bedroom, he raised his hands and shook his head. His gestures, in any language, meant that she could not enter. In words which would have been understood in South Carolina or Washington she insisted that this was her room, and that she had left it only a short while before. But the gentleman was firm—she could not enter. The ladies finally retreated to the office to plan a campaign to capture the bedroom. They enlisted the help of the Army by calling upon one of the MPs stationed in the hall. He spoke no more Russian than they did, but the uniform apparently convinced the Soviet guard that the ladies could be trusted in the apartment. His orders no doubt had been that no one could enter the suite. With the help of the MP, another crisis in Russo-American relations was avoided.

Probably Mr. Molotov is neither aware of nor responsible for the somewhat unusual methods of the guards assigned to him. These security officers are perhaps directed by an organization similar to our Secret Service. I suspect Mr. Molotov sometimes shared my own desire to escape the constant surveillance to which all of us were subjected—by our host government if not by our own.

In London, Scotland Yard assigned Captain Black, a most efficient officer, to watch me and he never let me get out of the hotel without him. In Paris, an English-speaking plain-clothes officer, René Houvenaghel, was always on the job. I got away from him only once—and that was after a particularly depressing meeting during the peace conference. Mrs. Byrnes, who shared my depression, suggested that we take a walk. I was not only depressed, I was tired of being watched. And, over Mrs. Byrnes' objections, we slipped out a side door of our hotel to escape detection. I thought we had escaped our security officer and that idea alone tended to raise my spirits. After we had walked half an hour I happened to look back—there was Houvenaghel. An employee of the hotel had reported our leaving and he had followed us. With both "the law" and my wife against me, I did the only thing a man could do under the circumstances: I confessed my guilt and promised not to offend again.

Many times when the security officer was with me I felt in much greater danger than I was that night. Every day we were driven to the meetings; our car traveled behind two motorcycle policemen, who raced through Paris traffic at fifty miles an hour, each of them blowing a tiny whistle. Paris streets are crowded with bicyclists and every one of them dislikes traffic policemen and has utter contempt for a whistle. I tried to get the escorts to go slower. But they persisted in dashing madly through red lights. To protect ourselves we had to keep up with them, even though our tenseness increased with every jump in the speedometer.

I have digressed from the dinner with Mr. Molotov, but it was just about as relaxed as one of those rides through Parisian traffic. Before we reached the dining room, Mr. Molotov began to complain bitterly about the attitude of the United States in the Iranian case, which had been argued in the Security Council at New York since our last meeting. He charged that our actions were not those of a friend and that his government was the victim of an "anti-Soviet campaign" in which the Iranian case and the Security Council were being used to advance an offensive. I first reminded him of the efforts made at Moscow, both with him and with Generalissimo Stalin, to deal with the Iranian situation. These talks had had the specific intent of preventing the Iranian case from being brought before the United Nations. At that time I had clearly stated it would be necessary for us to oppose the Soviet Government if the case did become a Security Council issue. Mr. Cohen and I outlined in detail the actual course of events in the Security Council, and stressed that, once Soviet troops had remained in Iran beyond the treaty date, it was no longer possible to arrange matters privately; the issue then had to be met in the light of public opinion.

Because the dinner opened on this note of discord, it is not surprising that our later discussions of the treaties, and the United States' proposals about Germany and Austria, met with little success. The next morning I went over the situation with Vandenberg and Connally—we agreed there was little prospect for early agreement on the issues before the council.

The council, however, quickly agreed on the limitation of the Italian Navy, the disposition of surplus naval units, three minor rectifications of the French-Italian border, and on a committee to study a fourth French-proposed change in the Tenda-Briga area. Then we came to the question of the colonies. Mr. Molotov advanced a new proposal: two-power trusteeships with the Soviet Union and Italy together administering Tripolitania. This ran into strong British opposition and Mr. Bevin made a counterproposal that all of Libya, including Tripolitania and Cyrenaica, should be given immediate independence. The French joined the Russians in opposing this suggestion. Finally, Mr. Molotov said he would accept the French proposal for Italian trusteeship. We continued our stand for a collective trusteeship but later said we would accept the French proposal if the others were in agreement and if there were a definite promise to give the colonies their independence in ten years. The French could not agree to this, and the British would not approve the French proposal. So I announced that we would stand by our collective trusteeship plan.

The discussions on the transfer of the Dodecanese to Greece continued to produce no results as Mr. Molotov insisted settlement of this question had to await the disposition of the colonies.

Our longest and most difficult hours were spent on the question of the Italian-Yugoslav border. The four-man commission that had gone to the province of Venezia Giulia spent four weeks there, and then had submitted four individual recommendations. The Soviet representative's recommendations corresponded closely to the claims of the Yugoslavs. The boundary lines proposed by the American, British and French representatives were identical in the north but they separated going southward. The French line, which represented roughly a compromise between our line and the Soviet line, did not take certain geographic and economic considerations into account, but it did appear to balance the two minority groups most equitably. The available population statistics were quite unreliable but our best estimates showed the French line leaving 130,000 Italians in Yugoslavia and 115,000 Yugoslavs in Italy. Only the Soviet member of the commission recommended that Trieste, with a population that was 80 per cent Italian, should be taken from Italy.

On May 3, Vice Premier Kardelj of Yugoslavia and Premier de Gasperi of Italy presented the arguments of their governments. They were largely the same ones we had heard in London. Nor was the situation advanced after more than five hours of debate by the Ministers the following day. Mr. Molotov gave full support to the Yugoslav claims. He charged that Italy would use Trieste as a military base, a springboard for the extension of Italian influence into adjacent territory populated by Croats and Slovenes. We must not punish our ally Yugoslavia, he declared, by severing Trieste, which he termed the head, from the body of the province, even though the city was predominantly Italian. I pointed out that a line giving Yugoslavia over 300,000 inhabitants and several thousand square miles of territory it had never had before could hardly be called punishment. I offered to go still further and accept as a compromise the French line which would give the valuable Arsa coal mines to Yugoslavia. I also suggested the holding of a plebiscite in the disputed area. Neither of these proposals was acceptable to Mr. Molotov and, as neither Mr. Bevin, Mr. Bidault nor I were willing to make further concessions, there was nothing to do but turn to consideration of the other treaties.

In a final effort to bargain, Mr. Molotov invited Mr. Cohen, Mr. Bohlen and me to dinner in his suite at the Soviet Embassy. He suggested that, if we would agree to cede to Yugoslavia all Venezia Giulia, including Trieste, it would be possible for him to take a different attitude about the colonies and about reparations. But he indicated that his concession on the latter point would be at the expense of Greek and Yugoslavian claims. The Soviet Union, he stated flatly, could not renounce its claim for 100 million dollars, which it thought an excessively modest sum. When we stated our inability to make such an agreement, he and Mr. Vyshinski launched into a whole series of propaganda charges that the United States was engaged in a policy of "imperialist expansion." They cited the presence of American forces in Iceland and in China, and charged us with seeking bases in Turkey, Egypt and Iran. I was tempted to answer in the same spirit, but instead pointed out how ridiculous it was to describe 720 air-base mechanics and service troops in Iceland as an "imperialist" threat to the Soviet Union, and reminded him that we had discussed the Chinese situation in detail at Moscow and had issued a joint statement on the subject. As for the Middle East, we had no plans or desires for any bases.

"Our basic policy is to obtain the removal of troops from countries other than Germany and Japan at the earliest possible moment," I told him in our discussion after dinner. "For this reason we have urged the conclusion of a treaty with Austria so that our troops there may be withdrawn. But it is the Soviet Government, which has forces there many times larger than those of any other Allied nation, that refuses this suggestion. No one in the world fears the United States or its intentions. I am sorry to say this cannot be said of the Soviet Union."

Mr. Molotov, in support of the charges of Anglo-American imperialism, even went back to 1919 and the American expedition to Siberia during the postwar revolution. The next morning he talked to Mr. Bevin the same way, commenting that while Bevin claimed nineteenth century imperialism was dead it had to be pointed out that twentieth century imperialism was very much alive, as evidenced by British troops and bases in Greece, Egypt, Iraq, Indonesia, and elsewhere. Bevin's denial of these charges did not discourage Molotov from waging a similar propaganda campaign later in the Security Council and General Assembly of the United Nations.

It was on this note that we began work on the other treaties. It was not surprising, therefore, that Mr. Molotov regarded the American proposals to guarantee equality of opportunity in economic affairs and free navigation on the Danube simply as additional efforts at imperialist expansion and capitalist domination.

When I told Senators Connally and Vandenberg about our dinner conversation with Molotov, they shared my pessimism. In this atmosphere there was virtually no hope of securing agreement on any controversial issues. Therefore, on May 8, I proposed we acknowledge the first anniversary of V-E Day by calling the long-promised peace conference. I suggested June 15 as the date in order to give the deputies time to prepare and circulate a report on the agreed clauses and to present the views of the four delegations on the still unsettled clauses.

Both Mr. Bevin and Mr. Bidault indicated their agreement. Mr. Molotov maintained, that, in accord with the Moscow agreement, it would be impossible to hold the peace conference until there was unanimous agreement on all "basic issues." In effect, this gave the Soviet delegation a veto as long as there was disagreement on any issue it considered "basic." But my suggestion apparently had some effect because the deputies' report the next day showed that they had been able, overnight, to reach agreement on nineteen additional points. For the next week we continued our effort to call the peace conference, but throughout the hours at the conference table, at informal meetings and at private talks, Mr. Molotov remained adamant. He was evidently determined to delay the withdrawal of his occupation armies.

In an endeavor to make some progress we proposed the appointment of special deputies to begin work on the German treaty, but that too was rejected. The only accomplishment of the entire week was a revision of the Italian armistice which abolished the Allied Commission and removed most military controls.

On May 16, we wearily agreed to take a recess and meet in Paris again on June 15. "Building the foundations of a people's peace in a war-shattered world is a long, hard process," I confessed to the American public in my radio report on May 20. "A people's peace cannot be won by flashing diplomatic triumphs. It requires patience and firmness, tolerance and understanding. We must not try to impose our will on others, but we must make sure that others do not get the impression they can impose their will on us."

Having failed to make June 15 the date for the peace conference, I had tried July 1 and July 15, with no more success. But, I told the radio audience, "when a world short of goods and short of food is crying for the return of conditions of peace, we cannot indefinitely delay the making of peace and the withdrawal of troops from occupied areas," and I served notice that if a peace conference were not held during the summer the United States would bring the matter to the attention of the United Nations. Although it was never intended that the United Nations organization should become involved in the peace settlement, Article 14 of the Charter does authorize the General Assembly to "recommend measures for the peaceful adjustment of any situation, regardless of origin, which it deems likely to impair the general welfare or friendly relations among nations." We were fast approaching, I felt, such a "situation."

"We must take the offensive for peace as we took the offensive for war," I added, and expressed my faith that "there is no iron curtain that the aggregate sentiments of mankind cannot penetrate."

Mr. Molotov's reaction to this speech was quick and violent. He released a statement to the Soviet press repeating his charges that Anglo-American capital was instigating new aggressive wars and was aiming at world domination. My reference to an offensive for peace, he said, was in reality an "offensive against the Soviet Union in disregard of the interests of peace."

Nevertheless, when the deputies resumed their work during the recess the Soviet representative was at last willing to negotiate in concrete terms on the economic sections of the five treaties. Consequently, there were an appreciable number of additional agreed clauses ready for us when we returned to Paris.

Premier Nagy of Hungary visited Washington during this "recess." While here he publicly announced that he favored international control of the Danube—a surprising demonstration of independence on the part of a satellite state. He wanted to secure the return of Hungarian gold removed by the Germans and captured by our forces. We ordered the commanding officers of our zone to return the gold to Hungary and any other property which was clearly Hungarian-owned.

On June 14, we left again for Paris. This was my eleventh trip across the ocean in less than a year. For the trip, the President had placed his plane, the Sacred Cow, at our disposal. In the party, as usual, were Senator and Mrs. Connally, Senator and Mrs. Vandenberg, Ben Cohen, Chip Bohlen, Mrs. Byrnes, and my secretary, Miss Cassie Connor, who had acquired in this quest for peace treaties a mileage record almost as extensive as mine.

The American delegation returned to ornate Luxemburg Palace for the second Paris session determined to do all in our power to see that invitations for a peace conference were issued. We expected all kinds of delay but felt that when Mr. Molotov realized he could not get any more concessions, he would agree. The meeting opened with the almost customary preliminary skirmishes. The American delegation had circulated a draft treaty for Austria which we asked to have placed on the agenda. Mr. Molotov was unwilling to discuss our draft but did accept Mr. Bidault's suggestion that an "examination of the Austrian question" be included on the agenda. He then countered with a request that the "political situation in Italy" be examined, using the demonstrations which had accompanied the Italian referendum of June 2 on the abolition of the monarchy as an opportunity to criticize Anglo-American occupation policies. We surprised him, I think, by readily assenting to hold this discussion. But for the next eleven days progress was agonizingly slow. Then, on June 27, the log jam suddenly showed signs of breaking up.

The break came most unexpectedly at the end of a long meeting that had started with a fruitless discussion of our proposal to include in the treaties a mere statement of principle that the Danube should be a free waterway. With almost monotonous insistence, Mr. Molotov had maintained that the Danube must be controlled by the riparian states. We had spent the entire afternoon on such items as the limitation of the Bulgarian Navy, the rectification of the French-Italian border in the Tenda-Briga area, and miscellaneous clauses of the Rumanian treaty. Our agreement on some of the economic clauses of this treaty prompted me to say in humor as much as in hope:

"We should make it a good afternoon and settle the question of the Dodecanese."

To my amazement, Mr. Molotov replied that "the Soviet delegation has no objection to that proposal."

"Did Mr. Molotov say that he agreed the islands should go to Greece?" Mr. Bevin, who had tried repeatedly to settle the issue, asked in disbelief.

The Soviet representative promptly said that he had, and immediately asked that we proceed to the next question.

"Let me have a minute or two to recover," I exclaimed.

Mr. Molotov calmly suggested some other "good agreements" might be made. I proposed we discuss the question of the Italian colonies. He said that the matter could be settled on the basis of the American proposal to postpone a decision for a year after which, if agreement was not reached, the General Assembly of the United Nations would be asked for a decision. After drafting work by the deputies, this was subsequently approved.

But the twin issues of reparations and Trieste remained unsolved. In a discussion on June 18 the United States had renewed its suggestion that the Soviet Union be allowed 100 million dollars in reparations to be met from four sources: wartime industrial equipment not readily convertible to civilian use, Italian assets in the Balkan states, the Italian merchant ships, *Saturnia* and *Vulcania*, and naval vessels and other war booty captured by the American and British navies.

Molotov claimed that war booty could not be considered a source of reparations. Strictly speaking, he was correct. War booty belongs to the governments that capture it. But Molotov asserted the Soviet Union was entitled to a share of the Italian naval vessels because, at the Potsdam Conference, the United States and Britain had agreed to let Russia share in the allocation of German naval vessels which we had taken as war booty. We told Mr. Molotov that since naval vessels were war booty, the Soviet Union was not entitled to any of them; that the German vessels had been allotted to the Red Navy purely as a gift. There had been no promise that we would forever continue to make such gifts of our war booty. They did not divide their war booty.

The other three sources of reparations he accepted, but claimed our valuation of these assets was far too high. He placed the total at approximately 30 million dollars. The balance, he said, should be made up from current production. We left the question open by suggesting an inspection of the merchant ships and a study of means to determine the valuation of the other sources.

Three days later, Mr. Bidault took up the Trieste issue by suggesting, very cautiously, a temporary international regime for the city. The other three members of the Council received the suggestion with comparable caution. That evening, Messrs. Molotov, Vyshinski and Pavlov came to my rooms at the Hotel Meurice for a private conversation with Mr. Cohen, Mr. Bohlen and me. Mr. Molotov made what apparently was a final effort to obtain Trieste for Yugoslavia. We maintained we could never agree to Yugoslav sovereignty over this Italian city and suggested that both sides give some consideration to Mr. Bidault's proposal.

The next day I proposed that we issue invitations for a peace conference on July 15 and that we utilize the intervening period to seek settlement of the remaining issues. Those that remained unsolved on the fifteenth we would simply report to the assembled twenty-one nations.

Although Mr. Molotov maintained the suggestion was premature, both Mr. Bevin and Mr. Bidault joined in strong urging the immediate issuance of the invitations. We finally decided to begin, on Monday the twenty-fourth, a review of progress on all the treaties and, the following Friday, to consider again the American demand for the peace conference.

Monday morning, Mr. Molotov asked me to meet him again in my room that afternoon for another talk on Trieste. There, he proposed that Trieste and its adjacent area be declared an autonomous state under the sovereignty of Yugoslavia and controlled by an international statute to be drafted by the four powers. We pointed out that this was quite different from Mr. Bidault's idea which provided for United Nations administration and a governor appointed by the United Nations, but we promised to consider it. The next afternoon we repaid his visit.

"We have analyzed your suggestion and feel it would create an impossible situation," I said. "With Yugoslav sovereignty and a Yugoslav governor there would be little for the representatives of the four powers to do and there would be no connection whatever with the United Nations. The United States cannot accept Yugoslav sovereignty over the Trieste area. I recognize that the Soviet Union cannot accept Italian sovereignty. We are willing, therefore, to consider any proposal that offers a way out—either United Nations' administration as proposed by Mr. Bidault or leaving the issue to the peace conference for decision. I prefer the latter, for then the responsibility will rest upon the twenty-one nations."

Mr. Molotov then asked whether the problem of reparations could be disposed of "in a positive fashion" if the Trieste issue were settled. I stated I did not think this would create insuperable difficulties.

"The United States does not wish to finance reparations for others," I added. "But, a plan might be agreed upon whereby the Soviet Union could supply Italy with certain raw materials out of which Italy could manufacture goods the Soviet Union desires as reparations."

He then asked if the United States would sign all the peace treaties, including the one with Bulgaria, if agreement could be reached. I told him I saw no difficulties on that score but would meet that question when it arose. I then asked him if he could persuade the Bulgarian Government to carry out the Moscow decision. The only reply he would give was that his government had tried, but the opposition parties in Bulgaria had refused and the failure thus rested on them. With this "position sounding" we parted.

The following afternoon, Mr. Bidault suggested a restricted night meeting at which each Foreign Minister would be accompanied by only two advisers.

As on all such occasions, Senators Connally and Vandenberg accompanied me. Mr. Molotov at first reiterated the proposal he had made at our private conversation and then took one more step toward the French proposal. Instead of a Yugoslav governor, he proposed two governors, one Italian and one Yugoslav, to administer in concert. This idea naturally aroused no enthusiasm and finally Mr. Bevin remarked that the procedure of the conference seemed to be not to decide anything. Mr. Molotov's wry rejoinder was that the Briton should not underestimate his own services in producing that result.

Having concluded on this note, it is little wonder that the agreement the next day on the Dodecanese and on the Italian colonies took us by surprise. Even then, there was still much to be done and the yielding process was slow and grudging. To keep the log jam moving, I asked that the calling of the peace conference be placed on the agenda of our next meeting. Mr. Molotov objected but I served notice that I, at least, would discuss it. The next day everyone but the Soviet representative agreed that the conference should be called on July 20. And he maintained the decision must be postponed for a few days to consider a new proposal on Trieste that Mr. Bidault had presented.

The Trieste issue then entered a crucial phase. We didn't like the free territory idea but, since this was the only way out of the dilemma, we were determined that the regime would be set up so that it had a chance to work. Mr. Molotov first proposed a territorial outline that was impossible: It cut the port off from its shipyards, it severed the city from its water supply, and placed its power transformers in Yugoslavia. He wanted four-power rather than United Nations supervision. We refused to budge from our position that responsibility should lie with the Security Council rather than with a rival four-power commission.

We felt that the success of the free territory would be a matter of vital interest to all the United Nations and not merely the four powers. The four powers had not shown ability to work harmoniously elsewhere and there was no reason to expect a different situation in supervising the free territory. By placing responsibility in the Security Council, eleven states would share the obligation. There was no excuse for a rival organization. We also felt that the United Nations would have greater prestige than a four-power organization created for this sole purpose. We believed that if the integrity and independence of the free territory were threatened by aggression, it would be the duty of the Security Council to furnish military protection and it would be unwise for a four-power commission to have a military force for the same purpose.

On July 3, we renewed our campaign for the peace conference. This time, Mr. Molotov said he could not agree until the question of reparations was settled, but he was finally pressed into suggesting September 1 as a possible date. The other three Foreign Ministers objected to such delay but at least we had his commitment in principle. We ended our session at 8:30 with the feeling that July 4 would be a decisive day.

The morning of the Fourth was a glorious morning. Senator Connally Senator Vandenberg, Ambassador Caffery and I took part in ceremonies arranged by the American Legion near the monument to George Washington, and then we marched to the statue of Rochambeau where we also placed flowers in memory of the Frenchman's contributions to our freedom.

We met that day at 5:00 P.M. As soon as the deputies had made their customary report, Mr. Bidault suggested the meeting be adjourned for half an hour to permit the four Ministers to meet in his office for a private discussion of the question of setting a date for the peace conference. In his office he explained he had proposed this meeting in the hope that we could settle the question of the peace conference and reparations simultaneously.

I immediately declared we had repeatedly stated our willingness to re-examine the questions of reparations and would do so once the date of the peace conference was set. The United States objects, I said, to being told what it must do on other questions in order to secure agreement on the holding of the conference. Mr. Molotov denied that such tactics were being employed. Mr. Bidault then renewed his efforts at compromise and, in response, Mr. Molotov asked about reparations from current production. At this point I interrupted to say that, while we appreciated Mr. Bidault's efforts, we could not discuss reparations until a date was set for the peace conference. The American people would not like the appearance of a threat, I asserted, and would interpret any agreement under such circumstances as a deal in order to obtain a peace conference.

Mr. Bevin was even more pointed in his remarks. He said he could not face Parliament if he went out of this room with the implication that he had bought the peace conference from the Soviet Union for 100 million dollars.

Mr. Molotov appraised the situation and made his decision. There was no intention of buying anything, he said. He merely asked that the legitimate claims of the Soviet Union be considered. He therefore agreed that the council should take up in regular session first, the date of the peace conference, and then reparations, with the expectation that both questions would be settled that day. With that, we returned to the council room and in five minutes reached agreement on July 29 as the date for convening the peace conference and instructed the deputies to draft the invitation.

The United States delegation then submitted a reparations proposal—which immediately became the center of six tiring hours of debate. At one o'clock, the morning of July 5, we wearily agreed that the Soviet Union should receive 100 million dollars in reparations. This figure is to be made up from industrial equipment not necessary for Italy's peace economy, Italian assets in the Balkan states, and the balance from current production for which the Soviet Union would furnish the necessary raw materials. Mr. Molotov was willing to let the other claims for reparations be fixed at the peace conference.

We expected that the invitations would be issued the next day, but we grossly underestimated the resourceful stubbornness of Mr. Molotov. He objected to the invitations being issued in the name of the Council of Foreign Ministers because that would make China one of the sponsoring powers and, more importantly, he insisted that we must first agree on rules of procedure for the conference. Four more days of bitter controversy ensued. Mr. Molotov proposed rules of procedure which would have left the peace conference virtually powerless to do anything but approve the work of the four Ministers. Mr. Bevin, of course, could not agree to rules that would give the British dominions little opportunity to present their views effectively. Again and again, I told Mr. Molotov the United States would not agree to the imposition of rules on an assembly of sovereign nations, and maintained that the conference had a right to determine its own procedure.

At Mr. Bidault's suggestion, we finally resorted to another private conference. The Soviet representative accepted the proposal that draft rules of procedure accompanying the invitations should merely be "suggestions" from the Council. Included in these rules was the provision that recommendations would be made by a majority vote of two-thirds. Mr. Molotov had sought persistently to negotiate the rules point by point, but I had refused. I had made it clear the United States would not be bound by these rules, and I could not permit "suggestions" to achieve through point-by-point negotiation the same status as agreed treaty clauses. At the end of the discussion I repeated a statement I had made many times:

"I wish it clearly understood," I said, "that when the conference convenes the United States will feel entirely free to accept or reject on its merits any amendment or new proposal which might be offered."

This statement, which is but one of many like it that I made during this discussion, is important because Mr. Molotov's later effort to ignore it provided one of the bitterest controversies of the peace conference.

Agreement at last was reached and the invitations to the peace conference finally went out the next day, July 9.

The story of this agreement would be incomplete without acknowledging that it was brought about by the mediation of Mr. Bidault. He is, in fact, quite a remarkable man. Before the war he was a professor. During the war he became a leader of the underground forces, and was taken as a prisoner of war. When he was released and returned to France, he entered politics. For a man who had no experience in that field, he showed unusual aptitude. Under his leadership, the party known as the Mouvement Republicain Populaire (MRP) elected the largest number of delegates to the Chamber of Deputies, and as a result, he was called upon to form a government. Later he became the provisional President of France as well as Foreign Minister. He had a coalition government composed of Communists, Socialists and members of his own party. When a man can be successful directing such a government in France even for nine or ten months he is certain to be helpful in presiding over the deliberations of the Council of Foreign Ministers. With his constructive mind and engaging personality he brought about agreement on several very controversial questions.

When Mr. Bevin dropped the chairman's gavel late in the evening of July 12 with the declaration, "Gentlemen, we will meet at the peace conference," I was tired and sorely tempted to follow the suggestion of the President and the members of my staff to take a vacation in Switzerland prior to the conference.

But much could be done in two weeks at home. The foreign service legislation and other such matters were pending; there were Far East and South American problems to be dealt with. Therefore, on Monday night, July 15, I found myself once again before the radio microphones in Washington delivering another report to the American people.

"The draft of treaties agreed upon are not the best human wit could devise," I admitted. "But they are the best which human wit could get the four principal Allies to agree upon. They represent as satisfactory an approach to the return of peace as we could hope for in this imperfect and war-weary world."

After outlining the major provisions of the drafts and the agreements reached I spoke of the "great struggle and tremendous difficulties the four governments had in harmonizing their views" and then added:

"I am ready to believe it is difficult for them to understand us, just as it is difficult for us to understand them. But I sometimes think our Soviet friends fear we would think them weak and soft if they agreed without a struggle on anything we wanted, even though they wanted it too. Constant struggle, however, is not always helpful in a world longing for peace."

Chapter 8

The Paris Peace Conference and Its New York Finale

WE PREPARED for the peace conference believing that the voice of the United States could be raised on behalf of both political parties and a large majority of the American people. This spirit was reflected by the response of the people of Washington to a friendly suggestion from the Washington *Post* that the American delegation be given a hearty send-off. The huge crowd that lined the road to the National Airport and crowded the field to cheer us on our way was a source of genuine encouragement during the eleven weeks of the conference. This moving demonstration of our people's desire for peace made the twelve months of work and over sixty thousand miles of travel to obtain the conference and its promise of peace more than worth while.

The French Government and people did everything they could to provide an appropriate setting for peace making. The French excel as hosts but even their best efforts failed to dispel the harsh feelings that held over from the closing days of the Council of Foreign Ministers meetings.

Social activities constitute a physical endurance test and I had to decline all invitations except those extended by the heads of government and the Foreign Ministers. I must admit, however, that there is virtue in the social life at such gatherings as the peace conference. As long as men meet socially and continue to discuss their problems there is a chance to solve them. This idea exists in many ways, among many people. It is recognized even by our Supreme Court where each Justice, upon entering the conference room from which the group marches into the Court, shakes hands with every other Justice present. It seemed to me, when I first became a member of the Court, that this was absurd because I had often just concluded talking with one or more of the Justices. I learned, however, that many years ago a Chief Justice established the custom on the theory that no matter how heated the arguments of the Justices might have been the previous day, they would be able to reconcile their differences if they started the day with a handshake and on speaking terms. I did not forget this lesson from the Court in my dealings with the representatives of other countries. It was especially valuable during the tense days of the Paris Conference.

We approached the conference from a point of view entirely different from that of the Soviet Government, and that fact produced conflict from the very start. We believed the discussions should be full and free; that the countries which had helped to win the war should have the widest latitude in suggesting amendments and proposals for the peace, and that their recommendations should carry great weight. We believed that a lasting peace had to be a people's peace.

The Soviet attitude, however, seemed to be that the conference should simply and speedily confirm the agreements made in the Council of Foreign Ministers and that establishment of the conditions of peace was primarily, if not exclusively, the concern of the great powers.

In accordance with our belief, I announced in my opening speech that the United States would support the agreements made in the council, but, as I had stated in the council, I would vote on each proposal of procedure regardless of the suggestions submitted by the council. Should the conference, on any question of substance not agreed to by the council, make a recommendation by a two-thirds majority, I would exert every effort to secure adoption of that recommendation by the council regardless of how the United States voted in the peace conference. Mr. Molotov immediately charged that our position, which was also taken by the United Kingdom, was a violation of an agreement made in council on rules of procedure for the conference. The first time I overlooked his accusation, but when it was renewed with the evident purpose of giving offense, I read from the record of the council six different statements I had made reserving for the United States the right to vote for any amendment on procedure. I stated I had made the reservation so often only because I knew the tactics of Mr. Molotov.

"In the light of this record," I declared, "only Mr. Molotov would say that I had agreed to support the suggested rules of procedure."

I pointed out that, when he had lectured the United States and the United Kingdom for "inconsistency" in supporting an amendment to the rules of voting procedure, he had closed his statement by offering an amendment himself to the same section of the rules.

"Now, only Mr. Molotov would do that," I added.

The debate on procedure was as long as it was bitter. For nearly three weeks Mr. Molotov and Mr. Vyshinski used all their talent as parliamentarians to restrict participation by the small and medium powers. This was contrary to the interest and desires of these powers. In addition, the tactics of the Soviet delegation in questioning the motives of those who differed from them and in charging the formation of blocs when there was no justification for the charge were so offensive that some delegates who had come to the conference thinking the Foreign Ministers of the western states were unfair to the Soviet Union changed their minds. From that time on these delegates were very critical of the Soviets and generally were found voting against them. The Soviet delegation declared that when the treaties were returned to the Council of Foreign Ministers they would disregard, as lacking in authority, any recommendation passed by a simple majority. But on many of the votes the Soviet proposals were defeated by more than a two-thirds majority.

Mr. Molotov assumed that we and the British had organized a bloc against him. The fact is I never attended a meeting that would even suggest such an effort. Later in the conference he even charged that we instigated amendments offered by the smaller powers. Many of these amendments supported objectives that had been included in our original proposals for the treaties. But we had been obliged to drop them because of the Soviet veto in the council. Because Molotov exercised a tight control over the votes and the actions of his supporters, he assumed that we did the same. It was inconceivable to him that Belgium, the Netherlands, South Africa, Australia or New Zealand, for example, could have ideas of their own, and that we would hesitate to try to influence their views. So he charged us with the formation of "blocs" aimed at destroying the work of the council.

"Whence comes this talk of blocs?" I was finally impelled to ask. "By what right do those who vote ballot after ballot with the Soviet Union call those of us, who do not always agree with the Soviet Union, a bloc? When the New Zealand proposal to have all recommendations made by a simple majority vote was defeated in the commission by a bare 11 to 9 votes, no one complained that the proposal had been rejected by a Soviet bloc; but when the Soviet proposal on voting procedure is defeated by the overwhelming vote of 15 to 6 here in this conference, the charge is made that the defeat was brought about by an Anglo-Saxon bloc. What loose and wicked talk this is!"

When the fight on procedure neared its end, I cabled Senator Connally and Senator Vandenberg, urging them to join the delegation. I needed them to defend the United States against the criticism now being directed against us by the satellites as well as the Soviet Union. As in the past, they immediately responded to my request. And they did a most effective job.

Senator Connally became the American representative on the commission handling the political sections of the Italian treaty, assisted by Assistant Secretary of State James C. Dunn and an outstanding foreign service officer, Sam Reber. Senator Vandenberg represented us on the commission in charge of economic questions in all the treaties, with the aid of Willard Thorp, now an Assistant Secretary of State. The other American commission assignments were as follows: The Commission on the Rumanian treaty, Mr. Averell Harriman, then our Ambassador in London; the Bulgarian Commission, our Ambassador in Paris, Mr. Jefferson Caffery; the Commission on Hungary, our Ambassador in Moscow, General Bedell Smith. On the Military Commission which dealt also with naval questions, we had Vice Admiral Richard L. Connally, Brigadier General Jesse D. Balmer, and Captain Roland K. Pryce.

At nine o'clock each morning these gentlemen would meet with me and various State Department experts. Each representative on the commission would make a report so that every member of the delegation knew the status of the discussions in all the commissions and, when desirable, could obtain the judgment of the delegation on a controversial issue. It was a harmonious and smooth-working team. No Secretary of State ever received more loyal or more capable support.

At one of the first plenary sessions, Prime Minister de Gasperi of the new democratic Italy, appeared in order to present his country's cause. He and his delegation were treated as representatives of an enemy state. No delegate greeted him except Mr. Bidault, who was presiding and who, in a formal way, presented him. The Italian Prime Minister presented his case tactfully but with dignity and courage. As he left the rostrum to return to the seat assigned to him on the last tier, he walked down the center aisle of the silent chamber, past many men who knew him. No one spoke to him. It impressed me as unnecessarily cruel. Like others, I had met him in London. So, when he approached the United States delegation I stood and shook hands with him. I then sent him a message inviting him to my apartment that afternoon. I wanted to encourage this man who had suffered personally at the hands of Mussolini and now was suffering at the hands of the Allied nations.

Before leaving Washington for Paris I had secured authority to help the new government of Italy in a matter of great importance to them. We had paid for supplies furnished our armies in France but the House Appropriations Committee had objected to our Army paying for supplies purchased in Italy on the ground that Italy was an enemy state. Because of their action, payments were held up by the Treasury. I presented this matter to Representatives Clarence Cannon and John Taber, chairman and ranking Republican, respectively, of the House Appropriations Committee. These two gentlemen frequently are criticized by free-spending officials. From my long experience I know they strive only to protect the money of the taxpayers and I have always found them sympathetic to a deserving cause. When I told them the supplies were furnished after Italy was fighting on the side of the Allies, they promptly stated they would withdraw their objection.

Knowing that Prime Minister de Gasperi was humiliated by his reception at the peace conference, I took the occasion that afternoon to inform him of the United States Government's decision. But I warned him our decision would not be announced until agreement was reached on the Italian treaty. Otherwise, I explained, the claimants for reparations from Italy might increase their claims.

There were times when we thought the conference would never end. On every subject where there was the slightest controversy, the Soviet Union would present its views and then several of the satellite states would make supporting speeches. Since each speech was made in three languages, progress was difficult. Not until representatives of other states, without any formal meeting or understanding but by general accord, began refraining from making speeches, and calling for votes instead, did the work start moving forward.

Nevertheless, it seemed to me that the course of the Soviet delegation and its satellites was not wholly discouraging. It seemed incredible to me that Mr. Molotov and Mr. Vyshinski would devote so much time to the consideration of the proposals before the commissions and in the plenary sessions and thereafter refuse to give consideration to the recommendations of the conference.

In the course of these debates, there were few accusations which were not directed against the United States and the United Kingdom. We were charged with seeking alliances with "Fascists," with attempts to "enslave" Italy through "foreign trusts and cartels," with using our capital to "subjugate" weaker nations, and numerous other crimes as heinous as they were ridiculous.

We sought, in so far as possible, to avoid indulging in debate of this kind, but there were occasions when answers had to be made. One of these was the speech made by Mr. Molotov after the ex-enemy states presented their views on the treaty drafts. It was an intemperate speech in which he supported the attacks of the former enemy states against our ally, Greece, and contrasted Italy unfavorably with the Russian-dominated Balkan governments. It also constituted a direct attack on American and British peace policies.

"Peace in this interdependent world," I told the conference in reply, "cannot be furthered by ignoring the repeated abuse and misrepresentation which have been leveled against America from this floor." I strongly objected to "the Soviet Government's giving the impression to the conference that other ex-enemy states are more democratic than Italy because they have harmonized their viewpoints with the Soviet Union. . . . The United States believes in the sovereign equality of nations. We are opposed to making the small nations satellites of the larger states."

I referred to Mr. Molotov's charge that certain large powers had enriched themselves during the war and asked if he could possibly mean the United States, which has spent over 400 billion dollars in fighting the war, and had sent over 11 billion dollars of lend-lease aid to the Soviet Union. I pointed out that we sought no territory nor reparations in contrast to the large territories and hundreds of millions of dollars allotted to the Soviet Union by the treaty drafts.

"The United States must also repudiate the suggestion of the Soviet delegation that the economic clauses proposed by the United States and based upon the principle of equality . . . are part of an effort to exploit the ex-enemy countries for the selfish advantage of the United States."

On one occasion when Mr. Vyshinski was repeating the charge that the United States was trying to dominate the world with "hand-outs," I noticed he was heartily applauded at the end of his remarks by two of the Czechoslovakian delegates seated two rows in front of our delegation. I had just been told that the Czechoslovakians had been allotted a credit of 50 million dollars for the purchase of surplus property. The credit had been given because of representations that the government needed financial help for the reconstruction of the country. I inquired and learned that the Czechoslovakian government had entered into a contract to transfer to Rumania 10 million dollars of this "emergency" credit. The transfer was to carry an interest rate of 6 per cent plus an administration fee of 7 per cent, giving the Czechs a very nice profit, since they were to pay only 2⅜ per cent interest on the money borrowed from us.

I immediately cabled instructions to the State Department to stop the extension of credit to Czechoslovakia. A few days later the very able and attractive Foreign Minister of that country, Mr. Jan Masaryk, came to see me, bringing with him Clementis, a member of his delegation, who was a Communist representative in the government. Mr. Masaryk asked what was disturbing the friendly relations between our two countries. I told him our friendly relations need not be disturbed but that there would be an end to relief appropriations or credits to a government whose officials could applaud a denunciation of the United States as a government seeking to dominate the world by "hand-outs." I assured him we wished to be friendly with Czechoslovakia and we did not want to offend them further by giving them hand-outs, particularly in view of the violent arguments against us in the Czech press. I also told him how shocked I was by the Rumanian transaction and said the credit was extended to Czechoslovakia because we relied upon their representations that they needed it. If Rumania needed assistance from us, I said, they should ask for it; Czechoslovakia could not act as a broker for us.

Mr. Masaryk advised me—and I knew he was sincere—that he had known nothing of the transaction with Rumania and he regretted such action. He said he would inquire into the facts. The other gentleman knew the facts, but explained that the bargain was not completed. With that, I told him it had not been completed because I knew about it and stopped it.

Later, I received information which mitigated slightly the action of the Czech government. A representative of our Treasury Department, visiting in Czechoslovakia, was approached by a Czech official. The Czech asked the Treasury representative about the Rumanian transaction. The American replied he had nothing to do with such matters but then added that the proposition might be submitted to our government for consideration. Czech officials later cited this statement in justification of the agreement with Rumania, saying that they assumed the United States would not advance the credit if we were opposed to the Rumanian transaction.

During this same period a crisis in our relations with Yugoslavia— a country about the size of New York and Pennsylvania, containing 16 million people—occurred. There, Marshal Tito, who had fought in the Russian revolution and was a thoroughly trained Communist leader, had worked his way into control. We had had difficulties with him a year earlier when it had appeared that Yugoslav troops would seek to take Venezia Giulia by force. The Yugoslavs had finally withdrawn to the Morgan line but skirmishes continued intermittently all along the line. The other source of friction had been airplane travel. The Army's Air Transport Service operating between Rome and Vienna passed through Udine in northern Italy to Klagenfurt in Austria. It was impossible for our planes to travel the sixty-five miles between these two points in a straight line because the northwest tip of Yugoslavia jutted out between them and, because of Yugoslav protests, our planes had been ordered to stay away from that territory. The order was often difficult to obey as the territory is rugged and many navigational hazards exist. Pilots must fly through a pass where mountains are 9,000 feet high and surrounding peaks reach as high as 18,000 feet. In bad weather it was easy to get lost and in any weather it was a temptation to clip the corner. No friendly country would have complained, but the Yugoslavs charged us with 176 violations of her frontiers. Our Army denied the charges.

On August 9, an army transport, carrying seven Americans, a Turk, and a Swiss, lost its way, strayed over Yugoslav territory, was attacked by two Yugoslav fighter planes, and forced to make a hazardous landing in a wheat field. The Turkish Army officer was wounded. The other eight were immediately interned in a Belgrade hotel. On August 19, another transport en route to Rome radioed Udine that it was over Klagenfurt. It was never heard from again, but Klagenfurt reported it had been attacked and sent down in flames by Yugoslav fighters. The bodies of the five Americans were found five days later.

The State Department asked for information and Marshal Tito made a belligerent speech in which he charged us with sending "whole squadrons" of military planes over Yugoslavia. I sent for the Vice Premier of Yugoslavia, Edward Kardelj, who headed his country's delegation to the peace conference. I told him the news I had received and asked for an explanation. He said he had none other than the general information that our planes had flown over his country on several occasions although they had been told not to do so.

"Yugoslavia claims to be a friendly government and your planes can fly over our territory at any time," I told him. "But even if you were not friendly and one of your planes, flying over Canada, got lost and happened to fly over the United States and was grounded, the officials of the United States would feel it their duty to do everything in their power for the safety and comfort of the Yugoslav crew and its passengers. Any official who failed to do so would be reprimanded by our government. The idea of a United States Army plane, under such circumstances, firing upon a plane of Yugoslavia, killing its crew and passengers, is something the American government would never be guilty of and is something for which the American people will not forgive Yugoslavia."

I demanded that he communicate with his government to obtain an explanation. At the same time I communicated with Under Secretary of State Dean Acheson and he sent an official demand through diplomatic channels. Upon receiving a very unsatisfactory reply, I issued instructions to notify the Yugoslavs that unless we received a satisfactory reply to our demands within forty-eight hours we would call upon the United Nations Security Council to take appropriate action.

The atmosphere at the conference was tense as the news of the American ultimatum spread among the delegations. Before long, I noticed a member of Mr. Molotov's group leave his delegation and go over to the Yugoslav table and whisper to Mr. Kardelj. Both Mr. Molotov and Mr. Kardelj then walked out of the conference chamber through different doors. A member of our delegation saw them in earnest conversation in the anteroom and noticed that Mr. Molotov was doing most of the talking. It may not have been a conference about our message, but, in any event, we received a satisfactory reply before the forty-eight hours were over.

During this period the pilot and co-pilot of the first airplane were flown to Paris to see me. The pilot told me that, while they were being kept prisoners in a hotel in Belgrade, they were prevented from communicating with the American Ambassador or any other American. He learned that one of his passengers was an UNRRA official and suggested he try to communicate with UNRRA officials in Belgrade. The UNRRA man did so, but his request was denied. Within an hour after this request was rejected, they looked out the window and saw an American-made locomotive over at the railroad depot with the letters UNRRA printed on it. They knew that 70 per cent of the cost of that locomotive had been furnished by the American taxpayers and the thought contributed little to the comfort of their internment.

The incident was ended, but it was not obliterated from the minds of the American people. And this, together with the experience with Czechoslovakia, led me to believe that when UNRRA expired, any new appropriations by Congress for foreign relief should be allocated by the United States and should go to those countries who would not denounce us for granting them the relief they asked for. I felt that if our representatives could get sufficient information to pass judgment on loans made by the Export-Import Bank we should be able to acquire the data needed to pass judgment on requests for relief.

Meanwhile, the tiring work of the conference went on, with sessions lasting into the early hours of the morning. I was chairman during much of the debate on the economic clauses, and I congratulated myself on succeeding in moving the adjournment hour from 2:30 A.M. to 1:00 A.M. The economic clauses of the five treaties were almost identical and, when a roll call was taken on the economic section of the Italian treaty, I hoped that roll calls would not be demanded on the same provisions in all the other treaties. But the Soviet delegation had other ideas.

Notwithstanding the fact that the commissions for each of the enemy states were made up of all the countries that had been at war with that particular state, and that in the commissions roll calls had been taken on all important issues, most of the arguments were repeated in plenary session and then roll calls were demanded again. The results rarely varied, but Mr. Molotov never gave up trying. Even when a resolution of a subcommittee had received a two-thirds majority vote in the plenary session, he would demand a roll call on the minority motion as well. The result was two roll calls on a resolution each time it came up for consideration in each of the five treaties. Tactics such as these by Mr. Molotov and his satellite associates served to create the western bloc that he charged us with seeking to build. Had we wanted to create a bloc he did the job far too effectively for us to have interfered.

Many nights I returned to the hotel from the conference depressed as well as exhausted. A few weeks before, when I left Washington, a reporter at the airport asked how I felt as I returned to the conference, and I replied that, in the words of the old Negro spiritual, I was "standing in the need of prayer." One night, when the prospects for peace were indeed gloomy, Mrs. Byrnes handed me a package of mail forwarded from Washington. Most of the letters were from persons who had heard or read my statement at the airport, and they told me they were praying for the success of the conference and for my efforts. None of them were from chronic letter writers. They were from good people who yearned for peace and believed in the efficacy of prayer. They will never know the comfort their messages gave me.

Toward the end of the conference, Mr. Molotov made a quick trip to Moscow. I assumed he desired to confer with his associates there and I was pleased. The attitude toward the United States adopted by him and by Mr. Vyshinski had been so unfriendly throughout the conference that I felt that any change resulting from his Moscow discussions would be a change for the better. It could hardly be for the worse.

When consideration of the treaties was completed, the Yugoslav delegation declined to attend the last meeting of the conference. The chairman of that delegation sent a letter to the President of the conference stating that because of dissatisfaction with the recommendations on Trieste, Yugoslavia would not attend the meeting and would not sign the treaty. Because of their continued threats not to sign the treaty unless the conference acceded to their views on Trieste, our delegation had offered, and the conference had approved by a majority vote, a proposal that no state refusing to sign the treaty could receive the benefits provided in it. Later, at the Council of Foreign Ministers' meeting in New York, I urged this proposal and when Mr. Molotov agreed to the provision I no longer doubted that Yugoslavia would sign the treaty.

The conference began with twenty-six unagreed articles before it in addition to all the articles agreed upon in the council, and in all, some three hundred amendments were considered. But the real issues of the conference focused on Trieste, the total of reparations obligations, and the control of the Danube.

The council had been unable to agree on the terms of a statute to govern the free territory of Trieste and had appointed a special commission to work out a report. As might be expected, this committee presented to the conference four different draft proposals. We had prepared our draft with an eye on the unhappy experience of the League of Nations with the free city of Danzig. Because the High Commissioner appointed by the League had been powerless to protect the integrity of that city after a well organized Nazi minority had captured control of the local legislature, we were determined that the Governor of Trieste should be invested with strong powers. This created the anomaly of the western democracies advocating appointment by the Security Council of a governor having almost dictatorial powers, while the eastern dictatorship sought to place control in a popularly elected legislature. We were determined, however, to do our utmost to protect the area from infiltration and similar tactics that would pave the way for a coup aimed at delivering Trieste to Yugoslavia, as Danzig had been delivered to Germany.

In addition to giving the Governor the role of a figurehead, the Soviet draft would have joined Trieste to Yugoslavia, and provided for joint administration of Trieste's railways, and the right of free settlement and employment in each other's territory. The conference finally approved, by a vote of 15 to 6, a French compromise on the statute much closer to the American and British drafts than to the Soviet proposal.

The reparations debate was equally difficult, but the conference finally approved for the Finnish, Rumanian and Hungarian treaties the figure of 300 million dollars which had been fixed in the Soviet armistice terms in 1945. We urged the council to take cognizance of the economic chaos prevailing in Hungary by advocating a reduction in reparations payments of one-third, but without success. Bulgaria's reparations payments to Greece and Yugoslavia were set at 125 million dollars, although the figure was opposed by the Slav bloc as being too high.

The biggest reparations fight, of course, centered on Italy. The smaller Allied states submitted claims totaling billions. Since we had agreed in the council to support 100 million dollars for the Soviet Union, these claimants could not be wholly denied, but we did try to give them some sense of proportion by showing that we could, if we wished, present reparations claims totaling 20 billions. The British submitted a similar claim for 11 billion, which they also had no intention of pressing. The conference finally recommended 100 million dollars each to the Soviet Union, Yugoslavia and Greece, and 25 million to Ethiopia. Albania's claim was denied. We sought to lighten Italy's burden by liberalizing the other economic clauses in the treaty for such items as compensation for Allied property, assets in Allied countries, and costs of occupation.

Harsh words were piled high on the American and British proposals aimed at guaranteeing equality of economic opportunity in the Balkan states and for unrestricted use of the Danube. The Soviet representatives professed to believe our purpose was to challenge their control of eastern Europe. We took the position that we wanted to put into action, in the treaties, the principles that had been agreed upon at Yalta. But we were charged with plans to accomplish capitalist "enslavement" of the Balkan people. During much of this debate, the United States was ably represented by Senator Vandenberg and Mr. Willard Thorp, assisted by Mr. Jacques Reinstein. They managed to obtain provisions in the treaties requiring that the ex-enemy states must grant to each of the United Nations, on a reciprocal basis, nondiscriminatory treatment in matters of trade and equal status with their own nationals in conducting business within the country. Also, guarantees were included for equal economic opportunity and for equal rights in negotiating civil aviation agreements for a period of eighteen months, by which time the ex-enemy states, it was assumed, would come within the jurisdiction of the United Nations agreements in these fields.

Senator Vandenberg led our fight for freedom of commerce and navigation on the Danube. He and Mr. Bevin pointed out that there had been international control of the Danube since 1856, but Mr. Molotov dismissed these agreements as "imperialistic treaties" and maintained that the Danube rights concerned the riparian states alone. In an eloquent speech on September 30, Senator Vandenberg urged adoption of a joint Anglo-American resolution affirming the free commerce and navigation principle; it called for convening, within six months after the treaties come into force, a conference to establish a new international traffic regime on the Danube; the Big Four and the riparian states would participate. The resolution, slightly modified, was adopted by the conference and was included in the final draft of the treaty.

While these three issues were the principal centers of controversy at the conference there were, of course, many other difficult questions such as the territorial and minorities disputes which had proved so troublesome after World War I. These included Hungary's loss of Transylvania to Rumania, the latter's transfer of northern Bukovina to Russia, and Russia's acquisition from Finland of Petsamo and naval base rights at Porkkala. There were also such claims as that of Greece for northern Epirus in southern Albania, which was countered by a Soviet-supported claim by Bulgaria for the Greek province of western Thrace.

In the midst of all these claims and counterclaims, Italy and Austria provided the conference with a timely demonstration of statesmanship by working out an enlightened agreement insuring basic human rights for the German-speaking peoples in South Tyrol, which remained with Italy. We tried to use this as an example of reasonable bilateral negotiations to help solve such problems as Czechoslovakia's desire to transfer back to Hungary its Magyar minority, but met with indifferent success.

In all, the peace conference passed on to the Council of Foreign Ministers fifty-three recommendations voted by at least a two-thirds majority and forty-one others adopted by a simple majority. This list made it quite clear, when the conference finally adjourned on October 15, that the Council of Foreign Ministers was faced with more weeks of tedious effort before the treaties would be completed.

Although the conference had not accomplished all we had hoped for, we did feel that our months of effort to obtain it were well and wisely spent. Our contention that wisdom was not a monopoly of the Big Four and that the smaller powers could make important contributions to the treaties had been thoroughly vindicated. The value of their recommendations is proved by the number subsequently included in the treaties.

The council opened its meeting in New York on November 4, 1946, and for once, there was no debate on procedure. We immediately began consideration of the peace-conference recommendations for the Italian treaty. Otherwise, there was little change. In fact, if the setting had not been the tower of the Waldorf-Astoria Hotel, I might have thought I was back in London a year earlier.

The setting, however, was a matter of concern to us for, this time, we were the host government and were responsible for making all the arrangements. Finding suitable accommodations in New York was a major problem. The shortage of hotel space had been made even more acute by the arrival of several thousand delegates for the session of the United Nations General Assembly, which had opened on October 23. The problem was not solved until the president of the Waldorf-Astoria, the late Mr. Lucius Boomer, volunteered to give up his thirty-seventh floor suite for use as the council chamber and for committee meetings, and arranged to clear large areas on the sixth and seventh floors where we established seventy-three offices.

After months of unrelenting negotiation, I thought I appreciated the difficulties involved in preparing peace treaties. But the duties of acting as host gave me still greater understanding. For example, we had to recruit switchboard operators who not only were skilled and thoroughly reliable but who could also speak the languages of the council group. A special switchboard was installed so that each delegation flashed a different colored light on the board whenever a member of its staff picked up the telephone. Thus it was possible for an operator speaking the language of that delegation to take the call. Providing reasonable security for the leading delegates and their papers required a detail of 150 military policemen and an untold number of FBI agents and New York City policemen.

Never before had I realized the magnitude of some of the mechanical aspects of treaty making. In the five weeks of the New York session, 855,000 pages of documents were mimeographed. The minutes of each meeting, the record of each motion made and agreement reached had to be checked and rechecked in each language and with each delegation. This painstaking work of supervising documents was ably handled by L. E. Thompson and Edward Page of the State Department's Eastern European Division, who worked with me also on policy questions affecting that area.

The work of preparing documents, in fact, went on for two months after the delegates went home. Language experts had to check the texts of the treaties in the three official languages and prepare a text in the language of each ex-enemy country. This meant four language versions for each of the five treaties. Approximately 143,000 maps had to be cut, folded and inserted into the treaty texts. The entire job, which required the production of twenty versions totaling, in all, 44,000 volumes, was under the direction of Dr. Warren Kelchner, the chief of the State Department's Division of International Conferences.

While these were new situations, the ones at the conference table were old. Mr. Molotov and Mr. Vyshinski entirely disregarded the recommendations of the conference and argued just as they had been arguing for the past thirteen months. The representatives of Yugoslavia came before the council and presented their case for control of the city of Trieste in substantially the same words they had used at London in September and October, 1945, and which they had persistently voiced at Paris.

I confess it was tiresome. It must have been particularly so for Senators Vandenberg and Connally who, as usual, sat at my side while I, as Secretary, did all the talking. It did not help that each time I made a statement it would be repeated in Russian by Mr. Bohlen and then in French by another interpreter. The best statement cannot be interesting in three languages. Usually, during these translation periods, the Senators, Ben Cohen, and other members of our delegation would hand me notes suggesting how to meet a new proposal or answer an argument that had been made. But, at times, there was nothing to do but wait for the translator to finish. During those periods the Senators would draw doodles. They were quite artistic; I think an artist would say they belonged to the "futuristic" school. Ben Cohen would sketch the persons sitting at the table, and some of his sketches actually were recognizable.

By then, the Senators had become quite expert in diagnosing Mr. Molotov's tactics and motives. They are realists to begin with, and their long experience in the Senate has enabled them to judge whether a man is trying to improve the language of his proposal or whether he is simply killing time. Ben Cohen possesses a different type of mind. Because a thing is right, he cannot understand why Mr. Molotov does not agree to it. For instance, he felt very strongly about the Austrian situation and the hardships the Austrians were enduring as a result of continued occupation. Several times when I had exhausted efforts to induce Mr. Molotov to proceed with the Austrian treaty, Ben would write a note suggesting a new approach and urging me to make one more effort. It was utterly impossible, Ben would feel, for Mr. Molotov to object to this new approach—but he would.

Vandenberg and Connally would admire my patience as much as they would deplore my lack of judgment.

The council in New York took up a great number of the peace conference recommendations before an agreement was reached on one. And that agreement was due to the action of Mr. Bevin. The article dealt with early deliveries of goods for reparations. The British delegation had fought very hard against it at Paris but it was adopted by a vote of 14 to 7. When we came to it, Mr. Bevin said:

"The clause acquired authority through a two-thirds vote in the conference. I withdraw the objection."

"Then, may we consider that this recommendation is accepted by the Council of Ministers?" Mr. Couve de Murville, who had taken Mr. Bidault's place in the Council, asked.

"I ought to say I was very strong on this in Paris," Mr. Bevin replied. "I do not propose to stand in the way in spite of that. I confess it will impose great difficulties on Italy, but I withdraw the objection."

"Mr. Chairman," I put in, "I think it might be noted that this is the first recommendation of the conference to be adopted."

"Britain still leads in some things," Mr. Bevin added.

At this point, Mr. Molotov made his first comment on the clause. With an attempt at humor, he turned to Bevin and said:

"We wish her as much success in the future."

We proceeded to go through all the recommendations of the conference, and with each article the Soviet representative made more emphatic his refusal to follow Mr. Bevin's example in acknowledging the majority will of the peace conference.

Personal relations between us, however, had greatly improved. From the day of his arrival in this country, Mr. Molotov refrained at the council meetings from directing criticism at the United States. During the peace conference there had been no private dinner conversations such as Mr. Molotov and I had had during council sessions. In New York, with the improved relationships, we reverted again to pleasant social exchanges. During the fourth week of the meeting, Mr. Molotov came to see me at my apartment in the Waldorf Hotel and asked what could be done to make better progress in our deliberations.

"I must tell you frankly," I replied, "that since you have rejected practically all of the recommendations of the peace conference adopted by at least a two-thirds vote, I see no hope for agreement. Beginning with London, over a year ago, I have done everything in my power to secure agreement on the treaties. It is with the greatest reluctance, therefore, that I have come to the conclusion we will not be able to agree upon the treaties. Having become reconciled to this, I think we should agree to disagree without having any of the bitter exchanges that marked some of the debates at Paris."

Mr. Molotov was surprised. He was not prepared for such a statement from the United States delegation which had worked so unceasingly for the treaties through so many months. He replied he was not so pessimistic; he thought we could reach agreement.

"For months I have refused to be pessimistic," I told him. "But I have at last realized that we do not share the same desire for treaties of peace. If we do not have the same objective, there is no purpose in further debate. I am particularly anxious that we should not announce our inability to agree in such a way as to frighten the peace-loving people of the world. Time is a great healer and a year from now other individuals may find it possible to agree."

Although Mr. Molotov was reluctant to believe my statement was serious, I closed our conversation on a strong note of resignation to the impossibility of securing treaties.

The day after my visit with Mr. Molotov, the Yugoslav representative, Mr. Simic, who then was also the Yugoslav Ambassador to the United States, requested an interview with me.

He opened the conversation by urging a modification in the boundary line between Yugoslavia and the free territory of Trieste. In return, he said, Yugoslavia was willing to make concessions on Italy's reparations payments. It was obvious to me that Mr. Molotov was merely employing this method to test our position. If I showed willingness to negotiate with Mr. Simic, it would be a good indication to Mr. Molotov that I had not meant what I had said to him about ending our efforts to reach agreement.

"Mr. Ambassador, there is not the slightest use in our discussing your proposal," I told him. "We have reached the conclusion that under the present circumstances it is not possible to obtain treaties that will genuinely contribute toward peace. I have told Mr. Molotov that I think we should end our work and avoid the recriminations that have marked many of our past discussions. Therefore, it is futile even to discuss your suggestion."

Mr. Simic said he thought it would be most regrettable to toss aside the efforts of months. I agreed, but said that I saw no alternative. He tried to reopen the subject, but each time I would simply state that we had exhausted our efforts. The demands made by Mr. Molotov for the conclusion of treaties, I said, made continuation of the status quo the more attractive alternative. I told him that the Italian Government would be satisfied if we announced disagreement and that I did not see how Yugoslavia would be hurt.

In a conversation the following day Mr. Molotov inquired if I held to the view I had expressed during our private conversation. I told him I did. He said again that he thought I was too pessimistic.

"If you really entertain that view," I replied, "I would be glad if you would express some justification for your hope."

Mr. Molotov indicated he was ready to agree to some of the recommendations of the peace conference. I told him that if he took that attitude, I might revise my opinion on the outcome of the treaties.

When the council met for its next formal session, Mr. Molotov announced his agreement to some of the peace conference recommendations and proposed slight modifications for others. He realized that I meant what I had said and that he could secure no further concessions.

When Mr. Molotov decides the time has come to agree, he does it in a big way. He proposed amendments to some of the recommendations which were merely changes in words rather than substance. We were quite willing to co-operate in this face-saving and within a few days we had reached agreement on all the controversial issues. His abrupt change in attitude is accurately reflected by the fact that when the council session opened he objected to virtually all the conference recommendations; but the treaties, as finally approved, contained forty-seven of the fifty-three recommendations adopted by at least a two-thirds majority, and twenty-four of the forty-one which failed to receive a two-thirds vote but were adopted by a simple majority.

These agreements were all the more notable since they had been reached in the midst of a debate on armaments control at the General Asssembly of the United Nations a few miles away at Flushing Meadows, and during continued friction on the familiar issues of Greece and Iran. But on all of these questions, reasonable measures of progress were made.

With the close of the Assembly on December 16, five days after the adjournment of the council session, we were able to return to Washington believing that at last we had passed one important milestone on the long road to peace.

The treaties, as I stated in my radio report at the end of the Paris Conference, were "not written as we would write them if we had a free hand," but I was convinced they were as good as we could hope to get by general agreement for a long time to come. They did represent an important step in the restoration of stability. As long as the armistice terms remained in effect, all five of these countries were subject to uncertainty and interference in every phase of their national life. No planning for the future, particularly in respect to economic development, was possible under these conditions.

The treaties also paved the way for the withdrawal of Allied forces from Italy, Bulgaria and Finland and the reduction of garrisons in Rumania and Hungary. The Trieste issue was settled in such a way as to give reasonable hope that serious conflict may be avoided in the future. Italy has been disarmed so that aggressive action cannot be supported, and Yugoslavia, despite its militant nationalism, will hesitate, I believe, to challenge the authority of the Security Council in this area. While the reparations penalties against Italy were heavier than we believed wise, at least we succeeded in arranging for alleviating the methods of payment.

Perhaps most important of all, the treaties will make possible the entry of the ex-enemy states into the United Nations and their participation in the benefits and responsibilities of such specialized agencies as the International Bank, the Monetary Fund, the Food and Agriculture Organization, and the International Trade Organization. Thus, these countries will be able to join the other United Nations in cooperative action to stabilize and improve their living conditions and their economic, social and cultural relations with the rest of the world.

CONFERENCE TABLE AT POTSDAM

Reading left to right around the table from President Truman: Bohlen, Davies, Cadogan, Eden, Churchill, Birse (interpreter), Attlee, Clark Kerr (now Lord Inverchapel) in striped suit behind Attlee, Vyshinski, Molotov, Stalin (other Russians unidentified), Admiral Leahy, Byrnes.

BOOK III
UNFINISHED TREATIES

Chapter 9

Central Europe—the Crucial Test

IN GERMANY and Austria we face the crucial test of our ability to create the conditions of peace in Europe and, in fact, the world. Geographically, this area is the heart of the European continent. Economically, it has provided much of Europe's lifeblood through its mines, its industries, its agriculture and its transportation system. And politically, it is the tinderbox which has ignited two world-wide conflicts within twenty-five years and which holds the fuel that—without skill, effort, patience and statesmanship—will start still another.

Sincere and well-intentioned people have held the view that the German problem should have been settled first. Virtually everything that has happened since the end of the war has confirmed in my mind the wisdom of concluding the lesser treaties first. The record of those negotiations amply demonstrates the ingenuity of the Soviet delegation at bargaining and log rolling in the pursuit of their objectives; it illustrates their willingness to block agreement on a noncontroversial, universally accepted proposal in order to obtain concessions on some wholly unrelated issue they consider important. Such tactics would have had free play if all the complex problems of the German and Austrian settlements had been added to those of the five lesser treaties. The restoration of peace in any area would have been delayed for years to come.

We have opened the way for withdrawal of occupation armies from a large segment of Europe. When the armies are gone, 80 million people in these five countries will have a reasonable chance to select the kind of government under which they wish to live and to work out their destiny. We have stripped away countless opportunities for confusion, procrastination, and pressure. We are now able to face more directly and clearly the crucial problem of Germany and Austria.

We should recognize that the Soviet Union, alone of all the major powers, was not eager to obtain an early peace settlement. Particularly in the case of Germany, the Soviet Union was content with any policy that contributed to delay. This permitted them to continue occupying the productive zone assigned to them, to continue drawing off its resources, to continue indoctrinating the population in the Soviet way of life, and suppressing those who maintained other beliefs. Delay also permitted them to keep armed forces in Poland for the ostensible purpose of protecting lines of communication to Germany.

Soviet armies, unlike ours, live in large part off the land. They are subject to little, if any, pressure from a public or parliament that is eager to remove from the tax rolls the burden of maintaining armies of occupation. Even the men of the Red Army, unlike ours, are often content to remain where life, in all the rubble of defeat, still is richer than most of them have ever known.

The same considerations have helped to delay a settlement with Austria, where the continued maintenance of armies of occupation not only serves immediate Soviet purposes there but also permits the retention of troops in Rumania and Hungary to protect lines of communication. In the past we have learned that the Russian phrase, "protection of lines of communication," has a very broad meaning when translated into action in the internal affairs of these countries.

The case of Austria is one of the most unhappy illustrations of our difficulty in making an agreement mean the same thing to the Russians that it means to us.

In October 1943, at Moscow, Cordell Hull—one of the greatest Secretaries of State this country has known, a man I am proud to call a friend, and a counselor I had the privilege of consulting during my service in the Cabinet—scored an outstanding success of his diplomatic career. Among the agreements he helped achieve was a Big Three declaration that Austria should be restored as an independent and democratic state.

The Red Army broke into Austria early in April 1945, and soon thereafter captured Vienna. Almost immediately, it was announced that a provisional government had been formed, a government we declined to recognize primarily because it was chiefly Viennese rather than national in its composition.

A congress of political leaders from all sections of Austria was held late in September as a result of which the power of the Communist Minister of Interior was sharply restricted. The control of election machinery, the police and public security were taken from the Interior Ministry and placed under a five-man commission on which the three major parties were represented.

On October 20, 1945, we recognized Austria's Provisional Government, and, on November 23, under the supervision of the Allied military authorities, it held a "free and unfettered" election. The elected government—headed by the veteran Socialist, Karl Renner, as President, and Leopold Figl as Chancellor—was recognized by the four occupying powers on January 7, 1946.

The fate of Austria, however, continues to lie in the hands of the Allied Council. Until a treaty is concluded defining Austria's position as an independent state, the council will remain the supreme authority. As in the case of Germany, Austria (which is only slightly larger than South Carolina) and its capital city, Vienna, are each divided into four separate compartments; and, as in Germany, the Soviet zone is not only the largest but it contains important industries and the best agricultural land.

The elections of 1945 reflected a general return to the political line-ups that prevailed prior to the Nazi Anschluss with the Socialist and the People's parties predominant, representing roughly a division between the urban and the rural areas. The Communist Party received less than 5 per cent of the total vote. Since these elections, Soviet policy toward Austria has altered noticeably. It is not unfair to describe this policy now as one that seems to punish the Austrians for their association with the Germans during the Nazi occupation, and one that tries to make Austria an economic if not a political dependent of the Soviet Union.

But when we were at Potsdam, the elections had not taken place. Decisions on Austria were made with relative ease. In fact, it was the Soviet delegation that suggested that the authority of the Renner provisional government be extended into all the zones. With the British, we finally agreed to examine the question once our troops had entered their zones.

The question of Austria first entered the Potsdam discussions when Prime Minister Churchill complained that although the country had fallen to the Allies in April, it was then July 20 and British forces had not yet been permitted to move into their zone of occupation. The situation, he declared, was "not satisfactory"—a typical bit of British understatement.

Stalin pointed out that agreement on zones had just been reached, owing largely, he said, to the delay of the French. He chided Churchill for being indignant and said the situation had been made difficult because Field Marshal Alexander had acted "less skillfully" than the British and American commanders in Germany. Alexander, he said, "behaves as if Russian troops were under his control."

The affair was straightened out quickly. Two days later Stalin announced that Soviet troops had begun withdrawing to their own zone. Later in the conference he acceded to Churchill's request for assistance in feeding the Viennese in the non-Russian zones since the city's food supplies normally came from the eastern, Russian-occupied area.

With this issue amicably settled, we turned to the question of reparations. Mr. Molotov proposed that Austrian reparations should be fixed

at 250 million dollars, payable in goods over a six-year period. He
designated the Big Three and Yugoslavia as the recipients. The British
and the United States not only renounced any desire for reparations
from Austria but maintained that, in accordance with the Moscow
Declaration of 1943, we should treat Austria as a liberated area and not
as an enemy country, and should exact no reparations from her.

The United States, Mr. Molotov replied, had not been occupied by
Austrian troops, whereas the Austrians had wrought great devastation
in the Soviet Union; they could not, therefore, go unpunished.

We appreciated, I told him, the sacrifices of the Soviet people in
human lives for which there could be no material compensation. Mr.
Molotov said he was talking about property and not about lives. I
reminded him of our huge war expenditures and asserted that, in
computing losses, there was little difference between losing a building
and paying for the cost of such a building. He then asked if we would
agree to the taking of plants and materials as reparations from Austria
and Italy.

I replied that we could not agree to the theory that Austria, a liberated
country, should pay reparations but we would agree that plants that
could only be used for war purposes might be taken from Italy as
reparations.

He dismissed this qualification by saying materials used for war purposes were "war booty" and could be taken anyway. I also pointed out
that Austria, even then, required relief from UNRRA; that it would
be wrong for a country to pay out reparations to the Allies while
receiving relief from those Allies.

At the next-to-the-last meeting of the Big Three on August 1, when
the conference protocol was being examined, the new British Prime
Minister, Mr. Attlee, said he understood Generalissimo Stalin had agreed
previously that Austria would not be called on for reparations. He was
not quite clear on it, he said, and asked if this were a "firm" decision.

"It is," Stalin replied. "The agreement should be stated in the
protocol."

We soon found, however, that Mr. Molotov was determined to get
at least the equivalent of reparations in a somewhat different fashion.
The loophole is in the section of the protocol dealing with reparations
from Germany—it makes available for reparations "German assets" in
the Soviet zone of occupation in Austria. During seven years of occupation, the Nazis, often through transfers made under duress or by use
of outright force, had acquired large interests in the entire Austrian
economy including the oil fields, the banks, Danube shipping, and so on.
The Soviet Government claimed that this made such properties "German
assets" and, therefore, available to Russia. No one of the other three

occupying powers could have anticipated this interpretation of the Potsdam agreement, and no one could accept it. It certainly is in conflict with the declaration issued by the Allies in London in January, 1943, which declared that transfers of property obtained by force or duress would not be recognized. Removal of the assets claimed by the Soviets would wreck Austria's economy; leaving them in Austria under Soviet ownership and control would mean the end of Austria as a sovereign state.

The Austrian government sought to curb Russian seizure of all these assets by nationalizing them, but the Soviet authorities ignored the law on the ground that it violated the Potsdam agreement. Up to this writing, all efforts to solve this issue through diplomatic channels—in the Allied Council and in the Council of Foreign Ministers—have been unsuccessful. The experience of our representative on the Control Council, General Mark Clark, and my own experience in the Council of Foreign Ministers force me to the conclusion that the Soviet Union has no intention of concluding a treaty with Austria as long as it can be avoided; that it desires a prolonged occupation during which time every effort will be made to gain control of the economic and political structure of the country and firmly tie it into the Eastern bloc.

At Moscow, in December 1945, I tried to discuss the problem of German assets in Austria and proposed lightening Austria's economic burden by reducing the occupation forces. On the first point, all I could get was Mr. Molotov's promise to give the subject consideration. On the second, my proposal first stimulated a charge that the Austrians were seeking to "insinuate" Fascists into the government. Then a paper was presented charging the British, particularly, with rebuilding the Austrian Army and also Nazi and anti-Communist White Russian units with the ostensible purpose of directing them against the Soviet Union.

Mr. Bevin replied with a blunt memorandum declaring that the allegations, "which are entirely without foundation, are categorically rejected." They displayed, he said, a distrust that is "deeply resented." He asserted that Soviet representatives in Austria must be "listening to fictitious tales maliciously recounted to them by persons seeking to create suspicion and ill feeling between the Allies." He pointed out that a four-power commission was now investigating these charges in all the zones and proposed that this procedure be followed in all such cases both in Austria and in Germany.

That was as far as we progressed at Moscow in our talks about Austria.

In February 1946, the United States informed the other members of the Council of Foreign Ministers that we wanted to discuss the treaty with Austria at the next meeting in Paris. On April 25, the first day of the session, I tried to have the question included on our agenda. Mr. Molotov immediately objected, saying his delegation had not had an opportunity to study the paper we had submitted.

"There is no parallel between Austria and the other countries and the treaty with Austria calls for special consideration," Mr. Molotov said. "The Soviet delegation is not ready to give it consideration at this time. Of course, we will study with full attention the proposal of Mr. Byrnes and will advise when we are ready to discuss it."

I tried again, during a private conversation with Mr. Molotov and Mr. Vyshinski, on April 28, and was told the Austrian Government had not shown itself capable of cleaning out the Nazis, and occupation forces would have to remain for at least another year. I proposed that the deputies begin a study of an Austrian treaty and was told it was a matter that had to be considered by the Ministers.

Toward the end of the meeting, when we were considering the agenda for our session to begin June 15, I proposed that the Austrian treaty be included and that the deputies prepare a treaty draft for all of us to consider. Mr. Molotov contended that such action was "inadvisable" since the deputies would have their hands full with the five treaties under consideration. Mr. Bevin then suggested that the four powers exchange drafts of treaties in the interim and plan to discuss them in June. Mr. Molotov refused to make any commitment except to "take steps to intensify and expedite the preparation for discussion of the question of a treaty with Austria"; whereupon Mr. Bevin served notice that the British delegation would press, "in whatever way was open to it," for the consideration of an Austrian treaty in June.

Mr. Molotov reiterated that the council was completely occupied with the treaties already under consideration and added:

"May God help us to complete the work on the treaties which are now before us."

Since it was clear that Mr. Molotov was lending little assistance, I could only reply that I hoped, indeed, that God would do so.

That was the extent of our progress on Austria at the first Paris council session.

During the recess, the United States sent the other members of the council a draft treaty with Austria so that there would be a basis for discussion when the council reconvened. This time, Mr. Molotov did not directly oppose the inclusion of the subject on the agenda, he merely asked that a decision be postponed. The council then accepted Mr. Bidault's suggestion that we place at the end of the agenda the subject, "Examination of the Austrian Question." On June 26, the British submitted a second draft, but no action was taken until the final day of the session, July 12. Then I asked that the deputies be instructed to study these two drafts and any others the French and Soviet delegations might submit, with a view to arriving at an agreed proposal. It was "inconceivable," I said, that we should conclude treaties with ex-enemy states before even considering a treaty with Austria, which all the council members regarded as a liberated country whose sovereign freedom they were pledged to restore.

Mr. Molotov thereupon presented a four-point resolution which, first, called attention to the recent agreement in the Allied Council increasing the authority of the Austrian Government. Second, it asserted that there were 437,000 displaced persons in the western zones of occupation, many of whom were pro-Nazi Yugoslav Chetniks and Ustashis, Hungarian Salashists, Russian and Ukrainian White Guards, and members of General Anders' Polish Army, whom he described as "Fascists." Mr. Molotov proposed that the council find that these displaced persons "constitute a grave danger to the neighboring democratic states," and agree to their "imperative and urgent" evacuation. Third, the resolution stated that the "successful accomplishment" of this evacuation was a necessary prerequisite to restoring Austria's full independence. And, last, Molotov's resolution would permit the deputies to begin preparing an Austrian treaty only after the other five treaties were completed.

We immediately agreed that the problem of displaced persons was urgent, and pointed out that the United Nations was then considering it. Both Mr. Bevin and I objected to making the solution of this question a prerequisite for beginning work on a treaty. Nor could we endorse the allegations in the resolution without first determining the facts. Mr. Bevin then referred to the problem of defining German assets in Austria and asked that a four-power commission be appointed to find a solution. Mr. Molotov refused to discuss it, saying it was not on the agenda. I pointed out that the matter of displaced persons had not been on the agenda either, but we had discussed it.

With that, the Austrian discussions stopped. We made no further progress in Paris.

In New York we tried again. This time Mr. Molotov responded with a proposal that both Germany and Austria be considered at a meeting of the council to be held at Moscow in March. Mr. Bevin and Mr. Couve de Murville, who was acting in the absence of Mr. Bidault, joined me in urging that deputies be appointed to begin preliminary work at once. Two days later, on December 11, Mr. Molotov agreed to the appointment of deputies for both the Austrian and the German treaties and it was decided they should begin work in London on January 14. Then, again, I raised the question of German assets in Austria; Mr. Molotov said he was not prepared to discuss it. I agreed not to press the issue as long as it was understood that the deputies would consider it.

Having sought from February to December to initiate work on a treaty for Austria, I realized that the end of the task was far ahead of us, and that a German treaty belonged to the still more distant future. The United States delegation decided that the next best thing was to try again to reduce the Allied occupation forces throughout Europe. Such action, we contended, would lift a heavy burden from the victors as well as the vanquished. We proposed that the four powers agree to reduce their forces to 10,000 in each of the four zones in Austria by April 1, and in Germany to the following numbers by that date: 200,000 in the Soviet zone, 140,000 each in the American and British zones, and 70,000 in the French zone. This reduction, we asserted, would permit a corresponding cut in the number of troops along lines of communication. We proposed a limit of 20,000 in Poland and 5,000 each in Hungary and Rumania.

Mr. Molotov said that this was a new question and that he was not prepared to consider it. Mr. Bevin asked if Mr. Molotov would be prepared to discuss it if it were raised at the meeting in Moscow and the latter indicated his assent. But, at Moscow, when Secretary Marshall again presented the proposal, Mr. Molotov would not agree.

During the Moscow meeting, the efforts of Secretary of State Marshall to conclude a treaty with Austria met with little success. The Austrian Treaty Commission, then created, has made virtually no progress. We will find at the council meeting, scheduled to take place in November, that the issue was merely postponed six more months. There is no certainty that we will reach agreement on a treaty even at that meeting. Our past experience certainly does not encourage optimism.

We must remember that we are not dealing with an enemy state. The treaty involved has the relatively simple objectives of re-establishing Austria's independence and fixing its frontiers. But we will be fortunate indeed if April, 1948—the third anniversary of its liberation from the Nazis—finds Austria restored to the freedom and independence that were pledged it by the Big Three in 1943.

In the case of Germany, our initial agreements were as satisfactory as the subsequent developments have been discouraging. At Potsdam, we gave primary consideration to the German problem. Even while we pressed successfully for the agreement to conclude the lesser treaties first, we took the initiative in securing approval for a set of political and economic principles to govern the occupation of Germany. These principles could have opened the way to an early and equitable peace settlement.

Politically, these principles not only provided for removal and punishment of all Nazis, but they set up the framework within which German political life could be reconstructed on a democratic basis. They directed the reorganization of the judicial and educational systems in accordance with democratic ideals, and they promoted the cause of free local governments and free trade unions. While insisting upon decentralization of the German political structure, they provided for central German administrative agencies in the fields of finance, transportation, communications, foreign trade and industry.

In the economic sphere, these principles called for prohibiting all armaments production, restricting the peacetime needs of industries convertible to war uses and eliminating centralized economic controls such as cartels. The three powers agreed that Germany should be treated as a single economic unit in which primary emphasis would be placed on the development of agriculture and peaceful domestic industries. There were to be common Allied policies on industrial production, mining, transportation and communication, agriculture, wages and prices, foreign trade, currency and banking.

Reparations, we originally had hoped, would be included in this list as well. But the wholesale removal of property by the Red Army prior to Potsdam forced us to conclude that an over-all accounting was an impractical hope and we turned to the plan of handling reparations on a zonal basis. Even then, it was provided that production available for export should be used to pay for necessary imports first and then for reparations; a provision which clearly called for over-all economic planning and administration.

Another aspect of the reparations agreement made at Potsdam has not received the attention it deserves. The recommendation made at Yalta that the "use of German labor" should be considered by the Reparations Commission as a possible source of reparations was dropped by the Big Three at Potsdam and the protocol signed there contained no provision for, or reference to, the use of labor as reparations. Yet it is a deplorable fact that thousands of Germans and Japanese are still being held as enforced laborers in violation of solemn international pledges.

In the closing days of the war against Germany we took so many prisoners it was difficult to care for them behind the lines, and guarding them required so many troops that General Eisenhower decided to transfer many of them to the custody of the liberated nations. But these prisoners surrendered to the United States Army and we therefore retained responsibility. The prisoners held in the United States we endeavored to return promptly. We encountered some resistance from their employers who found the labor profitable, but both Secretary of War Patterson and I were insistent. Notwithstanding the problems in getting necessary transportation, the last of the German and Italian prisoners in this country were returned home in the fall of 1946.

The Geneva Prisoners of War Convention, in letter and spirit, contemplates the repatriation of prisoners as soon as possible after the end of actual fighting. The Soviet Union was not a signatory of that convention but Great Britain and France were.

Because of the obligations I felt the convention placed on the Allied powers, I thought they, too, should exert every effort to expedite the return of prisoners. But, I could not well complain of others until we had returned our prisoners. On September 12, 1946, the British announced a program that would return the last of their prisoners to their homes in October, 1948. This seemed to me to be very slow, but at least it was a planned schedule. That same month, I suggested informally to the French a program for returning these prisoners for which we were responsible.

At that time, France still held approximately 600,000 of the prisoners transferred by General Eisenhower, of which 40,000 were working in coal mines, 280,000 were working on farms and the balance were in miscellaneous occupations.

The French asked me to withhold any formal action for a short time, which I did. But on December 2, 1946, I asked all three governments holding prisoners for us—France, Belgium and Luxemburg—to agree to complete repatriation by October 1, 1947. My message pointed out that eighteen months had elapsed since the end of hostilities and that, since the idea of forced labor was repugnant to the American people, we believed those prisoners not charged with war crimes should be returned. The French answered that while they realized the prisoners must be returned, they were so short of labor that they needed a longer period to complete the repatriation.

In mid-1947 we had in our zone in Germany approximately 573,000 displaced persons. We support them and will not force them to return to the countries of their origin as long as there is reason to believe they would be punished for political reasons.

I had suggested to French officials that they offer work to these people, but when their representatives went to Germany they expressed a preference for German workers. I believe it was the French Communists who objected to bringing in the anti-Communist Poles, Balts and Slavs. But the more quickly the German prisoners in France are returned to Germany, the more quickly will France want to find employment for the displaced persons now in camps in Germany and Austria.

On March 13, 1947, our government announced that an agreement had been reached with the French under which approximately 450,000 prisoners, including those captured by French forces as well as our own, would be released at the rate of 20,000 per month. This means that the last of the German prisoners will not be returned home until about four years after the end of the war. The agreement further provided that the prisoners, upon release, would be given a choice of repatriation or of remaining in France as voluntary workers. We should be certain that contracts are offered to the prisoners for whom we are responsible, under circumstances that protect their freedom of choice.

We know little about the prisoners of war in the Soviet Union, German or Japanese. Generalissimo Stalin told Mr. Hopkins in June, 1945, that they had about two million prisoners of whom 1,700,000 were German. He said they were being used in the Ukraine, White Russia and in the Moscow area on reconstruction projects, in the coal mines and in the timber industry. The Germans, he observed, had been so underfed that they were poor workers; he preferred the Hungarians, who were better fed. In March, 1947, the Soviet Government claimed to have returned over one million Germans and to have 890,000 left.

An over-all agreement on the repatriation of German prisoners finally was obtained at the last meeting of the Council of Foreign Ministers in Moscow. The agreement, reached on April 23, provides that all German prisoners shall be returned by December 31, 1948, and thus will have virtually the same effect as the French-American understanding. I still believe that we should have insisted that France return the prisoners for whom we are responsible by October 1, 1947. In any event, I hope that this issue, which should have never become a part of the reparations question, will be settled by the dates now agreed upon. Forced labor camps are a symbol of Hitler's regime that we should eliminate as rapidly as possible.

This story provides one more example of the many instances where what we thought was an understanding turned out to be no agreement at all. That is why I have stated that the Potsdam agreements on Germany failed. Because they failed it has become popular to criticize them. But the fault does not lie with the agreements. The refusal of the Soviet Union to join wholeheartedly in the collaborative effort necessary to fulfill them was and is the very heart of the German problem. This fact, however, did not become evident to us until some months after Potsdam because the French, without intending to, assumed much of the burden that the Soviet Union was quite willing to share.

France was not represented at Potsdam and therefore did not feel bound by the agreements made there; in fact, it objected strongly to some of them. These objections were placed before President Truman and me by General de Gaulle and Mr. Bidault during their visit to Washington a few weeks after our return from Germany.

Their worries centered on the plan to establish central German administrative agencies and on the disposition of the Rhineland, the Ruhr and the Saar. General de Gaulle feared that these acts were the prelude to the reconstruction of a centralized German state. To re-establish

German unity now, he contended, would be even more dangerous than in the past, because Germany might come under the influence of a strong and powerful Slav bloc rising in the east. The very fact that Germany was now weak, he said, "makes that country all the more susceptible of becoming the political instrument of other powers." The extension of Poland into eastern Germany, both of the French leaders argued, shifted Germany's center of gravity toward the west and therefore endangered the security of France. They asked for the separation of the Rhineland from Germany for administration by France, for the annexation of the Saar, and the transfer of the Ruhr to an international regime.

President Truman and I tried to convince them that the establishment of a central administration for such things as transportation and currency was not creating a highly centralized German government. The security of France, we asserted, could be promoted far more effectively by the United Nations than by slicing away sections of German territory. Only through joint action of all nations, we argued, could the maximum of security be realized.

We were unsuccessful in our efforts, and Mr. Bidault renewed his arguments at the first meeting of the Council of Foreign Ministers in London. France, he said, would continue to oppose creation of a central German authority in the absence of a decision on Germany's western frontier. The French feared that extension of German administration into the Ruhr and the Rhineland would prevent them from acquiring in the peace settlement the control they desired. In proposing an international regime for the Ruhr they were tactfully vague because they did not wish to precipitate the issue of Russian participation in the regime. Nevertheless, this provided Mr. Molotov with an opportunity to renew his proposal for four-power control of the Ruhr. It was suggested that the issues be studied by the deputies but the three of us finally agreed to Mr. Molotov's proposal that the matter should be pursued for the time being "through diplomatic channels."

All the political parties in France insisted that the government take the position stated by Mr. Bidault, but that position has blocked revival of healthy economic activity; it has also given the Soviets an excuse for delay for which they do not have to assume responsibility. I understand why the French are fearful, but I believe they should take a fresh look at the situation. They should withdraw their opposition to central administrative agencies essential to economic unity. There is even less reason for their position since Mr. Bevin and I, long ago, gave assurances in writing that in the peace settlement we would support the cession of the Saar to France. The continuation of their stand will not affect the Soviet position. Russia will maintain its opposition to the cession of the Saar until the final hours and then seek to secure, in exchange for agreement, French support on some other question.

As might be expected, little progress was made after London "through diplomatic channels"; and so, before going to Paris in April, I determined to insist that we start work on the German settlement. The American delegation, therefore, proposed the appointment of special deputies who would undertake two distinct tasks: prepare a report on immediate occupation problems and begin work on a German treaty. The division of Germany into four water-tight compartments, preventing the exchange of people, commodities, and even ideas, I pointed out, was forcing the United States to spend 200 million dollars a year to furnish food which ordinarily would come from the Russian zone. Production of goods for export would have to be increased in order to pay for the food we were bringing in; in such a situation we could not continue dismantling industrial plants to send to Russia for reparations.

The second duty assigned to the deputies, we urged, need not wait until a German government was established. We should agree among ourselves, we maintained, on the nature of the peace settlement and the kind of German government that should be created. Then, both the occupying powers and the German people would know how to proceed.

Our proposal was generally acceptable to France and Britain but Mr. Molotov refused to consent to the appointment of deputies. Even more disappointing was his rejection of our additional proposal for a twenty-five year treaty among the Big Four to block a resurgence of German militarism.

I had first discussed this proposal with Mr. Molotov informally at London in September and had been encouraged by his interest. But when we heard no more from him about it, I put it on the list of items to be discussed with Generalissimo Stalin during the Moscow meeting.

I waited until the Christmas Eve dinner which the Russian leader hospitably tendered us. After a toast-laden dinner marked by its cordiality, we moved into the drawing room for coffee. While it was being served, the Generalissimo and I sat down for a quiet chat; only his interpreter, Mr. Pavlov, was with us. I told him I had been disappointed not to hear from Molotov about the treaty we had discussed in London. He said his Foreign Minister had mentioned it to him, but it was evident from the questions he asked me that no serious consideration had been given to the proposal.

"Such a treaty will give all European states assurance that the United States would not return to a policy of isolation," I told him. "I have often recalled how you expressed at Yalta your fear of another invasion by Germany. You then asserted that the continued co-operation of the four Allies in keeping Germany demilitarized would relieve your fears and perhaps influence your actions in the Balkan states."

Stalin replied that it was the best proposal he had yet heard.

"The United States has always been reluctant to enter into such treaties," I added, "but our experience in trying to stay out of Europe's wars has been so disastrous I am confident our people would support a treaty under which the major powers would join forces to keep Germany disarmed. The Senate will have to ratify such a treaty but I think they will do so and I am willing to make the effort."

"If you decide to fight for such a treaty," Stalin said, "you can rely on my support."

With this conversation in mind, I started preparing a German treaty draft as soon as we returned to the United States. To minimize the possibility of misunderstanding, I followed as closely as possible the language agreed upon in the Allied declaration of June 5, 1945, on demilitarization during the occupation period. I also included a provision in which I have had a deep interest: That, following the conclusion of a peace treaty with Germany, the four major powers should maintain an inspection force. On this force would be men with engineering knowledge and similar specialized skills, to prevent the establishment of or conversion of industries capable of producing weapons of war. Should these technically skilled inspectors report a treaty violation, the four powers would call upon the German Government to order the manufacturer to stop these dangerous activities. A refusal would permit the four powers to take whatever steps they thought necessary to force compliance.

Such a compact would eliminate the need to maintain large armed forces in Germany. A disarmed Germany would never fail to comply with an order from the Allied headquarters if the government knew a violation would bring the air forces of one or more of the four powers over their land within a few hours.

Action under the treaty I proposed could be taken upon a majority vote. Of course, with four powers, it would take three to constitute a majority. The obvious purpose of this was to prevent any one state from blocking prompt action. This elimination of the veto power may be one reason for Soviet opposition, but if so, it is one reason Mr. Molotov has never mentioned. Under Article 107 of the United Nations Charter, punitive action is permitted against a former enemy state by the governments responsible for such action.

President Truman heartily approved of the proposal. He was so sure it would be accepted he began referring to it as the Byrnes treaty. I also discussed it with Senator Connally and Senator Vandenberg. The latter, in fact, had forcefully presented a similar idea in his notable speech to the Senate in January, 1945. In addition, I presented the plan to a group of Senators who had been appointed by the chairman of the Foreign Relations Committee to confer with me on matters such as this. These Senators, of course, had to reserve their decision until the treaty was before them in final form but they endorsed the plan in principle.

After receiving this general concurrence, in early February I sent copies of the proposed treaty to the Soviet Union, the United Kingdom and France with the request that they regard it as a basis for discussion and feel free to suggest amendments or alternate drafts. Mr. Bevin and Mr. Bidault quickly said that they endorsed the treaty, subject to some amendments they would offer. Just before leaving Washington for Paris, I received a message from Mr. Molotov stating simply that he had certain objections.

At dinner with Mr. Molotov on April 28, I asked him to let me know what those objections were. To my surprise, he stated that the treaty appeared to postpone the question of German disarmament until after the occupation. An agreement already existed, he said, that Germany should be disarmed immediately and he proposed that a commission be appointed to verify how it was being carried out. When this investigation was completed, he added, the question of future controls could be embodied in a separate treaty.

He already knew, but I nevertheless outlined for him, the whole background leading up to our drafting of this treaty, beginning with the conversation at Yalta in which Stalin had expressed fear of a revival of German militarism.

"This treaty," I said, "will serve as added insurance against your fears of a renewed attack by Germany and it will remove any element of doubt about the United States bearing its full share of the burden of safeguarding the peace. I must tell you frankly that there are many people in the United States who are unable to understand the exact aim of the Soviet Union—whether it is a search for security or merely expansion. A treaty such as this, and a similar treaty for Japan, will effectively take care of the question of security."

The Soviet Union, he replied, is "in favor of a twenty-five year demilitarization treaty both for Germany and Japan," but he emphasized the importance of carrying out the previous agreement for the immediate disarmament of Germany. We had a long discussion in which we were joined by Mr. Vyshinski and Mr. Cohen. Ben and I did our best to persuade Molotov and Vyshinski that our treaty did not postpone the disarmament of Germany but on the contrary was based on the assumption that disarmament would be completed at once and that the treaty would insure the maintenance of Germany's demilitarization.

The next day I raised the subject in the council and Mr. Molotov repeated substantially the same arguments. He said he would consider our proposal carefully but thought that the "burning question" before the council was the proper completion of the present agreement. I read to him the opening words of our draft which referred to the previous agreement between our governments "to effect the total demilitarization and disarmament" and went on to say that nothing in the proposed treaty "shall delay or prevent the completion of that process."

To meet Mr. Molotov's argument regarding lack of action on the existing demilitarization agreement, I communicated with General Clay in Berlin. A few days later he proposed to the Allied Control Council the apopintment of a commission to visit the four zones and report on the progress of demilitarization. When I reported this action to the council, Mr. Molotov said his government would support it. However, it did not alter his views on the treaty.

When the treaty was again considered, Mr. Molotov adopted a tactic the Russians often employ—he assumed the offensive. The period of the treaty, he said, was not long enough; it should run for at least forty years. I immediately agreed to make it that. It was, he went on, "completely inadequate" and "cannot be a reliable guarantee of security in Europe and the world," as its provisions for disarmament and demilitarization were not sufficiently comprehensive. I reminded him that when I had submitted the treaty I had told him that the language of the disarmament and demilitarization sections had been taken from an agreement issued June 5, 1945, on behalf of our governments by Generals Zhukov, Montgomery, deLattre de Tassigny, and Eisenhower, and that I knew of no better qualified men to draft a demilitarization program. However, if it was not sufficiently comprehensive, I suggested that we amend it.

Mr. Molotov then returned to his previous statement that such a treaty was useless in the absence of any immediate action to disarm Germany. I pointed out that General Clay in the Allied Control Council in Berlin had proposed the appointment of a commission to investigate the status of disarmament in all four zones; that Mr. Molotov had said his government would support it but that every member had agreed except the Soviet representative, who insisted the inquiry should not extend to the demilitarization of industrial plants. If he really wanted an investigation, I said, he could instruct his representative in Berlin to agree and the inquiry would be started promptly.

He then complained that the treaty "evades and disregards" such problems as democratizing Germany. I explained that economic and political objectives for the future would be set forth hereafter in any treaty agreed upon at a peace conference. I said, further, that this particular treaty which provided the method and the necessary force to require compliance should not be confused with a political-economic treaty.

The discussion made it clear that he had no idea of discussing the treaty in a serious manner but was simply looking for excuses for delay. And my patience was exhausted when he continued: "The treaty ignores the necessity of delivering to the Soviet Union reparations totaling at least 10 billion dollars, which President Roosevelt had agreed to at Yalta." Reparations payments, he continued, "naturally" must include commodities out of current production as well as equipment, and he then referred to the "unlawful statement" by General Clay that no more reparations deliveries would be made.

"When the United States is willing to make a drastic departure from its policies of the past and offers this treaty in order to help insure security for Europe," I replied, "we resent having that offer met with irrelevant arguments on reparations and minor difficulties of the occupation.

"You have misquoted President Roosevelt," I added. "My shorthand notes as well as the protocol itself show that the President stated simply that the Soviet proposal should be referred to the Reparations Commission as a basis for discussion." At Potsdam, President Truman and Generalissimo Stalin agreed to a reparations program which recognized the impossibility of obtaining this sum and which deliberately and intentionally stated no amount in dollars.

"Other agreements were made at Potsdam," I continued, "including a provision that reparations payments should leave enough resources to permit the Germans to live without external assistance. Still another agreement provides that exports should first be used to pay for necessary imports. Notwithstanding this, the United States is having to support the people in its zone at a cost of 200 million dollars a year. It was also agreed that Germany should be treated as an economic unit but this is not being done. Therefore, when you complain about General Clay's action, you should remember his action is taken only to obtain justice for the United States under the Potsdam agreement."

By the time Mr. Molotov and I had finished our exchange it was 8:30 P.M. Our tempers as well as our appetites were on edge so I quickly accepted Mr. Bevin's suggestion that the discussion be continued the following day.

The next morning, Mr. Bevin and Mr. Bidault made strong statements in general support of our position. The British people regard the resurgence of Germany as the greatest menace to peace, Mr. Bevin said, and, although he might have some amendments to offer later, his government warmly approved the treaty for the long-term disarmament and demilitarization of Germany. There are three approaches to maintenance of peace in Europe, he continued: first, a balance of power between states of equal strength; second, domination by one power or by two blocs of powers; and third, united control by the four powers with the co-operation of their Allies. It is this last approach, he stressed, that the British Government believes is the most likely to produce stability.

Mr. Bidault, in his statement, declared it was necessary that measures be undertaken to destroy the "militaristic Prussian character" of Germany, and the American treaty should constitute "the crown of the edifice." It would not be an obstacle to reparation, denazification, or any of the other essential tasks of the occupation, he insisted, but would make more concrete the solidarity of the Allies against the danger of a resurgent Germany and would guarantee the security of Europe with the "indispensable" support of the United States.

Both these statements were impressive but they were unsuccessful in swaying the stand taken by Mr. Molotov. When Secretary of State Marshall again proposed consideration of the twenty-five or forty-year treaty at Moscow in April, 1947, the Soviet Foreign Minister offered new reasons for opposing it. Some of the reasons and the amendments he offered were so irrelevant and absurd they indicated a deliberate intent to make certain they could not be accepted.

I have been forced to the conclusion that following Stalin's promise, on December 24, 1945, to support the treaty, the Soviet High Command or Politburo concluded they did not want the United States involved in the maintenance of European security for the next twenty-five or forty years. The pressure of American power would restrict the freedom of action which the Soviet Union, as the predominant military power in Europe, might otherwise enjoy. The same assurance that made the treaty attractive to Mr. Bidault caused Mr. Molotov to disagree. I feel satisfied it is Mr. Molotov who is responsible for the Soviet position. From the very first, his indifference was in contrast to Stalin's enthusiasm.

It does not follow that Mr. Molotov will continue to oppose the treaty. He should be convinced by now that, treaty or no treaty, we intend to maintain our interest in Europe. But when he decides to support it, he will probably announce: "The Soviet Union offers a paper for consideration," and he will produce a draft of a treaty containing some reasonable amendments. He will offer it as a great concession to us and probably ask that we in turn agree to give him the two things he wants: 10 billion in reparations and a part in the control of the Ruhr.

When we made no progress at Paris in the discussions on our treaty, the council, on July 10, turned once again to the American proposal for the appointment of deputies to work both on immediate German problems and a draft treaty.

Mr. Bidault opened what proved to be a highly significant three-day discussion. He outlined the French position that, until the boundaries of Germany were set, no determination of policy could be made. He renewed the French plea for the Saar, international control of the Ruhr, and separation of the Rhineland from Germany. His second objective was assurance of larger coal deliveries from Germany. This request was directed primarily at the British as he was highly doubtful that he would ever get much coal from the Polish-operated mines in Silesia. But he agreed that deputies should be appointed to begin work on these and other problems.

Mr. Bevin also agreed to the appointment of deputies and asserted that Britain would support France's claim to the Saar. He placed particular emphasis on the necessity of securing a decision for immediate implementation of the Potsdam compact to treat Germany as an economic unit. Support of their zone, he said, was costing the British taxpayer 320 million dollars annually and it could not continue. The reason, he went on, was that surplus food from other zones, primarily the Soviet zone, was being removed from Germany.

Mr. Molotov said "no"; deputies could not be appointed until the Ministers had settled other issues. One, of course, was the Soviet demand for 10 billion dollars in reparations, and the other was control of the Ruhr. He coupled with this latter proposal the charge that disarmament and demilitarization were not being carried out in the western zones.

This was a familiar issue by now. The previous November, the Russians had charged that the British were maintaining remnants of the Nazi armies in their zone. The British had proposed an investigation by the Allied Control Council in all the zones with the understanding that a precedent would thereby be established for handling similar allegations. The matter was then dropped by the Soviet representative. Later the British submitted to the Control Council in Berlin reports that war matériel was still being manufactured in the Soviet zone and proposed an investigation of the industrial demilitarization of the country. When we had proposed an investigation early in May, Mr. Molotov had said he would support it, but his representative in Berlin blocked any action. Now, when the charges were renewed, I proposed again that the Allied Control Council set up a commission to investigate progress both in the dismantling of war plants and the destruction of arms and armed forces. Mr. Molotov contended in reply that such an investigation would be meaningless until we had decided on an over-all plan for Germany's economic disarmament.

Mr. Bidault then entered the argument. He had the impression, he said, that the members of the council "were on a merry-go-round," in which case he was "going to ride his own horse and say something more about coal."

I urged that we could get off the "merry-go-round" by appointing deputies who would narrow the points at issue and thus permit a more fruitful discussion at another session of the council. Mr. Molotov asked why I would not agree to holding a special session of the council in November.

"I have no objection to such a meeting," I replied, "but why put off until November what we can do today? What I fear is that when November comes and we propose to take up this question, the Soviet representative will suggest referring it to the deputies and another five months will pass before they get to work. I would like to get to work now."

We know now that this fear was fully justified. Mr. Molotov withheld agreement on the appointment of deputies for Germany until December 11 at the Council of Foreign Ministers meeting in New York. With Ambassador Robert D. Murphy representing the United States, the deputies met in London in January to hear the views of the smaller Allied nations who had fought against Germany and to consider the procedure for drafting a German peace treaty. We know what little progress was made at the meeting in Moscow during March and April 1947. The world now is looking toward the next meeting of the council scheduled for November, two and one-half years after the surrender of Germany, hoping for the first signs of genuine progress toward a settlement.

Chapter 10

A Course of Action

THE EARLY conclusion of peace treaties with Germany and Austria is essential to the restoration of Europe's political and economic health. The barriers of military zones, the burdens of military occupation, and the uncertainty of the future, all of which paralyze Europe's "heart land," cripple our friends and Allies as much as they bring indiscriminate punishment to Germany and Austria.

As this is written, it is almost two years since we gathered around the big table at Cecilienhof Palace in Potsdam, preparing what we believed would be an adequate blueprint for a lasting structure of peace. The blueprint has failed to fulfill our hopes. It is necessary, therefore, to evaluate the situation and plan a new course of action.

The most significant statement of Soviet policy toward Germany was made by Mr. Molotov in the Council of Foreign Ministers at Paris on July 10, 1946. The importance he attached to the speech is shown by the fact that it was released to the press in advance—an act as unusual for Soviet diplomats as it is routine for us. This first and still authoritative expression of Soviet atttude toward Germany is worthy of special note in any effort to plan for the future.

Mr. Molotov opened his speech with a strong appeal to the Germans— criticism of all suggestions that Germany should be transformed into a primarily agrarian state.

"It would be incorrect," he said, "to adopt the course of Germany's annihilation as a state or that of its agrarianization, including the annihilation of its main industrial centers." He reiterated the point in various ways. "Our purpose is not to destroy Germany," he went on, "but to transform Germany into a democratic and peace-loving state which, besides its agriculture, will have its own industry and foreign trade. . . . The policy of Germany's annihilation as a state or that of her agrarianization and annihilation of her principal industrial centers will result in making Germany a center where dangerous sentiments of revenge will be nourished and will play into the hands of German reactionaries and will deprive Europe of tranquility and peace."

Then he turned to the Ruhr, where he managed to create a two-headed horse.

Talk about the separation of the Ruhr from Germany originates "in the same policy of destruction and agrarianization of Germany, for it is easy to understand that, without the Ruhr, Germany cannot exist as an independent and viable state." But, he added, "the Ruhr should be placed under an interallied control of four countries with the object of preventing the revival of war industries in Germany." Thus he tried both to leave it and to take it away.

The future form of the German state was his next concern and he criticized the "fashionable" talk of splitting Germany into autonomous states and similar proposals, such as federalizing Germany. Allied authorities in the western zones, he said, "have encouraged the idea of a federal structure for Germany," without regard for the desires of the German people, while the Soviet Union holds "it is incorrect to impose upon the German people some one or other solution of this question." No action of this kind should be taken, no territory should be separated from Germany, except as a result of a plebiscite. He did not, of course, make any reference to the Soviet Union's support of Poland's claim for Silesia and all the territory east of the Oder and Neisse rivers.

"We should not put obstacles in the way of the increase in the output of steel, coal and manufactured products of a peaceful nature in Germany," he stated. He then mentioned the recent action of the Allied Control Council in fixing the levels at which German industries would be allowed to operate in the future, and added: "It should now be admitted that peaceful industries in Germany must be given an opportunity to develop on a wider scale. . . ." He avoided admitting that, when the levels of industry were fixed by the Control Council, the Soviet representative had voted for the lowest figure and it was only by the most urgent insistence of the American and British representatives that a higher figure was set.

He dealt finally with the question of a German peace treaty.

"Before talking about a peace treaty with Germany it is necessary to solve the question of setting up an all-German government. . . . But even when a German government has been set up *it will take a number of years* to check up on what this new German Government represents and whether it is trustworthy. . . . A future German Government must be such a democratic government as will be able to extirpate the remnants of Fascism in Germany and which will at the same time be able to fulfill Germany's obligations toward the Allies. Amongst other things and above all it will be bound to carry out reparation deliveries to the Allies. Only when we become satisfied that the new German Government is able to cope with these tasks and is really honestly fulfilling them in practice will it be possible to speak seriously of concluding a peace treaty with Germany."

Here, in this last statement, was confirmation of our fears that unless forced by world opinion to do so, the Soviet Union would not agree to a treaty of peace with Germany for years to come. They would utilize their veto power on the Allied Control Council and in the Council of Foreign Ministers to secure adoption of their conception of a "democratic" government; to secure a part in the control of German industry, the industries of the Ruhr in particular, and to enforce the payment of 10 billion dollars of reparations.

It was an effective speech. It was timed to win the favor of the German people who were about to vote in various municipal elections. Their dislike of the quietly enunciated claim for reparations was more than offset by his announced opposition to dismemberment and to cession of territory without approval by plebiscite. But the part of the statement that was particularly heartening to the Germans was that which denounced all proposals to annihilate German industry and to "agrarianize" the country. I realized at once the strength of this appeal. It was clearly calculated to play on the widespread German fear of the so-called "Morgenthau Plan," which had been widely discussed in the American press.

In October 1944, while the war was still in progress, I was in Paris. At the Guest House, where I lived, there was a sergeant who spoke German. Each night he would interpret for me the Berlin broadcasts; these invariably included an appeal to the people of Germany not to consider the proposals of the Allies to surrender. Surrender, they warned, meant enforcement of the "Morgenthau Plan" which would destroy all industry and turn Germany into an agricultural state. The plan was greatly exaggerated to inspire the Germans to fight and die rather than surrender. Molotov's speech was aimed at the German people who had listened to those broadcasts day after day, and had been educated to expect only the harshest treatment from the United States. He capitalized on the confusion in the minds of the German people about American policy.

I had to admit the effectiveness of the effort because there *had* been confusion in our own country on the policy of the United States toward Germany. The truth is, there had even been much confusion in the Cabinet on the subject.

My mind went back to an occasion at the White House, in the latter part of August 1944, when President Roosevelt had discussed the kind of peace he proposed for Germany. He said that some well-meaning but misguided officials of the State Department were planning what he regarded as a "soft" peace for Germany. That, he said, was not his plan.

The German people should be taught their responsibility for the war and for a long time should have only soup for breakfast, soup for lunch, and soup for dinner. It did not sound like President Roosevelt. He was angry.

About that time he appointed a Cabinet committee to consider the peace for Germany, consisting of the Secretary of State, Mr. Hull, the Secretary of the Treasury, Mr. Morgenthau, and the Secretary of War, Mr. Stimson.

There was a wide difference of opinion among the members of this Cabinet committee. On September 9, 1944, they held a meeting in the President's office which was also attended by Mr. Hopkins.

Secretary Stimson took the position that they were all trying to devise protection against a recurrence of attempts by Germany to dominate the world. They differed, he said, as to the method. He contended that Mr. Morgenthau's remedy would substantially obliterate the industry of Germany. He quoted Mr. Morgenthau's plan for the Ruhr and surrounding industrial areas as providing that:

"This area should not only be stripped of all presently existing industries but so weakened and controlled that it cannot in the foreseeable future become an industrial area—all industrial plants and equipment not destroyed by military action shall either be completely dismantled and removed from the area or completely destroyed, all equipment shall be removed from the mines and the mines shall be thoroughly wrecked."

These resources, Secretary Stimson argued, constitute a natural and necessary asset for the productivity of Europe. He urged that such assets should be conserved and made available for the benefit of the European continent. His thought was that the internationalization of the Ruhr or the trusteeship of its products would constitute a treatment of the problem in accord with the needs and interests of the world.

Secretary Stimson objected also to the proposal in Mr. Morgenthau's plan that so-called archcriminals should be put to death by the military without provision for any trial and upon mere identification after apprehension. Mr. Stimson contended that the procedure should embody at least the rudimentary aspects of the Bill of Rights. If these criminals were punished in a dignified manner consistent with the advance of civilization, he asserted, it would have a greater effect upon posterity.

About the same time, the President and Secretary Hull asked me to consider becoming the American High Commissioner for Germany. I had previously told the President of my desire to leave the Office of War Mobilization and Reconversion at the end of hostilities but this new proposal did not appeal to me. Nevertheless, I promised to consider it and to study the plan that had been outlined for the occupation. Mr. James Riddleberger, who has ably directed the administration of German affairs in the Department of State through the postwar period, brought me the plan for occupation and offered to answer any questions. It impressed me as intended to enforce a punitive peace somewhat along the lines suggested to the President by the Secretary of the Treasury. I shared the President's opposition to what he regarded as a "soft peace" but I thought the plan was unnecessarily harsh and not wise for the future of Europe.

One provision struck me particularly. Its phraseology was tantamount to saying that the principal war criminals should be tried and hanged. I asked if any consideration had been given to the possibility that some of those charged might be acquitted or that a mistrial might occur. Mr. Riddleberger agreed that the language was questionable. In justice to the State Department, he added, I should be informed that much of the plan, including that section, had been prepared by representatives of the Treasury Department. Shortly thereafter, I informed the President and Secretary Hull that I could not accept the appointment, since I did not think I was qualified for the task.

The difference in the Cabinet committee did not come to a head until President Roosevelt and Prime Minister Churchill met in Quebec in September 1944. Secretary Hull did not attend because, he told me, the President had said that only military matters would be discussed. There evidently was a change of plan because Secretary Morgenthau did attend. Nor did Secretary Stimson go, but after the meeting was under way he sent the President his views on the postwar program for Germany.

It developed that the Quebec Conference was very important. Agreements were reached, for example, on the zones to be occupied by the British and American forces in Germany. We accepted the southern zone after Mr. Churchill agreed that Bremerhaven in the British zone, should be made part of the American zone to insure us the use of a major port for the transportation of men and supplies.

Another important decision, on September 14, dealt with the continuation of a very generous lend-lease program to Britain during the war with Japan.

Differences arose about this agreement. In a memorandum handed the Secretary of State by the Secretary of the Treasury, on September 20, it was stated that "the President thought a committee should be set up and suggested that Mr. Morgenthau should head it, representing him, and that Mr. Stettinius who had taken such a large part in lend-lease should also be a member." However, the memorandum from the White House contained simply the record of the conversation in Quebec and did not include this paragraph. Mr. Leo T. Crowley, then in charge of Foreign Economic Administration, presumably was to administer lend-lease. Mr. Crowley and the President discussed carrying out lend-lease for the British. He said that the President had instructed him to continue administering lend-lease and to consider British requests as he considered all other requests and without regard to the Quebec agreement.

The question of how the lend-lease program for the British should be carried out did not become an acute controversy between the departments because of President Roosevelt's death and because of the short time that elapsed between the surrender in Europe and the Japanese surrender.

Mr. Churchill and Mr. Roosevelt, however, on September 15, had approved with their initials a memorandum on postwar Germany, which was subsequently called the "Morgenthau Plan." The President followed the views held by the Secretary of the Treasury instead of those held by the Secretaries of State and of War. The portion of the agreement which immediately attracted the attention of officials in Washington was the reference to the "metallurgical, chemical and electric industries in Germany." The memorandum stated that experience had shown that these industries could be converted from peace to war and that the governments which had suffered at the hands of the Germans should be entitled to remove the machinery they needed to repair their losses.

"The industries referred to in the Ruhr and in the Saar would, therefore, necessarily be put out of action and closed down," the memorandum stated. "It was felt that these two districts should be placed under somebody under the world organization which would supervise the dismantling of these industries and make sure they were not restored by subterfuge.

"This program for eliminating the war-making industries in the Ruhr and in the Saar is looking forward to converting Germany into a country primarily agricultural and pastoral in its character;

"The Prime Minister and the President were in agreement upon this programme."

Secretary Hull did not approve of this program. On September 25, he advised the President to effect a firm agreement with the governments of Great Britain and the Soviet Union on policy to be adopted regarding Germany, stating that we had followed a principle of placing matters of this kind on an agreed tripartite basis. As of that date, he added, the State Department had no indication that the British Government would be in favor of completely eradicating German industrial productive capacity in the Ruhr and Saar. He said he did not know the views of the Soviet Government.

It is difficult to understand how Mr. Churchill approved the memorandum of the "Morgenthau Plan." Certainly, later at Yalta, he deplored a peace that smacked of vengeance. And at Potsdam, he argued that heavy industries should not be reduced to a point that would necessitate financial assistance from other governments to maintain Germany's economy. After Potsdam, when the four powers agreed upon a level of industry for Germany, the British government advocated a higher level of production than any of the four powers.

It is equally difficult to understand President Roosevelt's attitude in view of what occurred immediately thereafter.

In reply to the Secretary of State, the President sent him a memorandum, dated September 29. However, it did not reach the State Department until October 2.

In it the President stated that he did not think any good purpose would be served at that stage by having the State Department, or any other department, sound out British and Russian views on the subject of German industry.

"The real nub of the situation," the President asserted, "is to keep Britain from going into complete bankruptcy at the end of the war." The President said that somebody had been giving statements to the newspapers "which are not fundamentally true." And, he added, "No one wants to make Germany a wholly agricultural nation again and yet somebody down the line has handed this out to the press. I wish we could catch and chastise him."

The President stated further that he could not go along with the idea of seeing the British Empire collapse financially while Germany at the same time was building up a potential rearmament to make another war possible in twenty years. While mere inspection of plants would not prevent this, the President concluded, "no one wants complete eradication of German industrial productive capacity in the Ruhr and Saar."

On the same day that the President's memorandum was written, September 29, Secretary Hull was submitting to the President a paper obviously drafted before the receipt of the President's message. Mr. Hull said:

"The Cabinet committee has not been able to agree upon a statement of American policy for the postwar treatment of Germany. The memorandum submitted by the Secretary of the Treasury is decidedly at variance with the views developed in the State Department. In the meantime I have received your memorandum of September 15 with the statement of views respecting the Ruhr, Saar, etc. and the conversion of Germany into an agricultural and pastoral country, which was formulated at Quebec. This memorandum seems to reflect largely the opinions of the Secretary of the Treasury in the treatment to be accorded Germany. I feel I should, therefore, submit to you a line of thought that has been developing in the State Department on this matter."

This, Secretary Hull followed with a statement of policy. In the economic section he stated that, among others, our objectives were to make Germany incapable of waging war and to eliminate German economic domination of Europe permanently. To achieve these two objectives, the Secretary said, it would be necessary (a) to destroy all war plants that could not be converted to peaceful purposes, and to prevent their reconstruction; and (b) to force conversion of all other war plants to the manufacture of peacetime goods.

Secretary Stimson seemed to share, in a general way, the views of Secretary Hull. In a conversation with the President he expressed his attitude. The President told Secretary Stimson that they were not far apart in their ideas, and that he had no intention of turning Germany into an agrarian state. The Secretary, however, called the President's attention to the language of the Quebec agreement stating that the program "is looking forward to converting Germany into a country primarily agricultural and pastoral in its character." Mr. Stimson had genuine affection for the President and great admiration for the part he had played throughout the war. He expressed the hope that the President would not approve a peace of vengeance. The President agreed with Mr. Stimson and told the Secretary of War he did not know how he had initialed that particular language in the Quebec agreement. It must have been done, he said, without much thought.

That the Quebec agreement on postwar Germany became a cause of considerable anxiety to the President is evident from the fact that the day before he wrote his long memorandum of September 29 to Secretary Hull, the President sent a memorandum to Mr. Crowley reading as follows:

"You have been making studies from the economic standpoint of what should be done after the surrender of Germany to control its power and its capacity to make war in the future. This work must be accelerated and, under the guidance of the Department of State, you should be furnished assistance in the work and when requested to do so, in personnel, by making available specialists to work with the military authorities, the Foreign Service, and such other American agencies, to see to it that Germany does not become a menace again to succeeding generations."

The President told Crowley he would make public the fact that he had requested him to make the study. Mr. Crowley's report was furnished to the State Department and considered in drafting the plan finally agreed upon.

The interdepartmental discussion on a German program continued until March 25, when a paper prepared by the State Department, after consultation with the Secretary of the Treasury and the Secretary of War, was signed by representatives of the three departments, and then was approved by President Roosevelt. This memorandum was used by Assistant Secretary of State Clayton when he represented us on the Economic Committee at Potsdam. It said nothing about making Germany an agricultural and pastoral state. Nor did Mr. Churchill, who had initialed the Quebec program, mention it to President Truman or to me. The fact is, it was not mentioned to us by anyone at Potsdam. There, our proposal formed the basis of the program of economic and political principles for Germany and was approved by the heads of government.

Mr. Molotov, of course, had learned from our press about the confusion in our government as a result of the agreement between President Roosevelt and Prime Minister Churchill at Quebec. Knowing how the German people feared any plan that would turn a nation of skilled industrial workers into a nation of farm workers, Mr. Molotov successfully played on those fears. The Soviet-controlled press in the Soviet zone misrepresented our views almost daily. Communist leaders in Berlin spread rumors that the United States was disgusted with the European situation and within a short while would withdraw its armed forces.

On July 11, the day following Mr. Molotov's significant declaration of Soviet policy toward Germany, I made a general statement of the American position. I made it brief because I wanted to keep attention focused on the immediate objectives of appointing deputies and putting them to work. I intended to withhold a detailed statement of our German policy until the Council of Foreign Ministers was prepared to act on the German question. Later I changed my mind. Since the Soviet delegation had forced a postponement of action on Germany until November, and since the Soviet campaign of misrepresentation in Germany continued, I decided to make a full statement of our German policy immediately. I did not think it proper to make such a declaration in Paris while the peace conference was in session; therefore, I decided to go to Germany and talk to the occupation forces, military and civilian, in the American zone. General Clay encouraged me to do this. He informed me that a policy statement in Germany would be very helpful to his organization and he quickly initiated arrangements for a meeting at Stuttgart.

At his request, we went first to Berlin where we took a train in order that, en route to Stuttgart, we might see the country and the destruction wrought by the war. We traveled in the train that the Nazi government had built for Hitler's personal use. It certainly was more luxuriously equipped than the train used for the President of the United States. Hitler's suite consisted of two rooms and a large lavender-tiled bathroom. Mrs. Byrnes and I felt a little strange in these rooms formerly occupied by Hitler and Eva Braun.

We welcomed the diversion of seeing the many American GIs who were in evidence all along the route. At one station there was a troop train on the opposite side of the platform and one of our boys was out on the steps of the train making a speech to some fifty or sixty Germans. I am sure they did not understand a word the youngster was saying, but that didn't discourage him. Suddenly he stopped in the middle of a sentence and flattered me by crying out, "Look who's here! Hi, Jimmy."

We arrived in Stuttgart shortly before noon on September 6. At the bomb-scarred station the minister-presidents of the districts of Württemberg, Bavaria and the Duchy of Hesse, in the American zone, were waiting to see us. I was anxious to meet them because they represented our first experiment in re-establishing local self-government and democratic processes in Germany. They reported the progress they were making and expressed a belief that the Germans in the British zone would like to have similar efforts at local self-government initiated but had not yet made much progress. Senator Connally and Senator Vandenberg asked them some questions. We spent half an hour with them and then proceeded to the Württemberg Staatstheater, the only large gathering place still standing in Stuttgart.

Generals McNarney and Clay had made every effort to provide an impressive setting for a declaration of American policy, but I am sure their plans did not include one item that was on the program. As I walked on the stage with General McNarney, Ambassador Murphy and the two Senators, the band was playing "Stormy Weather." I was tempted to ask the general if he had instructed the band to play symbolic music. General Clay, who seeks to avoid the spotlight, was seated in the audience.

I opened the speech by declaring that the American people have learned that we live in one world, that "peace and well-being are indivisible and that our peace and well-being cannot be purchased at the price of the peace and well-being of any other country.

"I hope the German people will never again make the mistake of believing that because the American people are peace loving, they will sit back hoping for peace if any nation uses force or the threat of force to acquire dominion over other people and other governments. . . . We intend to continue our interest in the affairs of Europe and of the world. We have helped to organize the United Nations. We believe it will stop aggressor nations from starting wars. Because we believe it, we intend to support the United Nations organization with all the power and resources we possess."

I then turned to the question of the kind of peace the United States believed should be enforced in Germany. We had long since, I said, stopped talking of a hard or a soft peace because what we wanted was a lasting peace. "We will oppose harsh and vengeful measures which obstruct an effective peace. We will oppose soft measures which invite the breaking of the peace."

We must first of all free Germany from militarism and give the German people an opportunity to "apply their great energies and abilities to the works of peace" and "in time, to take an honorable place among the members of the United Nations."

"It is not in the interest of the German people or in the interest of world peace that Germany should become a pawn or a partner in a military struggle for power between the East and the West."

With this general statement, I then turned to specific actions that were required. Germany should do her part to repair the devastation that had been inflicted on her neighbors twice in a generation. The United States wanted to see the Potsdam agreements on demilitarization and reparations fully carried out so that Germany's war potential would be reduced by the elimination of her war industries and by the reduction and removal of heavy industrial plants not required for her peacetime economy. This should not be carried so far as to deprive Germany of the levels of industry necessary to maintain average European living standards without assistance from other countries.

"In fixing the levels of industry no allowance was made for reparations from current production," I stated. "Reparations from current production would be wholly inconsistent with the levels of industry now established under the Potsdam agreement," and I then added that the United States would not agree to greater reparations payments than those agreed on at Potsdam.

The Potsdam agreements had not been carried out, I explained, because the Allied Control Council had been unable to agree on the treatment of Germany as an economic unit. It was impossible to achieve the standards set by the Allied Council in the absence of economic unity. It was the American view, I added, that central German administrative agencies should be established to develop a common financial policy; and a nation-wide organization of transportation, industry and foreign trade.

"Germany must be given a chance to export goods in order to import enough to make her economy self-sustaining," the speech continued. "Germany is a part of Europe, and European recovery, particularly in Belgium, the Netherlands and other adjoining states will be slow indeed if Germany with her great resources of iron and coal is turned into a poor house."

With this statement of economic principles, I turned to the political sphere. The purposes of the occupation did not contemplate "a prolonged alien dictatorship" of German economy or political life, but rather the building of a political democracy "from the ground up." We believed the German people should be given primary responsibility for running their local affairs. We should administer them so that the political structure would be decentralized and local responsibility developed. We do not believe, I stressed, "that large armies of alien soldiers or alien bureaucrats, however well motivated and disciplined, are in the long run the most reliable guardians of another country's democracy." We wanted the Allied governments to lay down the general rules "under which German democracy can govern itself" so that Allied occupation forces could be limited "to a number sufficient to see those rules are obeyed." That was why, I explained, we had proposed a treaty that would make certain a force would be available for a twenty-five or forty year period to insure that Germany did not rearm. I then made a statement that the army newspaper, *Stars and Stripes,* described as being "just what the doctor ordered."

"Security forces will probably have to remain in Germany for a long period. I want no misunderstanding. We will not shirk our duty. We are not withdrawing. We are staying here and will furnish our proportionate share of the security forces."

Meanwhile, we favored the early establishment of a provisional government, which "should not be hand picked by other governments" but which should be composed of "democratically responsible" chief officials of the several states or provinces established in each of the four zones. Under the authority of the Control Council, this government should see that the central administrative agencies functioned properly and it should prepare a draft of a federal constitution.

"The time has also come to define the boundaries of the new Germany," I continued. Austria already was recognized as a free and independent country. At Potsdam, the heads of government had agreed to support the Soviet desire for the transfer to Russia of the city of Königsberg. As for Silesia and other eastern areas, I pointed out that their transfer to Poland for administrative purposes had been made by the Soviet Union before the Potsdam meeting. But, I emphasized, the Protocol of the Potsdam Conference makes clear "the heads of government did not agree to support at the peace settlement the cession of any particular area." We did agree at Yalta that territory east of the Curzon Line should be transferred from Poland to Russia, and we did believe that there should be a compensating revision of Poland's northern and western frontiers. The extent of the area to be ceded, however, "must be determined when the final settlement is agreed upon."

We could not deny the right of France to the Saar, I said, but so far as the Ruhr and Rhineland were concerned, "the United States will not support any encroachment on territory which is indisputably German or any division which is not genuinely desired by the people concerned." We were determined that the resources of these regions must never again be used for destructive purposes. We, therefore, will "favor such controls over the whole of Germany, including the Ruhr and Rhineland, as may be necessary for security purposes" but "will not favor any controls that would subject the Ruhr and Rhineland to the political domination or manipulation of outside powers."

I closed the speech by declaring that the German people must realize it was German arms that had sought "to dominate and degrade the world." The United States consequently could not "relieve Germany from the hardships inflicted upon her by the war her leaders had started," but we would seek to give the German people "an opportunity to work their way out of these hardships so long as they respect human freedom and cling to the paths of peace."

As I finished, the army band struck up our national anthem and the entire audience, including the German leaders, rose to their feet. The place, the occasion and particularly the audience of civilian and military occupation authorities made it an especially moving moment. As the last notes died away, Senator Vandenberg, who had been away from the United States many weeks, turned to me and said, "The 'Star Spangled Banner' never before gave me such a thrill."

This declaration of American policy was given wide publicity in the American and British zones, and to a slightly lesser degree in the French zone. A German translation was superimposed over my voice in a radio transmission carried by radio stations in all except the Soviet zone. In the Soviet zone, the Soviet-licensed newspapers, with one exception, ran the story on the second page, and the longest reference to it was 140 lines.

After a short delay, the Communist-controlled press throughout Europe launched a campaign of severe criticism. In Poland, the declaration on the Polish-German frontier especially was attacked. It was claimed that the United States was violating an agreement reached at Potsdam. But the facts clearly showed otherwise. It will be remembered that, when we complained about the unilateral action of the Soviets in assigning a portion of their zone to Poland, Stalin told the President "the western frontier question is open, and the Soviet Union is not bound," and the final protocol stated: "The three heads of government reaffirmed their opinion that the final delimitation of the western frontier of Poland should await the peace settlement." Stalin's statement to the President was true when he made it, but, on August 16, just fifteen days after the signatures were affixed to the Potsdam Protocol, the Soviet Union concluded a treaty with Poland which recognized the Oder-Neisse line as the western boundary of Poland.

The Stuttgart speech made it impossible for the Soviets to continue talking one way to the Poles and another way to the Germans. Forced to choose, they announced they would support Poland's claim to the territory. German leaders then asserted that this stand was in conflict with promises made to them and much of the support of the Communist cause in Germany began melting away. I am confident that, as a result of our statement of policy, the sphere of influence the Soviets had hoped to extend into Berlin was moved back into Polish-controlled territory.

Upon our return to Paris, representatives of several European governments expressed to me their approval of the American program for Germany. Mr. Bevin was among those who offered congratulations. He said the program was substantially that which the British were prepared to offer. Mr. Molotov never mentioned the subject, but from what some of his staff were quoted as saying, my speech received no applause at the Soviet Embassy.

From Switzerland, Winston Churchill sent a message of congratulations and, as he was stopping in Paris en route to London about a week later, asked if we could meet. I immediately informed the British Ambassador that I would be happy to come to the Embassy to see Mr. Churchill. The Ambassador was anxious to keep Mr. Churchill's presence in Paris a secret. Mr. Churchill, who had just received a great ovation in Geneva and in Brussels, was not hiding from anyone and seemed irked by the steps taken to insure secrecy. I shared his irritation. To this day I do not know the reason for the secrecy, but I co-operated with the Ambassador, and, to my surprise, he succeeded in keeping the visit a secret. I scarcely suspected I could get away from the Hotel Meurice, go to the British Embassy, and spend two hours with Mr. Churchill, without being detected by the watchful eyes and ears of the exceedingly alert American correspondents. The only explanation was that it was Saturday afternoon and our correspondents had adopted the French habit of declaring a holiday for that afternoon. It was even more difficult for me to understand how Ambassador Duff Cooper with only grudging co-operation from Mr. Churchill could get the former Prime Minister in and out of Paris without the press knowing it.

Mr. Churchill simply wanted to state his approval of the American stand at Stuttgart and to discuss current problems. He did not criticize any official of His Majesty's Government, but I gathered that, as leader of the opposition, he was not informed about what was happening in Britain's foreign relations and he was not happy about it. We talked of many things. Toward the end of our conversation, Field Marshal Smuts called, and we continued our discussion of world problems. Then I left these two great men. May they never grow old.

To some of the political leaders of France, the Stuttgart speech was disappointing because of our stand against separation of the Ruhr and the Rhineland, and our insistence on central administrative agencies. They were, however, gratified at our pledge to support French claims to the Saar at the peace conference, and by the positive declaration that we intended to keep in Germany our proportion of occupation forces.

Because of the reaction of some French leaders, I accepted the opportunity offered by the American Club in Paris to emphasize further our determination to help maintain European stability and peace, in a speech I delivered on October 3.

"The people of the United States did their best to stay out of European wars on the theory that they should mind their own business and that they had no business in Europe," I stated. "It did not work. The people of the United States have discovered that when a European war starts, our own peace and security inevitably become involved before the finish. They have concluded that if they must help finish every European war, it would be better for them to do their part to prevent the starting of an European war."

I then urged upon the French the value of our proposed forty-year treaty. The United States, I stressed, not only wanted to see Germany disarmed and demilitarized before the peace settlement but also wanted to make sure that Germany would remain disarmed and demilitarized for forty years *after* the peace settlement.

"So long as such a treaty is in force," I said, "the Ruhr could never become the arsenal of Germany or the arsenal of Europe. That is a primary objective of the proposed treaty.

"The United States is firmly opposed to the revival of Germany's military power. It is firmly opposed to a struggle for the control of Germany which would again give Germany the power to divide and conquer. It does not want to see Germany become a pawn or a partner in a struggle for power between the East and the West."

I also explained we were seeking to develop a sense of local responsibility in Germany so that the people would look to the states rather than to the central government.

"We want to see the federal government of Germany created by the states, and not the states created by the central government."

The speech helped to reassure the people of France that the United States wanted to see a Germany created that would respect the freedom of her own inhabitants and would not threaten the security of her neighbors, particularly the security of France.

The Stuttgart speech, Secretary Marshall announced at Moscow in the spring of 1947, continues to represent American policy toward Germany.

The policy of the Soviet Union also remains as it was revealed by Mr. Molotov at Paris in July 1946. The last day of that session of the council, and two days after Mr. Molotov's pronouncement on Soviet policy toward Germany, Mr. Cohen, Mr. Bohlen and I were the dinner guests of the Soviet Foreign Minister. At the end of the dinner I told him that, since he had known beforehand he would not agree to starting work on the German and Austrian treaties, I deeply regretted that he had not come to me and frankly told me so. We would thus have prevented much heated debate which did not accomplish anything but was calculated to do harm. In a perfectly disarming way, he agreed that I was right and said it would have been better if the debate had not taken place.

"Why, then," I asked, "don't you tell me what is really in your heart and mind on the subject of Germany?"

The Soviet Union, Molotov replied, wanted what it had asked for at Yalta—10 billions of dollars in reparations, and also participation with the United States, the United Kingdom and France *in a four-power control of the industries of the Ruhr*.

Since that time there has been much speculation on the ambitions of the Soviet Union in Germany. Soviet representatives probably will make many other claims for themselves and the satellites, but I am sure the statement made by Molotov that night represents the real desires of the Soviet High Command.

Of the two demands, the Russians have greater interest in participating in the control of the Ruhr industries. The coal and iron of that area cause the Soviets to regard it as the arsenal of Europe. They want to share in all decisions on the allocation of Ruhr products. Our experience in the Allied Control Council demonstrates how impractical this proposal is. For over two years the Control Council has been trying to come to some agreement on relations between the zones. The members of the Control Council have had just as much difficulty in reaching agreements as have the Foreign Ministers. We can find another example in Korea, where we are supposed to have a joint administration with the Russians. Only in June were we able to resume discussions that were discontinued a year ago because of our inability to agree. If it is impossible to reach agreements on any front, except after months of discussion, it would not be practical for the four powers to control the various industries of the Ruhr. They would be able to agree upon few questions connected with any industry. Four-power control would be an effective way of destroying the industries of the Ruhr, which, properly supervised, are vital to an economically healthy Europe.

During discussions on the Ruhr, France indicated that it favored control by the Allied governments of western Europe. France did not mention participation by the Soviet Union. The idea of the Soviets agreeing to any international supervision of the Ruhr which does not include them is so unrealistic it has not been seriously discussed by other governments.

The industries of the Ruhr should be considered in the peace treaty along with the rest of Germany's industries. When a treaty is agreed upon, the control of German industries should be turned back to the owners. Our interest and our duty is to see that these industries are not thereafter converted to the manufacture of weapons of war. That can be done by the kind of joint inspection contemplated in the forty-year treaty I have proposed. I think this is one of several reasons why the Soviets oppose the treaty. They know there are many people who have advocated international control of the Ruhr industries. If the forty-year treaty should be agreed to, most of these people would be satisfied, and it would lessen the Soviet's chances of getting hold of the Ruhr industries.

Wisdom and justice will prevent the United States from ever acceding to the Soviet demands either on the Ruhr or on reparations. Mr. Molotov, however, has said these are essential prerequisites to any peace settlement. Since we believe an early peace settlement is of vital importance to the restoration of stability throughout Europe, we are forced to consider what we must do.

The first step already has been taken. At Paris, on July 11, 1946, I announced the action which we had determined to take only as a last resort—the merger of the zones of occupation, with or without the Soviet Union.

I began by expressing the hope that the council would agree "at this meeting" to the establishment of the central German administrative agencies necessary to secure economic unity in Germany. To satisfy Mr. Bidault's fears, I stated that we would agree to the continuation of French administration of the Saar until Germany's western boundaries were determined. But if, I added, the council could not agree to these central agencies, the United States "as a last resort makes another suggestion." I declared that no zone of Germany was fully self-sustaining and the treatment of any two zones as an economic unit would improve conditions in both zones. I pointed out that officials in our zone had recently discussed common agricultural policies with British officials for the exchange of some products.

"Pending agreement among the four powers to implement the Potsdam agreement requiring the administration of Germany as an economic unit," I announced, "the United States will join with any other occupying government or governments in Germany for the treatment of our respective zones as an economic unit.

"The continuation of the present situation will result in inflation and economic paralysis. It will result in increased costs to the occupying powers and unnecessary suffering to the German people. The United States is unwilling to share the responsibility for the continuance of such conditions. We feel it our duty to exhaust every effort to secure the co-operation of the occupying powers in administering Germany as an economic unit."

The following morning, Mr. Bevin announced that His Majesty's Government would agree in principle to the American merger proposal. General Clay, in Berlin, then began negotiations with Lieutenant General Sir Brian Robertson representing the United Kingdom; these continued until the meeting of the Council of Foreign Ministers in New York.

During the negotiations in Berlin and Washington, agreement was reached on all questions except one—the share of the annual deficit which should be borne by each government. The deficit in the American zone for 1947 was estimated at 200 million dollars and that for the British zone was placed at 400 million. Both the American and British representatives believed the deficit would be progressively reduced and that the merged zone could be made self-sustaining in three years. In these terms, the issue was placed before Mr. Bevin and me.

Officials of the British Treasury contended, Mr. Bevin told me, that Britain did not have the necessary dollars to meet the deficit for the next three years and he therefore urged the United States to carry 60 per cent of the burden. I replied that, in view of the much larger deficit in the British zone, we were assuming an additional 100 million dollars anyway when we agreed to an even division and that we, therefore, could not approve the 60 per cent suggestion. Our representatives in Germany might be mistaken in their self-confidence, I added, but they firmly believed that, if they had charge of the British zone with its industries and coal mines, they would wipe out most, if not all, of the deficit. I then proposed quite seriously that we would pay 60 per cent of the total deficit if Britain would exchange zones with us.

With a smile, Mr. Bevin replied, "You know His Majesty's Government would not agree to that." I admitted that I had doubted that Britain would want to trade their heavily industrialized zone and its rich natural resources for our largely scenic and agricultural zone. I pointed out, however, that my suggestion would provide him with a good answer to make to the British Treasury officials, who were pressing him. He then agreed to an even division of the cost. I thought it unwise for Britain to be put in the position of a poor relative or a junior partner by contributing less than 50 per cent. They are a proud people. It would be apt to cause irritations. It seemed much better to aid Britain in some other way.

The difficulties of the British in meeting the estimated deficit in their zone should not be minimized. When they were negotiating for the loan we made them in the spring of 1946, they had not counted on having to use dollars to provide food for Germans. This was a large, unforeseen drain on their dollar balances. This fact, quite correctly, I believe, influenced my judgment on another point: the date on which we would begin to pool exports from the merged zones. I supported the British contention and the resulting decision will save them 30 million dollars.

I had hoped the French would join us in the merger. That was one of the reasons I announced our decision in regard to the Saar. The French wanted the Soviets to agree to the Saar proposal also, but Mr. Molotov reiterated his opposition. This was disappointing because I knew the French coalition government would be hesitant to join us in a move that certainly would offend the large French Communist Party. The French Communists were greatly embarrassed by Mr. Molotov's refusal to assist a universally supported French objective, and would have welcomed another issue to divert attention from the Russian stand on the Saar. Subsequently, in September 1946, I advised the French Government in writing that, in the peace settlement, we would support the claim of France to this region. The United Kingdom extended a similar assurance. But the Government of France did not join us.

It is my hope that the French, before long, will accept our invitation, which is a continuing one, and merge their zone and its 6 million people with the British and American zones, where there is hope of making 46 million people self-supporting within three years. The offer remains open to the Soviet Union as well, so that all four powers may carry out the Potsdam pledge to treat Germany as an economic whole.

Allied co-operation, however, is not a part of the Soviet program and Soviet officialdom has greeted the merger with loud protests. Probably no other single event since the end of the war has been so bitterly and continually attacked by Moscow. It is a signal to the Soviet officials that the veto they have exercised so effectively since Potsdam is no longer inviolate. It is evidence that we refuse to follow indefinitely a course that conforms only to Mr. Molotov's conception of what is best. It is a demonstration that the western powers are willing to act in support of their interests and what they believe to be the interests of the vast majority of European peoples, and also of the Soviet Union.

Our next action must be the conclusion of treaties with both Germany and Austria. The key to the problem is Germany.

By July 1946, the best agreement I had been able to obtain on the preparation of a peace treaty with Germany was a promise to consider the question in New York in December. In New York, the best we could do was to agree to take up the German and Austrian questions at a meeting in Moscow in March of 1947. After six weeks of negotiation in Moscow, the German question was virtually where it had been the previous July. The Ministers adjourned to meet again, in November 1947, to resume the discussion. Unless the Soviet Union changes its position by November, there will be no agreement except to adjourn to another date in 1948. Secretary Marshall, Mr. Bevin and Mr. Bidault did everything in their power at Moscow to reach agreement on questions of importance. They were unsuccessful because of Soviet opposition.

We must bear in mind Mr. Molotov's statement at Paris on July 11, 1946, that "even when a German government is formed, *several years* must elapse before it would be wise to sign a treaty with them." We must also recall his further statement that there is no necessity for us to hurry; that "we should spend the next year thinking about what should be done with Germany."

Nor should we forget what happened during the consideration of the treaty with Italy and the Balkan states. At Moscow, in December 1945, we agreed after long argument that a peace conference would be held at Paris not later than May 1, 1946. At Paris, after long discussion, Mr. Molotov took the position that, notwithstanding this agreement, invitations to a peace conference could not be issued until the Council of Foreign Ministers unanimously agreed upon all provisions of the treaties the Soviet Union regarded as fundamental. We argued that we should issue the invitations, agree as far as possible, and then submit to the conference those questions still unsettled when the conference convened. In this way, the Soviet representative has the power to deny the Allied nations not members of the Council of Foreign Ministers even the opportunity to consider a treaty with an enemy state until every question that the Soviet Union considers important has been settled to its satisfaction.

World opinion may force the council at its forthcoming session in November 1947, at London, to give serious consideration to the German question blocked by the Soviet Union at the last meeting in Moscow. But we must realize that even then the Soviets will exercise the same veto weapon to obtain concessions from the United Kingdom, France and the United States before they will agree to issue invitations for a peace conference.

We have had one experience of this kind. It is enough to last for a long, long time. The Indian was right when he said: "Fool me once, shame on you; fool me twice, shame on me."

Because I first proposed to President Truman that the Council of Foreign Ministers be established as the machinery to prepare drafts of all the peace treaties, one will realize how reluctant I am to conclude that it can no longer serve the purpose for which it was established. In proposing it, I assumed that all the members of the council would be anxious to secure peace. We accepted the idea that there should be unanimous agreement among the members of the Council. We never conceived that such a worthy principle would be employed by one member of the Council to enforce his views on all the others. We did not conceive it because we assumed that we were all animated by a common purpose, the early restoration of peace. Now I am not sure that is true. And, if the leaders of the Soviet Union continue in every possible way to delay the restoration of peace, and continue to keep their troops in Germany, in Austria, and in the adjoining states through which they maintain lines of communication to Germany and Austria, other means of making peace will have to be found.

There are more controversial problems involved in the German settlement than in all the Italian and Balkan treaties. Consequently, it would be easy for any member of the council to delay the work and to give plausible reasons for the delay.

Even if we cleared these hurdles and made such concessions that invitations to a peace conference could be issued, we still would not be heading down a clear track. The Paris Peace Conference was in session from July 29 to October 15, 1946, and we may safely assume that a peace conference for Germany will continue much longer. Then, if our previous course is followed, the recommendations of the peace conference will be submitted to the Council for a final decision on which of the recommendations are to be included in the treaty.

Viewed in this light, the procedure we have followed, under the most favorable circumstances we can presently imagine, places prospects for a peace settlement in Europe in the far distant future. In the interest of peace and security, of the economic and political well-being of millions of people in Allied as well as ex-enemy states, we cannot permit such prolonged delay.

Secretary of State Marshall, during the meeting of the council in Moscow, announced that if agreement could not be reached soon on a treaty for Austria, the United States would consider submitting the problem to the General Assembly of the United Nations, for recommendations under Article 14 of the Charter. I understood his attitude and sympathized with him. Confronted with a similar situation during discussions on the Italian and Balkan treaties, I made a similar statement in my radio report to the American people after the first Paris session of the Council of Foreign Ministers.

Upon further consideration, however, I concluded that this course could not be helpful. The Charter of the United Nations does not give the General Assembly power to take action. It has power only to recommend. Formerly, I had hoped that if the General Assembly made recommendations, the power of world opinion, as reflected in those recommendations, would induce the Soviet Union to accept them. Now I am inclined to believe this would not occur.

The Soviet Union would argue to the world that the recommendations were made by an Assembly which includes among its members many states that were not even at war with Germany. The Soviet spokesmen would point out that determination of important and controversial questions, such as control of the Ruhr, would be decided by the votes of South American states, Arab states, and other smaller states which made no substantial military contributions to the defeat of the German armies. To make the General Assembly of the United Nations the center of such a controversy would be to place upon it a burden it was not intended to bear. Rebuff would seriously impair its prestige and undermine it in the confidence of the people of the world.

We should adopt another course of action. The United States should ask those powers that constitute the Council of Foreign Ministers, including, of course, the Soviet Union, to agree to the holding of a peace conference early in 1948.

At Moscow, Secretary Marshall proposed that the next peace conference should include all the states at war. He suggested that a resolution, to be adopted, must receive not only two-thirds of all votes cast but also two-thirds of the votes of the states that made military contributions. This proposal is in accord with the objective we held from the outset—participation in the making of the peace by all the United Nations that helped to win the war. At the same time, the proposed voting procedure would prevent the states that made only economic contributions from having an undue amount of power in the conference.

If one member of the Council of Foreign Ministers rejects our proposal for an early peace conference, the other members should proceed to call it. They should do it in such a manner that the way would be left open for the dissenting member of the council to join and to become one of the sponsoring powers if it should later decide to do so. France, for example, chose not to be one of the sponsoring powers for the San Francisco Conference although it later became one of the permanent members of the Security Council. As in that case, the other powers should continue to urge the dissenting power, or powers, to join them in sponsoring and sharing in the peace conference.

Each of the sponsoring powers should be asked to prepare treaty drafts for the peace conference. Undoubtedly, they would try to agree on as many clauses as possible before the conference. It has been nearly two and a half years since the German surrender and during that time the German question has been discussed by the four powers time and time again. At Potsdam, three of the Big Four discussed and concluded agreements on political and economic principles and reparations. The French have formulated and expressed their views at length. If, after all this, the four powers don't know what their positions are, they never will.

In the Paris Conference we have ample precedent for handling these drafts and all other questions of procedure. As at Paris, the conference should appoint, from its membership, commissions to consider different phases of the treaty drafts submitted by the sponsoring powers. There would, for example, be a commission to consider political questions, one for economic questions, and another for military questions. If desired, subsidiary bodies could be set up to consider different phases of these issues. These commissions could then prepare drafts of those sections of the treaty within their jurisdiction. In this way, all the states that fought the war against Hitler would have a part in drafting the treaty. If we are going to hold a peace conference ultimately and have a treaty considered by commissions, as we did at Paris, why not hold it now?

We must make it plain that we are not trying to make a separate peace or to dictate the terms of the peace. We would not attempt to force the acceptance of any particular plan. We would submit our plan and urge the British, the French and the Soviet Union to submit plans as well. The members of the conference could then make their decision.

In view of our experience we must face the possibility that the Soviet Union may refuse to join its war partners in a peace conference. This would indeed be disheartening to the peace-loving people of the world and every sober-minded person must hope that this will not occur. The possibility need not, however, stop us from initiating the course I suggest.

By the time the conference takes place, the merged British-American zone probably will be operating successfully. I hope, in addition, that the 46 million people in this merged zone will by that time be joined by the 6 million people of the French zone, if not those of the Soviet zone. The treaty of peace can be signed by the government or governments in the zones that have been unified.

There are, in fact, several ways in which German ratification could be obtained. At Moscow, Secretary Marshall proposed that when a constitution is presented to the German people for approval in a plebiscite, they should also be asked to vote on a directive to whatever government is established to accept an Allied peace treaty. This is a good proposal. If it is not agreed to, we might then consider submitting the treaty itself to a plebiscite. The German people then would have to decide whether to accept the treaty or continue to live indefinitely under military government and military occupation.

It may be objected that the latter course creates the impression that the treaty must be acceptable to the German people. But I think such an impression would be offset by removing from the accepted German government the political handicap of having negotiated a treaty that many Germans will probably regard as oppressive. I do not believe, however, that they will consider it as oppressive as the continuation of the present situation.

Before acting without the Soviet Union, we should once again invite the Soviet Government to join us in the treaty.

That treaty, like the treaties with Italy and the Balkan states, should provide that a country that does not sign it shall not share in any of its benefits. If the Soviet Union declines to sign the treaty, it certainly should not receive any further reparations payments from the western zones and should receive none of the other benefits that would surely accrue to them as a result of the settlement.

One may say: But suppose the Soviet Union declines to sign the treaty, what then?

If Soviet troops are withdrawn from Germany, no action by other nations will be necessary. But if the Red Army is not withdrawn, we must, as a last resort, go to the Security Council of the United Nations. The problem then will no longer be one of drafting peace treaties—a function the United Nations was never intended to perform. We will then be facing a situation likely to endanger the peace—the kind of situation the United Nations *was* created to meet.

The Soviet Union has declared its adherence to the Atlantic Charter which states that none of the signatories seek territorial aggrandizement. The Soviet Union has solemnly pledged in the United Nations Charter to refrain "from the threat of force or use of force against the territorial integrity or political independence of any state, or in any other manner inconsistent with the Purposes of the United Nations."

Eastern Germany, like all other parts of Germany, is to be held by armies of occupation temporarily and only until a treaty of peace is agreed upon. For the Soviets to keep troops there after an overwhelming number of the Allied nations have reached a peace settlement would be evidence of their intention to hold indefinitely territory allotted to them only for the period of occupation. Such action would constitute a threat to the peace of the world and the United Nations should therefore require the Soviet Union to withdraw from Germany.

But, one may add, the Soviet Union will veto any action by the Security Council.

Because I do not believe it is wise to suggest a course of action unless one is willing to carry it through, it is proper to discuss the contingency that might arise. We should not start something we are not prepared to finish.

First of all, let me say I do not believe the Soviet Union will force us to take measures of last resort. The Soviet Government will not, I believe, remain away from the peace conference and thus isolate itself from the rest of the world. If it should, I do not believe the Red Army would try to hold permanently all of eastern Germany. However, if I misjudge them, and they do go to the point of holding eastern Germany and vetoing a Security Council directive to withdraw occupation forces, we must be prepared to assume the obligations that then clearly will be ours. If our action is to be effective, we must be clear in our own minds and must make it clear to all that we are willing to adopt these measures of last resort if, for the peace of the world, we are forced to do so.

By "we" I do not mean the United States alone. The United States wants no separate peace. We trod that path once before. We want to make the peace collectively—with all the Allies if possible. But if it is not possible to secure the co-operation of all states, we should seek to enlist the assistance of as many as are willing to join in the task.

In the Charter of the United Nations, all of us have pledged "to unite our strength to maintain international peace and security" and "to take effective collective measures for the prevention and removal of threats to the peace, and for the suppression of acts of aggression or other breaches of the peace." A veto by one member does not relieve the rest of us of these obligations. They are pledges we must be prepared to fulfill.

I hope, believe, and I pray that the leaders of the Soviet Union will never force us to this course of last resort. But they must learn what Hitler learned—that the world is not going to permit one nation to veto peace on earth.

Chapter II

Toward Peace in Asia

WE MUST never forget that World War II began in the Pacific.

The first scene of the drama that ended on board the USS *Missouri* on September 1, 1945, took place in Manchuria in the same month in 1931. The scenes that followed were of varying interest to us in the United States—Italy's invasion of Ethiopia in 1935, civil war in Spain in 1936, Japan's attack on China in 1937, the fall of Austria and Czechoslovakia in 1938, and Hitler's invasion of Poland in 1939. But all of them led us inexorably to the tragic action at Pearl Harbor on December 7, 1941.

If we regard Europe as the tinderbox of possible world conflagration, we must look upon Asia as a great smoldering fire. There, civilization faces the task of bringing a huge mass of humanity, the majority of the people on this earth, from the Middle Ages into the era of atomic energy.

In China, unfortunately, the end of one war has brought the beginning of another. Our most earnest efforts there, for the present at least, have failed. But Japan has made heartening progress toward matching in the political, economic, and social fields its earlier swift absorption of the technical aspects of modern civilization.

The feudalistic control of Japan's economy by a few families has been proscribed; state religion and the worship of the Emperor as a deity have been abolished; the right of the people to organize and to elect their representatives freely has been established. These, and similar changes are a start toward a democratic society; they and the speed with which they have been effected is in contrast to the usually slow tempo of human affairs. Much of this progress is due to the wise administration of General Douglas MacArthur. Some of it comes, I believe, from our decision to continue the institution of the Emperor under our own conditions and to use it as an instrument for carrying out the instructions and policies of the Supreme Allied Commander.

Immediately upon becoming Secretary of State, I learned about the differences of opinion in the State Department as to whether, at the time of surrender, we should insist on the removal of the Emperor. Before we left for Potsdam, I was presented with memoranda setting forth

the varying views. These went into a brief case bulging with the problems
of war and peace in the Pacific.

President Truman and Generalissimo Stalin discussed Russia's entry
into the war against Japan at their first meeting on July 17. The Generalissimo said he had not yet succeeded in reaching an agreement with the
Chinese—a prerequisite to the Soviet declaration of war. He told the
President that his negotiations with Premier T. V. Soong would be resumed again after the conference. Among the questions still unsettled
was a regime for the port of Dairen. President Truman declared that the
United States wanted to make sure Dairen was maintained as an open
port. Stalin replied that, if the Soviet Union obtained control of the port,
it would have that status. I pointed out that, under the agreement President Roosevelt had entered into at Yalta, China was to retain control
of Dairen.

We received a report that Soong had told his government the Soviet
Union was making claims extending beyond the Yalta agreement. Since
the negotiations were taking place in accordance with a commitment made
by President Roosevelt, I was interested. I was afraid Soong would find
it difficult to resist Soviet pressure and would make additional concessions
if he were in doubt about our attitude. Therefore, with the approval of
the President, I sent a message to the Chinese Government saying we
would not advise making any concessions that went beyond the terms of
the Yalta agreement.

The Chinese and Russians subsequently reached agreement, but events
have shown that our concern about Dairen was justified. Two years after
Japan's defeat, Dairen still is not a free port. Before a ship can enter the
port, it is necessary to obtain clearance from Moscow, not only for the
vessel but also for its personnel.

At a later meeting Stalin told the President and me that the Japanese
Ambassador in Moscow had asked whether the Soviet Union would agree
to act as a mediator to bring about the settlement of the war. This request,
Stalin said, did not indicate a willingness to surrender unconditionally as
the Allies demanded; it was phrased so generally that Mr. Molotov simply told the Ambassador that he would discuss the matter with him later.
Subsequently, Stalin said, the Japanese Ambassador presented another
message. This stated that the Emperor wished to send Prince Konoye to
Moscow with a message saying that Japan wanted to end the war but
had decided to fight on with all its strength as long as unconditional surrender was demanded. Stalin added that a letter was then sent to the
Ambassador stating that the character of the indicated message was general, contained no specific proposal, and therefore it was impossible to
give a definite reply. President Truman expressed his approval of Stalin's
action.

Meanwhile, Secretary Stimson informed us that he had received reports from New Mexico on the test of the atomic bomb on July 16. The reports made it clear that the bomb had met our highest hopes and that the shock of its use would very likely knock our already wavering enemy out of the war. Before the experiment we had agreed that, if it proved a success, we would not use it without issuing a final solemn warning to the Japanese.

Secretary of War Stimson, on July 2, had submitted to the President a wise memorandum setting forth a proposed message to Japan. Using this memorandum as a basis, the President prepared a draft of a declaration to be issued jointly by the United States, the United Kingdom and China. The President and I spent some time on it. Then Prime Minister Churchill made some suggestions which were adopted. The declaration to which Mr. Churchill agreed followed the general lines of Secretary Stimson's proposal except that it did not contain a reference to the future status of the Emperor. The proposed declaration then was sent to Chiang Kai-shek for his approval.

On Thursday, July 26, the conference recessed to enable Mr. Churchill and Mr. Attlee to go to London to receive the results of the British election. President Truman utilized the opportunity for a trip to the headquarters of the American zone of occupation at Frankfurt. I accompanied him. Wherever the President reviewed troops abroad, commanding officers managed to have the band play "The Missouri Waltz," and presented to the President the Missourians among the commissioned officers of the outfit. Like all Senators and ex-Senators, the President is "state conscious." He liked it, and by the end of the day he had almost concluded Missouri had won the war. He enjoyed making to me the facetious charge that South Carolina had not participated in the war. The President rode in an open car, first with Brigadier General Doyle O. Hickey and later with Major General A. G. Bolling, commanding the Third Armored and the 84th Infantry Divisions. After each stop he would tell these officers that I had not yet found any South Carolinians among the troops. Finally, Pfc. Warren E. Baker, who was driving the President's car, could stand it no longer. He swung around in the driver's seat and said:

"Mr. President, I would like to say that I am from South Carolina, and I live just around the corner from the Secretary of State."

The President laughed heartily and at the next stop told me the story. He liked the courage of the young private in telling the President of the United States in the presence of a Major General that he was mistaken. The boy did demonstrate pride in his state and also the spirit that helped to make what I believe was the greatest army in the world.

When we returned to the "Little White House" that evening there were two messages for the President. The first one was from Ambassador

Winant with the surprising news of Churchill's defeat and the second was from Generalissimo Chiang Kai-shek approving what is now known as the Potsdam Declaration.

The declaration was immediately released for publication and a copy was sent by special messenger to Mr. Molotov. It pointed out that the combined forces of the three Allies "are poised to strike the final blows upon Japan," and that the experience of Germany "stands forth in awful clarity as an example to the people of Japan." It warned that the might converging on Japan "is immeasurably greater" than that which laid waste Germany.

"The full application of our military power, backed by our resolve," the declaration continued, "will mean the inevitable and complete destruction of the Japanese armed forces and just as inevitably the utter destruction of the Japanese homeland."

The declaration then set forth in seven paragraphs the terms under which the government of Japan was called upon to proclaim its unconditional surrender. They were phrased so that the threat of utter destruction if Japan resisted was offset with hope of a just though stern peace if she surrendered. It is tragic that the Japanese chose to reject this offer.

Mr. Molotov telephoned later in the evening asking that the declaration be held up two or three days. When he was told it already had been released he seemed disturbed. The next day I explained it had not been submitted to him before release because we did not want to embarrass the Soviet Union by presenting it with a declaration affecting a country with which it was not yet at war. He did not say he desired to make any change but said simply that we should have consulted him.

Two days later, on July 29, Mr. Molotov called again. It had been agreed that the President and I would meet with him and Generalissimo Stalin, but Mr. Molotov informed us that Stalin was ill that day. He had instructed Mr. Molotov to discuss with us the immediate cause of the Soviet Union's entry into the war. The Soviet Government, Molotov said, considered that the best method would be for the United States, Great Britain, and the other Allies to address a formal request to the Soviet Government for its entry into the war. He added that the Soviet Government was assuming, of course, that the agreement with the Chinese Government would be signed before his country entered the war.

The request presented a problem to us. The Soviet Union had a non-aggression pact with the Japanese. The Soviet Government also had had a similar pact with Hitler, but it was the Nazis who had violated that one. We did not believe the United States Government should be placed in the position of asking another government to violate its agreement without good and sufficient reason. The Soviet Union had notified Japan a few months earlier of its intention to abrogate the treaty but it would still be in force for nearly a year. The President was disturbed.

As for myself, I must frankly admit that in view of what we knew of Soviet actions in eastern Germany and the violations of the Yalta agreements in Poland, Rumania and Bulgaria, I would have been satisfied had the Russians determined not to enter the war. Notwithstanding Japan's persistent refusal to surrender unconditionally, I believed the atomic bomb would be successful and would force the Japanese to accept surrender on our terms. I feared what would happen when the Red Army entered Manchuria. Before it left Manchuria, my fears were realized.

When the agreement on Russian participation in the war was reached at Yalta, the military situation had been entirely different. President Roosevelt and our military leaders wanted the Soviet Union in the war. No one of them could have anticipated the difficulties we encountered after Yalta. However, an agreement had been made and we had to stand by our obligation.

Ben Cohen and I spent hours trying to decide how the President could properly reply to the Soviet request. It was Ben who suggested that we call the Soviet Government's attention to its obligations under the Charter of the United Nations.

The President approved the idea. It was late at night. The staff had gone. With Ben's suggestion as a starter I went to a typewriter and drafted the letter which the President later approved.

It first mentioned the Moscow Declaration of October 30, 1943, signed by the Soviet Union, the United States, the United Kingdom and China. That declaration provided that "for the purpose of maintaining international peace and security pending the re-establishment of law and order and the inauguration of a system of general security, they will consult with one another and as occasion requires with other members of the United Nations with a view to joint action on behalf of the community of nations." The letter then pointed out that Article 106 of the proposed United Nations Charter provided that the four powers would continue to act on the basis of the Moscow Declaration until the Charter came into force. It then cited Article 103 of the Charter, providing that "in the event of a conflict between the obligations of the Members of the United Nations under the present Charter and their obligations under any other international agreement, their obligations under the present Charter shall prevail."

The President's letter then concluded:

"Though the Charter has not been formally ratified, at San Francisco, it was agreed to by the Representative of the Union of Soviet Socialist Republics and the Soviet Government will be one of the permanent members of the Security Council.

"It seems to me that under the terms of the Moscow Declaration and the provisions of the Charter, above referred to, it would be proper for the Soviet Union to indicate its willingness to consult and co-operate with other great powers now at war with Japan with a view to joint action on behalf of the community of nations to maintain peace and security."

The President later told me that Generalissimo Stalin expressed great appreciation of the communication. He should have. The Soviet Government's statement announcing its entry into the war did not include a reference to Section 103 of the Charter, but our finding it for Mr. Molotov will enable the Soviet historian to show that Russia's declaration of war on Japan was in accordance with what they like to claim is their scrupulous regard for international obligations.

We arrived back in Washington the afternoon of August 7. The day before, we had received word aboard ship that the first atomic bomb had been dropped on Hiroshima. The day after our return, Nagasaki received its atomic blast and the Soviet Union declared war on Japan, to be effective August 9. In the early morning hours of August 10, we received, through the Swiss Government, a message from the Japanese that they were ready to accept the terms of the Potsdam Declaration "with the understanding that the said Declaration does not comprise any demand which prejudices the prerogatives of His Majesty as a Sovereign Ruler."

The message had come in during the night, but the President and I were not called until early morning. I immediately rushed to the White House where the Secretaries of War and Navy soon gathered. Admiral Leahy urged that the Japanese offer be accepted promptly. I told the President I would like a little time to think about a reply to the message.

"I do not see why we should retreat from our demand for unconditional surrender," I said. "That demand was presented to Japan before the use of the bomb and before the Soviet Union was a belligerent. If any conditions are to be accepted, I want the United States and not Japan to state the conditions."

The President agreed with me, and asked me to draft a reply.

In my office I drafted a reply, which the President approved when I presented it to him an hour later. About noon Secretary Stimson telephoned to say he had seen the draft and highly approved of the message. It stated:

> From the moment of surrender, the authority of the Emperor and the Japanese Government to rule the state shall be subject to the Supreme Commander of the Allied powers who will take such steps as he deems proper to effectuate the surrender terms.
> The Emperor will be required to authorize and ensure the signature by the Government of Japan and the Japanese Imperial General Headquarters of the surrender terms necessary to carry out the

provisions of the Potsdam Declaration, and shall issue his com-
mands to all the Japanese military, naval and air authorities and to
all the forces under their control wherever located to cease active operations and to surrender their arms, and to issue such other orders
as the Supreme Commander may require to give effect to the surrender terms. . . .

The ultimate form of government of Japan shall, in accordance with
the Potsdam Declaration, be established by the freely expressed will
of the people.

The message was sent on August 11, and we waited tensely for a response. I was confident the Japanese would accept, but the feeling of
responsibility for thousands of lives was inescapable. I telephoned our Minister in Switzerland, Mr. Leland Harrison, and asked him to call me as
soon as he received a Japanese reply and say whether or not the Japanese
accepted unconditional surrender. I wanted to eliminate the hours a coded
cable would consume.

A few minutes after 4 o'clock on August 14, I got the telephone call;
it ended the longest wait I have ever experienced. As soon as Mr. Harrison had read me the contents of the Japanese note, I asked the War
Department to set up a radio circuit with London, Moscow and Chung-
king and then rushed out to the Pentagon Building to carry on a teletype
conversation with the Foreign Ministers in these three capitals. I informed each one of Harrison's message, said we regarded the Japanese
reply as a complete acceptance of the Potsdam Declaration, and suggested
a time for simultaneous release of the news. The teletype clicked off so
many different replies I realized it would be impossible to reconcile them
quickly.

On the other hand, I did not believe this happy news should be withheld
from the people of the world because of an argument on the time of release. So I ended the discussion by stating that at 7:00 P.M., Eastern
War Time, the hour that seemed most suitable, President Truman would
announce the surrender, and invited the other governments to do likewise. By 5:30 I had reported the conversation to the President and received his approval for the arrangements. At 6:00, the Chargé d'Affaires
of the Swiss Legation, Mr. Max Grassli, arrived at my office with the
Japanese message read to me over the transatlantic telephone. An hour
later President Truman announced the end of the world's most horrible
conflict.

Some day the complete story will be written of the events in Japan
preceding the surrender. From the interrogation of high-ranking officials
and from the documents that came into the possession of our authorities,
it is evident that five weeks before the surrender Japan had no idea of
Stalin's intentions. In fact, the Japanese were no more certain of the
Soviet Union's entry into the war than the Soviets had been of Hitler's

intentions five weeks before he invaded Russia. Nor were they any more certain than we had been of Japanese intentions five weeks before Pearl Harbor.

Not until July 6, 1945, when China's Foreign Minister, T. V. Soong, was in Moscow, did the Japanese become suspicious of Soviet intentions. At that time, Foreign Minister Togo said, "Soong, we know to have been received well by the Russians and to have conferred with Stalin. . . . This may result in some sort of treaty." And he added with evident surprise, "It is *even* reported in some quarters that the Soviet Union would soon enter the war against Japan." This would indicate that, even then, the Japanese intelligence was not very efficient.

It is evident that at the time Ambassador Sato, the Japanese envoy in Moscow, presented Japan's mediation request to Mr. Molotov, the Emperor already had concluded that their cause was hopeless. His advisers, however, apparently believed they could avoid the Emperor's removal and also save some of their conquered territory.

Also clear, from his messages to the Japanese Foreign Office, is the fact that Ambassador Sato in Moscow was a realist and a courageous representative. He advised the Japanese Government that the message sent to him was so general in character the Soviets would not consider it; that they would not be convinced by pretty phrases having no reality and that, unless Japan was ready to surrender, there was no use wasting time sounding out the views of the Soviet Government.

Ambassador Sato told his Foreign Office that the Soviets had insisted upon the unconditional surrender of Germany and certainly would join the Americans and British in insisting upon the unconditional surrender of Japan. He said he knew his views were not in accord with the communications from His Majesty and even though "my offense is great," nevertheless "I want to preserve the lives of hundreds of thousands of people who are about to go to their death needlessly." And he stressed that "Japan has no choice but to accept unconditional surrender."

Had the Japanese Government listened to Sato and surrendered unconditionally, it would not have been necessary to drop the atomic bomb. But his advice was ignored as the militarists clamored for a negotiated peace. On July 21 the Japanese Government advised its representative in Moscow:

> We cannot consent to unconditional surrender under any circumstances. Even if the war drags on and more blood must be shed, so long as the enemy demands unconditional surrender, we will fight as one man against the enemy in accordance with the Emperor's command.

The Japanese Government communicated with the Soviets instead of Sweden or Switzerland in order to advise the Russians that they were prepared to meet fully their demands in the Far East. They hoped, by granting Soviet demands, to secure Soviet aid in negotiations. They also hoped, by such discussions, to find out definitely whether the Soviets were going to enter the war.

The Japanese Cabinet did not decide to surrender until the atomic bomb had been dropped on Hiroshima.

The records of the Japanese Foreign Office show that on August 10 the Soviet Ambassador to Tokyo presented Togo a message stating the Soviet's endorsement of the Potsdam Declaration and the existence of a state of war with Japan. In return, the Foreign Minister handed the Soviet Ambassador, for transmission to his government, a copy of the message sent that morning through Switzerland, announcing Japan's willingness to surrender upon condition that we made no demand prejudicing the prerogatives of His Majesty as a sovereign ruler. This was the message I answered on the eleventh which resulted in the surrender on the fourteenth.

The Japanese surrender had come earlier than we expected, but it did not find us unprepared. A co-ordinating committee, composed of representatives from the State, War and Navy departments had been at work for some time preparing general orders to govern the surrender and the occupation. One crisis, however, immediately confronted us: Who should have the honor of accepting the surrender of the Japanese?

The Great Powers had agreed that General MacArthur should act as their representative as well as ours in accepting the surrender. But officers of the Navy soon registered their keen disappointment at this arrangement. Secretary Forrestal presented their arguments: The war in the Pacific had been their show primarily; the bluejackets and Marines had advanced island by island from Pearl Harbor to Tokyo; they had destroyed the Japanese Navy. Therefore, MacArthur could sign for the Allies but Admiral Nimitz should sign for the United States. My service in the Senate as chairman of the Committee on Naval Appropriations may have influenced my view, but I responded sympathetically to Mr. Forrestal's arguments; I wanted the Navy in the picture. Arrangements had already been made, but I promised Forrestal I would try to think of a way by which Admiral Nimitz could take part in the signing along with General MacArthur.

When Secretary Forrestal is really interested in a cause, he doesn't sleep, and he doesn't let others sleep. That night the telephone awakened me. It was Secretary Forrestal, suggesting that the surrender ceremonies take place on board the battleship USS *Missouri*. I was sufficiently awake to recognize what the Army would call a "Navy trick." Had he said simply, "a battleship," it would have remained a debatable question, but when he named the Missouri, I knew the case was closed. The President, upon receiving the suggestion, of course, thought it an excellent idea. Thus was averted a great crisis in army-navy relations.

The people of the Soviet Union, however, may not know of Forrestal's victory. After the Christmas Eve dinner that Generalissimo Stalin gave during our meeting in Moscow in December 1945, a moving picture of the Soviet Army entering Manchuria was shown to us. It pictured Japan's preparation for war as being directed only against Russia; the tumultuous reception given the Red Army by the people of Manchuria and, finally, the signing of the terms of surrender. According to the film, the principal participants in the surrender ceremonies were representatives of Japan and the Soviet Union. The Supreme Commander, General MacArthur, was in the background. The scene was described as "signing the surrender terms" on "a battleship." There was no statement that the battleship was the *Missouri* or even that it was a United States' ship. The entire scene might well impress many Russians as the ending, on a Soviet battleship, of a private war between Russia and Japan. It showed me that the Soviets are keenly aware of the effectiveness of propaganda through moving pictures. I was not surprised to learn that the Soviet Government is now promoting the exhibition of Soviet films in European countries.

While we had borne the major burden in crushing the military power of Japan, we had always regarded the war as one war against the Axis, and we intended that the occupation of Japan should be an Allied responsibility. As early as August 22, we invited the Soviet Union, Great Britain and China to join us in setting up a ten-power advisory commission to carry out the aims of the Potsdam Declaration and the surrender terms. The Soviet Union and China promptly accepted, but Great Britain objected because the commission would have only advisory powers. Australia and New Zealand wanted more decisive roles. Consequently, the establishment of a commission was delayed.

As soon as the Council of Foreign Ministers met in London in September, I began talks with Mr. Bevin in an effort to settle our differences. But before we had progressed very far a new element was injected into the situation. Mr. Molotov came to see me, on instructions from Moscow. He wanted to complain of the way in which the surrender terms were being carried out. He complained particularly about the way the Japanese Army was being demobilized. It was dangerous, he said, merely to disarm the Japanese and send them home; they should be held as prisoners of war. We should do what the Red Army was doing with the Japanese it had taken in Manchuria—make them work.

I pointed out to him that the Potsdam Declaration, to which the Soviet Union had adhered, pledged that "Japanese military forces, after being completely disarmed, shall be permitted to return to their homes with the opportunity to lead peaceful and productive lives." I assured him that we would hold all those suspected of war crimes but said that we would not hold prisoners to work for us.

No one can say accurately how many Japanese prisoners have been taken to the Soviet Union. In mid-1947, the best guess was that approximately 500,000 were still there. Transportation difficulties delayed the return of many of our Japanese prisoners, but they *have* been returned. As long as we were holding either Japanese or Germans, we could not very well insist that our Allies comply with the Geneva Convention on Prisoners of War and the clearer promises of the Potsdam Declaration. I have described in an earlier chapter our efforts in returning the Germans. The positive statements concerning prisoners in the Potsdam Declaration make the use of Japanese as slave laborers even less excusable. The time has come when the United States should demand that its Allies comply with the Potsdam Declaration.

At London, however, when Mr. Molotov said that Japanese should be made prisoners, he even expressed the fear that our policy would lead to a revival of Japanese aggression. Assistant Secretary Dunn pointed out to him that our proposal to set up a Far Eastern Commission would give his government an opportunity to express its views on Japanese policy, including the disarmament of prisoners. I said that I thought we should have a demilitarization treaty for Japan similar to the German Treaty. I assured him that, when I returned home, I would discuss it with President Truman.

Despite our assurances, Mr. Molotov two days later opened the session of the council by reading a prepared statement in which he suggested the establishment of an Allied Control Council for Japan. The council would be composed of the United States, Great Britain, the Soviet Union and China, with the American representative acting as chairman. The council would have far-reaching powers, much greater than those Mr. Bevin had suggested. Through two long meetings, I argued against including on the agenda the subject of establishing a Control Council in Japan. The other members, on the whole, supported me, for they were eager to proceed with the European treaties, and at the time Mr. Molotov's request appeared to be just another phase of his campaign for delay.

On September 26, at my request, Mr. Bevin, Mr. Molotov and I met in an effort to solve our differences on the right of France and China to participate in all the discussions of the council. But Mr. Molotov immediately reverted to the Soviet proposal for the establishment of a Control Council in Japan. The policies being pursued by General MacArthur made him wonder, he said, whether it was "useful for the Soviet Government to continue having a representative in Tokyo." I repeated that I was not prepared at this session of the council, called to begin work on the

European treaties, to discuss the Japanese question. I again assured him that I would go into the matter thoroughly as soon as I returned home, and would communicate with him.

The Soviet delegation, he said, was unable to understand why it was impossible to discuss this question during the present meeting, and he wished to ask whether or not the one or two billion dollars of gold which the Americans had found in Japan, according to newspaper reports, had anything to do with this situation.

Had the Foreign Minister of Great Britain, France or China made such a statement, one would have known that it was deliberately intended to be insulting. But, from the way in which it was expressed and particularly in the light of Soviet actions elsewhere, I concluded Mr. Molotov did not intend it as an insult.

Mr. Molotov had admitted at Potsdam that the Red Army had indulged in large-scale removals of property and had suggested that one billion dollars be deducted from his reparations claims to cover them. Notwithstanding the embarrassment he seemed to feel about this at Potsdam, the Red Army repeated a few weeks later in Manchuria its performance in Germany. Soviet troops removed from the soil of their Chinese Allies everything they could carry away. It was therefore quite understandable that when Mr. Molotov read the story, later proved to be untrue, that our soldiers had found two billion dollars in gold, he should expect us to do just what the Red Army would do under similar circumstances—remove the gold and refuse to talk about Japanese affairs until the wealth was safely hidden in the United States.

In London, I tried once again, in a private conversation with Mr. Molotov, to persuade him that the establishment of the Far Eastern Advisory Commission was logically the first step in considering how the occupation of Japan was to be directed. But my efforts met with no success.

Meanwhile, I had been urging Mr. Bevin to agree to our proposal, submitted on August 22, for the creation of the Far Eastern Advisory Commission. I agreed informally that when the commission met, we would support a proposal that it should be authorized to meet in Tokyo as well as in Washington and that India should be made a member. The Cabinet then authorized Mr. Bevin to accept our proposal. With Britain's approval obtained, I hoped Molotov would withdraw his new proposal and revert to his earlier approval of our August 22 proposal. I immediately wrote him a letter stating that, since the four powers now were agreed, a meeting of the commission would be held on October 30, and I hoped a Soviet representative would be there. He replied that the situation had changed since the Soviet Union had agreed to our August 22 proposal and that his government now asked for the establishment of a Control Council. As I left for Washington, it still was uncertain whether a representative of the Soviet Union would be on hand for the commission's first meeting.

This situation was a part of the whole state of our relations with the Soviet Union which deeply disturbed me during October 1945. I felt that as long as we continued to communicate with each other concerning our problems, they might be reconciled. But during those weeks there was no communication.

I thought it wise to give the Soviets the benefit of every doubt, since we wanted to progress in the task of peace making. Therefore, we prepared a modification of our proposal for a peace conference on the European treaties—the issue we thought was mainly responsible for the deadlock of the London session of the council. I wanted this proposal to get to Stalin, who was then on vacation. A message to the head of a government must be signed by the President, so we drafted a letter and asked the President to have Ambassador Harriman deliver it for him personally. The President made the letter a most cordial one.

On October 25, Ambassador Harriman called on Stalin at Gagri. After he had read the President's letter, which had been translated into Russian, Stalin looked up and said, "The Japanese question is not touched upon."

When this message came in from Harriman, I immediately realized that we had miscalculated at London. We had thought it was the peace conference issue that was behind Molotov's obstructive tactics. Stalin's question made us realize that they were more angry about Japan.

Harriman was equally surprised, but fortunately he had been with us in London and was able to explain our August 22 proposal in detail to Stalin. He made it clear he was not authorized to negotiate regarding Japan. He added he knew I was most anxious to devise a method of informing and consulting with the Soviet Government and our other Allies on Japanese policy, provided that, if there was disagreement, the United States would not be interfered with in carrying out the occupation policy.

Although Harriman was able to steer the conversation back to the question of the peace conference, Japan remained uppermost in Stalin's mind. He opened the second day of his talks with our Ambassador by returning to the subject.

He was unwilling, he said, to send a representative to the forthcoming meeting of the Far Eastern Advisory Commission because, as Molotov had stated in London, the situation had changed since our invitation had been accepted. Stalin had, in fact, recalled his representative in Tokyo, Lieutenant General Derevyanko, because, he claimed, the general was neither informed nor consulted and, under such circumstances, could not accept responsibility for actions taken by General MacArthur in the name of the Allies.

The Soviet Union, Stalin declared, was being treated as a satellite state and not as an Ally, and this did not become the dignity of his nation. He complained that the Japanese press and radio had been allowed to vilify the Soviet Union; that changes in the government had been made without informing or consulting him; and that Japanese banks had been closed without any information being issued on the disposition of their assets.

Ambassador Harriman explained that General MacArthur was carrying out the surrender terms agreed to by the Soviet Government and that all assets were being held for eventual disposition by the Allies. He pointed out that, even before the surrender terms had been signed, we had proposed the establishment of the Advisory Commission to consider just such matters as the Generalissimo was mentioning, and he urged that a Soviet representative be sent to the forthcoming meeting in Washington where he could get the information his government wanted.

Stalin was not satisfied. He said his representative in Tokyo had been treated "like a piece of furniture" and he feared further differences would arise if he sent a representative to the Washington meeting. If the United States wished to come to an agreement with the Soviet Union, he insisted, it could only be done properly in negotiations between our two governments. He called attention to the fact that Russia had maintained thirty to forty divisions on the Manchurian border throughout the war, had engaged the Japanese with seventy divisions and had been ready, if their offer had been accepted, to assist in the occupation of Japan.

Because this statement undoubtedly will be heard frequently in the discussion of the Japanese peace treaty, it should be recorded that while Generalissimo Stalin's statement was correct, it is also true that Japan's thirty or forty divisions on the Manchurian border did not seriously affect the Japanese war effort. As a result of the successful operations of the United States Navy, the Japanese early in the war lacked the ships necessary to move men and supplies to the battlefields of the Pacific. With their forces immobilized, it was just as easy for the Japanese to maintain their divisions on the Manchurian border as elsewhere. Conceivably, the Japanese could have used these forces for land operations in China, but we know now that this would not have materially affected the final outcome of the war.

We had barely received Harriman's report on his conversations when the Far Eastern Advisory Commission gathered for its first meeting, and elected Major General Frank R. McCoy, the United States representative, as chairman. It then adjourned for a week to give the Soviet Union another chance to send a representative.

The fact is, the commission was unable to operate effectively from the very outset. Although the United Kingdom and Australia were willing to co-operate with us, they were not satisfied with a purely advisory role. I soon realized we must try to work out an arrangement which, while protecting General MacArthur from undue interference, would nevertheless meet the desire of our Allies for more extensive participation.

Many conferences and long debates took place before we finally agreed upon a draft proposal for a Far Eastern Commission and an Allied Council. This proposal was approved by the President, and I presented it at the first meeting of the three Foreign Ministers in Moscow on December 16. Discussion of our proposal extended through six meetings. The chief issues were Mr. Molotov's opposition to making India a member of the commission, his desire to insert the word "Control" in the name of the Allied Council, Mr. Bevin's request to include Australia on the council and, finally, the voting procedure in the commission.

For a while I feared that agreement would be delayed so long that it would be impossible to obtain China's concurrence before we adjourned. But on December 24, Mr. Molotov announced his willingness to admit India to the commission. It was agreed that the commission would act upon majority votes of the eleven members, including the votes of the United Kingdom, the Soviet Union, China and the United States. Mr. Bevin likewise accepted a suggestion that on the four-member Allied Council in Tokyo, the United Kingdom, Australia, New Zealand and India should have one representative in common.

The new Far Eastern Commission began functioning in Washington on February 26, 1946. It has authority to decide upon the principles which control the administration of Japan, and its decisions are put into directives issued to the Supreme Allied Commander by the United States Government. This means, of course, that no basic policy may be adopted without our concurrence, and, pending agreement in the commission, we are free to give interim directives on all urgent matters.

Only three questions were excepted from this authority. These three questions, on which the commission must decide by a majority vote which includes ours, are: (a) changes in the control system as set forth in the surrender terms, (b) fundamental changes in the Japanese constitutional structure, and (c) changes in the government as a whole as distinguished from shifts involving individual officials. It has not been our policy to dictate wholesale alterations in the government, and the authority of General MacArthur to make individual changes or fill vacancies has been unimpaired.

The council continues to advise and consult with the Supreme Commander in Tokyo. At the time the commission and the council were established, I stated that the authority of General MacArthur should not be obstructed by the inability of the commission to agree on policy or of the council to agree on advice for carrying out that policy. Nearly two years have passed and events have proved that the two bodies have not interfered with MacArthur's administration. He and his staff have continued to carry out their difficult task with an efficiency that has won the plaudits of the people in other Allied nations besides the United States.

There were other Japanese questions on Mr. Molotov's mind at Moscow. He asked first about plans for disposing of the Japanese Navy and, secondly, about the Japanese islands. Two months before the Moscow meeting, we had proposed that what was left of the Japanese Navy should be scuttled. Britain and China had agreed, but Mr. Molotov had replied that his government wanted one-fourth of all surface vessels from destroyers on through the lesser tonnages. He also had asked about the merchant fleet. Secretary Forrestal had said the naval vessels requested had little practical value and, with his approval, we had agreed rather than argue the point with Mr. Molotov. The merchant fleet, I told Mr. Molotov, was being used to repatriate Japanese, and we believed it should ultimately be considered in connection with the reparations settlement.

I don't know why Mr. Molotov felt it necessary to raise the issue again in the Council unless he wanted me to restate our position before the other Foreign Ministers. Apparently, he did not know that I had sent them the same message I had sent him. His other motive may have been to create an opportunity to submit a claim for a part of the Japanese fishing fleet. Mr. Bevin quickly pointed out that the fishing fleet was essential to maintain Japan's food supply. Even though the Japanese were defeated, he said, "It is necessary for them to go on living somehow."

Mr. Molotov then turned to the question of the Japanese mandated islands.

The United States, I replied, had not yet formulated its views and I knew of no agreements concerning Japanese islands in the Pacific except two: (a) the declaration at Cairo in November 1943 that Japan should be required to surrender territories acquired by conquest, and (b) the Yalta agreement regarding South Sakhalin and the Kurile Islands. The last of these I had learned about only some weeks after becoming Secretary. Mr. Bevin said the British Cabinet had not known of the Yalta agreement until some time after it was made, nevertheless they had no intention of going back on it.

After the Moscow meeting and through most of 1946 we studied actively the question of what should be done with the islands entrusted to Japanese care by the League of Nations. Shortly before the meeting of the Council of Foreign Ministers in New York in November, the President held a meeting of the Secretaries of State, War and Navy to determine our policy.

The State and War departments felt that, since Japan had received these islands under a mandate from the League of Nations, our rights were not superior to those delegated by the League and that therefore, if possible, the United Nations should declare them a strategic area to be administered by us under a United Nations trusteeship agreement. We pointed out that at San Francisco the United States delegation, by direction of President Roosevelt, had been a strong advocate of the trusteeship system. We argued that we could not properly adopt a policy that would show a lack of confidence in the system we had urged upon the United Nations. Japan had violated her mandate and therefore we could seek a decision from the United Nations on these mandated islands, while those islands that belonged to the Japanese, such as the Ryukyus, would have to await disposition by the peace conference.

The Secretary of the Navy was very reasonable. He did not want us to do anything that would show lack of confidence in the United Nations, but because he felt keenly the loss of life these islands had cost us, he wanted to make certain that the terms of the arrangement would permit the Navy to maintain adequate bases. He expressed fear that once negotiations were under way, subordinate officials of the State Department or some delegate to the United Nations might compromise and accept an arrangement that would jeopardize the proper maintenance of the bases. When I assured him that no changes in the United States proposal would be accepted without the approval of the President or the Secretary of State, he said he was satisfied with the trusteeship proposal. Shortly thereafter, our able representative to the United Nations, Mr. Warren R. Austin, placed our proposal before the Security Council.

The United Nations General Assembly was in session during the meeting of the Council of Foreign Ministers in New York, and some of the pending trusteeship proposals were up for approval, in the hope that the United Nations Trusteeship Council could be established.

The Charter provides that each trusteeship agreement must be acceptable to the "states directly concerned." I held that while the trusteeship agreement for strategic areas had to be approved by the Security Council, the United States, as the country in possession of the mandated islands, was the only state "directly concerned." Mr. Dulles, who was our representative on the Trusteeship Committee in the General Assembly, had taken the position that the definition of "states directly concerned" should not be determined until the Trusteeship Council was established but he had been strongly opposed by the Soviet representative, Ambassador Nikolai V. Novikov.

Mr. Molotov asked me to agree that the five permanent members of the Security Council should be regarded as "states directly concerned" in all cases. He suggested that the five powers exchange letters confirming this understanding. The Soviet Union probably would have no objection to the United States' proposal for a strategic trusteeship over the Japanese mandated islands, he said; nevertheless his government would like to have an agreement that all trusteeship proposals must have the approval of the five permanent members. If this were done, he added, two or three trusteeship agreements could be approved at that session of the General Assembly so that the Trusteeship Council could be organized.

Such a definition of "states directly concerned," I replied, was a matter of Charter interpretation within the United Nations itself, and should not be the subject of a bilateral arrangement between our two governments. I then added that I would bear his position in mind when considering the ultimate disposition of the Kurile Islands and the southern half of Sakhalin. This brought a very quick response. The Soviet Union, he said, did not contemplate a trusteeship arrangement for the Kuriles or Sakhalin; these matters had been settled at Yalta. I pointed out to him that Mr. Roosevelt had said repeatedly at Yalta that territory could be ceded only at the peace conference and he had agreed only to support the Soviet Union's claim at the conference. While it could be assumed that we would stand by Mr. Roosevelt's promise, I continued, we certainly would want to know, by the time of the peace conference, what the Soviet Union's attitude would be toward our proposal for placing the Japanese-mandated islands under our trusteeship. Mr. Molotov quickly grasped the implications of this remark. When the United States trusteeship agreement was voted upon later by the Security Council, I was delighted, but not surprised, to see that the Soviet representative voted in favor of our proposal.

The other Far Eastern territorial question that figured prominently in our discussions at Moscow was Korea.

The United States, United Kingdom and China had agreed at Cairo on December 1, 1943, that "in due course Korea shall become free and independent." At Yalta, President Roosevelt and Generalissimo Stalin had agreed informally that Korea should win its independence and that if a transition period were necessary, a trusteeship should be established. For forty years Korea had been exploited by Japan. The Japanese had permitted relatively few Koreans to secure an education and had made it difficult for them to obtain the important positions in trade and industry that would have given them administrative experience. As a result, there was some question whether the people were sufficiently trained to assume the responsibilities of government immediately. The desire to help the Koreans develop the skills and experience that would enable them to maintain their independence was the inspiration for President Roosevelt's acquiescence in the trusteeship idea.

When we went to Moscow we were troubled by the fact that Korea had, in fact, been split in two. At the time of the Japanese surrender, the military leaders agreed that all Japanese troops north of the 38th parallel would surrender to the Red Army and all troops south of that line would surrender to our Army. This arrangement was accepted by the Soviet

Union and was included in Order No. 1 issued to General MacArthur. But what was intended as a division for military convenience has become a closed boundary between the Soviet and American zones of occupation.

Our delegation therefore submitted a paper to the conference proposing the establishment of a Joint Soviet-American Commission to unify the administration of such matters as currency, trade and transportation, tele-communications, electric power distribution, coastal shipping, and so on. It also proposed that a four-power trusteeship be established which would "endure for no longer period than necessary to allow the Koreans to form an independent, representative and effective government."

A few days later, Mr. Molotov submitted a Soviet proposal for a Joint Commission on urgent problems of economic unification, the establish-ment of a provisional government and a four-power trusteeship to last for five years. In the interest of promoting agreement, we accepted the Soviet draft with a few amendments and it was included in the Moscow protocol.

But "trusteeship" to the Koreans meant only a continuation of outside control, which under the Japanese had brought them much suffering, and the postponement of their long-sought independence. The complaints against the Trusteeship proposal prompted me to issue a statement saying:

"The joint Soviet-American Commission, working with the Korean provisional democratic government, may find it possible to dispense with a trusteeship. It is our goal to hasten the day when Korea will become an independent member of the society of nations."

This hope, unfortunately, has not been sustained by subsequent events. The Soviet-American Commission met in January 1946 to carry out the mandate of the Moscow agreement. But what seemed to us unequivocal language, once again, apparently, was different in Russian. To us it seemed clear that the country should be considered as an economic and administrative whole. The Soviet commander, however, saw the problem as one of arranging exchanges between and the co-ordination of two en-tirely separate zones. Today, a year and a half later, they are still separate zones, and progress toward setting up a provisional government has been equally disappointing.

The Soviet representative has insisted that only those political parties which had not opposed the idea of trusteeship should be consulted in forming a government. But most Koreans, with the exception of the Communists, had opposed it. The United States maintained that, in accordance with the doctrine of free speech, an expression of opposition should not keep anyone from being consulted. We insisted on meeting with representatives of all political parties; as a result, the commission adjourned in a deadlock in May 1946. In the spring of 1947, at Moscow, Secretary Marshall succeeded in arranging for the Joint Commission to resume negotiations, but these have as yet produced no concrete results.

In the United States zone, Koreans rapidly are replacing Americans in administrative positions. An interim legislative assembly composed of forty-five elected members and forty-five appointed members met for the first time in December 1946. The purpose was not to encourage a movement for separate governments in Korea but to prepare the Koreans for responsibilities of self-government.

Whenever a provisional government is established, I fully expect the Soviet Union will propose that the Soviet-American Commission be withdrawn and that the proposed period of trusteeship be eliminated. This latter proposal, particularly, will be popular with the Koreans. But the Soviet Union may have another purpose in mind. In the Soviet Zone, the Red Army has trained an army of Koreans estimated to number from 100,000 to 400,000 men. The withdrawal of the Joint Commission and Soviet-American occupation forces would leave the Soviet-trained army the only effective military force in Korea. Undoubtedly, this army would attempt to take charge of whatever government then existed. Therefore, as a condition to withdrawal of the commission, we must require that this army be disbanded.

Korea does not need an armed force trained either by Russians or by Americans. What it needs is economic assistance. The fertilizer plants in the Soviet zone were converted by the Japanese to the manufacture of explosives. The Soviet commander has refused the American zone adequate shipments of fertilizer. Consequently, fertilizer will have to be imported in the immediate future if the depleted soil of the southern zone is to be productive.

Korea's industrial plants need rehabilitation. This requires coal, raw materials, and replacement parts. If the Joint Commission remains for two or possibly three years and American representatives can supervise financial assistance, the United States might furnish the help that is needed to set Korea's industrial machinery in motion.

The United States and the Soviet Union are committed to the establishment of a unified, independent and democratic Korea. Our government must continue its interest until that promise is fulfilled and Korea is able to take its place as a sovereign equal in the family of the United Nations. This is one of the important steps toward lasting peace in Asia.

Another essential step is to conclude an early peace treaty with Japan. Nearly two years of occupation experience have given us sound basis for judgment. Under the policies administered by General MacArthur great progress has been made. The time has come when we should agree upon the terms of the peace treaty so the people of Japan may know what the future holds for them and may begin the work of rehabilitation, guided by the blueprint provided by the Allied nations.

For reasons I have given in connection with Germany, I do not think the Council of Foreign Ministers should prepare the preliminary draft of the Japanese treaty. The Soviet Union, which entered the war a few hours before the first offer of surrender, should not insist upon peace machinery which gives them the power of veto. On the other hand, it is quite understandable that a government like Australia, whose armed forces fought the Japanese from Pearl Harbor to the day of surrender, feels that it should play a larger role in the Japanese peace settlement than it had in the drafting of the five European treaties.

We should immediately announce that we believe a peace conference should be held, and fix an early date. The eleven governments on the commission are those that made substantial military contributions in the war against Japan and are the ones that should prepare the preliminary draft of the peace treaty. Through their work on the commission, all eleven have been giving careful consideration to Japanese problems for nearly two years. They should be able, without difficulty, to prepare drafts of a treaty for consideration by the peace conference.

The peace conference should include all the states at war with Japan.

Decisions of the drafting powers and of the peace conference should be by a two-thirds vote, including two-thirds or seven out of eleven powers that made substantial military contributions. Every effort should be made to secure unanimity, but a two-thirds vote should be decisive and a treaty based on such decisions should be submitted to the governments for signature. The veto power, of course, cannot be entirely eliminated since there is no way in which an Allied nation that is a member of the peace conference can be forced to sign a treaty. But it cannot prevent others from signing it.

The governments unwilling to accept the decision of a two-thirds majority would remain in a technical state of war with Japan. I believe, however, that the treaty with Japan, like those with Italy and the Balkan states, should provide that any government refusing to sign it will not receive any of the benefits of its provisions.

In adopting the procedure recommended here we would, of course, be giving up our right to veto any provision with which we disagree. This would be a magnanimous gesture on the part of the country which was largely responsible for defeating the Japanese. It also would be an expression of confidence in our Allies and in our ability to reach, by a two-thirds vote, satisfactory agreements on the treatment of Japan.

In drafting the peace treaty there should be no serious controversy on territorial questions. The United States undoubtedly will stand by President Roosevelt's agreement on the Kuriles and Sakhalin. I see no objection to Japan's keeping the islands of the Ryukyu group north of Okinawa. From Okinawa south, it is my hope that the islands will be placed under a United Nations trusteeship. For sentimental reasons, the United States will want a trusteeship interest in Okinawa.

The question of reparations is certain to be most controversial. The Far Eastern Commission's discussions on this subject have been marked by the Soviet representative's insistence that the industrial equipment removed from Manchuria must be excluded from any reparations settlement. These removals, the Soviets insist, must be regarded as "war booty." One Soviet representative has placed an estimated value on these removals of 97 million dollars. Reparations Commissioner Pauley, on the basis of his investigation in June 1946, has placed direct damage at more than 858 million dollars and the total damage, including deterioration and cost of replacement, at over two billion dollars.

The Soviet position is indefensible. Of course, this industrial equipment must be included in the reparations settlement. It cannot be war booty. It does not include weapons of war. Its return to Manchuria is impractical, but the least that can be done to repair the damage is to charge it against the Soviet Union's share of reparations.

We have taken this position in the Far Eastern Commission. We have been supported in it by nine other nations. But the Soviet Union, through its use of the veto, has been able to block action in the commission.

At the time of the Peace Conference we should propose a forty-year treaty to insure the demilitarization of Japan, similar to the treaty we proposed for Germany. In this case, however, any violation of the treaty should be reported to the Ambassadors or Ministers of the states that drafted the treaty, who would constitute a Commission of Enforcement. As in the German treaty, decisions would be made by a majority vote.

Both in the peace treaty and the demilitarization treaty we must look forward to a long period of involvement in Japanese affairs. The great progress we have made in the last two years can be lost if we do not make sure that the changes become a permanent part of the Japanese way of life. The spiritual disarmament of a people is a much more difficult task than their physical disarmament. To instill the democratic concept of the individual in the Japanese requires a major social revolution. It can be accomplished permanently only if we make certain that a whole new generation of Japanese is educated in accordance with this democratic ideal. Unless this is done, the newly won rights of labor to organize, of farmers to own their land, of women to participate in public life, and of political parties to operate without fear, can be dissipated and destroyed. We must work intelligently with the new generation and we must make a just economic settlement so that that generation will have a promise of stability and an opportunity to create a better way of life than under the old order.

I have said relatively little about China. This is primarily because the record of our effort there is well known. Unhappily, that record shows little success. China still is a long way from peace. The future which could hold so much for that great country and its millions of people is still only a promise. It is one of the great tragedies of our times that a nation so rich in human and material resources is split by fratricidal conflict.

The one safe generalization that can be made about China is that it stands on the threshold of great change. We should encourage and assist that change whenever possible. China needs the physical and human engineering skills that we possess. The intelligent and persevering application of those skills can prevent China's change from becoming an upheaval that could well endanger the peace of the world. But the initiative for applying them must come from within China herself if they are to succeed.

Awareness of China's importance is by no means confined to the United States. My own experience as well as events have made clear the interest of the Soviet Union in this great area bordering its eastern frontiers. Outer Mongolia has become virtually a Soviet protectorate. At Yalta, Stalin successfully quoted as his price for entering the Japanese war, joint control of the two railway systems in Manchuria, a free port at Dairen, and a naval base at Port Arthur. And, when I went to Moscow in December 1945, Mr. Molotov's great interest in China was clearly revealed by his insistent efforts to discover what aims, hidden or otherwise, the United States might have toward China.

Fortunately, I arrived in Moscow well prepared for Mr. Molotov. Before Ambassador Hurley's resignation, the State Department had prepared a statement of policy on China, the first draft of which I showed the Ambassador a few days before he resigned. As soon as President Truman appointed General Marshall his personal representative in China, I asked the General to study the draft so that he could help prepare the final statement for presentation to the President.

The Sunday before I left for Moscow, Under Secretary Acheson, General Marshall and members of his staff met in my office. By the end of the morning's discussion, we had agreed upon the statement of policy that subsequently was approved by the President and released to the public on December 15. Thereafter the President made no change in that policy except upon the recommendation of General Marshall or with his approval.

At our very first meeting in Spiridonovka House, Mr. Molotov asked that the question of American troops in north China be discussed. I agreed and presented him with a prepared statement giving the exact number of troops in north China. I explained that they were there at the request of the Chinese Government to assist in disarming 325,000 Japanese. I assured the Soviet Government the troops would be withdrawn as soon as this mission was completed, and pointed out that General Marshall had gone to China as the President's personal representative to help effect a truce that would end China's internal strife and permit the disarming of the Japanese.

The next day I presented to the council President Truman's statement of American policy toward China. It reiterated that our troops were in north China to disarm the Japanese, a mission that was being delayed by the country's internal strife, and it stressed our belief that the antagonists should cease fighting and join in a national conference of all political parties to unify the country.

These statements did not satisfy Mr. Molotov and he raised the question again two days later. This time I explained in detail our obligations to the Allies to make certain that the Japanese in north China were disarmed, how this task had been assigned primarily to the Chinese Nationalist forces, how they were prevented from accomplishing it because the Communist armies stood between them and the Japanese troops, how we had delayed taking action to disarm these Japanese ourselves because it was a duty that had been assigned to the National government by the Supreme Commander, and since we all recognized that government, we thought they should be given a fair opportunity to discharge it. I assured him that if it became necessary we would go in and disarm the Japanese so that our troops could then return home.

Mr. Molotov said he felt Chiang Kai-shek's government exaggerated the strength of the Communist forces. He observed that Chinese never wished to do any fighting themselves but prefer that others do it for them. The continued existence of these Japanese forces, he asserted, was "intolerable" and dryly remarked that after eight years of war Chiang Kai-shek should have learned how to handle the Japanese, particularly after they had capitulated.

A few days later, Mr. Molotov resumed the offensive by suggesting that a date be fixed for the simultaneous withdrawal of American and Russian troops from China. Once again I explained that the disarmament of the Japanese was a different problem from the one the Red Army had faced in Manchuria. But a few minutes later he was asking the same question he had been asking since the first day of the session.

"Mr. Molotov, you must be asking these questions because you like the sound of my voice," I said. "I can only give you the answer I have given you every time you have asked the question. For your advance information, when you ask the same question tomorrow, you will get the same answer."

That evening I was to see Generalissimo Stalin. I was weary of going through my routine with Molotov so I added this question to the items to be discussed.

I told Stalin of my discussions with Molotov, who was present, and I reminded him how he had declared at Potsdam that Chiang Kai-shek's government was the only possible government in China and that the Chinese Communists were not real Communists at all. In response, he pointed out that the Soviet Union had a treaty recognizing Chiang. He had no objection to the presence of our troops there, he added, but he merely wished to be informed about it. If the Chinese people became convinced Chiang Kai-shek was depending on foreign troops, Stalin remarked, Chiang would lose his influence.

Taking some matches, I placed them on the table, indicating the relative location of the Japanese troops and the Communist troops along the railroad in North China and the troops of the National government. Stalin became deeply interested and inquired about the size of the Communist forces in the Tientsin area. I replied that Mao Tse Tung, the Communist leader, claimed to have 600,000 in that area. Stalin laughed at the statement. Pointing to the match representing National government forces in the North China area, which I said numbered about 40,000, he asked me what had become of the army of one and a half million that Chiang was supposed to have. I told him our Navy and Army had not seen them. Stalin laughed heartily and said all Chinese were boasters who exaggerated the forces of their opponents as well as their own. He paid a compliment to General Marshall, saying that, if anyone could settle the situation in China, he could.

As a result of this discussion with Stalin the council reached an agreement the following day on the statement that was included in the protocol. It reaffirmed that the three governments recognized the need of a unified and democratic China under the National Government, and stated that the Foreign Ministers of the United States and the Soviet Union were "in complete accord as to the desirability of withdrawal of Soviet and American forces from China at the earliest practicable moment consistent with the discharge of their obligations and responsibilities."

In September 1946, General Marshall reported to the President that it seemed useless to remain in China much longer. President Truman authorized him to return whenever he thought his mission should be concluded. In Paris, I told China's Foreign Minister of our decision. He immediately expressed fear that General Marshall's departure would suggest to the Chinese people that the United States had lost interest in China's affairs. I assured him of our friendly interest but emphasized that the general could not remain indefinitely when neither faction would accept his advice.

Every effort had been made to insure the success of General Marshall's mission. In addition to his own great prestige, he was accorded the prestige and authority of a personal representative of the President of the United

States. At Moscow, we had secured from the Soviet Union an official re-affirmation of their support of the National Government as the only legitimate government in China. And the President, in his statement of policy on December 18, 1945, had held out to the Chinese this attractive promise:

"When conditions in China improve we are prepared to consider aid in carrying out . . . projects, unrelated to civil strife, which would encourage economic reconstruction and reform in China and which, in so doing, would promote a general revival of commercial relations between American and Chinese businessmen."

General Marshall continued his efforts until January 1947, but the warring groups were still no nearer settlement. We then had to decide whether Ambassador Leighton Stuart should continue the efforts to bring the two factions together. John Carter Vincent, chief of the Far East Division and an experienced foreign service officer, took the position that he should not; that, if General Marshall could not bring about unity, it would be unwise to ask any other official to force our views upon the factions. I agreed with Vincent.

Many of us have had the unhappy experience of intervening in the domestic quarrel of some couple, and we have learned that, when our advice is not wanted by either, the best course is to withdraw. This is as true of nations as it is of married couples. In both cases our action is motivated by friendship. But if we are to stay friendly with the couple it is always necessary to wait until at least one of them is tired of fighting. In international as well as domestic affairs, there are times when the best thing to do is—to do nothing.

In our approach to the myriad troubles of Asia we should always remember that we start with a tremendous reservoir of good will. The fulfillment of our promise of independence to the Philippines and our acts of friendship toward the independent Kingdom of Siam stand as beacon lights to millions of Asiatics who are looking toward an expansion of their political and economic freedom. In all the change that inevitably lies ahead in Asia, we must make sure our actions do not drain this reservoir of good will. Our own safety and security, as well as the peace of the world, depend upon our success in being on the side of progress in Asia.

King George VI, Ernest Bevin, and James F. Byrnes following a dinner discussion of the atomic energy resolution and other matters then pending before the United Nations General Assembly. St. James Palace, January 1946.

BOOK IV
WORK AHEAD

Chapter 12

Building a People's Foreign Policy

THIS GENERATION of Americans has learned that the United States is a principal trustee of the world's peace and freedom. What the United States says and does affects the lives of people in the most remote areas of this earth. The words and deeds of a member of the Cabinet or of the Congress often reaches into more homes than those of many Kings and Presidents. Even Generalissimo Stalin, in his last talks with Harry Hopkins, acknowledged the world-wide interests and responsibilities of the United States and declared that our country has more reason to be a world power than any other.

Leadership and its inherent responsibilities we have accepted with reluctance—reluctance that two costly wars have not wholly overcome. But without our initiative, the United Nations probably would not have been created to promote and maintain international peace and security. Without our determined effort, it is doubtful whether ravages of war can be removed quickly enough to give the United Nations a chance to work.

The responsibilities that clearly are ours will be discharged in the years ahead only if we develop in international affairs a policy that truly reflects the will of our people. I am convinced that to build a people's foreign policy we must pursue three primary objectives.

First, we must have a foreign policy that is bipartisan in its origin and development; that is national rather than political in its conduct and its character; and that, consequently, is a continuing policy worthy of the confidence of other nations.

Second, we must have an institution that is responsive to the will of the people and able to translate our policies into effective action.

And, third, we must leave behind the era of secret diplomacy. We must make sure that our people have an opportunity to know the problems their diplomats confront so that they can judge properly the proposed solution. The right of the people to know is a basic element in the development of a people's foreign policy.

These objectives, I know from experience, are not easy to attain. But the story of what I encountered in my pursuit of them may be of some service in the work that lies ahead.

My conviction on the first objective stems from World War I. In November 1918, I was in Paris with Representatives Carter Glass and Richard S. Whaley of South Carolina. Out of all our talks with military and diplomatic representatives, I was particularly impressed by the comments of General Tasker H. Bliss, our military representative on the Supreme Council at Versailles. Among other things, he told us that, with the approach of peace, his associates lost much of their idealism; they talked less about ending all wars and more about reparations and territorial gains. He thought there was little chance of establishing international machinery to preserve peace unless President Wilson came to France and could make a successful appeal over the heads of politicians.

When I returned to Washington, I spoke to President Wilson about my conversation with General Bliss. He told me that in the latter days of the war he relied on Bliss more than on any other representative in Europe. However, he could not do as General Bliss suggested, he said, because he could not speak French and any appeal he might make would lose its force when translated into another language. When I visited him again a short time later, he then told me he had decided to go to Europe. To this day, I remember his words:

"I am going," he said, "in the hope that I may redeem the pledge I made to the mothers of the world that we were fighting a war to end wars."

He was not making a speech to me. He stated it simply as the reason for his decision.

In the early days of World War II, I told this story to President Roosevelt and expressed the opinion that Wilson lost his great fight for the League of Nations because he did not take with him at least one Republican Senator. President Roosevelt shared my opinion.

At Yalta, immediately after the Big Three agreed to support the Dumbarton Oaks proposal and before he left the conference table, President Roosevelt instructed Secretary Stettinius to name, as members of the delegation to the San Francisco Conference, Senator Connally and Senator Vandenberg. They worked in harmony with Secretary Stettinius at San Francisco and their wholehearted co-operation was largely responsible for the almost unanimous vote by which our adherence to the United Nations was approved by the Senate.

Before the first meeting of the Council of Foreign Ministers, I decided to invite a prominent Republican, well informed on international affairs, to accompany me. It did not occur to me then that a Senator could be away for as long a time as the treaty-drafting business was likely to consume. I consulted Senator Vandenberg. He suggested that I invite Mr. John Foster Dulles, who for years has been keenly interested in our foreign relations and is exceptionally well qualified. Mr. Dulles accepted the invitation, notwithstanding his business commitments, and was of great assistance. Later I recommended to President Truman that Mr. Dulles be a member of our delegation to the first meeting of the General Assembly of the United Nations. He accomplished much and continued his service at the meeting of the General Assembly in New York.

Our participation in the United Nations constantly and deliberately has been bipartisan. At both sessions of the General Assembly, our delegation included, in addition to Mr. Dulles, the top-ranking Democratic and Republican members of the Foreign Affairs Committees of both the Senate and the House, Senators Connally and Vandenberg and Representatives Bloom and Eaton. At the first session at London one of the delegates was my friend John G. Townsend, former Senator from Delaware, chairman of the Republican Senatorial Campaign Committee, and a man respected by all Senators.

When Edward R. Stettinius resigned as head of the permanent delegation to the United Nations, I recommended to the President that he appoint the Vermont Republican, Senator Warren R. Austin, as chief of our permanent mission to the United Nations. The President was delighted with the suggestion. He liked Austin, having been closely associated with him in the Senate. Throughout his Senate career Austin had shown an extensive knowledge of and a keen interest in foreign relations. He had made a great contribution to the success of the Chapultepec Conference and, in fact, since 1939, has co-operated wholeheartedly in the prosecution of the war and the preparations for the peace.

After we agreed at Moscow to resume work on the preparation of peace treaties at Paris, I asked Senators Connally and Vandenberg to go with me as advisers. They generously agreed and served through the meetings of the council and also during the peace conference. I discussed with them every phase of our foreign relations. In 1946 they spent 213 days away from Washington attending international conferences. No two legislators ever served their country more loyally or more efficiently than they did at those meetings.

Because Senator Vandenberg represented the political party opposed to the administration, and because he enjoyed the confidence of the overwhelming majority of his party, his support enabled us to speak of our foreign policy as the American policy.

At the conference of the Council of Foreign Ministers each delegation has five seats at the table. Seated with me were the two Senators, the deputy in charge of the work on the treaty under discussion, and the interpreter. Each Foreign Minister can bring to the conference room an additional eight or ten members of his staff. It makes quite an audience. Consequently the Ministers frequently hold private meetings in the hope that the absence of an audience may promote agreement. When these meetings are held each Foreign Minister is allowed to bring two associates in addition to the interpreter. To all such meetings, I asked the two Senators to accompany me. I preferred to have their counsel rather than the aid of the technicians of the State Department, as helpful as these gentlemen always were. Also, I wanted the Senators to know at first hand every stage of the treaty making.

The political party in power cannot ask the opposition party to share responsibility for the conduct of our foreign relations unless the leaders of the opposition are fully advised of our policies. This is true when the Congress and President are of the same party. It is particularly true when a majority of the Congress and the Chief Executive are not of the same political party. The executive branch of the government cannot announce a policy of importance requiring congressional action and then inform the leaders of the opposition. Even if the opposition leaders think the proposal unwise they must support it or create abroad the impression of dissension. A policy of by-passing the Congress would make impossible a bipartisan policy.

While Senator Vandenberg and Senator Connally were with me I sought their counsel not only on the treaties but on other matters connected with our foreign relations that were submitted to me by the Department each day. They were helpful and, though I know they were frequently and skillfully tempted, not once did either of them give to newspaper friends advance information of our plans.

The participation of Senators Connally and Vandenberg in the meetings of the Council of Foreign Ministers, the peace conference and the United Nations served to let the people of the world know that the foreign policy of the United States was a continuing policy and would not end with the defeat of a political party. It enabled me, during the ceremony at the Washington airport which marked our departure for the Peace Conference, to address this statement to the people of the world:

"The situation is entirely different from that which existed after World War I. Then we were badly divided. This time there is no division between the Executive and the Congress as to the making of peace. This time there is no division between the great political parties as to the making of peace. . . . We are all working together not as partisans of any political party or of any branch of the Government; we are working together as Americans. . . . We are deeply conscious that if we as a nation are to exert our influence on the affairs of the world, we must be united."

But during our stay in Paris, I was to experience one more demonstration that bipartisanship does not necessarily insure unity. Long before the Paris meeting, I had learned that the most conscientious effort to make a just peace would not receive united support at home. I have already reported the criticism I encountered when, at London, the Council of Foreign Ministers could not agree. I was prepared for that. But I was not prepared for some of the criticism I received when, at Moscow, we did agree.

The story of the Moscow meeting, I have told; the long negotiations, the final session which ended at 3:30 A. M., our take-off for the United States four hours later at 7:30 A. M., December 27. My statement that we were thoroughly exhausted when we landed at Washington at noon on the twenty-ninth will be fully understood. Nevertheless, I went directly to the State Department and to work.

Upon asking when I could see the President, an employee at the White House told me that the President was cruising down the Potomac and expected to remain on his boat for several days. I requested that a message be sent to him saying that I had returned and would like to report to him at his convenience and that I expected to make a radio speech the following evening about the work of the conference.

Shortly thereafter, I received an invitation to visit the President that afternoon on his boat, which was anchored near Quantico. I took a plane and reached Quantico about 4:30.

After I had reported to the President on what had happened at the conference, he expressed wholehearted approval of my action. He asked me to remain for dinner. There were present, as I recall, members of the President's staff who frequently accompanied him on such trips: Admiral Leahy, George Allen, General Vaughan, Clark Clifford, Charles Ross, Matthew Connelly, General Graham, and Judge Rosenman, who was working on a speech the President was to deliver the following week.

While we were at dinner, the President asked me to repeat what I had said to him about the conference, and I did so. From time to time the President interrupted to express his approval. There was no expression of disapproval or approval by any other except Admiral Leahy, who said that my report made him feel much better about the situation but that he did not approve of the agreement on Rumania and Bulgaria. I reminded him that both of us had been at Yalta and at Potsdam when President Roosevelt and President Truman had entered into agreements on the same subjects, seeking to establish provisional governments that would include representation of all political parties and that would provide for free elections and the four freedoms. These agreements, I added, had not been kept by either of the two states or by the Soviets. The Moscow agreement, I told him, was simply one more effort to achieve the objective of the Yalta and Potsdam agreements. At Moscow we had secured what previously the Soviets had opposed—the agreement to send Ambassador Harriman, Ambassador Clark Kerr, and Mr. Vyshinski to Rumania to seek ways to carry out the agreement. The effort might not be successful, I said, but the result could not be any worse than the previous situation. I asked what he would have done. I received no information.

Immediately after dinner I asked to be excused because I had to fly back to Washington; because of the rain and sleet then falling I feared a low ceiling at Washington. There was no further discussion of our foreign problems.

The President invited me to come back New Year's Eve and spend the night on the ship, and I promised to return.

When I went ashore I found that the sleet had covered the wings of my plane and it was impossible to use it. Therefore, I had to return to Washington by automobile. The marine officer who kindly offered to drive me to Washington found he had undertaken an exceedingly difficult task as the sleet kept all the windows and windshield of the car covered with ice. Consequently, it was late when I reached home. That automobile trip, following the long journey from Moscow, made December 29 a far from perfect day. But when I walked in the door at home, Mrs. Byrnes handed me a message that gave the day at least a perfect ending. It was from my thoughtful friend and counselor, Cordell Hull. It said:

My dear Jim: My heartiest congratulations on the splendid progress made at the Moscow Conference. Understanding, confidence, friendliness, and the whole spirit of international co-operation have been greatly improved by the work of this conference.

The next night I made to the people my radio report on the conference. I explained the agreements reached and observed that they "should bring hope to the war-weary people of many lands." I also expressed the belief that "the meeting in Moscow did serve to bring about better understanding."

When I returned to the President's ship, the night of the thirty-first, he congratulated me on the report. He said the party on board had listened the previous night and considered it a convincing statement.

Within a few days, however, one or two newspaper columnists wrote that the President had wired me to come to his ship and had expressed strong disapproval of my agreements. They stated that there was ill feeling between the President and the Secretary of State. There was a general understanding among the newspaper correspondents that the information came from the White House and critics felt encouraged to attack me when it was rumored that the criticisms were shared by the President's official family.

The fact is the President did not on that occasion nor at any other time express to me disapproval of any position I took at the meetings of the Council of Foreign Ministers or any other meetings. Nor did he ever express to me disapproval of any statement I made on our foreign policy.

In the President's letter to Stalin written before the Moscow Conference, the President approved most of the proposals agreed to at Moscow.

My experience with the Moscow agreements demonstrated that in the pursuit of a truly national foreign policy one has to be prepared for criticism from both the right and the left. Had these agreements been as favorable to the Soviet Union as some critics have charged, the Soviets would not have violated them. And the fact that ever since then we have been protesting against these violations indicates that they were in the best interests of the liberated states.

However, the person or persons inspiring the stories of dissension between the President and myself continued their efforts. In at least one press conference the President denied such dissension, but the stories persisted. A man who holds public office learns to disregard misrepresentations, but I admit these untrue stories did not make life any easier for me in the strenuous days of early 1946.

My hope for united support of our foreign policies received a serious setback when, on September 12, 1946, while I was in Paris, Secretary of Commerce Henry A. Wallace made a speech at Madison Square Garden contending that the policy which had been approved by the President, and carried out by me, was too harsh to the Soviet Union and that a more conciliatory approach to them was necessary. I was not greatly surprised by the Secretary's action. Previously, he had made a statement to the New York *Times* referring to our negotiations with Iceland for the use of the airfield we had built there. His statement was effectively used by the Communists in Iceland and it had obstructed the efforts of the State Department to secure an agreement important to the defense of this hemisphere.

In Paris, the importance of Mr. Wallace's Madison Square Garden speech was magnified in the minds of the representatives of foreign governments by newspaper reports quoting President Truman as saying at a press conference that he approved the Wallace speech in its entirety. This report stimulated widespread discussion among the govermental representatives attending the peace conference; it inspired inquiries to our representatives in various capitals. Foreign Ministers wondered whether in my various public statements I had correctly presented American policy.

Senator Vandenberg issued a statement saying that he wanted to co-operate with the administration but he could co-operate with only one Secretary of State at a time.

Senator Connally declared that he supported the policy we had announced and had been following.

I concluded that I should not make a public statement; that the matter called for correction by the President.

Of course, the position of our delegation was a very unhappy one. So far as possible, I tried to avoid delegates to the conference or the other Foreign Ministers because I wanted to avoid answering questions about whether the policy of our government had changed. Our difficulties were increased rather than lessened when Mr. Wallace announced on the White House steps that he and the President had agreed that the Secretary of Commerce would make no more speeches until after the peace conference. To the delegates in Paris, this implied that the President had not objected to a later renewal of his attacks on our foreign policy.

While I had no direct communication with the White House, I learned of developments from the press and from several messages sent to me by Assistant Secretary of State Donald Russell. As a result, on September 18, I sent the President a message, reminding him that, on the advice of a physician, I had given him my resignation in April. By agreement, my resignation would take effect upon the completion of the treaties. My message further stated:

> "If it is not possible for you, for any reason, to keep Mr. Wallace, as a member of your Cabinet, from speaking on foreign affairs, it would be a grave mistake from every point of view for me to continue in office, even temporarily. Therefore, if it is not completely clear in your own mind that Mr. Wallace should be asked to refrain from criticizing the foreign policy of the United States while he is a member of your Cabinet, I must ask you to accept my resignation immediately. At this critical time, whoever is Secretary of State must be known to have the undivided support of your administration and, so far as possible, of the Congress.
>
> "I shall, of course, remain here until my successor arrives. In case you are not ready to make that appointment promptly, you can, of course, appoint someone other than the Secretary of State to head the United States delegation at the Peace Conference."

The following day I was informed that the President wished to talk with me over the telephone. We had difficulty getting a clear signal and finally I was told that a third party was on the channel and the telephone company's operator was unable to "clear the line" for our conversation. I then asked the President if we might arrange for a teletype conversation. He kindly consented. There is a teletype instrument in the White House, and one in our Embassy in Paris. I went to the message room of our Embassy and dictated to the operator this statement:

> I realize that in reaching the agreement announced by Mr. Wallace you were trying to reconcile the difference in views held by us on the one hand and by Mr. Wallace on the other.
>
> But Mr. Wallace's last statement leaves the representatives of our government abroad, as well as other governments, in more doubt than ever as to just what American foreign policy will be.
>
> Mr. Wallace has reiterated that he stands by his New York speech which he does not deny was intended to be critical of our foreign policy. There is little difference in a member of the Cabinet issuing

to the press statements that he stands by his criticism of your foreign policy and making such criticisms from a platform.

Mr. Wallace has promised to refrain from speaking until the present Paris Peace Conference concludes, but the form of his statement indicates that he will continue to press publicly his own ideas on foreign policy which differ from your ideas and that you recognize his right as a member of your Cabinet to do so.

When the administration itself is divided on its own foreign policy, it cannot hope to convince the world that the American people have a foreign policy.

The position of the delegation in this particular conference is not restored by Mr. Wallace's agreement not to speak during this conference when he remains a member of your official family and indicates in effect that he will renew his criticism of your present foreign policy as soon as the conference is over. We are promised only a moratorium from criticism of your policies by your own administration.

The world is today in doubt not only as to American foreign policy, but as to your foreign policy.

This particular peace conference is only a stage in the peace-making process. The conference makes only recommendations to the Council of Foreign Ministers which upon the adjournment of the conference will meet to draft the final treaties. Then while the Foreign Ministers are at the most critical stage of their negotiations, Mr. Wallace can resume his public criticisms of our policies and says he will do so.

Moreover, this conference deals only with some of the treaties, and the making of peace with Germany, Austria and Japan is still ahead of us. This conference is only a start and nothing done will have finality if there is not continuity in our foreign policy.

You and I are confronted with most serious problems entirely disassociated from the conference and demanding unity at home.

When the representatives of other governments know that as soon as the conference ends we will again have conflicting statements made by your Secretary of State and your Secretary of Commerce, your delegation here cannot contribute much to the making of the peace. As a matter of fact, since these attacks upon us by a member of the Cabinet, our efforts have been greatly handicapped.

When the conference ends and the Council of Foreign Ministers meets to make the final decision, each day I would be confronted with statements of Mr. Wallace in conflict with views expressed by me. I would then have to insist upon being relieved. It is far better for the administration to let us come home now, rather than for us to return October 23, by which date we hope the conference will adjourn.

If Wallace is influenced by any ill feeling toward me it is possible that if you accept my resignation he might be willing to support your foreign policies or at least refrain from attacking such policies.

To me the important thing is to try and restore confidence in our policies.

I sincerely hope that when you appoint someone you can announce that you are wholeheartedly and undividedly behind the foreign policy of the United States as it has been heretofore determined by you and as it is being carried out; that our foreign policy is an American foreign policy and not the policy of any party or faction; that no change in American foreign policy is desired or contemplated by you. If for any reason you wish to modify your policy in any way, I hope that whatever policy you determine upon you will announce it as the American policy to which we are going to adhere, and that while a private citizen can express his views in opposition, that no member of your cabinet can express views in conflict with your policies.

I have been urging on every Foreign Minister with whom I have talked that the American policy as fixed by you was a permanent bipartisan policy and they could rely upon it that it would not be shifting from time to time and it would not even shift if there were a change in parties because for the first time we had the co-operation of the Republicans. Any statement that in six weeks the policy will be re-examined and discussed with Mr. Wallace whose statements have caused such consternation will cause these Foreign Ministers to doubt the stability of our policy.

I respectfully submit that if Mr. Molotov believed that on October 23 there would be a re-examination of the question of permitting Wallace to again attack your policy he would derive great comfort. No other member of the Cabinet would claim the right or be allowed to criticize your policy. The fact that it is not decided now that a man who stays in the Cabinet must support your policy is bound to hurt us. The work of our delegation is at a standstill. Representatives of the other delegations keep our delegation busy asking whether the administration will permit Wallace to make another speech attacking us. These governments would never permit a member of the Cabinet to do such a thing and they cannot understand how we would permit it unless his views were shared or there was a serious division of sentiment among the people. I do not want to ask you to do anything that would force Mr. Wallace out of the Cabinet. However, I do not think that any man who professes any loyalty to you would so seriously impair your prestige and the prestige of the government with the nations of the world. This is particularly true, if you showed him telegrams such as we have received from Greece. You and I spent 15 months building a bipartisan policy. We did a fine job convincing the world that it was a permanent policy upon which the world could rely. Wallace destroyed it in a day.

It is not proper for me to quote the President's statements. But I think it is proper to say that, as a result of the conversation, I knew he did not intend to change his policies or leave any doubt about his views. He did not tell me what action he would take. However, the following day the

President settled the matter in a manner satisfactory, I hope, to the over-whelming majority of the people of the United States.

With the resignation of Secretary Wallace, confidence in the American policy was restored. Senators Connally and Vandenberg continued to serve in support of our foreign policy with unswerving loyalty. The Wallace incident took place during a national campaign which resulted in the shifting of the majority rule in Congress from the Democrats to the Republicans. Senator Connally met opposition in his primary election, but would not abandon his work in Paris where he was helping his country and come home to help himself. Senator Vandenberg, who also was a candidate for re-election, not only took no part in the campaign but was barely able to get back to Michigan to vote; he urged other Republicans to support the bipartisan foreign policy.

The results of our efforts to maintain a bipartisan foreign policy were clearly indicated by the overwhelming approval of the Senate in its vote on June 5, 1947, ratifying the five treaties thus far concluded. When I was informed of the vote, I could not help but recall again the unhappy months after World War I when President Wilson struggled with a disgruntled and determined Senate that finally defeated his efforts for peace. And I renewed my hope that never again would our policy makers repeat President Wilson's mistake; that hereafter the responsible leaders of both parties would be kept informed of our policies from the beginning of their formulation to their ultimate conclusion.

The second element in the development and maintenance of a people's foreign policy is the caliber of the institution responsible for our foreign affairs. It has often been popular to use the State Department as a whipping post for shortcomings in the conduct of our foreign affairs that actually are due to our own indifference.

The organization and operation of the State Department still needs continuing study. It grew from an organization that numbered nine hundred people before the war to one of some 3,000 people who were scattered in eighteen buildings throughout Washington. A few months after I assumed office, the personnel of the Department had been almost doubled by the transfer to it of all or part of such war agencies as the Office of Strategic Services, the Office of War Information, the Foreign Economic Administration, and the Surplus Property Administration. The transfer of these wartime agencies did not make me very happy. The job of acting as "undertaker" for war agencies necessarily is a bad one. The most capable people are impelled to leave a dying organization, to find permanent work with a live and growing organization. Morale sags and problems multiply.

But, more important, I do not believe that functions primarily administrative in character should be assigned to the State Department.

The State Department must be a policy-making department. It cannot be run like one which is charged with conducting a variety of operations. The amount of time a Secretary of State must give to decisions on carrying out operating functions, necessarily is taken away from the important questions of foreign policy.

Because I thought the State Department should be maintained as a policy-making department, I opposed the efforts of the War Department to transfer to the State Department control of our occupation organizations in Europe and in the Pacific. The State Department is not adapted for such work. It cannot recruit an efficient organization because the appointees could, at best, be promised only temporary employment far removed from their homes. If the burden of carrying on shipping, maintenance of transportation, policing, inspection and all the myriad duties of occupation forces were transferred to the State Department, its capacity to define wisely important foreign policies would be seriously hampered. We should retain the efficient organizations that have been developed by Generals McNarney and Clay in Germany, General Clark in Austria, and General MacArthur in Japan.

The proponents of the transfer argue that there is a division of authority between the War Department and the State Department, but I do not believe the argument is sound. There is such a division in all matters affecting foreign policy. The President determines our foreign policy. He makes his decisions upon the recommendations of the Secretary of State. The policy as determined must be executed by the War and Navy departments whose personnel, by training and experience, are best qualified to conduct the necessary operations. Until there is a treaty of peace, the job of occupation is as much the job of the Army as is the job of making war. Of course, it is a disagreeable task, but the army of no other power has quit the job and our army should not.

There must, of course, always be close co-ordination between the State, War and Navy departments. A policy which, in today's world, is not defined with one eye on our power to back it up, is hardly a policy at all. Since the early days of the war not only have the Secretaries of State, War and Navy held frequent consultations but a Co-ordinating Committee made up of representatives from these three departments meets regularly to consider common problems.

In February 1946, I agreed to a proposal made by the Joint Chiefs of Staff which eventually will greatly promote the efforts to achieve coordination. This was the proposal to establish the National War College as a combined training institution for high ranking officers of State, War and Navy. It began its operations July 1, 1946. Foreign service officers have been assigned to the college and the new institution is already doing a most effective work.

In October 1945, I proposed that the President issue an executive order establishing a Council of National Defense consisting of the Secretaries of State, War and Navy, so that our foreign and our defense policies could be fully co-ordinated. The draft order provided that the Chief of Staff of the Army and the Chief of Naval Operations serve as advisers to the Council on military matters. In addition to maintaining its own secretariat, the council also would have under it a unified intelligence service. The proposal was never approved, but many of its objectives were incorporated into the legislation to merge the Army and Navy into a Department of National Defense. As this legislation is put into practice, the problem of co-ordinating our foreign and our military policies must be given continuing study.

One who was Secretary of State a total of 562 days, 350 of which were spent at international conferences, cannot claim to have effected many fundamental changes in an institution like the State Department. In fact, during the early months of my tenure we made a conscious effort to help the Department recover from an acute attack of "reorganization jitters." But one innovation was introduced. It did not win any public attention but I regard it as one of the more significant undertakings in the conduct of our foreign affairs.

When I became Secretary, I attempted to obtain a broad statement of our policy. I thought there should be a basic operating guide for a realistic foreign policy. No such document had been drawn up. Many officials of the State Department could outline our policy for a particular area, but it was readily apparent that the statement was only their idea of what our policy was. There was no authoritative text, duly considered and approved, which set forth our national objectives the world over. I asked that the formulation of statements of policy be given a top priority in the work of the Department.

Country committees for every nation in the world were created. These committees sought to draw up a rounded program that tied our political, economic, intelligence and information activities into a commonly conceived program. After this group had prepared a draft statement it was sent to our Missions abroad for review and criticism. It was my opinion that too much policy was determined without consulting the man on the spot who was in daily contact with the situation in that country. Also, I thought, if he helped to shape the policy he would be better able to follow a consistent program. Certain of the larger Embassies received many or all of the statements for comment. When the suggestions from the field had been received and studied a final policy statement was prepared by the men who lived with these problems. As they were approved, these became our operating guides. To meet changing conditions, I directed that these policy statements be reviewed and revised every six months.

There is little sense in determining policy in the Department unless that policy is made known to our representatives throughout the world. In past years I have visited Embassies where the representatives of our State Department and the Navy and Army attachés each had different opinions about our government's policy toward that particular country. When our own people didn't know our policy, one could not expect a foreign government to know it. Copies of our policy statements were also sent to the Joint Chiefs of Staff.

When these "country" statements were completed, I asked that "area" committees be set up to review the policies set forth for each country in that area to make sure that our aims were consistent. At this point, we decided to bring in fresh minds to review the statements with critical detachment. The "area" committee for Latin America was the first one created. It was composed of Professors Samuel F. Bemis of Yale University, Dana G. Munro of Princeton University, and Dexter Perkins of the University of Rochester, all of them outstanding scholars of Latin-American diplomacy. I had not had an opportunity to extend this program further when my resignation became effective.

I was glad to be able to hand to Secretary Marshall statements of American foreign policy on every country in the world and covering every facet of our interests. He may differ with some of those policies, but at least he can determine definitely and in a few minutes what they are, and change them to accord with his views.

These statements carry an added advantage. They require the development of a consistent program of action. And they force the responsible officers to look ahead, to plan for the crises of tomorrow.

The best planned organization, however, depends for its strength on the caliber of its people.

Immediately after becoming Secretary I found that attending conferences abroad made it impossible for me to attend many staff meetings so I requested Under Secretary Acheson to preside at these meetings. Each morning he met with the office directors of the Department. While I was abroad Mr. Acheson kept me informed about any important problems considered by the group. When I was home, he would confer with me about them, usually late in the afternoon. It was seldom that either of us left the Department before seven o'clock. I could not have devoted myself so completely to the task of peace making in the conferences abroad had I not known the work of the Department was being efficiently carried on under the direction of a man with the unusual ability and energy of Under Secretary Acheson.

I want to pay tribute also to the generally high quality of the men who have made the diplomatic service their career. The vast majority of the career foreign service officers I have met are able, conscientious, hard-working men, capable of earning far more than the comparatively low salaries our government has paid them.

And I would like to destroy the legend of the diplomat as a striped-pants cookie pusher. Today's diplomat knows that the social graces are far less valuable to him than the ability to work intensively for long hours with little opportunity for rest or relaxation. Members of my staff at the various international gatherings more than once found themselves working around the clock. The fact is that during my year and a half as Secretary of State, out of all the men in the service of the Department who called on me, I can recall only two who arrived wearing striped trousers and spats—and those two were political appointees!

It should be clear, then, that I intend no disparagement when I say that our foreign service was, and to a large extent, still is inadequate for the tasks we must discharge in world affairs. I am particularly pleased that during my period as Secretary of State action was taken to help remedy this situation. The passage of the Kee-Connally bill "to improve, strengthen, and expand the Foreign Service," which was signed by the President on August 13, 1946, was the first legislation dealing with foreign service personnel in twenty-two years—a period which brought vast changes in the scope and responsibilities of our foreign service.

Work to obtain this legislation had been started under Secretary Hull and was continued by Secretary Stettinius. It was pending before Congress when the Council of Foreign Ministers adjourned its first session in Paris on May 16 and was one of the reasons why I resisted the temptation to take a vacation during the one-month recess and returned home instead. Long experience had taught me that in Congress, as in other places, things do not happen unless somebody makes them happen.

With Assistant Secretary Donald Russell, I went to the Congress and enlisted the aid of friends. Thanks again to the co-operation of both political parties, the bill was given special handling to insure a vote before adjournment and was adopted in both the House and the Senate by unanimous consent. It marked a long step forward toward the fulfillment of the second objective I have stated.

As a result of this act, salaries can be raised so that no longer will it be necessary to appoint men of wealth as our Ambassadors. At the same time that salaries were advanced all down the line, more rigid requirements on training and promotion were provided. The bill seeks to make our foreign service truly representative of our government and people by making it possible for the best qualified men and women in the country, in or out of the government, to have tours of duty with the foreign service in any of its ranks. Among the most important provisions, in my opinion, was one that calls for more frequent and varied assignments in this country. Its purpose is to prevent these sentinels of the United States from losing touch with American life. I recall Woodrow Wilson saying, "It is easy to send an American to London or Paris, but it is hard to keep an *American* there." A man who represents his country abroad, no less than the man who represents his people in Congress, needs to return frequently to the "grass roots."

In other ways, too, the State Department is becoming increasingly sensitive to public opinion. Each day a digest of representative newspaper editorials and opinions of radio commentators is placed on the desks of Department officials and sent to our missions overseas. Letters and petitions from individuals and organizations are analyzed for evidence of opinion trends. The Public Liaison Division, for example, keeps in touch with all types of voluntary organizations throughout the country, not only to help them keep informed on foreign affairs but to get their criticism and suggestions on pending issues. Behind these efforts is the firm realization that our foreign policy must be responsive to and have the firm support of the American people.

A basic prerequisite to a people's foreign policy is, of course, a well-informed public. In the field of international relations the world is still suffering a hangover from the era when international agreements were secret and private arrangements between rulers. But the United States, at least, is rapidly leaving the habits of that era far behind.

The war interrupted the trend away from secret diplomacy. Military and political agreements then were often so interrelated, secrecy was required in the interests of the war effort. All the meetings between President Roosevelt, Prime Minister Churchill and Generalissimo Stalin were held in secrecy with the press excluded. Although many newspapermen may have learned indirectly of the conferences, the discussions and the agreements, they refrained from publishing them in accordance with the wartime voluntary press censorship.

But at Potsdam, even though the war in the Pacific was still continuing, the press was restless under the agreement denying them information on what was occurring at the conference. American newspapers and radio networks had many representatives stationed in Berlin to cover the conference. However, the suburb of Potsdam, which was the scene of the conference, was in the Russian zone, and they were not permitted to go there. The press complained bitterly, but they received no detailed report until the President returned and made his report to Congress. Because of the agreements in connection with the Japanese war, some secrecy was thoroughly justified. But since then I have often wished that more information could, at that time, have been supplied our people on European problems.

When the Council of Foreign Ministers met in London, there was no military reason for secrecy. But the best arrangement we could secure was for a daily issuance of a communiqué containing the subjects discussed and any agreement reached. It did not, however, report the statements or positions of individual members. This seemed an advance over Potsdam, but it turned out to be no advance at all. Each Minister assigned a representative to a committee charged with the drafting of a communiqué. But the communiqué, like everything else, required unanimous agreement. The Council itself reached so few agreements that there was little for the committee to report except the debates, which were prohibited material. Under these circumstances, the correspondents did the only thing they could do—tried to get information from someone connected with the delegations who presumably had been instructed not to give it. Consequently, the reports of the meetings not only were inadequate but were often inaccurate.

Trouble began with the very first communiqué. The Soviet representative did not want to give out any statement. The others argued that a communiqué should be issued stating at the very least that the Council had agreed to take up the Italian treaty and would begin with the study of a text submitted by the British delegation. After a long argument, the Soviet representative finally agreed to the release of the following uninformative communiqué:

The Council of Foreign Ministers held its second meeting at 4 P.M. and adjourned at 6:30 P.M. Owing to the number of documents which have to be translated and studied it was decided to meet next at 11 o'clock on Friday instead of tomorrow as planned.

A soothsayer rather than a reporter was required to get any news out of a statement like that. Similar statements followed. Our communiqués were shorter than the average weather report and soon an effort was made to make them less accurate than one.

The Council had discussed a complaint from the Soviet Union that France was failing to repatriate Soviet citizens. France in turn complained that the Soviet Union continued to refuse to repatriate nationals of France. That evening the communiqué contained no information other than this simple statement of subjects discussed. It was unanimously agreed to by the members of the Press Committee. But later that night, about eleven o'clock, a Soviet representative told Mr. Walter Brown, who represented the United States on the Press Committee, that Mr. Molotov objected to the communiqué and wanted it held up. Mr. Brown replied that it had already been given out by the representative of the United Kingdom who was serving as chairman for that day.

Next morning, Mr. Molotov complained to the council. Mr. Bevin stated that the chairman of the committee had issued the communiqué as a result of unanimous agreement. Mr. Molotov replied, "My actions cannot be controlled by any secretary or representative on a committee." He insisted that the council should issue another communiqué eliminating reference to France's complaint that the Soviets failed to repatriate French nationals. Mr. Bidault objected. Mr. Bevin and I maintained that it would be an incorrect statement of the proceedings; that the communiqué had correctly stated the facts and that we would not agree to issue a second one. Mr. Molotov stated that under such circumstances he would put out a communiqué of his own. And he did so.

Later I learned that it was important to him to issue another communiqué because the previous night he had wired Moscow to prohibit the publication of the committee's communiqué in any newspaper in the Soviet Union. Consequently, Moscow expected a substitute communiqué. Mr. Molotov's personal communiqué, therefore, was the only statement on the proceedings of the council that was released to the Soviet press.

The London press arrangements greatly embarrassed me because I had known many of the correspondents covering the conference during much of my public life. Some of them I knew from my days in the Senate, while others I had come to know since I had been in the White House and the State Department.

One day I met a group of them in the lobby. An old friend addressed me as "Senator," and asked whether I wanted to be called Senator, Justice or Secretary. I told him it made little difference, because I knew at that time the press representatives were not calling me any one of those three names.

When we went to Moscow in December we had the same arrangement we had had in London. I did not like it, but the meeting in Moscow was called at my request. I wanted to progress with the peace, and I did not feel I was in a position to dictate terms on press arrangements to the government I had asked to be our host. This was particularly true since any satisfactory arrangement would necessitate the Soviet Government's altering its own censorship rules. Once again, the communiqué furnished very little news and once again the people of the world received many incorrect impressions about the proceedings of the Council and the arguments leading up to the decisions.

During the discussion of the Iranian case at the Security Council in New York, for the first time it was possible to meet freely with the correspondents and frankly tell them the problems we faced. The proceedings in the Council were opened to the public and I refused to be bound by any pledges of secrecy in the closed meetings. I met with the correspondents and explained to them, for their background information, our view of the situation. When I couldn't do it, I designated a member of my staff to do it for me. The result was that the public received accounts that were written with full knowledge and understanding. And the force of public opinion thus stimulated was a vital factor in the ultimate outcome of the case.

I decided that what was good in the Security Council would be good also in the Council of Foreign Ministers. I realized I couldn't do the task myself and that I needed an officer who was familiar with all phases of our foreign relations and whose relationship to me was close enough to enable him to be fully informed on all issues so that he could properly interpret those with news value to the press. I persuaded Charles E. Bohlen to accept the assignment. Chip was not only a veteran foreign service officer but he had spent several years in Moscow, spoke Russian fluently, and had acted as interpreter for President Roosevelt and President Truman at all their international conferences. Chip and Michael J. McDermott, who for many years has handled press relations for the State Department capably and courteously, made an effective team.

When the Council of Foreign Ministers met in Paris, I told the Ministers that I would not again agree to the previous press arrangements and that I would insist on our right to give the press the American point of view on every proposal before the council. I was determined that, if the meetings of the council were to continue to be closed, so far as the American delegation was concerned, they would not be secret meetings.

After every session, Chip and Mike would meet with the press and "brief" them on everything of importance that had taken place. The newspapermen, of course, would have preferred to be present at the meetings but they soon learned that they were receiving objective, accurate and constructive reports. They recognized that closed meetings sometimes were helpful in reaching agreement; most of them were willing to sacrifice attendance at the meetings, particularly since they soon realized that our action was forcing other delegations to take similar action.

During the Paris session the council held several "private" meetings at which the Minister was accompanied only by two advisers in addition to his interpreter. At the first of these, it was suggested that we withhold from the press everything that took place in these gatherings. I refused. I said, "In the first place, I think it wrong. In the second place, the agreement will not be kept. Somebody present will advise other members of his delegation of what has taken place and then the information will leak to a favorite correspondent."

I had been bitten by that dog before. I told them that at London I had tried to live up to such an agreement. Then, I had read in the New York

Herald Tribune an absolutely correct description of the events of the previous day. I was embarrassed at the next meeting, assuming I would be charged with having "leaked" the story. Upon investigation I learned that the correspondent had gotten his information from a person connected with the *Herald Tribune* office in Paris.

I told them of similar experiences in London. A true story in an American newspaper came, my press representative learned, from information supplied by an official in the British Foreign Office. Shortly thereafter, an enterprising reporter secured a story for the Chicago *Sun,* which was a correct statement of a debate in the council, from a representative of Tass, the Soviet news agency.

The London experience was enough for me, I told my colleagues, and consequently I would not again join in any agreement that would prevent me from giving the press information about the American position.

From then on, the press could give the people accurate reports on the progress, or lack of progress, in the council as it appeared from the American point of view. This stimulated the others to present their point of view. I was glad to observe this development, because it placed the position of the individual countries on the various issues precisely where they belonged—before the bar of public opinion.

Eventually, even Mr. Molotov was influenced by this example. In July, when he made his important speech announcing the Soviet program for Germany, he adopted our custom. Mimeographed copies of his speech —which was delivered in a closed session—were distributed to the press in advance. When I learned of this action, I congratulated him. Since then, both Mr. Molotov and Mr. Gromyko, in his work at the United Nations, have frequently followed this course. Mr. Gromyko, I understand, now even calls in various newspaper correspondents to explain to them, as background information, the Soviet point of view on questions before the United Nations.

When the peace conference convened in Paris, I proposed that the press and radio representatives be admitted to all meetings. My motion was seconded by Mr. Molotov, who declared he was heartily in favor of it. I felt my efforts to remove the curtain from the peace negotiations had at last succeeded. My satisfaction was not lessened by the intensive efforts of the Soviet delegation and its satellites to use the conference proceedings for propaganda purposes.

In one of Mr. Molotov's propaganda attacks, he charged that the United States and the United Kingdom were violating agreements to support the adoption of certain conference-procedure rules. This was so baseless that I replied with a very sharp speech in which I repeatedly cited the record to prove that his assertions were without foundation. And after each citation I would say: "Only Mr. Molotov would make such charges." Toward the end of the speech I referred to our free press and assured Mr. Molotov it would print his charges impugning the motives of the United States. I then added:

"I challenge him to permit publication in the Soviet Union of the statement I have now made. . . . Today we have only admiration and respect for the people of the Soviet Republics and we will not permit that admiration and respect to be lessened by any attack by Mr. Molotov."

Within forty-eight hours my speech appeared in the Soviet press. As far as I know, it was the first and last time a speech of mine was so honored. I only regret it had to be a speech criticizing Mr. Molotov.

In New York, when Mr. Molotov invited the council to meet in Moscow, I agreed, provided the press would be free to report the proceedings as they had the council sessions in Paris and New York. He agreed, saying that Moscow's serious housing shortage would impose the only limitation. In a private conversation I tried to get assurances that radio correspondents would be included. Radio, he said, presented a different problem and he would have to take it up with his government. Later he said that the radio correspondents would be allowed to report from Moscow. The correspondents agree that Mr. Molotov fulfilled his promise to keep their dispatches free from censorship.

Early in 1946, I determined to find some way of telling the Russians and the people of the Soviet satellite states the truth about our position on matters affecting world peace. In all these countries our position was being misrepresented daily. I did not want a vehicle for propaganda but we were engaged in a battle for the minds of the people and I did want a method of making factual statements to correct untruths. The only possibility seemed to be to increase the power of our radio station at Munich.

When I told General Clay of my keen interest in the subject, he went to work on it. Assistant Secretary William Benton, with his energy and resourcefulness, also became active. He sent engineers to Munich to determine what was necessary to improve the equipment and perfect an organization. Additional equipment was transported from England where we had been using it during the war.

Between the first and second sessions of the Council of Foreign Ministers in Paris, I returned to Washington. While there, I was invited by some of my former colleagues of the Senate Appropriations Committee to discuss with them my proposal to add 18 million dollars to the State Department appropriation bill to carry on the Department's information work, including the operation of "The Voice of America." Some Senators expressed doubt about the wisdom of the appropriation because they felt that the views of some of the persons engaged in the work were too liberal, if not radical.

I explained that these employees had been transferred to the State Department from wartime agencies, that they were protected by civil service and could be removed only in accordance with civil service rules. The result was the enactment of the McCarran Amendment which gave the Secretary power to remove employees for the good of the service. I assured the Senators that a thorough investigation would be made of the personnel to be sure of their sympathies and loyalties. They then granted the full appropriation.

Before returning to Paris, I issued instructions for the investigation. Believing that prosecutors should not be judges, I directed that the investigators should present to an independent committee which had nothing to do with the investigation the evidence believed sufficient to justify removal. As a result of the recommendations of this committee, a number of employees have been removed under the authority of the McCarran Amendment.

Once again, serious opposition to the continuation of this program has arisen in Congress. As this is written, the outcome still is in doubt. It will be most unfortunate if Congress does not make an adequate appropriation for this work. I spent many hours helping to develop this program because I thought it very important to have some means of answering the false charges made against the United States. It is not enough for us to be conscious of the purity of our motives and the innocence of our actions. It is necessary that we convince the world.

While we are appropriating hundreds of millions of dollars to aid other countries, it would be wise to spend a few million to protect the good name of the United States.

One small but important technical barrier to the free flow of information to the public is the desire of many officials to "overclassify" documents. Every army officer has encountered the problem and I imagine many of them have shared my experience of receiving material taken from a newspaper with "confidential" marked over it, and in some cases even "secret." I found altogether too many State Department documents that were classified "top secret" when they did not merit even a "secret" classification. Since the war was over, I issued instructions to liberalize the classification of all messages. I am afraid that I did not make much progress. It will take some time to change the habits of years, but changed they must be.

Early in 1946 I found another way to remove diplomatic exchanges from the realm of secrecy. On February 28, instead of sending a "note," I made a speech setting forth our position on existing problems. I hoped it would result in bringing into the open the discussion of those problems. I followed this with other speeches and my efforts were more successful than I had expected. Thereafter, not only did the Soviet officials speak publicly explaining their position on current problems but Generalissimo

Stalin began giving newspaper interviews to correspondents of the United States and the United Kingdom.

There are, of course, some matters between governments which should not be discussed in this manner but, after all, there are not very many of these. This decision, as well as my decision not to agree again to secret conferences, was based on a conviction I reluctantly reached on the attitude of the Soviet Government. If, at the time of the London Conference, the American people had known about the communications exchanged by President Roosevelt and President Truman with Generalissimo Stalin, which I have reported in preceding chapters, they would have better understood the difficulties I encountered at London. Certainly, the people would have been more sympathetic with my position.

After the London Conference, in justice to our position, I was forced to describe in my radio report some of the difficulties we encountered. I did not tell all that I have now told because I still hoped and wanted to believe that the Soviets were moved by the same common purpose that moved us—the desire for an early peace. Whenever persons representing their own interests or the interests of their governments meet in conference and have a common purpose, it is advisable to minimize differences on methods in order to reconcile those differences more easily. This was the thought that President Roosevelt expressed just before he died when he advised Churchill to minimize our difficulties with the Soviets in his public address.

At Moscow I still hoped that the Soviet Union and the United States had a common purpose. However, by the latter part of January 1946, there was accumulated evidence that regardless of what might be their long-term plan, certainly their immediate purpose was to delay the peace in Europe and in the Pacific.

Stalin's speech on February 9, 1946, in which he announced the new Five-Year Plan with its emphasis on rearmament instead of the production of consumer goods the Russian people need so badly, was a shock to me. But even more threatening was the Soviet attitude toward Iran, the evidence of their willingness to violate the sovereignty of their little neighbor. It confirmed the ambition Molotov had expressed to Hitler for the control of the territory south of Baku. These things inspired my speeches beginning in February 1946, speeches which were correctly interpreted as reflecting a firmer attitude toward the Soviet Government. No longer was there any wisdom in minimizing our differences because no longer was there any justification for the belief that we were animated by the common purpose of an early peace.

And no longer was it necessary to minimize our differences because of the condition of our armed forces. In the fall of 1945 the American Army was being demobilized with greater rapidity than anyone expected and the point system of discharges left us with only skeleton divisions. As Director of War Mobilization, I had approved that system because I thought it fair and because I assumed the world would want peace quickly and permanently. However, it meant that the most experienced men were among the first to be discharged. Key men in all divisions were discharged at about the same time. Some of the people who yelled the loudest for me to adopt a firm attitude toward Russia, yelled even louder for the rapid demobilization of the Army. Theodore Roosevelt once wisely said, "Uncle Sam should speak softly and carry a big stick." My critics wanted me to speak loudly and carry a twig.

With the turn of the year the reorganization of the Army was under way and there was no longer reason for withholding from the people full information as to our differences with the Soviets.

With that decision there had to be a change in our information policy. The people had to know what was going on else we could not hope for their support. Thereafter, by speeches, daily conferences between Mr. Bohlen, Mr. McDermott and the correspondents, and by the frequent meetings I held with the correspondents, we kept the people fully informed of our relations and our negotiations with the Soviet Government.

I continue to think that, if we are to have a lasting peace, it must be a people's peace. The people can exert their full influence in the conduct of foreign affairs only if they know more about them.

That basic democratic right, the right of the people to know, must be applied increasingly to the conduct of foreign affairs. If that right is essential—as I believe it is—to the functioning of democracy here at home, it is at least equally necessary to apply it in the field of foreign affairs where the need for knowledge and understanding is so much greater. To carry this policy into action involves a break with the diplomatic habits of the past. Such habits are not easily broken. Time, effort, and a constant demand by the public to know what is happening will be needed.

People cannot act intelligently if, in all matters of importance affecting our relations with other governments, they are kept in the dark.

Let there be light—and lots of it!

Chapter 13

Control of Atomic Energy

I DO NOT REMEMBER just when it was that President Roosevelt told me about the atomic bomb. I do remember that it was a hot summer afternoon and the two of us were sitting alone in his oval office discussing certain phases of the war mobilization program. Suddenly, and for no apparent reason, he began to tell me the awesome story of the Manhattan Project.

I confess I thought the story fantastic. I was sure the President was exaggerating the possibilities just to watch my amazed reaction. I didn't disappoint him. And, as he noted my amazement, he proceeded with obvious pleasure to astound me with the scientists' prediction of what atomic energy would do. He told me that, prior to 1939, the Germans had made some progress with their experiments and he knew they were continuing their efforts. It was a race between us, he said, to see who could develop the first bomb.

At that time, which I believe was the summer of 1943, the President thought the Germans were ahead of us in the atomic race. It was evident that the information on which he based his belief contained more speculation than fact. Our Intelligence agents necessarily were restricted in securing accurate information on such a highly technical matter. From what we learned after the war, it was clear that the President had overestimated the progress of the Germans in this respect. Nevertheless, such reports served to stimulate the extraordinary efforts put forth on the Manhattan Project.

After the first discussion, neither the President nor I mentioned the atomic project to each other for many months. In fact, no one ever talked about it unless it was absolutely necessary. I remember once mentioning it to Secretary of War Stimson who, from its very inception, personally supervised the Manhattan Project. His reaction indicated surprise that I knew about it.

Even if the President had not told me about the project, as Director of War Mobilization I could not have avoided noting certain aspects of an enterprise as colossal as this. It, of course, held a top priority both for men and materiel. With manpower one of our most critical shortages, a project that at its peak claimed the labor of 125,000 men could not escape my notice, particularly since so many of the workers were highly skilled technicians.

However, I was not directly concerned with the project and was too busy to be curious. Thus it was not until December 1944, when another aspect of the labor situation brought me into the picture, that I learned definitely of the great progress we had been making.

An effort was being made to organize the workers at the Oak Ridge plant; controversies over the jurisdiction of the labor organizations involved had arisen and these had been referred to the National Labor Relations Board. The public hearing required under the circumstances had been postponed four times at the War Department's request; no further postponement was possible.

Under Secretary of War Robert Patterson and Major General Leslie R. Groves came over to the White House to discuss the problem with me. General Groves pointed out that the hearing would require the presentation of evidence on such things as the number of workers employed, the number to be employed, the relationship of a particular unit to the project as a whole, and so on. Such evidence, General Groves was convinced, would necessitate disclosures that would seriously jeopardize the security of the project. They thought it would be helpful if I would arrange a meeting at the White House for the three of us and the leaders of the labor organizations involved. I agreed.

During our discussions, Mr. Patterson said that the War Department would know by April 1, 1945, whether or not they could develop the bomb. Both he and General Groves thought the effort would succeed, and they were confident they would know one way or the other by that date. It was the first time I had heard anyone venture to name a date.

The conference was arranged for the morning of December 5. The union officials were Mr. Joseph P. Clark of the International Brotherhood of Firemen and Oilers and Mr. Al Wegener of the International Brotherhood of Electrical Workers.

We took these men into our confidence. We told them that few people knew about the project. At that time, I believe, only four members of Congress had been given any concrete information. We asked the labor officials to waive their rights under the Wagner Act and to co-operate with General Groves in protecting the security of the project. They were good and patriotic men. They agreed to help and left immediately to do so. They were given authority to explain the situation to the presidents of their respective unions, Mr. John F. McNamara and Mr. Edward J. Brown; both of these leaders likewise promised their full co-operation. Their promise involved sacrificing rights given them by the law, but they kept it. They convinced the local union leaders, and the secret was protected for the duration of the war.

As a matter of fact, it was always amazing to me that the project did not become more generally known. It also was surprising that the Congress was willing to appropriate approximately two billion dollars without demanding more information on the use to which it was being put. It is a great tribute to those few congressional leaders who did have some idea of the nature of the project that they resisted the temptation to tell their colleagues and thus share the great responsibility.

The April 1 deadline came, but the result of the gigantic effort still was in doubt. Secretary Stimson, however, was confident of success. He instilled his confidence in the President. I am glad he did. But I have always regretted that President Roosevelt died without knowing definitely that the project was a success: It had been undertaken and carried to a conclusion solely because of his vision and courage in the days when the effort seemed hopeless.

Shortly after President Roosevelt's death, Secretary Stimson told President Truman that the scientists and others who had been working under his direction felt confident they would produce an atomic bomb within a very short time. He suggested the appointment of an Interim Committee to consider and make recommendations to the President on such important questions of policy as the test of the bomb, its use in the war, and the postwar use of atomic energy.

President Truman approved Mr. Stimson's suggestion and asked him to serve as chairman. The President requested me to act as his representative on the committee. The committee also included Under Secretary of the Navy Ralph Bard; Assistant Secretary of State William L. Clayton; Dr. Vannevar Bush, Director of the Office of Scientific Research and Development; Dr. James B. Conant, President of Harvard University; Dr. Karl T. Compton, President of the Massachusetts Institute of Technology; and Mr. George L. Harrison, president of the New York Life Insurance Company and special consultant to Secretary Stimson. Mr. Harrison served as chairman in Secretary Stimson's absence. We were assisted in our work by a group of scientists who had been connected with the project. They were Dr. Arthur H. Compton, Dr. Enrico Fermi, Dr. E. O. Lawrence, and Dr. J. Robert Oppenheimer.

During May and June 1945, while the attention of the country was focused on the end of the European war and on the San Francisco Conference, this group worked quietly and intensively in Washington. It was an interesting—and exciting—task. Some of the newspaper correspondents noted my presence in Washington when I was supposed to be resting in South Carolina, and were curious about my activities. Of course, I couldn't tell them, so they resorted to speculation. Most of them speculated that I was there in connection with some appointment in the government service.

During that period I made several trips to the Naval Hospital at Bethesda, Maryland, to talk with former Secretary Hull and get the benefit of his advice about the work of the Department of State, which I was to take charge of in a few weeks. On one of these trips two young sailors showed me how unimportant was my war service.

They were hitchhiking, but were not making much progress. One, in fact, was leaning against a post, slightly intoxicated. I thought he needed a ride. They got in the front seat with me. The boy who sat next to me was very alert. I got the impression that he wished to divert my attention from his friend and, therefore, was doing a lot of talking. Finally he asked me what my business was. I told him I did not have a business; that I was out of a job. He sympathized with me and then asked what had I done. Thinking to impress him, I said I had been Director of War Mobilization. His expression clearly showed he had never heard of it. After being quiet for a second or two, he made another effort to satisfy his curiosity and asked: "Well, what did you do before that?"

"I was Economic Stabilizer," I said. I saw he had never heard of that one either.

"I mean before the war," he replied.

"I was a Justice of the Supreme Court," I told him. This time he was impressed, and asked: "You mean the High Court?"

"Yes," I said.

He nudged the redheaded boy next to him: "How would you like to be a member of the Highest Court?"

The young sailor replied: "I wouldn't like it. No chance for promotion."

In the first meeting of the Interim Committee, Doctors Bush, Conant and Compton described the destructive power of the bomb. After hearing them, I was confident that, when developed, it would bring a speedy end to the war in the Pacific. I remembered that as a member of the Senate committee handling naval appropriations I had often heard naval officers say that a new defensive weapon was developed for every offensive weapon. I asked the scientists what defense there could be against the atomic bomb. But these distinguished gentlemen, who had directed the advisory work on the bomb, could think of no defense. They did anticipate the development of still larger and more destructive bombs. I asked them if I should believe the only defense against further development was to kill off all the scientists. This suggestion did not appeal to them.

After listening to the scientists discuss the development of the project, we spent a day with the industrialists and engineers who had performed the amazing task of constructing the huge plants in Tennessee and Washington, and of installing the manufacturing processes that produced the bomb. Because it was a vital point in any decision on a system of control, I asked both groups how long it might take other governments to produce atomic bombs. The question, of course, was not only one of physics, but one of materials, of engineering skills, of technical know-how, and many other factors. From all the information we received, I concluded that any other government would need from seven to ten years, at least, to produce a bomb. And I think that to accomplish the task at such speed would require a quicker return to normal conditions than has taken place in any country within the last few years.

On July 1, 1945, the Interim Committee unanimously recommended to the President that the bomb be used against Japan as soon as possible. It added that the bomb should be used only where war plants or military installations were located. With the exception of Mr. Bard, the committee recommended that it be used without warning. This last question we had carefully considered.

We feared that, if the Japanese were told that the bomb would be used on a given locality, they might bring our boys who were prisoners of war to that area. Also, the experts had warned us that the static test which was to take place in New Mexico, even if successful, would not be conclusive proof that a bomb would explode when dropped from an airplane. If we were to warn the Japanese of the new highly destructive weapon in the hope of impressing them and if the bomb then failed to explode, certainly we would have given aid and comfort to the Japanese militarists. Thereafter, the Japanese people probably would not be impressed by any statement we might make in the hope of inducing them to surrender.

Arrangements for the test in New Mexico also were a problem for the committee. Because no one could be sure what the full results of the first atomic explosion might be, arrangements had to be made to evacuate the whole area if necessary. We knew that under the best circumstances the explosion would reverberate so far that secrecy would be difficult to maintain. News releases, with stories to meet every foreseeable contingency, were prepared and were to be issued to the public only if the circumstances required.

As the President's representative on the committee, it was my duty to report to him the reasons for our various recommendations. Throughout our deliberations, I told him, we relied on the estimates of the military situation presented by the Joint Chiefs of Staff. Their plans called for an invasion of Kyushu, the southernmost island of the Japanese homeland, on November 1. This was to be followed by an invasion of the main island of Honshu in the spring of 1946. The Joint Chiefs anticipated that more than five million of our armed forces would be engaged. The Japanese armies were then estimated at about five million—an estimate we later found was quite accurate. Secretary Forrestal had told me that the Japanese air force suicide attacks were increasing our losses in ships and in human lives. These attacks gained in intensity the closer we got to Japan; it was certain that an invasion force would be attacked with far greater fury and recklessness. The military experts informed us that, from the facts at their disposal, they believed our invasion would cost us a million casualties, to say nothing of those of our Allies and of the enemy.

I reported these conclusions to the President. I also told him what the scientists, engineers and industrialists, who had come before the committee, had to say. He expressed the opinion that, regrettable as it might be, so far as he could see, the only reasonable conclusion was to use the bomb.

While we were aboard the *Augusta* en route to Potsdam, the final preparations were under way in New Mexico for the crucial test. The day the greatest blast the world had yet known was reverberating over the sands of Alamagordo, the President, Admiral Leahy and I were looking at the rubble that had been Berlin. Reports of the test, which had to be transmitted in top secret codes, did not reach us for several days. By that time, the conference was in full swing; I was so busy that I have never been able to recall the time and circumstances under which Secretary Stimson brought us the news. Another reason the moment made so little impression on me was that my work on the Interim Committee had already convinced me that the bomb would succeed. News of the test seemed simply a confirmation of a well-known fact.

Prime Minister Churchill, whose co-operation with President Roosevelt had contributed so much to the success of the great gamble, was intensely interested in the reports. He discussed the project at length with President Truman and was eager to hear from me about the work of the Interim Committee. In addition to his tremendous interest in the effect of the bomb on the war with Japan, he foresaw more clearly than many others the possibilities presented by the release of atomic energy.

We faced a terrible decision. We could not rely on Japan's inquiries to the Soviet Union about a negotiated peace as proof that Japan would surrender unconditionally without the use of the bomb. In fact, Stalin stated the last message to him had said that Japan would "fight to the death rather than accept unconditional surrender." Under those circumstances, agreement to negotiate could only arouse false hopes. Instead, we relied upon the Potsdam Declaration.

As soon as we had studied all the reports from New Mexico, the President and I concluded we should tell Generalissimo Stalin that we had developed the bomb and proposed to use it unless Japan acceded promptly to our demand for surrender. The Soviet Government was not at war with

Japan, but we had been informed of their intention to enter the war and felt, therefore, that Stalin should know.

At the close of the meeting of the Big Three on the afternoon of July 24, the President walked around the large circular table to talk to Stalin. After a brief conversation the President rejoined me and we rode back to the "Little White House" together. He said he had told Stalin that, after long experimentation, we had developed a new bomb far more destructive than any other known bomb, and that we planned to use it very soon unless Japan surrendered. Stalin's only reply was to say that he was glad to hear of the bomb and he hoped we would use it. I was surprised at Stalin's lack of interest. I concluded that he had not grasped the importance of the discovery. I thought that the following day he would ask for more information about it. He did not. Later I concluded that, because the Russians kept secret their developments in military weapons, they thought it improper to ask us about ours.

Two nights after the talk with Stalin, the Potsdam Declaration was issued. We devoutly hoped that the Japanese would heed our warning that, unless they surrendered unconditionally, the destruction of their armed forces and the devastation of their homeland was inevitable. But, on July 28, the Japanese Premier issued a statement saying the declaration was unworthy of notice. That was disheartening. There was nothing left to do but use the bomb. Secretary Stimson had selected targets of military importance and President Truman approved his plans. Shortly thereafter Secretary Stimson left for the United States.

Despite the Japanese Premier's statement, I continued to hope the Japanese Government would change its mind. I was greatly disappointed when August 2, the day of our departure from Potsdam, arrived and no further word had been received. I recognized then that our hope of avoiding use of the bomb was virtually gone.

The President had accepted an invitation from King George for a brief visit at Plymouth Harbor, where we were to meet the USS *Augusta* for the trip home. Because the law of succession placed the Secretary of State next in line for the presidency in case of the death or resignation of the President, President Truman and I traveled from Potsdam to Plymouth on separate planes. We landed at Harrowbeer, near Plymouth. Shortly thereafter Admiral Leahy and I accompanied the President aboard the battleship H. M. S. *Renown,* where King George entertained us at luncheon.

The King had learned from Churchill of the successful experiment with the bomb and was eager to know all about it. Most of our luncheon conversation was devoted to the bomb. The only one of the group who was skeptical about its success was Admiral Leahy and the King enjoyed joking with him about his pessimism. Admiral Leahy felt that the scientists greatly exaggerated the bomb's capacity to damage. Throughout the entire discussion, King George showed that, contrary to the impression of some Americans, he was well informed on the diplomatic as well as the military situation. His views on pending problems, in my opinion, were sound. Later in the afternoon, the King paid a return visit to the *Augusta;* when he departed, the *Augusta* started for home.

On August 6, the President and I had lunch with the enlisted men. A few minutes before twelve, Captain Frank H. Graham, the watch officer of the White House Map Room, hurried into the mess hall and handed the President a brief message from the Navy Department saying that Hiroshima had been bombed a few hours before. Ten minutes later Captain Graham was back with a second message, this time from Secretary Stimson. His report indicated that the results of the bomb were even more successful than the test had led us to expect. The President read the message aloud to me, and then stood and asked the crew to listen for a moment. He announced that he had just received two messages informing him of the highly successful results of our first use of a terrifically powerful new weapon with an explosive 20,000 times as powerful as TNT. As the President left the mess hall with the two messages in his hand, the crew clapped and cheered. He went to the wardroom, where he made the same announcement to the ship's officers, and again applause rang through the ship. A few minutes later, the ship's radio began to carry news bulletins from Washington about the bomb and the statement about its development, which the President had approved just before leaving Germany.

I thought that the bombing of Hiroshima, southern headquarters and depot for the homeland army, would convince the Japanese that the Allied nations meant what they said in the Potsdam Declaration. Millions of leaflets were dropped warning the Japanese that one out of ten listed cities would be the next target. We received no communication from them and so, on August 8, the second bomb was dropped on Nagasaki, a major seaport with many war plants.

As at Hiroshima, the destruction in Nagasaki was terrific. The Emperor did not wait for further evidence of our intention to carry out the Potsdam Declaration. He broke the deadlock that had existed for several days in the Japanese Cabinet; on August 10, he submitted the offer of surrender. No one should doubt that the destruction wrought by the atomic bomb influenced the action of the Emperor and the Cabinet.

Those two bombs were all we then had ready for use, but others were on the way and some were expected to be even more powerful. In these two raids there were many casualties but not nearly so many as there would have been had our air force continued to drop incendiary bombs on Japan's cities. Certainly, by bringing the war to an end, the atomic bomb saved the lives of thousands of American boys.

No one who played a part in the development of the bomb or in our decision to use it felt happy about it. It was natural and right that men should worry about performing a duty that would cost so many human lives. Most of these men were civilians, but I have no doubt that all thinking men in the armed forces felt the same way about air raids, the dropping of incendiary bombs and similar actions which cost many lives. Being soldiers, they did not write to the press about their views as did the civilians. But the truth is, war remains what General Sherman said it was.

Shortly after Japan's surrender, many people demanded that we immediately give the world all the scientific and engineering information on the atomic bomb that we possessed. Most thinking people wanted international control of atomic energy. Some, however, were not so particular about safeguards necessary to protect us against a violator of the international agreement. I agreed with the scientists who argued that inevitably some other nation would produce an atomic bomb, but I felt that we should not shorten that period unless we were fully protected. I felt that if any nation were opposed to submitting atomic energy to complete control by an international organization, with safeguards against violations, then the longer we could keep the bomb out of the hands of that nation, the better it would be for the people of the world. I still feel that way.

On November 10, 1945, Prime Minister Attlee and Prime Minister Mackenzie King came to Washington to talk with the President about our future atomic energy policy. The day of their arrival President Truman invited his guests to accompany him on Sunday on a cruise down the Potomac aboard the presidential yacht, the *Williamsburg*. The party also included Lord Halifax, Sir John Anderson, Admiral Leahy and myself. That afternoon conversations began. They continued that night and for several days. On November 15, the President, Mr. Attlee and Mr. Mackenzie King held a press conference. They announced that the three governments agreed on the need for international action, under the auspices of the United Nations, to provide controls over atomic energy to insure its use only for peaceful purposes, to outlaw atomic weapons and other major weapons capable of mass destruction, and to provide for effective safeguards through inspection.

History will not disclose action by any governments comparable to this generous offer. It was only as a result of great expenditures that we, in co-operation with our Allies, the United Kingdom and Canada, developed a weapon so destructive as to frighten all thinking people. We could have held this weapon and used it as a threat to force concessions from other governments. Instead, the three governments hastened to offer the secret of this power to an international organization in order to have it used for peaceful rather than for destructive purposes.

I was scheduled to give a speech the following day at Charleston, South Carolina, on international trade. With the announcement of this historic agreement I rewrote the first half of the speech. I did not want to neglect a single opportunity to stress to our people the importance of controlling atomic energy "so that it may be used, not for war and destruction, but for the peace and happiness of the world."

In meeting the challenge of atomic energy, I said, we must "let our minds be bold." At the same time, I cautioned, "we must not imagine wishfully that overnight there can arise full grown a world government wise and strong enough to protect all of us, and tolerant and democratic enough to command our willing loyalty.

"If we are to preserve the continuity of civilized life, we must work with the materials at hand, improving and adding to existing institutions until they can meet the stern test of our time."

I described the plan announced in Washington the day before and said we realized that it was "a very modest first step in what is certain to be a long and difficult journey." I emphasized that even though we had advanced a program, "the creation and development of safeguards to protect us all from unspeakable destruction is . . . the responsibility of all governments."

"Without the united effort and unremitting co-operation of all the nations of the world," I said, "there will be no enduring and effective protection against the atomic bomb."

A month later, when Mr. Bevin and I went to Moscow, we took with us a very definite proposal based on the Washington agreement of November 15. It called for the establishment by the United Nations of a Commission on Atomic Energy and all weapons capable of mass destruction.

I proposed that we place the atomic energy resolution at the top of the agenda. Mr. Molotov objected and asked that it be placed at the end. I agreed, although I wondered why he took such a position. At first, I thought it might be because one of Russia's most distinguished scientists, reportedly an expert on nuclear physics, was reported by the press to be in Paris. I assumed Molotov wished to have him present for the discussions and therefore had suggested deferring the item. This theory was upset, however, when the scientist returned to Moscow and still did not attend the conference. I then came to the conclusion that Molotov's request had been made solely to give us the impression that the Soviet Government did not regard the atomic energy problem as important.

At Moscow, as at Potsdam and then at the Council of Foreign Ministers meeting in London, no member of the Soviet delegation expressed any curiosity about atomic energy. At Potsdam, neither Stalin nor Molotov had mentioned the matter after the President's talk with the Generalissimo. At London, Mr. Molotov showed no interest whatever; his only references to the bomb were a few offhand remarks about my carrying an atomic bomb in my pocket. I decided that I was right in the conclusion I had come to at Potsdam, that the Russians never disclose information about such a discovery to anyone else and so thought it would be improper for them to exhibit curiosity about ours.

Postponement of the atomic energy issue, however, meant considerable inconvenience for Dr. James B. Conant, president of Harvard University, who had generously agreed to accompany me to Moscow in an advisory capacity. He had done so expecting that, as soon as the atomic energy resolution was adopted, he could return home to the urgent business that was awaiting him. Instead, he had to sit through about ten days of discussion on totally unrelated issues.

Conant sat near me during most of the meetings. After being a silent observer for nearly a week, he leaned over to me one day and said:

"I think the President of every university in the United States should be forced to attend a conference of the Council of Foreign Ministers. They might then appreciate the patience required to reach agreement with our Soviet friends."

I felt like accusing him of harboring some secret animosity toward his fellow university presidents, but I appreciated his thought.

Dr. Conant's presence in our delegation was noted at length in the Moscow press. He and I fully expected that some of the Russian scientists would call on him. They did not.

One afternoon, Mr. Molotov entertained the three delegations. He is always a good host. In talking with Dr. Conant, Mr. Molotov remarked that, during his visit in Moscow, the president of a great university like Harvard should address the University of Moscow on the subject of atomic energy. That night Dr. Conant told me about Molotov's statement and said he was willing to make such a speech. He thought it would be one way to pierce the "iron curtain" and explain our views on atomic energy, but he was not sure Molotov really meant it. The following day I mentioned the matter to Molotov, saying that, if he were serious, Dr. Conant would be glad to address the university. Mr. Molotov said he had not been serious, that he had no authority to extend an invitation on behalf of the University, and that he had been only trying to be pleasant.

When we finally reached the subject of atomic energy, Mr. Molotov offered only a few amendments to our proposed resolution. With some revisions, we accepted the Soviets' suggestions. One dealt with the relationship between the proposed Atomic Energy Commission and the Security Council of the United Nations. As revised, the resolution provided that, in view of the Security Council's primary responsibility for the maintenance of international peace and security, the Security Council should issue directions to the commission in matters affecting security. It is obvious this must be done by the Security Council, which is in continuous session and which has the power to take action. The Assembly, on the other hand, is not always in session, and even when meeting it can only make recommendations.

The only paragraph of our proposal to which Mr. Molotov raised serious objection provided: "The work of the Commission shall proceed by separate stages, the successful completion of each of which will develop the necessary confidence of the world before the next stage is undertaken."

Mr. Molotov argued that this was a matter to be determined by the commission. I told him it went to the heart of our whole proposal and that without it we would not offer the resolution. I stated that this language had been agreed upon by the President, Prime Minister Attlee and Prime Minister Mackenzie King and we would have to insist upon its retention. He withdrew his objection. As a result, the proposal that we had expected would provoke extensive discussion was agreed to with less debate than any other subject on the agenda.

At the Christmas Eve dinner given by Generalissimo Stalin, I told him about Dr. Conant's distinguished service as an educator and more particularly as one of the contributors to the success of the atomic energy project. Stalin was not so indifferent as Mr. Molotov had appeared to be. He said that, although scientists spoke a language he did not clearly understand, they did a wonderful work and he thought those American scientists responsible for the discovery of atomic energy were to be especially congratulated.

A few minutes later, Molotov, acting as toastmaster, proposed a toast to Dr. Conant and, in a good-humored way, expressed the hope the doctor did not have an atom bomb in his pocket. Dr. Conant responded in like good humor to the toast. Generalissimo Stalin, beside whom I was seated, arose and said he was not satisfied to dismiss Dr. Conant's work thus lightly. He believed, he said, that Dr. Conant and his associates had rendered a great service and he wanted to congratulate them upon their success.

During the few days between my return home from Moscow and my departure to London for the United Nations General Assembly meeting, I acted in anticipation of the adoption of our resolution. I appointed a committee to begin work upon plans to be presented to the Atomic Energy Commission when it was organized. The committee was composed of Under Secretary of State Dean Acheson, as chairman, the former Assistant Secretary of War John J. McCloy, Dr. Bush, Dr. Conant, and General Groves.

In London, the British Government presented the resolution, drafted at Moscow, to the General Assembly on behalf of all five permanent members of the Security Council and Canada. On January 24, just before the resolution was adopted without amendment by a unanimous vote, I made a short statement to the Assembly emphasizing the common responsibility for controlling atomic energy.

"The problems presented by the discovery of atomic energy and of other forces capable of mass destruction cannot be solved by any one nation," I stressed. "They are the common responsibility of all nations and each of us must do our part in meeting them. In meeting these problems we must realize that in this atomic age and in this interdependent world our common interests in preserving the peace far outweigh any possible conflict in interest that might divide us."

The day before the adoption of the General Assembly resolution, the committee I had appointed in Washington appointed a board of consultants with David E. Lilienthal as chairman. The other members were Mr. Chester I. Barnard, president of the New Jersey Telephone Company; Dr. J. Robert Oppenheimer, director of the Los Alamos atomic laboratory; Dr. Charles Allen Thomas, vice president of the Monsanto Chemical Company, and Mr. Harry A. Winne, vice president of the General Electric Company.

The so-called Acheson-Lilienthal report was the work of the committee and its Consultants. It was adopted and released to the public on March 28, 1946. In a foreword to that report, I referred to it as a "suitable starting point for the informed public discussion which is one of the essential factors in developing sound policy," and emphasized that "the document is being made public not as a statement of policy but solely as a basis for such discussion."

The report succeeded in its purpose. The discussion was nation-wide and the objectives the report set forth were received generally with approval.

The essence of the report was summed up by Undersecretary Acheson in a radio discussion on April 23, 1946, in which he said:

"In plain words, the report sets up a plan under which no nation would make atomic bombs or the materials for them. All dangerous activities would be carried on—not merely inspected—by a live functioning international authority with a real purpose in the world and capable of attracting competent personnel. This monopoly of the dangerous activities would still leave a large and tremendously productive field of safe activities open to individual nations, their industries and universities. . . . The extremely favored position with regard to atomic devices which the United States enjoys at present is only temporary. It will not last. We must use that advantage now to promote international security and to carry out our policy of building a lasting peace through international agreement . . ."

For the task of translating the various proposals stimulated by the Acheson-Lilienthal report into a workable plan, I recommended to the President the appointment of Bernard M. Baruch. During the recent war,

as during World War I, he had rendered distinguished public service. He
had been official adviser to me when I was Director of War Mobilization,
meeting with me regularly and helping with many problems; he had been
an unofficial adviser to the President and the heads of several war agencies.
He had earned a rest from public service, but, appreciating the importance of the assignment, he agreed to undertake the job. The President sent
his name to the Senate on March 18, 1946. The appointment was greeted
by the public with deserved acclaim, and his nomination was quickly confirmed.

The law governing our membership in the United Nations stipulates
that our representatives in the organization and on its commissions must
follow the policy determined by the President, transmitted through the
Secretary of State. Accordingly, Mr. Baruch asked for a directive giving
the American policy on atomic energy control. I asked him to help draft
the policy. After several conferences between Mr. Baruch, his associate,
Mr. John M. Hancock, Mr. Acheson and me, we agreed upon an extensive, eleven-page statement of policy. I submitted it to the President for
his consideration. Later, the President, Mr. Baruch and I discussed it
further and made some changes; the President then gave it to Mr. Baruch
as his directive. In doing so, he advised Mr. Baruch to exercise his own
judgment on the methods most likely to accomplish the stated objectives.

The policy of the United States, as described in that directive, was presented to the United Nations Atomic Energy Commission by Mr. Baruch
on June 14, 1946. It was a noteworthy speech which began with this solemn
injunction to the commission:

"We are here to make a choice between the quick and the dead."

The United States proposed the creation of an International Atomic
Development Authority, to which should be entrusted all phases of the
development and use of atomic energy, starting with the raw material including:

1. Managerial control or ownership of all atomic-energy activities potentially dangerous to world security.
2. Power to control, inspect, and license all other atomic activities.
3. The duty of fostering the beneficial uses of atomic energy.
4. Responsibility for research and development intended to put
the authority in the forefront of atomic knowledge and thus to enable
it to comprehend, and therefore to detect, misuse of atomic energy.

Mr. Baruch said that when an adequate system for control, including
the renunciation of the bomb as a weapon, was agreed upon and put into
operation and when punishment was provided for violation of the rules of
control, then the manufacture of atomic bombs should stop; existing bombs
should be disposed of pursuant to the terms of the treaty; and the author-

ity given full information concerning the know-how for producing atomic energy.

The policy further provided that penalties be fixed for such violations as the following: (1) illegal possession or use of an atomic bomb or of atomic material suitable for use in an atomic bomb; (2) the seizing of any plant or other property belonging to or licensed by the authority.

Mr. Baruch drafted a group of men of unusual ability, including Mr. Hancock, whose services during the two world wars have been invaluable; Ferdinand Eberstadt, former Vice Chairman of the War Production Board; Herbert Bayard Swope, who had been an associate of Mr. Baruch in the War Industries Board in World War I; Fred Searls, Jr., who had served with me as special assistant in the Office of War Mobilization and also in the Department of State. He also called on Mr. Thomas F. Farrell and Dr. Richard C. Tolman, to assist him in representing the United States.

From the beginning, he insisted the plan should provide that, once the treaty was ratified, any government violating its treaty obligation and developing or using atomic energy for destructive purposes should be subjected to swift and sure punishment; and in case of violation no one of the permanent members of the Security Council should be permitted to veto punitive action by the council. Our position was that the permanent members of the council should in this special situation agree in advance to waive the veto power.

The public was kept fully informed of everything that took place in the Atomic Energy Commission from June until November. When the Council of Foreign Ministers met in New York, Mr. Baruch and his associates conferred with me about the advisability of asking the Atomic Energy Commission to vote immediately on the principles of the United States proposal.

These gentlemen had been studying the problem for six months and were certain the United States proposal was generally acceptable to every member of the commission except the representatives of the Soviet Union and Poland. Their description of the tactics of the Soviet representative, Mr. Gromyko, was simply a restatement of the delaying tactics I had encountered on other questions in the Council of Foreign Ministers for over a year. They called my attention to the fact that the terms of two members of the commission would expire on December 31; if no action was taken by that date, in January Mr. Gromyko probably would move to postpone further action on the ground that the two new members should have time to study the problem. I knew they were right and agreed that they should act at once.

On December 5, Mr. Baruch presented his plea for immediate action to the commission and proposed a series of general findings and recommendations which encompassed the American plan. He pointed out that the commission and its committees had held over seventy meetings and were qualified to take this step. The commission, with the Soviet Union and Poland abstaining, agreed to act. Subsequently, on December 30, it voted to submit its first report to the Security Council with a recommendation that a comprehensive international system of control and inspection be established and its functions be defined by a treaty in which all the United Nations should be entitled to participate. Again, the vote was 10 to 0, with the Soviet Union and Poland abstaining.

The report recommended the establishment of an international agency to promote among all nations the exchange of scientific information on atomic energy for peaceful ends; prevent the use of atomic energy for destructive purposes; and to exercise the controls necessary to insure its use only for peaceful purposes. It could carry out research and developmental responsibilities in order to remain first in atomic knowledge and would have the exclusive right to carry on atomic research for destructive purposes.

Representatives of the agency would be afforded unimpeded rights of ingress, egress and access for their inspections and other duties into, from and within the territory of every participating nation. The agency should have the right to prohibit the manufacture, possession and use of atomic weapons, provide for the disposal of any existing stocks of atomic weapons and insure the proper use of nuclear fuels adaptable for use in weapons.

The commission stated that the treaty should specify how to determine violations of its terms and should define the violations which would constitute international crimes. It also should establish how to enforce its measures and how to punish violators. Serious violations, it proposed, should be reported immediately to the nations that signed the treaty, the General Assembly and the Security Council.

The commission supported our contention that once the violations had been defined and the methods of enforcement and punishment agreed to, a violator should have no legal protection by veto or otherwise, from the consequences of his act. The report also stated that a violation might be of so grave a character that the inherent right of self-defense, recognized in article 51 of the Charter of the United Nations, might be exercised.

Finally, the report provided that the treaty should embrace the entire program for putting the international system of control and inspection into effect and should provide a step-by-step schedule for the completion of the process. The commission would determine when any particular stage or stages had been completed and subsequent ones were to begin.

While Mr. Baruch was pressing for action on atomic energy, Mr. Molotov presented to the General Assembly of the United Nations a proposal for general disarmament. I did not take it seriously. What the

Soviet delegation really sought was to combine the Atomic Energy Commission with a commission on general disarmament.

The record since January 1946 shows what would happen if this effort had succeeded. The Security Council has been unable to agree upon the relatively simple question of establishing military contingents to enforce the decisions of the United Nations. It is therefore easy to guess how long it would take a commission to agree on a general disarmament program, including the reduction of naval, air and land armaments—several years certainly. Therefore, if the two commissions were combined, there would be many more excuses for delaying an agreement on atomic energy control.

Despite the clear and obvious necessity for the control of atomic energy, and despite the existence of a plan which has won approval everywhere except with the Soviet Union and its satellites, agreement still seems remote. If we cannot agree upon the control of this one major weapon, we certainly cannot agree upon the limitation of all armaments. The Soviet Union does not take into consideration the fact that the United States proposals, as presented by Mr. Baruch, offer a pattern for control of more than atomic weapons. The resolution creating the Atomic Energy Commission specifically authorized it to investigate how to control other weapons of mass destruction. The pattern developed for atomic energy could be applied to these other weapons, such as bacteriological warfare. That pattern could mark the beginning of general and genuine disarmament, but the Soviet Union chose to ignore what could have been and what still could be a fruitful possibility.

The Soviet tactic was exceedingly smart. The word "disarmament" is very attractive to a war-weary world. But disarmament, to be effective, must look to the future. It is easy to see now what folly it would have been, when gunpowder was discovered, to start disarming by limiting the use of the bow and arrow. But that is what the Soviet Union, in effect, proposed.

The General Assembly insisted that the work of the Commission for the Control of Conventional Armaments be kept distinct from that of the Atomic Energy Commission. Nevertheless, the Soviet Union's representatives have continued their efforts to merge the two.

I think I know their motives.

Through such a merger of issues they want to get away from the Atomic Energy Resolution, to which they agreed at Moscow and which was adopted by the United Nations. That resolution provides for safeguards and adequate inspection. It provides that the work should proceed by stages and that the commission must be convinced by inspection that one stage of the work is proceeding satisfactorily before it begins the next stage. This is the clause to which Mr. Molotov objected at Moscow, but finally accepted. I think he has regretted that agreement ever since. That section prevents a full exchange of information until the system of inspection and control is operating effectively. It would make it possible for representatives of the international organization, who may be nationals of another state, to inspect Soviet plants. This is in conflict with their whole system, which is based upon and sustained by secrecy.

The Atomic Energy Resolution, therefore, is an agreement the Soviet Union wants the world to forget and which it urgently desires to see superseded.

The reason for this determined resistance to effective control is equally clear. Mr. Gromyko disclosed it recently when he stated that the American plan proposes that "a system of inspection be established in such a way that it should be given unlimited powers *and the possibility of interfering with the internal economic life of nations."*

It is unfortunate but apparently true that the Soviets think capitalist interference is more to be feared than atomic bombs. And protection of the Soviet economic system from that interference seems to be more important than the protection of humanity from the scourge of atomic warfare.

This fear also explains the Soviet stand on the veto as applied to atomic energy. Mr. Gromyko has said that the Soviet Union is not willing to subject the fate of its internal economy to a majority vote. The veto, he contends, is necessary to protect the sovereignty of the states. The Soviet leaders do not yet appreciate that civilization and not state sovereignty is at stake.

No one wants to interfere in the internal economic life of their nation, but Soviet suspicion of the outsider is so deep seated that they believe that any inspection made by representatives of the international organization, adequate to satisfy the rest of the world, would interfere in their internal affairs. Every statement Mr. Gromyko has made on the subject of disarmament and atomic energy control should be read and considered in this light and in the light of what the Soviet Union has done in these postwar years. One is forced to the conclusion that the United States must not agree to any plan that will make it possible for anyone, including the Soviet Union, to avoid effective inspection.

If the United States destroyed its bombs and agreed not to make any more and then desired later to violate our treaty obligations and make bombs, our alert and uncontrolled press soon would discover it and make public the violation of our pledge. But that is not possible in the Soviet Union. Should the Soviet Government obtain from the international organization the scientific information and the engineering know-how and decide to build a plant and produce bombs, no one outside the Soviet Union would know it until the Red Army was ready to use them. That would be too late.

I know the officials of the present Soviet Government assert that they scrupulously carry out agreements. I hesitate to charge them with violating agreements, but I do say they have a very peculiar way of interpreting some of them.

What, then, shall we do in case the Soviet Union refuses to join in a treaty containing the safeguards it accepted in principle in Moscow and in London, and which clearly are essential to effective control? The answer is not a happy one, but I see no other. We must pray that the Soviet leaders will change their minds, and while we pray, we must use our best efforts to develop better bombs and more of them. For our own protection, we must continue pushing forward the boundaries of our scientific knowledge.

This is a harsh judgment, but the nature of the weapon demands that we be realistic.

We have not been, and I do not believe we ever shall be, guilty of using "atomic diplomacy." Others might suspect us of it because that is what they would do under similar circumstances. But, as I said in Charleston, South Carolina, on November 16, 1945, the suggestion that we might use the atomic bomb "as a diplomatic or military threat against any nation is not only untrue in fact but is a wholly unwarranted reflection upon the American Government and people."

It is one of the inherent characteristics of our democracy that we can fight a war only with the genuine consent of our people. No President in the absence of a declaration of war by the Congress could authorize an atomic bombing without running the risk of impeachment. No one who knows the peace-loving temper of our people can believe that our Congress would adopt a declaration of war contrary to our obligations solemnly undertaken, under the United Nations Charter. The history of 1914 to 1917 and of 1939 to 1941 is convincing proof of the slowness of Congress to declare war. There is surely no reason to believe that it would be more eager to engage in a future war more terrible than any we have ever known.

While we wait for the realities of the atomic age to penetrate the fears and suspicions of the leaders of the Soviet Union, we must not permit the magnitude of the United States initiative to become blurred in the minds of men. It is a record that clearly shows we do not wish to continue making atomic bombs.

Within one year after the successful demonstration of atomic power, the United States had done these things:

1. Secured the agreement of our collaborators in the discovery of atomic energy to place that discovery under international control.

2. Secured the co-operation of the five major powers in initiating machinery to consider plans for international control.

3. Secured the unanimous adoption of that proposal by the United Nations.

4. Devised a detailed plan for world control of nuclear energy by an Atomic Development Authority representing all the United Nations.

5. Established by act of Congress a civilian commission to exercise strict control over all fissionable materials.

6. Released radioactive materials (isotopes) for medical, biologic, and scientific research.

7. Presented to the United Nations Atomic Energy Commission our detailed plan for international control of atomic energy; and, within a few months after the end of that first year, secured approval for our plan from all but two of the members of the commission.

I do not agree with those who predict that should the Soviet Union continue to block that record of progress, mass destruction must follow in a few years. In the war just ended, the Germans and Japanese had poison gas and death-dealing germs, as did the Russians, the British and ourselves. That war was no polite tea party. It was brutal. Nevertheless, no nation dared use these terrible weapons because they knew the same weapons would be used against them.

In saying this, I do not minimize the danger. It would be unfortunate if hostile governments possessed atomic bombs. But, it would be even more unfortunate if we threw our bombs away, gave our information to an international organization with inadequate power to exercise effective control, and thus enabled another government to manufacture bombs without our knowledge far sooner than otherwise would have been possible.

The years ahead pose no greater challenge to mankind. In the time we have at our disposal, fear and suspicion may yet yield to the wisdom of insuring the use of atomic power for human welfare rather than for deadly warfare.

Chapter 14

What Are the Russians After?

THE AMERICAN PEOPLE, in their deep and abiding desire for peace, look toward the Soviet Union with many anxious questions in their hearts and minds. The two I have encountered most often are:

What are they like?

What are they after?

Both are good questions. Our ability to acquire some understanding of the leaders and the people of the Soviet Union, and some idea of their objectives will govern to a large extent our success in framing policies that will promote peace.

The best way I can approach the first question is out of my own experience. And the first conclusion clearly indicated by that experience is that Russia's leaders are stubborn and resourceful negotiators.

I have had quite a broad experience in dealing with men. My active practice as a trial lawyer was rich with such experience. In my service in the House of Representatives and in the Senate I served with over two thousand Representatives and nearly two hundred Senators. I conferred with most of them in the adjustment of differences within each branch and between the two branches of Congress. As Justice of the Supreme Court, as Director, first of Economic Stabilization, and then of War Mobilization, I met many men with many interests, and settled many issues. But through all these years I had no experience that prepared me for negotiating with Mr. Molotov.

I remember once at London one of the newspaper correspondents, reluctant to believe that Mr. Molotov would break up the conference rather than meet the views of the rest of us, asked me incredulously:

"But are you certain you have explored every avenue of approach to the problems?"

"My friend," I replied, "I've not only explored every avenue, but I've gone down every lane, byway and highway. I've tried everything I ever learned in the House and Senate. But there I worked with a majority rule. This is more like a jury. If you have one stubborn juror, all you can expect is a mistrial."

I have often thought that dealing with Mr. Molotov would be good experience for an attorney, who represents a corporation constantly being sued for damages, whose task is to play for time in the hope that the complainant will get tired of waiting for a trial and settle for a small part of his claim.

I have mentioned Moiotov's tactics at the close of the Moscow Conference when the protocol of the conference had been signed and I had left the table. Mr. Molotov at that very late eleventh hour then announced that, after consideration, he had decided to accept the United States' proposal on the Balkan issue made the previous afternoon. That indicates his perseverance and patience.

If we are correctly informed about the patience exercised by Job, I am certain Mr. Molotov is one of his lineal descendants. He has unlimited patience as well as a fine mind and tremendous energy. Any exhibition of impatience or bad temper by others gives him amusement. At such times it is interesting to watch his serious, solemn expression as he protests his innocence of any provocation. These qualities were well demonstrated by Mr. Molotov's stand on the Dodecanese Islands.

At the first meeting of the Council of Foreign Ministers at London in September 1945, the other members of the council believed that the Dodecanese should be transferred from Italy to Greece and be demilitarized. But Mr. Molotov objected. He said that while he might finally agree to the transfer, he objected to the proposal for demilitarization. In view of the Soviet Union's well-known attitude toward Greece, it was certain he did not want the existing government to have the right to fortify the Dodecanese. It was evident he wanted to withhold action in the hope that the Communists would get control of Greece and would then fortify the islands, or that he could later use his consent to the transfer as a concession in driving a bargain for his territorial demands.

Every day the question was presented for action, but each time he would say he had to submit the matter to his government. We would ask if he would submit it promptly and get instructions. He would doubt that this could be done because his government would want to consider it. He still had not heard from his government when, after a month, we adjourned. When we met in Paris the following April, he could not then very well give the same excuse. He had a new one—he could not agree because Greece had never asked for the transfer of the islands. We pointed out at length and through many arguments that other transfers of territory had been made without formal requests. Finally, he said that in any event the matter should be settled in connection with the settlement of other territorial questions.

Shortly after we gathered at Paris for the second session of the council, we again reached the question of the Dodecanese. Mr. Molotov said he had hoped to be able to discuss the matter but he had been informed that morning that the Greek Ambassador was going to call on Mr. Vy-shinski and he would have to await the result of that conference! The rest of us laughed at this newest and lamest excuse. Even Molotov smiled.

After enough problems were settled to his satisfaction, Mr. Molotov then proposed that the Dodecanese be transferred to Greece and demilitarized. And he made the proposal as if the subject were being mentioned for the first time.

Mr. Molotov likes to discuss questions of procedure. In such discussions he has no equal. He will argue for hours about what subjects should be placed on an agenda. You must not only be patient but also must watch carefully even the manner in which your own proposal is stated. If you do not, you will later spend hours trying to get your complete proposal before the council for discussion. Mr. Molotov's answer will be "Nyet," the Russian word for "No," which I heard so often that I almost accept it as part of my own language. He can say in English "I agree," but so seldom does he agree that his pronunciation isn't very good.

In any conference, with or without the unanimity rule, he will win your reluctant admiration by the resourcefulness he exhibits in his delaying tactics. He will sit through it all imperturbably, stroking his mustache or spinning his pince-nez glasses as he waits for a translation and smoking Russian cigarettes in what seems to be an endless chain.

In one important respect, Mr. Molotov is typical of all Soviet representatives. When they conclude that they have exhausted their bargaining efforts, that further delay will result in no further concessions and they might as well agree, the Russians suffer no embarrassment whatever in changing their position—even if it involves a complete reversal of stands they have maintained for hours on end. As a rule, Mr. Molotov smilingly announces that the Soviet delegation, in order to bring about agreement, desires to make a proposal. He then presents your proposal, which has been the subject of controversy for weeks, with only a few unimportant changes. Having argued the question so long, the other conferees are so anxious to get rid of it that they receive the announcement with pleasure. And frequently they even express appreciation to Mr. Molotov for his doing what he should have done weeks or months before.

Another well-exercised tactic is the counteroffensive. Whenever Mr. Molotov suspects that the United States or another country is going to present a complaint about the failure of the Soviet Union to comply with an agreement such as that at Yalta on free press, free elections, and so on, he anticipates the discussion. He either makes an attack himself or gets one of the satellites to do it, and usually it is directed against Greece.

He charges the Greek Government with corruption; with aggressive intentions and unwarranted attacks upon its peaceful neighbors, Yugoslavia, Bulgaria, and Albania; he cries out against the domination of the Greek people by British imperialists who maintain troops in Greece solely to deprive the Greek people of their freedom and to support the Greek Fascists. Usually, he expresses deep regret that the United States Government should give its support to Britain and thus share responsibility for the British misconduct. He repeats his charges about Greece so often that I fear he comes to believe them.

The people of whom Mr. Molotov disapproves are always described as "Fascists." All Communists and Communist sympathizers are "democratic forces." It is a simple classification.

Senators Connally and Vandenberg were never called Fascists by Mr. Molotov directly, but the Communist press made up for his oversight. Both of them were characterized as representing the "big interests." Senator Vandenberg was selected by the Communists in Paris as the real representative of the Fascists, but Senator Connally managed to take the lead during the period when he was ably presenting the United States' position on Trieste to the peace conference. The Communist press intimated that, if left alone, I might possibly do the right thing, but these two "Fascist" Senators were always at my side to influence me against the "democratic" forces.

When I left Washington for the peace conference, the two Senators had to stay there because of some important matters pending in the Senate, but they agreed to come to Paris later. I joked with them about getting away from their "evil influence."

After the conference had been in session about a week, Molotov charged that the United States and the United Kingdom were violating agreements made in the Council of Foreign Ministers regarding the procedure for the peace conference. Knowing him by that time, I had anticipated that he would make such charges, and in the council I had consumed a lot of time making a record. In that record we reserved the right at all times to vote our views on procedural questions. The charge of bad faith was too much for me. I read the record and made some comments about Mr. Molotov which I disliked greatly having to make. It was the severest criticism I ever made of him. Members of our delegation suggested that I should send for the two "Fascists" who, they said, were peaceful individuals compared to me.

After a heated session in Paris one afternoon, Chip Bohlen remained behind talking to a member of the Soviet delegation. The Soviet representative said it was impossible for him to understand the Americans. They had a reputation for being good traders and yet Secretary Byrnes for two days had been making speeches about principles—talking, he said, like a professor.

"Why doesn't he stop this talk about principles, and get down to business and start trading?" the Soviet representative asked Chip in all sincerity.

Chip attempted most unsuccessfully to explain that there were some questions which, in the opinion of Americans, involved principle and could not be settled by bargaining.

Dealing with Generalissimo Stalin and Foreign Minister Molotov are entirely different experiences. Where Molotov is devious, Stalin is direct. But in all my dealings with Stalin, I could not forget a story President Roosevelt had told me in the early days of the war about his communications with Stalin. One day he received a message from Stalin that was very discourteous. He dictated a reply in the same vein, but decided to hold it a day. The next morning, while I was with him, he received a second message from Stalin which was couched in the most courteous language possible and contained assurances of great personal friendship. The President did not understand how such contradictory behavior was possible but it happened more than once.

When I first observed Stalin at Yalta, I also could not understand the President's experience. Stalin was unusually courteous to the President and generally appeared anxious to reach agreement with him. He was always in good humor, and enjoyed a joke. My favorable impression was not at all impaired when I would see him at an afternoon session beckon to a Red Army general who sat back of him, and send him out for a cup of tea. I knew a lot of GIs would pay good money to see a man who could order a general to wait on him.

Despite their differences in personality, one can be sure that the aims pursued by Mr. Molotov are those approved by Generalissimo Stalin. Only in the negotiations on reparations at Potsdam, and in the Soviet rejection of the forty-year treaty, have I ever felt that it was Molotov who influenced Stalin. Otherwise, it clearly has been Stalin who has called the tune—and Molotov who has made it last as long as a symphony. How much the Politbureau influences Stalin, I do not know. My guess is that he accepts Politbureau recommendations whenever he has no special interest or strong conviction. Like every successful leader, he recognizes the necessity of holding the support of his associates. However, in any matter affecting foreign relations in which he has strong convictions, I am certain the Politbureau has supported him. I have seen him make so many important decisions promptly that I do not think he worries very much about control by the Politbureau. Stalin and the gentlemen of the Politbureau realize they could not exact blind obedience to their decisions unless they gave the party workers and the people the impression of unity on all important matters.

I have said enough, I think, to indicate one cardinal fact that must be kept in mind in evaluating any Soviet action. The fact is that, to them, the ends justify any means. The question we must therefore ask is, what are the ends sought by Soviet leaders. In other words, what are the Russians after?

My experiences merely confirm an answer that actually is found in Russian history. Few Americans are well informed on Russian history. I do not profess to be. But I have learned enough to conclude that many of the problems which perplex us today have their explanation in that history. Despite the violence of the Russian revolution, the aims of Bolshevik diplomacy differ very little from those of the Czars. And the aims that Stalin and Molotov have pursued since the end of the war vary little from the demands they made of Adolf Hitler.

Russian expansionism, which has concerned us so deeply in the postwar years, was clearly exposed, and strangely enough, by the godfather of the Communist revolution, Karl Marx. In a series of articles written for the New York *Tribune* from London in 1853, Marx dealt at length with "The Eastern Question." Among his observations were these:

> As to Russia's antipathy against aggrandizement, I allege the following facts from a mass of the acquisitions of Russia since Peter the Great.

> The Russian frontier has advanced: towards Berlin, Dresden and Vienna, about 700 miles; towards Constantinople, about 500 miles; towards Stockholm, about 630 miles; towards Teheran, about one thousand miles. . . . The total acquisitions of Russia during the last 60 years are equal in extent and importance to the whole Empire she had in Europe before that time.

In another dispatch, Marx wrote:

> And as sure as conquest follows conquest, and annexation follows annexation, so sure would the conquest of Turkey by Russia be only the prelude for the annexation of Hungary, Prussia, Galicia, and for the ultimate realization of the Slavonic Empire which certain fanatical Panslavistic philosophers have dreamed of. . . . The arrest of the Russian scheme of annexation is a matter of the highest moment.

How contemporary that sounds!

Following 1853, the year of these dispatches, Russia continued to acquire territory right up to World War I. The total territorial gain of czarist Russia between 1853 and 1914 was 971,277 square miles, which brought the prewar area of the Russian empire up to 8,645,000 square miles.

The advent of Soviet power in Russia was accompanied by the loss of nearly half a million square miles of territory. The new Soviet Union excluded the areas of Finland, Estonia, Latvia, and Lithuania, which became independent states. Kars was ceded to Turkey; Bessarabia was returned to Rumania, and a large area was lost to the new Poland.

During the first twenty years of Soviet rule, the only extension of territory was the annexation in 1926 of certain islands in the Arctic. But in 1939 the Soviet Union embarked upon an active policy of expansion. Between December 4, 1939, and the end of 1945, the Soviet Union took control of the territories of Latvia, Lithuania, Estonia, Bessarabia, south Sakhalin and the Kuriles, parts of Finland and of Poland, the Königsberg area in East Prussia, the Transcarpathian Ukraine, and Tannu Tuva. It also took over Port Arthur where, although it did not acquire sovereignty, it did acquire the right for thirty years to maintain a naval base jointly with China. In all, nearly 300,000 square miles of territory have been acquired since 1939, bringing the area of the Soviet Union to 8,455,939 square miles, only slightly less than the greatest extent of czarist Russia.

It is clear, then, that expansionism is not an innovation of the Communist regime. It is rooted in Russian history. Only the personalities and the tactics have changed.

Russia's modern leaders nevertheless have given us an outstanding demonstration of the means they are quite willing to employ to achieve their ends. This is found in the story of Russo-German relations from the Munich agreement in September 1938, through the Russo-German Nonaggression Pact of August 1939, to Hitler's attack on the Soviet Union in June 1941.

In an after-dinner conversation at Yalta, Stalin said that the Soviet Government would never have entered into the Nonaggression Pact with Germany had it not been for the attempt at Munich to appease Hitler and the failure of Britain and France to consult the Soviet Union on the subject.

Certainly it is true that immediately after Munich, the Soviet press began to modify its campaign of criticism against Germany. By December 1938, when a trade agreement between the two countries was renewed, the press felt free to hail the action as a forward step in Soviet-German relations. Shortly thereafter, in an address to a Congress of the Communist Party, Stalin stated that the only differences between Germany and Soviet Russia were ideological, and these differences were exaggerated by others who wanted someone else to "pull their chestnuts out of the fire" for them.

In the spring of 1939, Stalin made known his disappointment over the results of Soviet negotiations with France and England. Foreign Minister Maxim Litvinov, known for his understanding of "the West" was removed and replaced by V. M. Molotov.

Hitler seemed indifferent to these overtures. It was not until the summer that Hitler evidently decided he would need the support of Russia to make his projected attack on Poland. Events followed so quickly that they mystified the governments of the world and frightened those of us who still hoped war might be avoided.

The history of those negotiations remained obscure until records of them were discovered among the captured archives of the Nazi government. They make an important contribution to our understanding of what it is the Soviet Union seeks. That part of the story which includes the conversations of the principal actors was reported by Gustav Hilger, counselor of the German Embassy in Moscow, who acted as interpreter for the negotiators. His report is from notes made at the time when he could have had no motive for making them inaccurate or false. The rest of the story is based upon official documents discovered in the files of the German Foreign Office.

The record, therefore, is German and has not been confirmed by Soviet sources. However, it cannot be disregarded by anyone seeking the truth about what occurred in that fateful year preceding Hitler's attack on the Soviet Union. Nor can it be disregarded by anyone seeking to understand what is in the minds of those in the Kremlin today. Do they merely desire security? To get what they regard as security, do they intend to expand their control over other states and peoples? Often it is possible to tell what is in a man's mind and heart by what he has said and done in the past in relation to the same issues. Let us, then, look at the record.

On August 15, 1939, the German Ambassador in Moscow, Graf von Schulenburg received instructions to advise Mr. Molotov: (1) ideological differences need not preclude friendly relations and there are no real conflicting interests between Germany and the Soviet Union; (2) Germany has no aggressive intentions against the Soviet Union and believes such questions as the Baltic states can be solved to their mutual satisfaction; (3) the capitalistic Western democracies would try to incite the Soviet Union to war against Germany, a fight which would benefit only the capitalistic powers; (4) English warmongering makes necessary a clarification of Soviet-German relations in order to avoid circumstances that would make German-Soviet friendship and the settlement of territorial questions in Eastern Europe impossible; and (5) therefore, Foreign Minister Ribbentrop is willing to visit Moscow to explain Hitler's views to Mr. Stalin.

When the German Ambassador presented his message, Molotov expressed keen interest, but thought there should be preparation for such a conference. He wanted to know what the attitude of the German Government would be toward a Nonaggression Pact between the two countries and whether Germany would use its influence on Japan to improve the Japanese-Soviet relations. He also wanted to make certain that the

Baltic states would be considered at the proposed conference. He immediately received affirmative replies.

Molotov expressed appreciation of the German Government's willingness to send its Foreign Minister to Moscow, in contrast to Great Britain's action in sending a civil service officer, such as Sir William Strang. He suggested that both governments prepare drafts of a Nonaggression Pact.

On August 19, a trade and commerce agreement between the two countries was signed in Berlin. On the same day Molotov transmitted to the German Ambassador a draft of a Nonaggression Pact.

Hitler was impatient. Evidently he was ready to attack Poland but was anxious to complete this pact with Stalin first. He sent a personal telegram to Stalin saying that he would accept Molotov's draft of the Nonaggression Pact. Germany, he said, was not interested in the Baltic Sea bay and the bordering countries of Finland, Estonia, Latvia and Lithuania. This assurance, he added, could be placed in a secret protocol attached to the Nonaggression Pact. The secret protocol, he suggested, also could set forth the spheres of influence to be observed by the two nations in eastern Europe.

Hitler ended his message by saying that Poland was increasing its provocative acts daily, and a crisis might occur at any moment. He therefore urged Stalin to receive, not later than August 23, Foreign Minister Ribbentrop who would have authority to sign the pact and the secret protocols.

The importance of Hitler's declaration was immediately appreciated by Molotov. Within thirty minutes after it had been delivered by the German Ambassador, the latter was asked to inform his government that the Soviet Union was ready to receive Foreign Minister Ribbentrop and discuss an agreement on the terms set forth in the telegram.

There is every reason to believe that Stalin was pleased by this unexpected turn of events. He was annoyed with Britain and France for failing to join in the pledges he desired. He wanted assurance that the Soviet Union would not be attacked by Hitler. He knew there would be war between Germany and Poland in the immediate future. He must have reasoned that, if the Nonaggression Pact prevented the Western powers from coming to Poland's aid, general warfare would be averted and the Soviet Union would have more time to develop its military strength. On the other hand, if the Western allies did go to war the balance of strength would be such that Russia would still have time to train and equip its armies. In addition, the pact would enable him to take over the Baltic states without the risk of war.

Ribbentrop arrived in Moscow on August 23. The conferees included Stalin, Molotov, Ribbentrop, Ambassador Schulenburg, and Hilger.

Stalin insisted that the secret protocol include a declaration of the

Soviet Union's special interest in Bessarabia and that the northern boundary of Lithuania be fixed as the line of demarcation between the Russian and German spheres of interest. This was accepted. The pact and the protocols were approved; the signing was celebrated; champagne was served; Stalin proposed a toast to Hitler; and Ribbentrop returned to Berlin the following day.

Only nine days had elapsed since Ambassador Schulenburg had made the first approach! The speed with which they reached agreement impresses me because I spent fifteen months trying to get Soviet agreement to five treaties of lesser importance. In the first case, they wanted to agree; in the latter case, they did not.

Although the propaganda machines in both countries had been trying to prepare the people for this about-face, the Russian and the German people must have been mystified by the sudden shift. The assumption is justified by the difficulty of the people in this hemisphere, including the Communist press, to understand what had taken place.

This pact, it seems to me, is a classical example of an agreement not worth the paper it was written on. Stalin's statement at Yalta confirms the line usually taken by Soviet representatives: the pact was entered into solely to gain time for a conflict Russia recognized was inevitable. Thus, it seems clear that the Soviet Government concluded the pact while fully intending to violate it. We have no statement of Hitler's intention, but we have his act of violation. It is therefore reasonable to doubt the good faith of either Stalin or Hitler in agreeing to this pact.

Hitler overran Poland more rapidly than Stalin had expected, and in pursuing the retreating Poles, Hitler's troops entered the Soviet sphere of influence. Stalin asked that Ribbentrop return to Moscow and make a new agreement on the line dividing Poland between them.

Ribbentrop arrived on September 27. This time Germany agreed that the Soviet Union should take over Lithuania. A boundary line was devised splitting Poland in half and Soviet plans to set up an autonomous Soviet Republic were approved. Germany permitted the Soviet Union to take over the oil sources of Drohobycz and Boryslaw, and the Soviets contracted to furnish the Nazis with 300,000 tons of raw oil from these sources. The new border and friendship pact was celebrated at a banquet given by Mr. Molotov on September 30.

Thereafter, Wagner's operas were once again heard in Moscow. The German war communiqués were featured on the front page of the official Soviet newspapers. On October 31, 1939, Molotov made a speech in which he said: "Germany is in the position of a state which is striving for the earliest possible termination of war and for peace, while Britain and France are in favor of continuing the war and are opposed to peace." And Hitler told friends that the Friendship Pact would last for years.

Estonia, Latvia and Lithuania were brought more tightly into the Soviet sphere. They were forced to cede bases to the Red Army. Finland, however, resisted similar proposals and, without the formality of a declaration of war, was invaded by the Red Army in November, 1939. The earlier concessions made by three Baltic states proved to be merely stepping stones; these nations soon were forced to join the Union of Soviet Republics. At this juncture rifts began to appear in the Hitler-Stalin partnership.

In the earlier division of territory, a small area in the southwest corner of Lithuania was allotted to Germany. But the Red Army, when it marched into the country, occupied this area. Germany protested. The Soviets admitted the protest was justified but argued that it was difficult to separate this area from the rest of Lithuania. The issue was pending for months until the Soviet Union finally agreed to pay Hitler 31,500,000 reichmarks for this Lithuanian territory.

In June 1940, the Soviet Union demanded Bessarabia from Rumania. Germany could not object because Hitler had declared he had no interest in this area. But next the Soviet Union demanded north Bukovina. This area had not figured in the earlier discussions or agreements and Germany objected. Mr. Molotov simply replied that he saw no reason for the objection since the area was settled by Ukrainians. He blandly added that the Soviet Union not only expected Germany's support for this claim but also for a claim they would make later for south Bukovina.

Hitler began to be irritated. Evidently, he felt that Germans were shedding blood for the territory they got, and the Soviet Union was insisting upon taking the spoils without the fighting. The German Ambassador in Moscow received instructions to inform Molotov that Germany was interested in guaranteeing Rumanian territory. Germany needed Rumania's food and oil. Germany felt the same way about Hungary. The Nonaggression Pact, the Ambassador added, obliged each party to consult the other on questions of mutual interest, yet Germany had not been consulted when action was taken against neighboring areas. He cited the Lithuanian area and Russia's sudden action in Bessarabia and Bukovina.

Molotov insisted (I can almost hear his words!) that the German procedure was not loyal to the agreement and Germany should have known that the Soviet Union would be interested in Rumania and Hungary.

Suspicions began to grow on both sides. On October 13, 1940, Ribbentrop wrote a nineteen-page letter to Stalin giving a detailed explanation of the steps taken by Germany in the previous months and the reasons for such steps. He invited Molotov to Berlin. Stalin's reply was noncommittal, but he agreed that an improvement in relations was entirely possible and said Molotov would arrive in Berlin on November 12.

Molotov had two conferences with Hitler, one on the twelfth of November and the other on the thirteenth, each lasting three hours. These discussions were recorded by Ambassador Paul Schmidt. In my opinion, these marked the turning point of the war. In fact, as closely as such things can be calculated, I believe these visits represent a decisive point in history. For Mr. Molotov greatly overplayed his hand. His interview with Hitler on the thirteenth, particularly, stands out as a major diplomatic blunder.

Hitler apparently was in a grandiose and expansive mood. Since Nazi victory was certain, he declared, Germany and the Soviet Union should reach agreement on the division of the British Empire which soon would fall into their hands. Germany, he thought, should look to the West and the Soviet Union should direct its attention toward the East. Russia needed an exit to a free warm sea which could be found by way of Iran, the Persian Gulf and the Arabian Sea. Hitler waxed eloquent as he described a world divided between Germany and the Soviet Union.

Mr. Molotov's precise, legalistic mind failed to respond to Hitler's grandiose scheme. He agreed that Hitler was presenting an interesting long-term program but the Soviet Government, he said, wished to discuss immediate problems. Evidently the existing arrangements between them "are not satisfactory to Germany," Molotov went on, because the agreements clearly placed Finland in Russia's sphere, yet German troops were there. They should be withdrawn promptly. Germany's guarantee of the Rumanian border the Soviet Union must protest, and he could not help but wonder at whom such a guarantee was directed.

What a let-down this must have been for Hitler's flights of fantasy! He explained that German troops had to be in Finland to protect lines of communication for the supply of Swedish ore and of oil which was of greatest importance to Germany's war effort. The troops would be withdrawn as soon as possible. Germany had interfered in Rumania because otherwise there would have been open conflict between Rumania and Hungary, which would have injured Germany's economic interests there. Rumania had suffered cessions of territory to Hungary and to the Soviet Union, Hitler went on, and the border guarantee was essential to preserve peace and order in Rumania. Germany had only a military mission in Rumania which was there at the request of its government. He emphasized that Germany had no political, only economic interest in the Balkan states; he wanted to protect the Rumanian oil sources from attack.

Molotov said bluntly that he was not satisfied with Hitler's reply. In addition, Molotov said, the Soviet Union wanted to enter into closer relations with Bulgaria and possibly sign a Mutual Assistance Pact with her, because of her position in relation to the Dardanelles. His final demand was for a new regime for the Dardanelles that would involve realistic guarantees rather than paper assurances.

Hitler replied that he was unable to give an answer without consulting the Bulgarian government and Mussolini.

It was here that Molotov made his worst blunder. He insisted upon a definite and immediate answer. The interpreter's report says that at this point Hitler showed great indignation.

I can picture the scene. Hitler had just said what he actually believed. He was certain of victory; he thought he dominated the world; and he had just painted a picture allocating an exceedingly generous portion of the world to the Soviets who had not lost a life nor spent a dollar in the war. But Molotov simply said that it was "interesting" and demanded an immediate answer to what Hitler must have regarded as relatively trivial things—Rumania's boundary, a mutual assistance pact with Bulgaria. It is easy to visualize the excitable and explosive Hitler wondering at the temerity of this man whose government, Hitler believed, was not prepared for war telling him—Hitler—that his answers were unsatisfactory.

Historians may discover when Hitler decided to make war on Russia. He may previously have considered it in a general way, but until I see other evidence, I shall believe that this interview with Molotov was the decisive moment. Certain it is that from this fateful November 13, Russo-German relations steadily declined.

Later that day, Ribbentrop read to Molotov a draft agreement and two secret protocols; he proposed the Soviet Union join the Axis powers in signing them. Evidently these were prepared before Molotov's arrival and before he saw Hitler. The agreement provided that the Soviet Union would co-operate with the other three powers, each to have a separate sphere of interest, and each to agree not to support any other power bloc directed against any one of the four. The first secret protocol set forth the territorial aspirations of the four, as envisaged by Hitler; for Germany, there would be central Africa; for Italy, north and northeast Africa; for Japan, the Asiatic area south of the Japanese islands; and for the Soviet Union, all the region south of the USSR in the direction of the Indian Ocean. The second secret protocol provided for replacing the Montreux Convention governing the Black Sea Straits with an agreement which would give the Soviet Union unrestricted rights to use the Straits; all other powers except the Black Sea states would abandon passage rights through the Dardanelles for their warships. In addition, Ribbentrop offered to mediate between Japan and the Soviet Union in an effort to promote a lasting understanding.

Molotov's response to this proposal is especially noteworthy. It should be read and considered in light of recent history.

Japan had already offered to enter into a Nonaggression Pact; the Russian Government awaited replies to some questions it had submitted, Molotov said. There would have to be "substantial" discussions about Iran, and the Soviet Union would insist on concrete guarantees for the Dardanelles. Molotov then brought up Bulgaria, Rumania, Hungary, Yugoslavia, Greece, the future of Poland, and Swedish neutrality. (When I first read this report it impressed me as sounding like an agenda for a meeting of the Council of Foreign Ministers!) He concluded with the statement that great questions of the future should not completely obscure the questions of the day.

Molotov gave no more definite answer than this during his visit. But on November 25, he asked the German Ambassador in Moscow to come to the Kremlin and he then presented a full reply to the Ribbentrop proposals of November 13. This, too, is worthy of special note in light of subsequent events.

The Soviet Government, Molotov informed the Ambassador, was ready to accept the Ribbentrop draft of the four-power agreement on four conditions: (1) that German troops be withdrawn immediately from Finland; (2) that Soviet security in the Dardanelles be guaranteed by a Mutual Assistance Pact with Bulgaria and by the establishment of a base for Soviet land and sea forces in the Straits; (3) that Soviet aspirations in the area south of Baku and Batum in the general direction of Iran and the Persian Gulf be recognized; and (4) that Japan abandon its concession rights to coal and naphtha in north Sakhalin.

Molotov apparently had not realized how ineptly he had played his hand in Berlin nor the degree of Hitler's indignation. The Soviet Government never received a reply to this message.

Both Stalin and Molotov began to worry about Hitler's silence. In January 1941, through their representatives, they negotiated a second economic agreement. The Soviet Union had scrupulously fulfilled the deliveries called for in the first agreement and now agreed to a further increase in the exchange of goods. Later in the month Molotov's concern about Hitler's failure to reply to his proposal prompted him to suggest further conversations. The German Government simply informed him that his proposal had been received, that communications had been sent to Italy and Japan regarding it, and that it was hoped discussions might be continued in the near future. Such a reply—two months after the proposal was made—showed clearly that Hitler was no longer interested. The conversations never took place.

Instead, the Germans increased their troop concentrations in the Balkans. They informed the Soviets of their action. On February 28, Ambassador Schulenburg told Molotov that Bulgaria had subscribed to the Axis three-power pact and would sign a concurring protocol on March 1.

Molotov received this communication with great concern. He emphasized that these developments in Bulgaria created a situation entirely different from that which had existed on November 25 when the·Soviets made their proposal. Apparently, Molotov did not realize that his November 25 proposal represented the final divorce decree ending the strange marriage between Hitler and Stalin.

On March 1, Schulenburg informed Molotov that Germany had decided to move troops into Bulgaria. Immediately, and in the presence of the German Ambassador, Molotov wrote a note expressing regret that the German Government had violated the security interests of the Soviet Union by such a military occupation.

On April 5, a Friendship and Nonaggression Pact was concluded between the Soviet Union and Yugoslavia, almost simultaneously with the German attack on Yugoslavia. It is not clear what prompted Stalin to take this step although it was said at the time that Russia's support of Yugoslavia might keep the Germans so involved in the Balkans that there would be less danger of their attacking Russia. Within a few weeks, however, it was evident that Stalin had miscalculated Yugoslavia's strength.

Thereafter, the Soviet Government avoided doing anything that might displease Germany. Raw materials were delivered promptly. When the foreign press published reports that German troops were concentrating on Russia's borders, the Soviet Government, through the official Tass News Agency, declared that the rumors were inspired by warmongers, that relations between the two countries were pleasant and that existing treaties made it clear there was no threat to the Soviet Union. Of course they did not believe what they were saying.

Ambassador Schulenburg did not believe it. He was so concerned that late in April he personally took to Berlin a memorandum setting forth the dangers of war with the Soviet Union. I do not know whether this memorandum reached Hitler. The evidence does not disclose that he mentioned it in his talks with Schulenburg but the Ambassador is quoted as saying that Hitler, in parting with him, said he would not make war on Russia.

Weeks of suspense followed. Meetings no longer took place between Molotov and Schulenburg. Finally, in June, the German Embassy received instructions to send all German women and children back to Germany without creating excitement.

On June 22, Molotov asked Schulenburg to visit him. He stated that German planes were making an increasing number of unauthorized flights over Soviet territory and insisted that steps be taken to prevent further violations. Schulenburg promised to refer the matter to his government. Molotov then said rumors were circulating over the world that there would be war between Germany and the Soviet Union, and now he had heard that the women and children of members of the German Embassy were leaving the country. He desired an explanation. Schulenburg was embarrassed. Molotov must have known Schulenburg was not telling the truth when he replied that he knew nothing of the rumors and that the departure of the women and children was due merely to summer vacations.

The next day, June 23, 1941, Schulenburg received instructions from Berlin to see Molotov and make the following statement:

"The increasing Soviet troop concentrations at the German border have reached such a proportion that they are intolerable to the German Government. The German Government, therefore, has decided to take countermeasures."

"Is this a declaration of war?" Molotov asked.

The Ambassador made a helpless gesture with his hands.

Molotov said he could not regard the message in any other light, since German troops had already crossed the Russian border and Nazi aircraft had been bombing several Russian cities for more than an hour. He described the attacks on a country with which Germany had a Friendship and Nonaggression Pact as a breach of faith such as the world had never seen. The alleged concentrations of Soviet troops, Molotov added, could only be a pretext since the Russian forces were merely engaged in customary maneuvers. Had the German Government questioned, the Soviet Union would have given an adequate explanation.

Ambassador Schulenburg did not say that "customary maneuvers" was the customary explanation. He simply said he was unable to make any further comments on the situation.

Thus ended the "enduring" twenty-two-month-old Friendship and Nonaggression Pact between Germany and the Soviet Union. Thus began the war between the Nazis and the Soviets.

Now let us see what guidance this history holds for us. I think it reasonable to assume that Soviet ambitions still include the territory Molotov desired when he sent his message to Hitler. Some of those desires have been fulfilled. However, the flush of victory has encouraged the Soviet Government to extend its ambitions.

In the North, their demands against Finland have been satisfied. During the war, Mr. Molotov explored the possibility of extending Soviet power a little through concessions from Norway. In November 1944, he asked Norway to grant the Soviet Union greater economic privileges in the Spitsbergen group of islands. He wanted outright possession of Bear Island and the right to establish military facilities on other islands of the group.

Mr. Molotov made this request despite the fact that the 1920 treaty— by which Norwegian sovereignty over these islands was recognized and which was signed by thirty-four countries, including the Soviet Union—contained a proviso that Norway could not construct fortifications and that the islands could "never be used for warlike purposes." The Norwegian Government, after first agreeing to discuss both subjects, has since declared it would consider only the economic issue and has pointed out that the military proposal must be a subject of multilateral negotiation.

In the East, the Soviet Union now has all of Sakhalin and, in addition, has taken over the Kuriles and has acquired rights in Port Arthur, Dairen, and on the Manchurian railroad. Whether Stalin will continue to resist the temptation offered by the successes of the Chinese Communist forces in Manchuria is a question which, at this writing, remains in the balance.

Soviet aspirations south of Batum and Baku have not been realized, but the effort has been made. Turkey was asked to cede the provinces of Kars and Ardahan south of Batum. The effort to extend south of Baku into Iranian territory was blocked by the Security Council.

The familiar technique of trying to install a puppet government under the protection of the Red Army was employed. The Red Army interfered with the armed forces of little Iran. The Soviets encouraged the establishment in Azerbaijan of an independent government. The case was brought before the Security Council. When the Soviets kept their troops in Iran beyond the date of their treaty, the council acted on the complaint of Iran. Every member of the council except the Soviet Union and Poland voted to protect the integrity of Iran. The Soviet Union complied with the Security Council's decision because it was not yet ready or willing to be isolated from the rest of the world.

Now, let us compare Molotov's 1940 demands with today's situation in Europe.

The Bulgarian Government, installed and protected by the Red Army, has now made a pact unnecessary. Thus the "safety zone" between the Soviet Union and the Straits, which Molotov requested, has been achieved. In Rumania, a similar regime has been installed by tactics I described earlier. The pursuit of Soviet ambitions in Hungary is a more recent story, but the pattern is old.

Poland has been subordinated to the status of a satellite. Albania and Yugoslavia are tightly clasped in the Soviet-dominated Slav bloc. Czechoslovakia is a captive of this bloc. Out of all the European areas toward which Molotov expressed an interest, only Greece and Turkey remain free. And the struggle for them is in progress.

The reports of our able observer, Mark Ethridge, have made it clear that a small, well-organized Communist minority, based in and supplied from Greece's Soviet-dominated neighbors, would have captured Greece long ago had it not been for two things: (1) the action by the United

Nations, and (2) the Soviets' realization that, if they took over Greece, the United States and the United Kingdom would demand that the United Nations act against such aggression.

The Security Council's Balkan Investigating Committee delayed and exposed the effort. But chaos still prevails and the fate of Greece hangs in the balance while the American mission headed by former Governor Dwight Griswold seeks to promote the economic and political health which alone can kill off the disease of Communist-agitated unrest.

As for Turkey, we must remember that Stalin declared at Potsdam the continuing interest of the Soviet Union in the Straits and that subsequently a demand was made for the right to build a land and naval base in the area. Our efforts to obtain collective guarantees to maintain the freedom of the Dardanelles have been unsuccessful. We now have taken other measures to protect the sovereignty of Turkey.

Karl Marx and other historians made it plain that Soviet aspirations differ little from czarist aspirations. And certainly, Mr. Molotov's 1940 demands are a good general signpost for the immediate future.

As to whether the Soviet Union seeks security or expansion, I suppose the Soviets themselves, in analyzing their motives, would find it difficult to tell exactly where security ends and expansion begins. And if they did know the dividing line, I am certain they would not admit it. In considering this question, I keep thinking of the kind of people—and many of us know them—who buy the house or farm adjoining theirs for protection. The difficulty always is that there is another adjoining house or farm. So it is with the Soviets who think the governments adjoining the Soviet Union or its satellites must be "friendly governments" for their security. The chief difference is that the Soviets do not buy the adjoining territory and they have no scruples about violating laws and pledges to acquire the property they want for security.

Frequently people ask whether, in the name of security, the Soviets intend to dominate all of continental Europe. I think they want in all European states a sufficient number of organized Communists so that they can dictate the policies of these states. I do not think they want to take over all European governments now. They fear the people of western Europe would not accept the form of government existing in the Soviet Union. They realize also that in most of those countries they have not yet trained leaders who could make such governments succeed, and failure would impair their prestige all over the world. For the present, while developing local leaders, they are satisfied to bide their time. By the threat of strikes and by encouraging discontent, they can in many states exert power without having responsibility. Greece is apparently their first objective. They are likely to seek next, through the usual infiltration method, control of the Italian Government. This would be because of the military effect it would have on Greece and Turkey. I do not doubt that their ultimate goal is to dominate, in one way or another, all of Europe.

In determining our course of action, Karl Marx is helpful. In 1853, about the Czar's demands on Turkey, he wrote:

"It would have been impossible for Russia to make more extensive demands upon Turkey after a series of signal victories. . . . *If the other powers hold firm, Russia is sure to retire in a very decent manner.*"

Should the Soviet Government get the impression that the United States and other members of the United Nations will only voice protests and will do nothing, Russia will continue the pursuit of these historic objectives. The Soviet Government will do as it did shortly after the Yalta Conference in connection with Rumania; it will take over a government and then say the matter has been settled and there is no excuse for further discussion.

But, on the other hand, if it is made to realize now that if it commits an act of aggression, we will appeal immediately to the Security Council of the United Nations; if we make it clear that a Soviet veto in the Security Council will bring a call upon the other United Nations to act collectively to support and enforce the principles of the Charter—if these things are made clear, I do not believe the Soviets will violate the integrity of Iran, Turkey, Greece, Italy, or any other country.

For many reasons the Soviets do not want war now. They will, I believe, "retire in a very decent manner." But if the other powers do not "hold firm" then, as Marx warned us of the czarist Russians, "conquest follows conquest and annexation follows annexation."

We must not indulge in idle threats. We must not start anything we do not intend to finish. We must meet aggression and pressure with firm resistance. At the same time, we must be just and objective in our analysis of each situation. We should always keep the hand of friendship extended. And we should constantly make clear our earnest desire to live at peace with our neighbors.

Soviet policy, as it stands today, is fairly well revealed by the historic record I have cited. I should like to point to one other guidepost. It is the speech Stalin made to his Communist Party comrades at the time of the first postwar election—February 9, 1946. A speech on such an occasion and to such an audience is a far more reliable guide, I believe, than the statements made to visiting Americans and foreign correspondents. In it Stalin had this to say of the future:

I have no doubt that if we render the necessary assistance to our scientists they will be able not only to overtake but also in the very near future to surpass the achievements outside the boundaries of our country. As far as plans for a longer period are concerned, the Party intends to organize a mighty upsurge of national economy which will enable us to increase the level of our production, for instance, three-fold as compared with the prewar level.

To achieve this, we must endeavor to see that our industry pro-duces 50 million tons of pig iron per year; 60 million tons of steel; 500 million tons of coal and 60 million tons of oil.

Only under such conditions will our country be insured against any eventuality. Perhaps three new Five-Year Plans will be required to achieve this, if not more. But it can be done and we must do it.

Time is not all on the side of the Soviet Government.

In seeking to answer the question, "What are they like?" I have said nothing of the Russian people. I have spoken only of the Russian leaders. They are the only Russians I know. Few Americans have been able to really learn much about the Russian people.

In evaluating present Russian policy, we can ignore the mass of Rus-sians: they have no more influence on Soviet foreign policy today than they did under the Czars. But in considering future policy, we must not ignore them. They are, I believe, our hope. I cannot believe that the Rus-sian peasant, who fought with such valor to defend his own home and land, really wants to impose foreign rule on people like himself. I cannot believe that the Russian worker, who only a few years ago emerged from conditions approaching slavery, would knowingly deprive other workers in other lands of their freedom.

I once said "there is no iron curtain that the aggregate sentiments of mankind cannot penetrate." I believe that. And I also believe there is a reasonable chance that we have enough time at our disposal to bring those sentiments to bear on the people and the leaders of the Soviet Union.

I also have said that "we must guard against the belief that delays or setbacks in achieving our objective make armed conflict inevitable." It is one of the beliefs held by the Soviet leaders that makes our task so diffi-cult. But we will never be able to rid them or the rest of the world of that belief if we ourselves become its victims.

Neither is time necessarily on the Russian side in the non-Soviet coun-tries.

Today the Soviets have armies in Germany, Austria, Poland, Rumania, Bulgaria, Hungary and Manchuria. An occupation army is an idle army and an idle army is a bad army. The very purpose of retaining soldiers in a foreign country is to restrict the lives and liberties of the people of that country. People who want to be free resent the presence of occupation troops and they grow to hate the country that keeps them there. They grow also to hate, perhaps even more intensely, the puppets who are kept in office by a foreign army. As long as the army is there, the people are cowed into submission. But when the Red Army leaves, the legacy of hatred it leaves behind will mean a difficult and uncertain future for the puppets in government and in the militia.

The Soviet Government cannot indefinitely find reasons for keeping troops in these states. Five treaties of peace already have been concluded. The Soviet Union has not yet ratified the treaties, but I think it will. Our Senate did not ratify them until four months after they were submitted. When they are ratified, it will be difficult for the Soviets to postpone for long the reduction in occupation forces that these treaties require. These states then become eligible for admission to the United Nations. Once they are members, it is then the obligation of all the United Nations to protect them from pressure and aggression. The sooner we prove to these countries that this obligation will be discharged, the sooner they will be encouraged to assert their independence.

I conclude that the Russians are after everything they set forth in the written statement to Hitler, together with a number of additional "aspirations" they have developed as a result of their success in the war.

The Soviets did not tell Hitler their aspirations because of their love and affection for him. They told him only because they feared that if they tried to take territory without his consent, he would use force to stop them. Today there is no military strength in Europe to restrain the Russians. Only the power of the United Nations can do it. The United Nations must make known its determination to act to protect the threatened states. And the United States must make known its determination to use all of its power to support the action of the United Nations.

Chapter 15

Where Do We Go from Here?

IN THE preceding chapters, I have tried to indicate where we are and how we got here. I have done so in the hope that it may help us to decide what to do and how to do it. Having gone thus far, I feel I should not avoid drawing out of my experience some thoughts on the question that is disturbing all of us: Where do we go from here?

There is no easy answer. For the ills of a war-torn world there are no speedy cures, no panaceas. I believe that mankind *can* build a lasting and a just peace. And I believe, also, that we must guard equally against the ready optimists who believe that only an act of faith is necessary to do it, and the reckless pessimists who are convinced that only another war can do it.

The charting of a course of action is always a hazardous enterprise. It is especially so when it is complicated by the fact that I deliver this manuscript to the publisher on July 1, 1947, and the book will not be ready for sale until mid-October. In these days of kaleidoscopic change only a prophet or a soothsayer would venture to predict what will happen in those three months. I am neither. I am keenly aware that each day brings a new crisis, and the crisis of today is frequently forgotten tomorrow. Obviously, then, opinions expressed today, based on existing facts and circumstances, may require extensive alteration or may even be entirely irrelevant in light of the facts and circumstances three months from now. With this qualification, I suggest some steps I believe we should take down the long road toward peace.

I believe we should immediately seek the early conclusion of treaties with Austria, Germany and Japan. In preceding chapters, I have suggested the course I would follow to secure those treaties and I earnestly hope the Soviet Union will see the wisdom of joining in this endeavor. But Russia's opposition must not deter the other nations from a course they know is right and indispensable to the reconstruction of the world. It is a course that requires dedication to the principle of collective action. It requires courage.

The importance of the objectives demands action. Continuation of a state of war, with its perpetuation of military governments and large armies of occupation, is a constant threat to peace and security. It jeopardizes the economic and political well-being of millions of people in Allied as well as ex-enemy states.

Even as we plan these peace settlements, many developments abroad have made us question the permanency of the peace. Ever since the war ended in Europe, we have had reason for concern in the Soviet attitude toward Greece and Turkey. The gallant Greeks, by their heroic stand against the Italians and later the Nazis, won the admiration of liberty-loving people the world over. Unfortunately, the withdrawal of enemy troops did not bring the difficulties and sufferings of the Greek people to an end. Almost immediately, they were confronted with civil war. The Greek Government believed the attacks were inspired, and certainly encouraged, by the Soviet satellites.

British troops finally took a hand and restored order. But since the summer of 1945, there has been unrest in Greece. Guerrilla warfare in the areas adjoining Albania, Yugoslavia and Bulgaria has kept the Greek Army occupied and prevented the restoration of the shattered economy of Greece. The Greek Government believes that guerrilla troops trained in Yugoslavia, Albania, and Bulgaria cross the border and, after raiding a community, return to foreign territory. This belief has been supported, in part at least, by the findings of the United Nations Balkan Commission of Investigation. The guerrillas are assisted by Greek Communists. Last year the people living in that area did not plant crops because they did not expect to be able to harvest them. Families left the farms and sought the greater protection of the city. In resisting these attacks and in protecting its citizens, the government resorted to measures that many people regarded as oppressive.

While in Paris in 1946, I frequently saw the Prime Minister of Greece, Mr. Constantin Tsaldaris, and members of his government. The Prime Minister's position was that those of us who did not receive daily reports of the killing of Greek soldiers and civilians might criticize what we considered oppressive measures, but that the problem was not easy for one with the responsibility of upholding the integrity of Greek territory.

In the election of early summer 1946, the Greeks voted for the monarchy and for the return of the King. Some persons, who were in Greece at the time of the election and whom I think well informed, believe that the people were not in favor of the monarchy but regarded it as the only alternative to Communism, to which they were genuinely opposed. After the election, the Prime Minister told me that the King was anxious, and so was he, to bring into the government representatives of liberal parties—a course which I had urged upon him. However, he did not succeed in his efforts.

During the peace conference, on about October 1, the Prime Minister told me that the need to devote a large part of the national income to military expenditures aggravated what, in any event, would be a bad economic situation. Greece, he said, needed financial assistance and its army needed additional military equipment. In response to my inquiry, he said that Britain had been furnishing them with military supplies and had agreed to continue such assistance. I told him we could help them with military equipment only to the extent that it was available from surplus property then in Europe. I requested the officer in charge of that property to assist Greece in every way possible. I also told Prime Minister Tsaldaris that in the absence of appropriations by Congress, I could not promise a financial advance for relief, but if Congress made the appropriation of 350 million dollars for relief which we intended to request, Greece would certainly receive a liberal share. I also told him I would urge favorable action by the Export-Import Bank on an application for a loan and would grant his request to appoint a commission to visit Greece and make an economic survey. This survey subsequently was made by a commission headed by Mr. Paul Porter.

Mr. Tsaldaris was in New York in December 1946, and again discussed Greece's needs with me. I invited him to Washington to talk with officials of the Export-Import Bank and Under Secretary Clayton about his request for assistance. Before his arrival, President Truman and I surveyed the situation with the directors of the Export-Import Bank. They said that, under the statute, they could not make a loan unless they had "reasonable assurance of its repayment," and they doubted whether this condition could be met for Greece considering the unsettled conditions there. They said they would consider the application, but I realized that there was little hope for a loan to Greece unless the law was changed.

While Mr. Tsaldaris was in New York, I discussed the Greek situation with Mr. Bevin. Britain, he told me, had been helping Greece both financially and militarily. His government would continue to help with military equipment but he hoped we would provide economic assistance. He said the British were anxious to withdraw their troops from Greece and several other places whenever and wherever it could properly be done. However, at no time did he indicate that, regardless of conditions in Greece, Britain would withdraw its troops on March 31, 1947, or any other specific date.

A somewhat similar situation existed in Turkey. Economic conditions in Turkey were better than in Greece, but Turkey's sovereignty was—and is—in just as much, if not greater danger. There may be some debate about the aspirations of the Soviet Union in Greece but there is no doubt about its aspirations in Turkey.

The record shows: (1) Molotov's request to Hitler in 1940 for approval of the establishment of a Soviet naval base in the Straits; (2) Stalin's reiteration of this desire at Potsdam; (3) the Soviet Government's direct request to Turkey for naval base rights and for the cession of the provinces of Kars and Ardahan. This war of nerves has required Turkey to keep under arms from 700,000 to 900,000 men. It is impossible for Turkey to maintain such an army without devoting to military expenditures the revenue needed to rehabilitate and develop its economy.

In the fall of 1946, I took the same position toward Turkey that I took toward Greece—we could not furnish military equipment but would do everything possible to help economically. I told Turkey's representatives that I would recommend that they receive a share of the 350 million dollars relief appropriation if Congress approved it, and that I would urge sympathetic consideration of a loan for reconstruction purposes.

At about the same time, the Turkish Government informed us of a communication from the Soviet Union renewing the demand for base rights in the Straits. We immediately advised Turkey that we adhered to our position of the previous November—that the revision of the Montreux Convention should be the subject of an international conference. We could not agree that control of the Straits was a matter of concern only to the Black Sea powers, or that Turkey and the Soviet Union should jointly organize for the defense of the Straits. Defense of the Straits, we said, should be based upon, and administered in accordance with, the purposes and principles of the United Nations. We asserted that we would insist upon this course.

This was the situation on January 20, 1947, when I left the Department of State. About March 1, the British Government informed the United States that it could give no further economic or military aid to Greece and Turkey after March 31.

On March 12, 1947, President Truman appeared before the Congress. He said that the United States had received from the Greek Government an urgent appeal for economic and military assistance without which Greece could not survive as a free nation. Britain, he said, was no longer able to furnish the necessary assistance.

"We must assist free peoples to work out their own destiny in their own way," President Truman declared. He urged Congress to appropriate 400 million dollars to aid Greece and Turkey with supplies and military equipment for the period ending June 30, 1948. In addition, he asked for authority to detail American military personnel to Greece and Turkey for the instruction and training of selected Turkish and Greek personnel.

Without having firsthand information, I am of the opinion that the disastrous weather conditions in Britain last winter, the labor strikes, and, particularly, the shortage of dollars, all combined to make British Treasury officials nervous, influencing the British Government to give us sudden notice of their intention to withdraw assistance from Turkey and Greece by March 31.

The financial condition of the British Government, I assumed, required it to stop financial assistance to these two countries. But I was certain, notwithstanding the statements made by some of our officials, that Britain would not withdraw its troops from Greece on March 31, or until we had an opportunity to determine our own course of action. The British do not act that way.

I did not misjudge them—their troops are still in Greece as of this date, July 1. They are reported to have approximately 8,000 troops there. We propose to send not more than seventy-five army and navy officers. Even our military authorities would admit that seventy-five American officers could not take the place of 8,000 British soldiers in protecting Greece against aggression. But the knowledge that we stand ready to do whatever is necessary to protect Greece against aggression gives comfort to the Greeks and a warning to potential aggressors.

While I think the British acted nervously in announcing withdrawal of assistance from these countries, I believe we were equally nervous—but right—in our response to this notification. I say we were "right" because, under the circumstances, we could not refuse to help. I say "nervous" because of some of the reasons given for the assistance; reasons which seemed to imply that we would oppose the efforts of Communists in any country to gain control of the government, even when they acted without the interference of a foreign government and through the free votes of their own people. That was not and should never be the position of our government. There is a vast difference between taking control of a government by honest ballots and taking control by bullets—or as a result of the threat of a foreign power. However, in a government like ours, different reasons may inspire different individuals in Congress and in the executive branch of the government to reach the same conclusion. The important thing is that the action in this case was correct—we had to give assistance.

We were justified in furnishing military supplies. We did not have to decide that the Turkish Government and the Greek monarchy were outstanding examples of free and democratic governments. We were not interfering in the internal affairs of those states. Greece had complained to the Security Council that her border was being violated by nationals of Yugoslavia, Bulgaria and Albania. If true, and if the aggression was countenanced by these governments, it constituted a threat to the peace of the world.

When Greece first asked for an investigation into this threat to the peace, the Soviet Union opposed it. The Council of Foreign Ministers was then meeting in New York. At that particular time Molotov had agreed with me on several questions and I was encouraged to ask for his co-operation. I told Mr. Molotov that the Soviet Union and the United States shared responsibility for maintaining the peace and I felt certain he could relieve the Greek situation by using his influence with Yugoslavia, Albania and Bulgaria. He said these three were not at fault; that the Greek Government was corrupt and did not have the confidence of the people. I disagreed and gave my reasons. In my second conversation with him, I told him that since his information was so different from mine, the sensible thing for us to do was to get the facts and then we might agree upon a remedy. Finally, to my surprise, he instructed his representative on the Security Council to support the resolution for an investigation. It was adopted, and I appointed Mr. Mark Ethridge to represent the United States.

From the outset, the commission met difficulties and delays—which our representative charged primarily to Greece's neighbors—even while the Greek Government continued to complain of more attacks from across its borders.

It was under these circumstances that the President addressed the Congress. He did not declare that it should become a permanent doctrine of the United States that, whenever we consider the independence of a free nation threatened, we should act unilaterally and, if necessary, use military power to prevent aggression. That is what the United Nations was created to do. The United States did not intend to by-pass the United Nations or to destroy or to cripple it. And the statement of the President does not warrant such an interpretation.

Senator Vandenberg made the position of the United States clear when he offered, and the Senate adopted, an amendment to the resolution authorizing assistance, which recognizes the right of the United Nations to assume jurisdiction over the situation in Greece and Turkey whenever it considers such action desirable.

Today the United Nations has no military force—owing again to the delaying tactics of the Soviet representative on the Military Staff Committee of the Security Council. The United States as one of the sponsors of the United Nations was compelled to let the Soviet Government and the world know that while the Security Council was investigating alleged acts of aggression against the Greek Government, we would act to maintain the status quo until the council could reach a decision, or had the military strength to control the situation. We were helping, not harming, the United Nations. And until it has such strength we must maintain the status quo in Turkey.

My belief that firmness brings results is also fortified by the Iranian case. There, as in Greece and in Turkey, the Soviet Union was seeking to fulfill one of its historic aims. The pattern was the same. Under the protection of the Red Army a puppet government had been installed in the province of Azerbaijan. We repeatedly warned the Soviet Union that the United States, as well as the Soviet Government, was pledged by the Teheran Declaration signed by Roosevelt, Stalin and Churchill to protect the sovereignty of Iran. I personally stressed to Stalin that, if Iran protested to the United Nations, we would support Iran. But all our efforts failed to convince the Soviet Government that we would fulfill our Teheran pledge. Therefore, when Iran appealed to the Security Council, we acted.

As so often happens in public affairs, the main battle was fought over a subsidiary issue; the right of Iran to present its case to the Security Council. I felt that if a precedent was established that denied any country the right of speedy access to the Security Council, the United Nations would be crippled from birth. I felt so strongly, in fact, about both the issue of Iran's sovereignty and the issue of ready access to the Security Council, that I personally argued the American case before the Security Council. Soviet resistance extended even to the point where Mr. Gromyko "walked out" on the Security Council. But firmness and the United Nations won.

Generalissimo Stalin announced the withdrawal of his troops in a telegram to the president of a news agency rather than to the Security Council. And then, last December, the puppet regime collapsed. The people of Iran were not fooled by Soviet propaganda. When Allied observers went into Azerbaijan with the Iranian authorities they were greeted with cries of "Long Live the United Nations." It is a cheer we should not forget in the months and years ahead.

The Security Council never took action in a formal sense, but it was the forum which made it possible for Iran to appeal to the conscience of the world. The Soviet Government may make renewed efforts to fulfill its aims toward Iran. Nevertheless, we can take heart from this example of firm and positive action within the framework of the United Nations.

Similar firmness is required in the case of Hungary. There, the Soviets have deliberately caused the removal of Hungarian government officials who received 57 per cent of the votes cast in an election which Stalin and Molotov have heretofore called free. The Hungarian Prime Minister has been driven from office and the Communists have taken charge. The Prime Minister declares that this action was dictated by the Soviet Government. There is corroborating evidence. If the Prime Minister's charges are true, the action in Hungary is a violation of the pledges made by the Soviet Union to its Allies at Yalta. I do not know what action the United States and the United Kingdom will take. But I know what I think they should do. They should call upon the Security Council to investigate and determine whether or not the facts constitute aggression. If the council makes that finding, it should require that the government be turned back to the political party that received 57 per cent of the votes of the people; or it should take some similar action that would assure the Hungarians their right to an independent existence free of the coercion of the Soviet Government.

We expect to act if there is aggression against Turkey and Greece. Why should we not act in the case of Hungary when there is evidence that the Soviets have already done there what we say will make us act in Turkey and Greece? Because of the events in Hungary, our government has canceled a credit of approximately 15 million dollars to buy our surplus property. If we have evidence to justify the suspension of credit and the filing of protests, we certainly have evidence sufficient to justify a request for an investigation.

We can not sit idly by simply because the Soviets have not formally ratified the treaty with Hungary. That treaty was agreed to by Foreign Minister Molotov and ratified by Great Britain, France and the United States. The Soviets should not be allowed to profit by their own delay. If, by the same methods, the Soviets tomorrow should take control of the Italian Government, we certainly would do more than protest, even though the Italian Treaty has not been ratified. I think the case of Hungary comes within the spirit of the declaration of policy made to Congress by President Truman on Greece and Turkey. Therefore, we should not now establish a precedent of inaction.

At all these points of present danger to the peace of the world—Iran, Greece, Turkey, Hungary and the other Balkan states—it can be argued that the national interest of the Soviet Union is involved or that fear and suspicion prompt her action. That may be true, but the unilateral pursuit of national interest, plus fear and suspicion, can lead to conflict—conflict that is contrary to the interest of all peoples.

Changes in power relations always tend to create uneasiness in the world. Russia long has been an important power, but never before has it been so clearly the dominant power on the European continent. When the power of any state has greatly increased, there naturally is concern regarding its possible further expansion. This is particularly true when the leaders of the expanding state have an aggressive ideology.

There is particular uneasiness in the world when a power—like the Soviet Union—acquires great strength in relation to others, but lags behind them in its own internal standard of living.

Other governments besides the Soviet Union seek territory. France wants the Saar. Greece has expressed a desire to annex Epirus. The Netherlands desires a slice of German territory adjoining its border. Belgium also may ask for adjoining German territory. The difference is that these governments seek changes through international machinery, either the peace conference or the Council of Foreign Ministers, whereas the Soviets apparently prefer to seek changes through unilateral action. That action frequently takes the course of political infiltration.

The Charter of the United Nations pledges all members to "refrain from the threat or use of force against the territorial integrity or political independence of any state." The definition is not restricted to armed invasion. It can mean coercion, pressure or subterfuge such as political infiltration.

The threat of political infiltration is especially grave in the countries whose political and economic structures were shattered by the war. Inevitably, it provokes countermeasures in retaliation. A situation can readily develop where all concerned come to believe they are acting in self-defense. Soon it becomes possible for a spark to start a fire that may engulf the whole world.

If we are to prevent such a holocaust, not only must we halt acts of aggression, but we must seek to eradicate the causes of those acts. In many countries, as a result of the war, the people are without adequate shelter and without adequate nourishment, and become easy prey to aggressive ideologies which offer them the illusion of escape from the hard realities of their daily existence. If we want these people to value freedom and respect law, we must give them at least the chance to feed, clothe and shelter themselves and their families, and give them the necessary means to keep internal order. We must give them the feeling that they can have an independent life without becoming satellites of Russia, the United States or any other power.

In extending economic aid, we must not seek to control the people of a country, but rather we must seek to make them free. We must have confidence that if we give people the opportunity to be free, they will not wish to be dependent upon us or upon any other power. Where there is no freedom, we must make sure that our economic aid is not turned against us.

We must make it unmistakably plain that we are not competing with the Soviet Union for the control of other states. Rather, we should stress that we would welcome a real and bona fide willingness on the part of the Soviet Union to collaborate in rebuilding and protecting political and economic independence.

I would not be speaking frankly, however, if I did not repeat that thus far our efforts to collaborate with the Soviet Union have met with little or no success. My efforts in this direction are told in the preceding chapters. And today we have before us Mr. Molotov's rejection of the plans advanced by Mr. Bevin and Mr. Bidault in response to the proposal made by Secretary Marshall on June 5. In his speech at Harvard University, Secretary Marshall called upon European nations to agree on "the requirements of the situation and the part those countries themselves will take in order to give proper effect to whatever action might be undertaken by this Government."

Secretary Marshall did not say the United States would furnish any specified amount to aid the program agreed upon. He said simply that we would support "such a program as far as it may be practical for us to do so." But other officials of the government have made statements which are quoted abroad, estimating that such a program would cost us from five to six billion dollars a year for four or five years. These estimates were made even before the European governments met, indicating that our officials have some idea of what the over-all program should be. Certainly the estimates have whetted the appetites of many European officials.

I welcome the initiative of Mr. Bevin and Mr. Bidault, but political realities demand that in welcoming this program to advance Europe's economic recovery, we should also express some words of caution. It should be made clear that the United States will determine, in the light of its resources, the amount of aid to be extended, where the money will be spent, and what conditions, if any, will be attached to its expenditure.

Some European governments and peoples do not understand that a member of the executive branch of our government cannot make a financial commitment until Congress actually appropriates the funds. We should make sure they do not proceed in the belief that any program agreed to by them will automatically be paid for by us. Unless this is done, a subsequent refusal by Congress to provide money for the agreed program will cause misunderstandings and disappointments which will dangerously affect our relations with European states.

In considering what the Congress may do, we must not overlook what has been done recently. We did not try to extend the life of UNRRA because it was decided that, instead of other governments allocating funds appropriated by us for relief, the United States should make the allocation. When the Congress authorized 350 million dollars for relief, it did not leave it to the executive department to determine where it should be spent. It specified that 335 million dollars would be available only in Austria, Greece, Hungary, Italy, Poland, Trieste and China, and only 15 million dollars should be available for relief in other states. It also provided for supervision and control of expenditures in every country by missions of American citizens.

And again, the recent legislation authorizing 400 million dollars for military and economic aid to Greece and Turkey, which was passed by Congress and approved by the President, provides that the money should be spent under the supervision of an American committee, the chairman of which must be approved by the Senate.

Mr. Molotov's action in late June in refusing to attend the Paris Economic Conference unless he could first know the terms and conditions under which the United States would furnish financial aid, and could receive certain assurances that the sovereignty of states would not be interfered with, was disappointing to all who favor world co-operation. However, I do not agree with some officials and editors who think this refusal is conclusive proof that the Soviets want chaotic conditions to continue in Europe.

Judging by the Soviets' refusal to co-operate in other matters, it is entirely possible that they may not object to a continuance of unrest in Europe. Nevertheless, Mr. Molotov's action in this matter is open to a different interpretation. The invitation of Britain and France placed him in an embarrassing position. The satellite states, like all people in financial distress, must have welcomed the invitation to inform the United States of the financial assistance they needed, particularly when the news reports indicated that the assistance would be a gift instead of a loan. If the Soviets now bring pressure on them not to accept financial help from the United States, the Soviets themselves will have to help the satellites economically, and consequently they will retard their own reconstruction projects.

I think that Mr. Molotov's refusal to participate is influenced by the same fear that has made him refuse to co-operate in our atomic energy proposal and many other proposals—the fear that they would be forced to agree to inspection by representatives of other governments who could demand the right to freely travel in the Soviet Union.

Mr. Molotov has consistently objected to every proposal that involves inspection by representatives of other powers in areas under Soviet control. Evidently, Molotov now thinks that if we require supervision or inspection in giving economic aid to friendly countries like Greece and Turkey, we shall insist upon similar arrangements in helping other countries. My guess is that the Soviets will continue to refuse to co-operate in the Paris Conference unless they have some assurance that there will be no inspection and supervision in the Soviet Union or in areas under Soviet control by representatives of the United States.

On this July 1, my opinion is that Mr. Molotov, by refusing to co-operate, has without intending to, settled a difficult problem for the United States Government. Had the Soviets and its satellites attended the Paris Conference, it is fair to assume that Britain and France, who are certain to recommend financial assistance for themselves, would also have recommended that we advance large sums for reconstruction in the Soviet Union and in its satellites. That would have posed for our Congress a question as embarrassing to it as the invitation of Britain and France was to Molotov. The proposal to help all needy European countries was, I assume, submitted to the leaders of both political parties before it was made. But even so, we can only speculate about the action of the Congress under those circumstances.

If Congress required the same supervision of expenditures that is required in the cases of Turkey and Greece and the relief appropriations, the Soviets and the satellites would have refused to accept the assistance. They would have declared that they should have been informed of those conditions when the offer of assistance was made. On the other hand, if Congress was asked to make a large appropriation for the Soviet Union and its satellite states without any supervision, the chances are that Congress would not make the appropriation. By refusing to attend the Paris Conference, Mr. Molotov has saved the Congress this difficult decision. He has assumed the burden of dividing Europe into two economic and political spheres.

The American people and the Congress realize that we must deal with the causes of unrest in the world and not merely with its symptoms. The need for help has proved greater than expected. And the rise in the American price level since the war makes necessary larger grants and credits than previously were thought necessary. Nevertheless, I am convinced they will make the sacrifices necessary to build the peace. But the program must be a reasonable one. If it is not, I fear the Congress will not appropriate adequate funds. Should that happen, it would have been better if aid had never been proposed.

As a first step toward restoring Europe's economy, we should concentrate on projects that will help to remove the economic bottlenecks which keep the individual states from increasing their trade and production. It does not require the agreement of all European governments or even an extensive inquiry to determine those bottlenecks—we know them.

First of all, we should use not only our money but our brains to devise means of increasing Europe's coal production. The need for coal is at the heart of nearly every European nation's economic problem. And the heart of Europe's coal problem lies in the Ruhr.

In the peacetime years before 1939, the mines of the Ruhr produced about 440,000 tons of hard coal per day. In May 1947, two years after the end of the war in Europe, those mines produced only 214,000 tons per day. Some of the shortage is being offset by purchases from the mines of the United States. But coal produced in the Ruhr region costs ten dollars a ton while West Virginia coal laid down in Naples, for example, costs twenty-two dollars a ton. This year, European states will pay approximately 600 million dollars for coal from the United States. The money will come in part from funds loaned to them by the United States. This is an uneconomic and wasteful process. It should be stopped at the earliest possible moment.

Disorganization and faulty administration of the Ruhr's production and distribution is a factor in this situation. Lack of improved machinery is another. But the main reason is much more understandable. A miner needs to work only two days a week to earn the money necessary for the limit of his rations. There is nothing else in the Ruhr for him to purchase. The future of his country is so uncertain that there is no incentive to save, and he has no confidence in the money he is paid. Improving the lot of the German coal miner may raise storms of protests from those who want to punish the Germans. But without such action, not only the Germans will be punished, but all Europeans.

We can start work on this problem now without waiting for other countries to agree. A substantial increase in the ration of the Ruhr miner, improved mine machinery from the United States, and some plan to provide more consumer goods for the miner and his family would be reflected almost immediately in an increased output of coal.

The coal mines of Silesia also are important producers. We should consider means of increasing production there. But our aid should be advanced only on the condition that a portion of the coal is made available to those countries of western Europe which prior to the war relied on Silesia for their coal. Even though Poland does not attend the Economic Conference at Paris, we can confer with its representative and try to solve this problem.

After coal, we should consider how to increase the production and availability of electric power. The last time I saw President Roosevelt, I introduced to him General Clay who was leaving for Germany. I told the President that Clay, who is an engineer, had built a great power project in Texas. The President immediately told us of his pet project—the building of a power project in Central Europe. He foresaw that fuel would be the main European problem.

We must be careful not to become preoccupied with the economic problems of Europe alone. The reconstruction of Asia's economy also is vital to world stability. There, as well as in Europe, the projects we help to finance should be the kind that give hope and increasing opportunities for self-support to those who are trying to rebuild their shattered lives. The advances of science have made it possible for all nations to preserve and increase their living standards if they work together to produce what they want and need.

The mere statement of the problem shows its immensity. What we in the United States do must be done within the limits of our resources. It would not contribute to the long-range goal of world stability if, in order to meet present emergencies, we drained away our economic lifeblood.

Prosperity, like freedom, must be shared, not on the basis of "handouts," but on the basis of fair and honest exchange of the products of free men and women. If we want repayment for the help we give, we must be willing to accept goods and services as part of that repayment. But we cannot realistically expect repayment until Europe's economy is placed on a self-supporting basis.

A world with working economies able to provide its people with food, shelter, clothing, schools and other necessities, will be a much easier world with which to deal. But while we are working toward economic recovery, we must continue working in other fields as well. Equally important is the building of a system of collective security.

Through collective action, Germany and Japan have been decisively defeated. Neither of them has the capacity to wage war. Neither of them will have the capacity to wage war for a generation unless the Allies, choosing to use them as pawns or as partners in a struggle for power, permit them to rebuild their armaments. Surely, we have learned enough from our experience following World War I to know that if the peace terms are to be changed it is better to revise them ourselves than to permit our former enemies to acquire the arms with which to dictate revision.

As a concrete demonstration of our desire to see that these countries stay demilitarized, I have proposed that the four great powers join in a forty-year treaty with provisions to insure that neither Germany nor Japan again threaten the peace of the world. The treaty provides for swift punishment if there is violation of its terms. And it provides for certain punishment by denying to any one of the four powers the right to veto action.

Acceptance of this treaty is a clear test of the sincerity of any nation's intentions of keeping these countries disarmed. Britain and France have endorsed it. It was agreed to in principle by Generalissimo Stalin but since has been opposed stoutly by Mr. Molotov. We should again call for acceptance of this treaty. If the Soviet Government continues to reject our offer, we will have reason to fear the future.

I still have hope that the treaty will be adopted. I believe that when the Soviets realize we are going to maintain American armed forces in Germany as long as there are occupation armies there, they will accept the treaty. It will take them a long time to get over the rapid disintegration of our military power in Europe after V-E Day. They were then inspired to hope that the United States was withdrawing its power from Europe. A conclusion nurtured by a desire is slow in changing, but this is one conclusion that the Soviet leaders, sooner or later and whether they like it or not, will have to change. As I stated at Stuttgart—"We are in Europe to stay."

Adoption of this forty-year treaty would be additional testimony of our belief in the principle of collective security which has reached its culmination in the Charter of the United Nations. I do not agree with those who declare that Russia's failure to co-operate has destroyed the United Nations. I still think our greatest hope for peace lies in supporting and developing the United Nations. It has much greater potentialities than is generally realized. And it gives us the opportunity to advance the co-operative ventures which alone can assure peace.

It has been said that the success of the United Nations depends upon the ability of the great powers to work together. Such a statement is only partly true. It is true that if the great powers co-operate to maintain peace, there is little chance that any one power will take the risk of breaking the peace. But co-operation of all the great powers, while devoutly to be hoped for and worked for, is not indispensable. I deny that the Charter of the United Nations—which unqualifiedly commits the member states to settle their disputes by peaceful means and to refrain from the use of force except in defense of the principles of the Charter—can be nullified by a single vote of a permanent member of the Security Council.

It is a fact that the Security Council can not *require* the member states to take action unless there is unanimity among the permanent members. But that does not mean that the members are not free to act, and should not regard themselves as morally bound to act, if there is a clear violation of the Charter.

Of course, a state in honest doubt about whether there has been a violation of the Charter ought not to be bound, morally or otherwise, to take action simply because one side or the other happens to get a certain number of votes in the council. But there are principles of law incorporated in the Charter which should be regarded as the law of all lands. These principles *will* be regarded as the law of all lands if we and all other members of the United Nations make it clear that we are determined, if need be, to defend them by force.

If we and the other powers are prepared to act in defense of law, the United Nations can prevent war. We must make it clear, also, that we will not use force for any other purpose.

But it follows, then, that if we are going to do our part to defend these principles, we must maintain our power to do so. We must not further reduce the appropriations for the Army and Navy. We must encourage and promote continued scientific research, and we must adopt some plan of universal military training. The force of an argument in an international conference is not lessened by the existence of military power at home.

Making clear that we are ready to enforce the Charter is not a threat or a hostile act against any nation. It is rather the spirit and vitality that will give strength to the rule of law among nations. It is the attitude toward the law that must be evident if law is to be respected.

I do not believe the Soviet Union wants war. But Soviet statesmen seem to believe it is their duty to struggle to the utmost to advance their power and interest. We must make it absolutely clear that, if they carry the struggle beyond definite limits, the law will be enforced against them. Otherwise, they may transgress those limits in the mistaken belief that we will not challenge their transgressions.

We must be ready to recognize, however, that many issues admit of honest differences of opinion. We cannot and must not claim infallibility for our policy decisions. We certainly must not expect less warmth in the arguments in the United Nations than we have in our own Congress, our own legislatures, and our own city halls.

Diversity of thought and competition in ideas can make both for progress and for peace if we are willing to meet one indispensable condition—respect for the right of others to ideas, opinions and ways of life we do not share. Others must equally respect our right to ideas, opinions and ways of life they do not share.

There is and always has been room in this world for more than one ideology and more than one way of life. There is room for the Soviet way of life and for the American way of life. The belief in the inevitability of conflict between ideologies is more likely to produce conflict than it is to enshrine any single ideology or way of life in this world. Even the unfortunate division of Europe into two economic and political spheres does not justify talk of the inevitability of conflict. There is too much talk of war and too little of peace. We need not fear the result if we use our power but we must fear the unnecessary use of our power. Should all our efforts for peace fail, we want to be sure in our own minds that the fault is not ours.

Even in these chaotic postwar years, the United Nations has been a powerful instrument for peace.

The Charter of the United Nations came into force as a fundamental law for the peoples of the world on October 24, 1945, when as Secretary of State I announced that the necessary number of ratifications had been obtained. As I look back over the events which have crowded the life of the United Nations since that date, I recall that the League of Nations was in existence nearly eleven months before its Assembly had its first meeting. The United Nations General Assembly, on the other hand, convened for the first time in London in January 1946. In October 1946, it met again in regular session and, in May 1947, in special session.

At its first meeting it brought into being the Security Council, the Economic and Social Council, the International Court of Justice, and it elected a Secretary General to begin the task of organizing a Secretariat—civil servants to the world.

The United Nations Security Council—unlike the Council of the League which met but four times a year—has been in almost continuous session. The clash of interests among the permanent members of the council has hampered its efficiency but has not yet sapped its vitality. The influence of the Council in the Iranian case I have cited. The integrity of Greece has been protected by the presence of a Security Council Commission of Investigation. British and French troops were withdrawn from Syria and Lebanon in accordance with a majority decision of the council. The negotiated settlement of the territorial dispute between France and Siam, and the prompt compliance by Yugoslavia with United States' demands in connection with attacks on our airplanes are examples where the *possi-*

bility of Security Council action stimulated peaceful adjustment of the situations.

We should not overlook these positive contributions in the midst of disappointment over the lack of progress in the Security Council's related agencies—the Atomic Energy Commission, the Commission on Conventional Armaments and the Military Staff Committee. To these agencies, the people of the world have entrusted the supreme task of building a system of collective security that will *develop and enforce* the rule of law. The principal reason they have not made the progress that their task demands is the Soviet Union's reluctance to accept the international controls, and the delegations of national sovereignty, that the overwhelming majority of the nations believe are essential.

The United States took the first step toward an effective system of international control of atomic energy and all other weapons of mass destruction. We should maintain our initiative. If such a system can be established, we then shall have safeguards that will enable the world to disarm with security. Until that is done, we cannot and must not disarm.

Meanwhile, we should press tirelessly for the special agreements, still to be prepared by the Military Staff Committee, which would give the Security Council adequate military strength to enforce its decisions.

We must continue building on the other structural foundations which have been laid. These include not only the principal organs of the United Nations established by the Charter—the General Assembly, the Security Council, the Economic and Social Council, the Trusteeship Council, and the International Court of Justice—but also the various specialized agencies, many of which have international operating functions. These specialized agencies include such bodies as the Food and Agricultural Organization, the International Labor Organization, the United Nations Educational, Scientific and Cultural Organization, the International Civil Aviation Organization, the International Bank for Reconstruction and Development, the International Monetary Fund, the International Refugee Organization, the proposed World Health Organization, and International Trade Organization. There is, in fact, scarcely a field of activity having a common interest for the peoples of the world for which continuing instruments of international co-operation have not been developed during the past two years.

The United States, the United Kingdom and Canada are the only countries which, by the summer of 1947, had become members of all the specialized agencies. The Soviet Union, on the other hand, had thus far announced its adherence only to one—the World Health Organization.

Notwithstanding all that I have said about the difficulty of getting along with the representatives of the Soviet Union, it is my firm conviction that we must continue our efforts to bring about world co-operation. We must do it in full recognition that the Soviets may not co-operate. Should our efforts fail, we must let the world know who is responsible for the failure. Experience has shown that Soviet policy is flexible and at any time Soviet spokesmen may change their views. We must let them know we are sincere in wanting their co-operation but nevertheless firm in the determination that if we do not get it, we will go ahead anyway with all those states that will co-operate.

In our efforts at world co-operation, we must be careful that we are not guilty of the offenses we charge to others. In international conferences we meet as equals, and there is no place for a "take it or leave it" attitude. For two years our patience has favorably impressed all fair-minded observers. Too much is at stake for us to lose our patience. Negotiating with the Soviets may affect the nerves of a few statesmen but another world war would more seriously affect the lives of millions of people. We must continue our efforts to develop through the United Nations a common law of nations to provide definite and agreed standards of conduct. It must rest upon something more than rules, something more than force, and something more than fear. It must be made to rest upon the growth of a common fellowship, common interests and common ideas among the peoples of the world.

In seeking the many-sided answer to the question, "Where do we go from here?" there is one course of action which I regard as the most important of all. That course is to take stock of our country and of ourselves. The leadership the modern world demands of us requires that we work from strong foundations here at home. We must enter international conference rooms with the firm but humble assurance that can come only from complete confidence in ourselves and our way of life.

If my public service has taught me anything, it is that the teachings of Thomas Jefferson and Abraham Lincoln can bring greater happiness and satisfaction to greater numbers of people than the teachings of Karl Marx and Nikolay Lenin. Nowhere is there an ideology that surpasses in its power and in its potential appeal to all peoples the ideology contained in such a statement as this:

"We hold these truths to be self-evident; that all men are created equal; that they are endowed by their creator with certain inalienable rights, and among these rights are life, liberty, and the pursuit of happiness."

No one has devised a system of government more lofty in concept or more responsive to the common good than "government of the people, by the people and for the people."

These ideals are part of our way of life. If we give evidence that we are striving unceasingly and progressing steadily toward their fulfillment, I have no fear of the outcome.

We are the world's greatest industrial nation. If we keep our own house in order, proving to the world that we learn from past mistakes; that our country is not one that booms and busts; and that we provide our people with the opportunity to live in expanding freedom and increased well-being, we can contribute immeasurably to the building of a politically free and economically stable world.

During the past two years, there were many times when I was deeply discouraged. Our repeated efforts to achieve co-operation in a peaceful world seemed to be meeting only with constant rebuff. But we persisted in our efforts with patience and firmness. I have not lost hope, but today I would reverse the order and alter the emphasis. I would say that our policy should be one of *firmness* and *patience*.

I remain confident that we can achieve a just peace by co-operative effort if we persist "with firmness in the right as God gives us the power to see the right."

To the goal of a just peace, freedom's past inspires us, and freedom's future calls us.

Index

Acheson, Dean, 92, 145, 226, 246, 268, 269, 270
Albania, 148, 149, 279, 293, 299, 302, 303
Alexander, Harold, 47, 56-57, 161
Allen, George, 237
Allied Control Council, *see* names of countries
Anders, Wladyslaw, 165
Anderson, Sir John, 265
Ardahan, 77, 293, 301
Argentina, 35, 39, 61, 63, 104
Arms Embargo, 7
Asia, peace in, 204-229, 310
Atlantic Charter, 33, 76, 202
Atomic bomb, 92, 206, 208, 209, 211, 212, 257-271, 274-276
Atomic Development Authority, 276
Atomic energy, 35, 109, 111, 122, 123, 124, 204, 257-276, 308, 314; Interim Committee for, 259-260, 262
Attlee, Clement R., 78-79, 84, 106, 108, 162; atomic energy policy, 265, 268; Potsdam Conference (July '45), 69, 78, 79, 206
Augusta, USS, 66, 67, 69, 262, 263, 264
Austin, Warren R., 7, 8, 220, 235
Australia, 39, 97, 102, 140, 213, 217, 218, 224
Austria, 7, 86, 107, 149, 151, 159-165, 190, 199, 296, 307; Allied Council for, 161, 163, 165; displaced persons in, 168; fall of, 204; occupation of, 163, 164, 166, 244; peace treaty, 91, 125, 127, 128, 131, 151, 159, 160, 163-166, 179, 194, 198, 199, 298; reparations, 161-162
Austrian Treaty Commission, 166
Azerbaijan, 118, 119, 293, 304

Baker, Warren E., 206
Baku oil fields, 119, 255, 290, 293
Balkan peace treaties, 70, 124, 198, 199, 202, 224
Balmer, Jesse D., 141
Bankhead, William B., 7
Bard, Ralph, 259, 261
Barkley, Alben W., 7, 11, 14
Barnard, Chester I., 269
Baruch, Bernard M., 269-273
Batum, 290, 293

Beaverbrook, Lord, 15, 16
Beirut, President, 80
Belgium, 114, 140, 168, 189, 305
Belgrade, Yugoslavia, 144, 145, 146
Bemis, Samuel F., 246
Benton, William, 92, 253
Berlin, Germany, 3, 24, 53, 65, 68, 82, 110, 187, 192, 248, 262, 282, 285, 291
Berlin Conference, *see* Potsdam Conference
Bern, Switzerland, 56, 59, 61, 71
Berry, Burton Y., 51
Bessarabia, 283, 286, 287
Bevin, Ernest, 75, 78, 79, 84, 94, 95, 99, 101-107, 113, 117, 120, 121, 123, 127-129, 131, 133-137, 149, 152, 163-66, 170, 173, 175, 177, 192, 196, 198, 213-215, 218, 219, 250, 266, 300, 306, 307
Bidault, Georges, 92, 94, 95, 103, 115, 124, 128, 129, 131-137, 141, 152, 164, 165, 169, 170, 173, 175-178, 195, 198, 250, 306, 307
Biddle, Francis, 13, 14
Black, Captain, 126
Bliss, Tasker H., 234
Bloom, Sol, 7, 235
Boettiger, Mrs. John, 22
Bohlen, Charles E. (Chip), 61, 64, 67, 69, 110, 113, 122, 125, 128, 131, 132, 151, 194, 251, 256, 280-281
Bolling, A. G., 206
Boomer, Lucius, 150
Braden, Spruille, 92
Brazil, 39, 112
Brown, Edward J., 258
Brown, Walter, 249
Bucharest, Rumania, 50, 51, 52, 74, 117, 123
Bukovina, 149, 287
Bulgaria, 73-75, 85, 100, 101, 107, 108, 115-117, 120, 121, 123, 131, 149, 208, 237, 279, 288-289, 290-291, 293, 296, 299, 302, 303; peace treaty, 91, 102, 103, 111, 112, 133, 141, 154; reparations and, 148
Bush, Vannevar, 259, 260, 268
Byelorussia, 39, 40, 42, 63
Byrnes, James F., appointed Secretary of State, 49, 65-66; Director of Economic Stabilization, 17-19, 277; Di-